What Is Direct Action?

Reframing Revolutionary Strategy in the Light of Occupy Wall Street

by Mitchel Cohen

& Marina Sitrin, Isis Feral, Jay Moore,
Arun Gupta, Jeff Goldthorpe, Rebecca Solnit,
David Graeber, John Tarleton, Sarah Jaffe, Dave
Lippman, Tom Angotti, Chris Williams, & Mickey Z.

A Red Balloon Collective Publication
Zen-Marxism Series

This book is written with much appreciation and love to my comrades, teachers & friends

Silvia Federici, George Caffentzis, Beth Youhn, & Chris Kinder

✶✶✶✶✶✶

and in memory of
John "Tito" Gerassi, Crysta Casey, Saralee Hamilton, Maria Kuriloff, Daniel Simidor (Andre Elizée), Dave Wycoff, Carl Lesnor, Alexander Cockburn, Len Weinglass, Dennis Brutus, Manning Marable, Howard Zinn, Dr. Philip Metling, Susan Blake, Bernie McFall, Steffie Brooks, Michael Shenker, Franklin Rosemont, Kathryn Shay, Tom Angress, Brad Will, Bob Fitch, Tuli Kupferberg, Ward Morehouse, Sol Yurick, Garda Ghista and Molly Goldstein, recently fallen comrades, my friends.

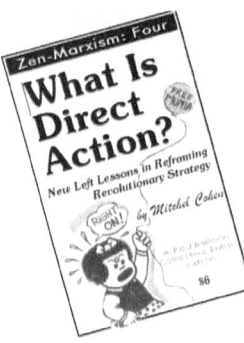

"What Is Direct Action?" was originally published in part as a pamphlet "Turning Motion Into Movement" in 1982 and significantly developed in 1992. It is one book in the series, *Zen-Marxism: Subjective Factors in Formulating Revolutionary Strategy.*

Anti-Copyright January 2013. Radical collectives, non-profit groups and individuals may freely reprint the text herein.

ISBN 978-1-57027-254-7

Red Balloon Collective Publications
2652 Cropsey Avenue, #7H
Brooklyn, NY 11214
mitchelcohen@mindspring.com

There are times when the operation of the machine become so odious, makes you so sick at heart, that you can't take part, you can't even passively take part, and you've got to put your bodies upon the gears and upon the wheels, upon the levers, upon all the apparatus, and you've got to make it stop. And you've got to indicate to the people who run it, to the people who own it, that unless you're free the machine will be prevented from working at all.

- Mario Savio
Berkeley 1964

America, I'm putting my queer shoulder to the wheel.

- Allen Ginsberg
"America"

What Is Direct Action?

PREFACE 5

FOREWORD by Richard Wolff
   Criticism, Violence and Roosting Chickens 9

INTRODUCTION
   Revolution is as American as Occu-Pie 15
   Storming the Pentagon 43
   Debates in the New Left 59
   Occupy Wall Street 65
   Global Revolt Takes Many Forms 90
   Occupy Did Not Come Out of Nowhere 95
   Dedication 99

ONE: What if We Were to Act? 109

TWO: Beyond Symbolic Politics 159

THREE: Reframing Issues 191

FOUR: Truths & Consequences 299

FIVE: APPENDIX of Related Essays
   Mitchel Cohen: How to Write Letters 347
   Occupy: How to Make a Bat-Signal 355
   Mitchel Cohen: People of the Dome:
      Direct Action in New Orleans 361
   Rebecca Solnit: Mad, Passionate Love/Violence 373
   Jeff Goldthorpe: Overthrowing the Ruling Class by Farce 387
   Mitchel Cohen: A Response to Chris Hedges 415
   David Graeber: The Violent Peace-Police 461
   Jay Moore: The Black Freedom Movement 476
   Marina Sitrin: Pulling the Emergency Brake 485
   Isis Feral: The Loving Embrace of Black Bloc 491
   Marina Sitrin: What Did Occupy Achieve? 499
   Arun Gupta: The Future of Occupy 510

SIX: OCCUPY SANDY
   Mitchel Cohen: Southern Brooklyn Sandy Diary 535
   John Tarleton: Changing the Political Climate 559
   Sarah Jaffe: Occupy Springs into Action 564
   Tom Angotti: On The Waterfront 569
   Chris Williams: Healing a Stricken City, Greening the Planet 576
   Mickey Z: Message to the New New Left:
      Occupy the Big Connections 588

PREFACE

As this book goes to press in January of 2013, Barack Obama has won re-election to the Presidency of the United States in a landslide vote. The pundits and TV wonks are up to their old tricks drooling all over the microphones in predictable Pavlovian barking at the nation's voters who thunderously rejected the Republicans and their right-wing policies. Not that the Democrats have much to brag about as they rush headlong into disassembling social security; cutting taxes on the rich (at the expense of everyone else); approving genetically engineered foods and nuclear power plants; sending drones to assassinate the President's "personally selected" targets or eavesdrop on U.S. residents; and starting new wars to extract resources and protect multinational corporate interests.

Third Party candidates, including Jill Stein of the Green Party (for whom I voted) and Gary Johnson of the Libertarian Party, among others, together received around 2 million votes — a significant though not overwhelming rejection of the twin corporate parties. Meanwhile, Occupy Wall Street, having reinvented itself as "Occupy Sandy," is using skills

> **Questionnaire: If "pro" is the opposite of "con", then the opposite of "*pro*gress" is ...**

brewed in the cauldron of last year's protests to organize food, water, clothing, blanket distribution and mold removal for communities hit hardest by the hurricane that devastated New York and New Jersey (and Cuba, and Haiti) last October — establishing networks of what the old Russian anarchist prince Peter Kropotkin termed "Mutual Aid."

Will those networks transform themselves into a force of resistance? As I look out my window across Gravesend Bay and the Coney Island Creek, the lights in the public housing projects in Coney Island are *still* off, while electricity to the private apartment buildings on the same blocks was restored months ago. FEMA's and the Red Cross' selective follow-up (or lack thereof) reveals yet again the racial and class privileging that has been a cancer in the soul of this country since its founding. Most people feel impotent, not apathetic. How do we — that expansive, catch-all "*we*" — focus the inchoate anger and despair, and cohere resistance to the policies of what we've come to call "the 1%", who are directly, through the financial, corporate and government apparatus they control, bringing down the curtain on even this shadow of democracy in what we in the U.S. call 'America'?

* * *

"What Is Direct Action?" is one book of several I've aggregated under the rather ponderous title, "Zen-Marxism: Subjective Factors in Formulating Revolutionary Strategy." It is meant to serve the 99%, discover new meanings in the history of our own movements, and provide conceptual tools for developing direct action as strategy to bring about revolutionary social and economic transformation right here in the U.S. of A. in our lifetime.

Direct Action — of which "Mutual Aid" is one important expression — is now the order of the day. I've written many essays over the decades staking out positions on any number of topical issues, but *Zen-Marxism* is different. It does not try to convince you, the reader, *that* the capitalist system needs to be overthrown and transformed. I take that as given. I am interested here in exploring the *how* rather than the *why*. What are the conditions that foster rebellion and resistance and how do we (there's that problematic pronoun, again) bolster them? What are the conditions holding us back, and how do we sidestep or undermine them?

I appreciate your feedback, and may include some of those experiences and insights in future editions.

Mitchel Cohen
Bensonhurst, Brooklyn
January 2013
mitchelcohen@mindspring.com

Foreword
Criticism, Violence & Roosting Chickens

by Richard Wolff

The 99 percent offered criticism of the 1 percent. They exposed and made clear what most Americans know. They struggled peacefully to inform and mobilize public opinion. They won huge numbers of hearts and minds. The 1 percent in the U.S. did what their counterparts in Tunisia, Egypt, Bahrain, and so on did earlier last year. First, they tried to deny the 99 percent the media access needed to reach the people. That failed. Then, they tried scattered police intimidation and pressure to stop the criticism. That failed. Then, Democratic Party operatives tried to convert the Occupyers to become Obama enthusiasts for the 2012 election. That failed, too.

So now, the weapon of criticism wielded by the 99 percent suffers the counter criticism of 'violence' by servants of the 1 percent. No one will miss which side resorted to organized, massive violence so early and so unnecessarily in this conflict. As in Iraq, Afghanistan, and elsewhere, having failed to win hearts and minds, U.S. government agencies cover their failure by resorting to violence. Chickens raised abroad often return home to roost. Consider the image: NY Police Department machines and personnel destroy the free library that had functioned so well in Zuccotti Park.

New York has acquired a newly renamed mayor: Mayor Mubarak (*né* Bloomberg). Situated atop the 1 percent, he gave the order to "clear and clean" Zuccotti Park. This mayor, who presides over some of the world's filthiest tunnels and stations that daily threaten the public health of millions of subway riders, suddenly acquired an obsession with cleanliness in little Zuccotti Park. This mayor — whose city handles garbage by piling it in bags that break and scatter their contents over the streets — wants us to believe he is concerned about public safety.

Will President Obama adopt the same autocratic policies as New York's mayor, and become known as President Mubarak? Or will the Arab Spring — so blithely praised by Secretary of State Clinton as "freedom struggles" — resurface here to confront the Clintons with their hypocritical complicity in repression at home?

The deepening economic inequality, the moneyed corruption of politics and the collapsing fortunes and prospects of the mass of Americans — none of those basic conditions and causes of Occupy Wall Street has been addressed by Bloomberg or Obama. Instead, they seek to repress those who expose and oppose those conditions.

Meanwhile, the system that keeps reproducing those conditions — a capitalism becoming increasingly intolerable — loses more bases of support. In times like these, the "criticism" by weapons risks losing to the weapon of criticism. Will the Arab Spring be reborn as the American Winter? ∎

Richard D. Wolff, Professor of Economics, UMASS Amherst, is currently a Visiting Professor at the New School for Social Research, NYC. He hosts "Economics Update" every Saturday at 12 noon on WBAI (99.5 FM), and archived at wbai.org. His website is http://RDWolff.com. This essay first appeared on www.TruthOut.org.

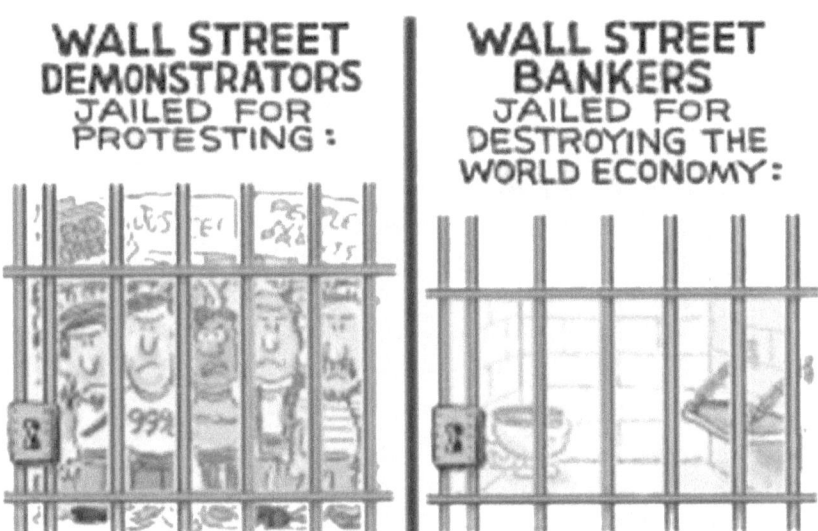

WHAT IS DIRECT ACTION?
Introduction

Paris, May '68

Until I was about ten years old I never realized that there were "warm" countries, places where you didn't have to sweat for a living, nor shiver and pretend that it was tonic and exhilarating. Wherever there is cold there are people who work themselves to the bone and when they produce young they preach to the young the gospel of work — which is nothing, at bottom, but the doctrine of inertia. My people were entirely Nordic, which is to say idiots. Every wrong idea which has ever been expounded was theirs. Among them was the doctrine of cleanliness, to say nothing of righteousness. They were painfully clean. But inwardly they stank. Never once had they opened the door which leads to the soul; never once did they dream of taking a blind leap into the dark. After dinner the dishes were promptly washed and put in the closet; after the paper was read it was neatly folded and laid away on a shelf; after the clothes were washed they were ironed and folded and then tucked away in the drawers. Everything was for tomorrow, but tomorrow never came. The present was only a bridge and on this bridge they are still groaning, as the world groans, and not one idiot ever thinks of blowing up the bridge.

Henry Miller, *Tropic of Capricorn*

REVOLUTION IS AS AMERICAN AS OCCU-PIE

> Nothing so effectively stifles our lives as the transformation into 'work' of the activities and relations that satisfy our desires.[1]
>
> - Silvia Federici

If you remember the '60s, the saying goes, you probably weren't there. But in actuality it is the huge political movements *of the '80s* that have been 'deep-sixed' by those assigned to patrol the repositories of official memory. Disco replaced punk; the political protests of the prior decades, we're told, dissolved into "me-ism" as the glitterati danced the nights away in *Studio 54;* star-struck spectators clambered all over each other to get a glimpse of someone famous, and good times were had by all. And if you believe that, I have a bridge in Brooklyn to sell ya.

In fact, radical protests surged in the 1980s, sparked by the anti-nuke, women's liberation, Latin America, gay and lesbian, and anti-apartheid movements. Ronald Reagan swept

---

[1] Silvia Federici, *Revolution at Point Zero: Housework, Reproduction, and Feminist Struggle,* PM Press, Oakland: 2012.

into office a month after John Lennon was assassinated in New York City, and immediately set to work crushing the Air Traffic Controllers union, replacing those trained professionals (even though many had campaigned for Reagan) with "scabs" — now prettified as "replacement workers". Airline safety plunged into a nosedive and took decades to recover. Workers began learning, once again, that they were expendable as far as corporate America was concerned.

Workers in the Soviet bloc, too, were learning that the U.S.S.R. was socialist in name only, as it moved to crush *Solidarity* in Poland, a mass-movement of workers responding to the austerity cuts being imposed on that country to pay off its multi-billion dollar debt to western banks. (Sound familiar?) In fact, the Soviet Union, on the verge of getting bogged down in an interminable war in Afghanistan, turned out to be the best friend Chase Manhattan ever had.

CAPITALISM SUCKS

In 1978, few in the U.S. had heard of El Salvador or Nicaragua, let alone were able to pick them out on a map. A year later, though, thousands of students were going door-to-door collecting funds for the "rock'n roll revolution" in Nicaragua and for the FMLN in El Salvador a year after that, following the assassination there of Archbishop Óscar Romero and, later, three catholic nuns from the U.S. (Ita Ford, Dorothy Kazel, Maura Clarke) and their friend (lay worker Jean Donovan). In July 1979 many of us cheered as the Sandinista Liberation Front rolled into Managua victorious, defeating Nicaragua's U.S.-backed dictator Anastasio Somoza, who had bombed his own cities with napalm supplied by President Jimmy Carter. Hundreds of college towns and churches in the U.S. set up projects with "sister cities" in Nicaragua, and sent brigades to pick coffee and build clinics, dams for electricity, and schools. "Liberation Theology" rose from the dead. U.S. citizens with no prior activist experience took to the streets in opposition to the policies of the U.S. government and provided sanctuary for those fleeing the death squads in El Salvador funded by Uncle Sam.

In Iran — a country whose oil sales filled the coffers of Exxon, Mobil, Chase Manhattan and the other Rockefeller-owned multinational corporations — a revolution succeeded in overthrowing the U.S.-backed monarchy. Independent leftists had been opposing the Shah's dictatorial rule for decades, and many of them had been tortured and murdered (with the U.S. government at best looking the other way). However, it was not the Left but a group of students from a militant Islamic faction supported by the Ayatollah Khomeini that took 52 American embassy staff hostage, claiming that the embassy was a viper's nest and a den of espionage. They demanded the return of the Shah for trial and execution. (The Shah had fled to the U.S. for cancer treatments. He died in early

1980). By taking a more militant anti-American stance than the Marxists, Khomeini's supporters managed to upstage the Left and reinforce his hegemony over the revolution. These were not the only methods, of course; they included wanton torture and assassinations of Leftists, and vile, violent anti-sexual, anti-gay and male supremacist "morality" campaigns.

Although popular within Iran, the taking of the hostages set off a chain of events that sunk the culturally progressive aspects of the Iranian revolution, drowning it in terror and bloodshed and guaranteeing the election in the U.S. of Ronald Reagan and George H.W. Bush. (Reagan had cut a secret deal with the faction's leaders (some say that they were in the pay of the CIA from the start) to hold onto the hostages until the U.S. election had ended — his "October Surprise". They were released a few minutes after Reagan was inaugurated.)[2]

The CIA was meanwhile busy installing a new strong man in Iraq, Saddam Hussein, as President. Saddam would spend a good part of the decade at war against Iran at the U.S. government's behest. Almost two million people were slaughtered in that war, as the United States, France and the Soviet Union armed all sides.

---

[2] A parallel scenario is playing out today in Egypt, but many Egyptians, caught between the military on the one hand and the Moslem Brotherhood on the other, seem to be aware of the implications of fanatical religious rule and are taking measures to curtail it. See, for example, "Dozens of progressive Egyptian women cut their hair in Tahrir Square to protest the passage of Egypt's new, fundamentalist constitution." Dec. 26, 2012: http://www.juancole.com/2012/12/protest-fundamentalist-constitution.html.

All of these mass movements, for better or worse, were direct actions on a massive scale. They not only set the context for, but directly influenced the movements erupting in the U.S. The Central America solidarity and the anti-nuclear activity, especially, were streams that flooded into an anti-Apartheid tidal wave that dominated the U.S. Left for the remainder of the '80s. By the end of that decade, the Red Balloon Collective — a small "new left" group founded in 1969 at the State University of New York at Stony Brook and deeply involved in all of the above — convened a gathering at the university of the newly formed Network of Alternative Student Press (NASP). Even without the possibility of quickly transferring information using today's technology (apparently Al Gore had not yet seen fit to invent the internet), copies of the presentations there, including my keynote address "What Is Direct Action?," wound the old fashioned way through the Alternative Student Press network and were published in radical newspapers on campuses across the country.

Participants thought of themselves as continuing in the *samizdat* or "underground" press tradition that had flourished in the late '60s and early '70s (even though many had become established as "campus clubs" and by the late '80s some were funded by student fees and were hardly "underground" any longer). Hundreds of alternative papers pumped the intellectual lifeblood of what was becoming the *new* New Left throughout the new generation, spreading leftist ideas and creating a strong cadre of young radical journalists who covered and, importantly, *participated in* all sorts of political activities. They were greatly influenced by *Yippie!* agitator Abbie Hoffman (who, in one of his last political acts a year before he died in April, 1989, helped organize a major radical student conference at Rutgers), and Ray Davis (executive director of the Washington D.C. Student Coalition against Apartheid and Racism (*D.C. SCAR*)). NASP included the young Lori Berenson (*The Thistle*, at M.I.T.) among many others. The activist–journalists exposed the way the government *used* our protests to upgrade policing strategies, infiltrate our movements, and test new weapons and instruments of repression. In fact, the alternative press debated the same questions that the Occupy movement, for one, wrestles with today, including "What to do, and how to do it?"

- How to advance the work of the anti-nuclear movement against nuclear weapons, nuclear power plants and nuclear family?[3]

---

[3] Thousands of women participated in the all-women's anti-nuclear missile encampments at Greenham Commons, England (1981-2000), the Women's Pentagon Action, and the Seneca Falls Peace Encampment in upstate New York (1983), which set up long-lasting communities and took on more and more issues (ecology, poverty, etc.) as the encampments grew. The women in the encampments also discovered that the military was subjecting them to experimental electromagnetic weapons, for which they were serving involuntarily as guinea pigs.

photo by Tony Savino

Mitchel Cohen speaking in front of the U.S. embassy in Managua, Nicaragua, Feb. 1984. The cartoon on his shirt reads: "It's simple Steve, Why don't you and your boys just get the fuck out of Central America?" Despite the vulgarity, it was shown live on Nicaraguan TV and replayed throughout the day.

- How to provide material aid (and not just generic "support") to the revolutions in El Salvador, Nicaragua, and South Africa?

- How to stay the fist of U.S. imperialism, which in the 1980s overthrew governments in Grenada and Panama and which was becoming increasingly belligerent in Iraq?

- How to promote resistance inside the U.S. military and convince the rest of the Left (let alone liberal intellectuals) to assist soldiers going AWOL or deserting, despite fears of being labeled "traitors" and isolated from one's liberal base and institutional funding?

- How to stop the clearcutting of primeval forests — home to some of the oldest living beings on this planet — and the flooding of native lands and rare wildlife habitats?[4]

- How to most effectively address the economic system that generates social crisis upon crisis and plagues "advanced" capitalist societies, especially their inner cities?

- How to end systemic racism and fight effectively for women's reproductive rights, prison abolition, and sexual liberation while grappling with the AIDS and cancer epidemics (and the emergence of the HIV paradigm promoted by the pharmaceutical industry)?, and,

---

[4] One of the first acts of the Quebecois movement for self-determination in Canada when they finally came to power was to override the self-determination of indigenous people who opposed the huge James Bay megaproject. That act entailed flooding Native lands in an area the size of New England to generate hydroelectric power to be exported to the U.S.

- How to construct our collectives and networks so as not to reproduce the top-down, centralized decision-making so prevalent in the Old Left Marxist parties?

Those are some of the questions that marked the 1980s for the Red Balloon Collective and many others involved in deepening the projects and politics of the '60s, and developing new ones. There is a continuity to our "struggles" (for want of a better word), just as there is to the interests of the ruling class opposing us. The Occupy Wall Street occupations of 2011-12 are the offspring of those direct action campaigns and strategic debates, as well as of the anti-war, radical ecology and anti-globalization movements of the '90s.

* * *

Direct action is not the same as symbolic civil disobedience. Some incorrectly use those terms interchangeably, and blur them into tactics aimed at lobbying those in power to change their policies. At other times, those same individuals denounce direct action activists as "destroyers" for using aggressive street tactics that end up alienating those the liberals seek to win to 'our' side. Both uses of the term "direct action" — symbolic and nonviolent civil disobedience, and alienating street tactics — miss the point: Direct action is not symbolic, nor is it a tactic for pressuring those in power.

Nor, for that matter, should it be allowed to provide a setting for individuals' "acting out" — behavior too often given a "pass" when so-called "anarchist principles" are invoked. (Such "principles" are often phony and self-absorbed rationalizations for tantrums and non-reflective behavior that have nothing to do with anarchism; they provide an excuse for simply regurgitating all the crap that U.S. individualistic-capitalism or Soviet-influenced state-capitalism has stuffed into our heads, and thus influencing the ways we relate to each other.) As Philip Slater observed, "Asking us to consider the manifold consequences of chopping down a forest, draining a swamp, spraying a field with poison, making it easier to drive into an already crowded city, or selling deadly weapons to everyone who wants them arouses in us the same impatience as a chess problem would in a hyperactive six-year-old."[5] Direct action is the opposite, a *way* not of faux rebellion but of accomplishing for ourselves, and not through intermediaries, some actual goal "directly" in the here-and-now. By *participating* in such goal-oriented projects, we expose and attack the system for exploiting our needs in its service to Wall Street, and at the same time we create models to build upon as we strive to create a different kind of society that values people and nature over the accu-

---

[5] Philip Slater, *The Pursuit of Loneliness: American Culture at the Breaking Point,* Beacon Press, 1970.

mulation of private profits.

In addition, direct action communities prefigure, to the extent possible, the new society we hope to create and the consequent non-capitalist ways of relating to each other. Thus, direct action draws from the future as well as the past; it is both a practical *tactic* for meeting the needs of our communities and also a utopian *strategy* for establishing parallel and truly democratic institutions that we then have to fight to defend, sustain and expand.

As such, direct actions contain very different moments within them — pushes and pulls that often clash, depending on which aspect is seen as most important to accomplish at any given time. In general, the tensions between tactics and strategy mirror those between organizations prioritizing the fight for reformist demands (much of the socialist Left) and the self-organized and prefigurative communities of resistance (often involving, in the U.S., anarchists and radical feminists, though not always). That tension is unavoidably present everywhere, in everything we do. For the last century-and-a-half, and with a little nudging from the police, it has played havoc with radical movements.[6]

The great Polish and German revolutionary Rosa Luxemburg

---

[6] The term "radical" is often misconstrued to mean "crazed" or "violent". But I and other radicals use the Miriam-Webster dictionary definition: "Arising from or going to a root or source; Favoring or effecting fundamental or revolutionary changes in current practices, conditions, or institutions."

wrote back in 1898 that just because capitalism is unable to reform its way to socialism, that does not mean that one should stop fighting for reforms. We are not free, she wrote, to pick and choose the one or the other — revolutionary mass movement or the fight for immediate reforms — as though they are hot and cold lentil patties on the counter of history.[7]

That age-old debate has come up repeatedly within Occupy Wall Street, where the initial participants continue to focus on the construction of alternative communities and new ways of relating to each other as key to building effective and long-term communities of resistance. Many of those in the various factions that make up the alphabet soup of the American Left, on the other hand, sneer at that emphasis and disparage its proponents' "lifestyle anarchism."[8] The parties are frustrated with what they see as the OWS founders' refusal to issue specific demands of the 1 percent.

These are factionalists who in every other setting exhibit hatred towards each other; they have not organized meaningful movements for decades. But now they have banded

---

[7] All right, it's true — Rosa referred to "sausages," not lentils. So much for Marxism-*Lentilism*! At any rate, see Rosa Luxemburg, *Social Reform or Revolution*, 1898-99, revised in 1909. In *Selected Writings of Rosa Luxemburg,* ed. Dick Howard, 1970.

[8] "Lifestyle anarchist" is a pejorative term coined by former anarchist Murray Bookchin, who used it to unnecessarily polarize, in my view, those mostly younger folks trying to "live the revolution" through lifestyle choices they were making (mostly around rejection of consumerism) but who — Bookchin argued (along with many Marxists) — were not appreciative of the history nor interested in contesting the power of the system itself.

together as a bloc to give marching orders to Occupy Wall Street, trying to impose their demands and ways of doing things on what is perhaps the most successful and sustained radical political action in a generation.

Until young activists, prompted by an article in the Canadian magazine *Adbusters,* took over Zuccotti Park on September 17, 2011 and set it up as a base for Occupy Wall Street, the most effective and sustained use of direct action in the U.S. for the last quarter-century were the campaigns of the AIDS Coalition to Unleash Power. ACT UP not only protested the policies of government and corporations regarding official definitions of AIDS and access to treatment, but its members turned themselves into human guinea pigs and organized systematic trials of self-experimentation with untested drugs and nutrients. Participants kept records of successes and failures, and, in one of the most productive early uses of the new technologies, used the internet to compare notes, compile results, and report them back to AIDS-ravaged communities.[9] ACT UP's *presence* fostered self-empowerment, and a disparate and in-your-face movement.

When Marcus Garvey, and later Malcolm X, referred to the need for "self help" they were talking about direct action,

---

[9] While there are many good books on the subject, one of the best and most accessible is by Bruce Nussbaum, *Good Intentions: How Big Business and the Medical Establishment are Corrupting the Fight Against AIDS, Alzheimer's Cancer, and More,* Penguin, 1990, which summarizes the battles over experimental treatments and alternative models.

in one of its guises. Direct action also involves shaking off the helplessness inculcated into us and taking personal risks. Take, for example, the work of Food Not Bombs, originating in the Bay Area of California. FNB feeds people who are hungry, no questions asked. The name of the project itself implies a non-too-hidden critique of government and the neoliberal policies that have resulted in hundreds of thousands of people going hungry, and making it a crime to feed them in the parks and on public sidewalks. Relevant here is the observation by Brazilian archbishop Dom Helder Camara: "When I feed the hungry, they call me a saint. When I ask *why* people are hungry, they call me a Communist."

Food Not Bombs co-founder Keith McHenry has been arrested over 100 times for serving free food in city parks. He refused to stop even in the face of arrests that could have led to *life imprisonment* under California's "three strikes and you're out" law, which the San Francisco Police Department used to try to bludgeon him into silence. Police Intelligence officers stripped Keith of his clothes, lifted him by his limbs and smashed him to the concrete floor ripping his ligaments and tendons. He was pushed into a tiny cage hanging from the ceiling and held in the dark for days. In 1995, Amnesty International and the United Nations Human Rights Commission took up his case and the international outcry brought about his release.

Others doing direct actions in the years that followed (just to give you an idea of the scope), included people who:

- systematically pulled up genetically engineered experimental fields and burned the crops, mostly in Europe (and sometimes in the U.S.)

- rebuilt sanitation, education and housing in New Orleans following Hurricane Katrina (*Common Ground* collective). In fact, Food Not Bombs' Keith McHenry helped coordinate shipments of food, clothing and other supplies for the survivors of Hurricane Katrina

- targeted the cosmetics industry's cruel experimentation on cats and monkeys (*Animal Liberation Front*)

- disabled nuclear missiles in their silos (*Ploughshares; Catholic Worker*)

- blocked Japan's whaling boats and Canada's baby seal-clubbing expeditions (*Sea Shepherd* and *Greenpeace*)

- fought the clearcutting of entire mountainsides of old-growth forest and natural habitat for so-called "development" by, among other actions, sitting in the trees — sometimes for many months (*Earth First!, Redwood Summer*).

Thousands of people changed their lives in order to remain true to their beliefs. Singer-songwriter Joni Mitchell's influential song, *Big Yellow Taxi*, was one of the first by a modern-day artist to decry the devastation of the planet in the name of *progress*: "They paved paradise and put up a parking lot," she sang. Social Ecology anthropologist Chaia Heller pithily tied pop culture to the shopping mall version of *progress* when she termed the tearing down of forests for big-box stores "The Texas Chain-Store Massacre." Indeed, as Philip Slater wrote in the influential New Left 1970 classic sociological review of American culture, *The Pursuit of Loneliness*, so-called development is "making it easier and easier to travel to more and more places that have become less and less worth driving to."[10] Hundreds of direct action activists remain in prison in the United States and Canada for participating in direct actions to save the planet. *Free all political prisoners!*[11]

Many of us in the '60s cut our political teeth on the free breakfast for children program that the Black Panther Party established — for many of us, it was our first experience with direct action. We not only helped prepare the food but physically defended those breakfast programs against police attacks and attempts to tear them down. Students for a

---

[10] Slater, *op. cit.*

[11] Listen to former Black Panther Ashanti Alston describe an attempt he was involved in that tried to break political prisoners out of jail in the early '80s, in an interview with Mitchel Cohen on "Steal This Radio," http://www.MitchelCohen.com.

Democratic Society's Economic Research and Action Projects (ERAP), and the United Farm Workers Union and Eastern Farmworkers Association built health clinics and "free stores" in poor communities. Those programs provided needed services. Why was the government letting children starve? Why didn't it provide free clinics for all? In the case of the MOVE collective in Philadelphia, why did it *bomb* their buildings, killing 11 (including five children) and burn down the neighborhood? Surely, the officials must have known. Didn't they care? More, why did they send in police to break up those much-needed service centers, arrest organizers and in some instances assassinate them?

When I was 15, I sent a very polite letter to Lyndon Baines Johnson, the President of the United States, informing him of the horrors being committed by the U.S. in its war on Vietnam. "If he only knew, he'd change things," I thought. A few months later I received a letter from the State Department thanking me for sharing my views. It concluded with, "We'll keep your name on file for future reference."

Of course government officials knew what was happening in Vietnam. It was not a question of ignorance, but of their service to the interests of capital. "Raising the consciousness" of such officials was beside the point; effectively *opposing* those interests seemed a lot more important.

Bertell Ollman, Marxist author and professor of politics at

NYU, warns not to abandon that moral and political battleground and cede control of State policies to ruling class interests. Victories depend on many factors, including our own level of mobilization and the ruling class's fear of revolt, which affects their long-term strategies as well as the immediate corporate "bottom line". We cannot allow the state, Ollman writes, to go unchallenged as a monolithic power lording over us and serving the interests of the one-percent; the State is — *like all institutions in capitalism* — an arena of class struggle where battles over policy can be won and things changed for the better through our political activity *as part of our revolutionary movements*. Ollman continues:

> For most people, their eyes are first opened politically when they grasp the state as an instrument of the ruling class; the society-wide dimensions of the problem only come into view when the state is also grasped as an objective structure tied in with capitalist economic structures. Their understanding is deepened — and the problem of organizing against capitalism better appreciated — when they also see the state as the illusory community and the hegemonic political ideology. But only when/if the state is also grasped as an arena of class struggle does Marxism become not only a way of understanding the world but *a means for changing it* through political activity.[12]

In a forgotten chapter of New Left history, the 1976 Peo-

---

[12] Bertell Ollman, "Thesis on the Capitalist State," *Monthly Review,* December 1982, reprinted as an Afterword in the Red Balloon Collective publication of Fredy Perlman's "The Continuing Appeal of Nationalism," 1998.

Photo by Mitchel Cohen

NYU Professor and Marxist scholar Bertell Ollman in Cuba, 1992.

ple's Bicentennial Committee sent carefully researched letters to family members of corporate executives outlining their fathers' and husbands' involvement in profiting from war production. The slickly produced packets outlined in graphic detail each individual's (and their company's) role in manufacturing components for the war machine used to kill people. The long arm of Truth reached into the inner sanctum of capital, breaching the sacred nuclear family. Reports abounded of the furor raised at the dinner table. Children and spouses challenged the decisions of the corporate patriarchs *inside their own homes,* adding another front to efforts to transform society.

Thousands continue to take part in those efforts, organizing *with* people to feed them when they are hungry, house them when they are homeless, wage peace with those besieged by invasions and bombings, ensure clean water and air for all, and act to save the polluted, despoiled environment. At the same time we expose and mobilize against the system for causing and perpetuating such misery and injustice. A popular poster puts it this way: "We don't inherit the world from our ancestors, we borrow it from our children."

Ours is a government that eats its children

Food — and its use as a weapon — was (and remains) a common motif. Henry Kissinger shook up many when he said: "To give food aid to a country just because they are starving is a pretty weak reason." But Kissinger's was a precise summary of U.S. capital's immoral policies with regard to food. Democrats and Republicans in government consistently betray people's needs, what else is new? But more important, are we prepared for betrayals by leaders of our own movements? The leadership of the largest antiwar coalition in the U.S., for example, refused to organize national demonstrations during the 2004 and 2008 presidential elections, fear-ing that they would embarrass the Democratic Party candidate and hurt his chances. The late historian Bob Fitch explained it well: "The Democratic Party is the Roach Motel of politics. The radicals go in and they never come out."

Recruiting vs. Self-Actuating

In Part One of this book I ask a number of "What if?" questions. "What if" students and longshore workers did *this*, nurses, health care practitioners, transit workers and Wall Street Occupyers did *that*? Through concrete proposals and historical examples we'll discuss how to devise projects to empower our social and environmental justice movements, aiming to mitigate oppressive and exploitative conditions even

(or especially) in today's dismal circumstances, and at the same time seek to understand what's causing them, so that we can also take action to overturn that system at its root.

I am writing for those who are enraged by injustice, especially when committed by our government and the corporate structure it serves, for they are acting in our name. What is *our* role at the present time? For one, we need to not only "support" but *participate in* the "Occupy" communities and scores of topical "working groups," which are emerging everywhere in response to the twin global crises of capitalism and planetary ecological collapse, and to strengthen what participants themselves are creating. There is as much to learn *from* those actions as there is to teach.

One day at Zuccotti Park, supporters of Ron Paul's campaign for President set up a table and distributed pre-printed signs. Around 8 or 9 Occupyers grabbed them and held them aloft proudly — no doubt because of the Congressman's call to end the war in Afghanistan and to dismember the Federal Reserve. Several astute activists tried to convince them to put the signs down, explaining that Ron Paul's views were *not* anti-capitalist or even anti-corporate, and that the Congressman wants to remove *all* government funding, even for socially necessary projects and institutions. But those arguments went nowhere. Just then, a thousand people came marching up Broadway for universal health care;

most of the Occupyers at Zuccotti, jazzed by the opportunity to *do* something about the deplorable state of health care in this country, flooded into the march including the very excited novice Ron Paul "supporters", who dropped their signs and picked up other ones for free universal health care — a position that Ron Paul opposes. In this instance, it was the physical and exciting presence of the large march to St. Vincent's Hospital — which had been shut down by the City and is in the process of being converted into luxury condos — that inspired the erstwhile Ron Paul supporters, and not the verbal jousting over Paul's positions. The question of "how do people actually learn?" could not be posed any more clearly: *People learn by participating.*[13] Our role — at least, those of us who have been at this for many decades — should be to nurture the "Occupy" communities, protect them from attack, and win for them the time and space that would enable them to flourish.

Unfortunately, many in Left organizations sabotage their own goals (let alone those of the larger movement) in two ways: 1) by neglecting and often ridiculing the so-called "subjective" circumstances in people's lives; and, 2) by pressuring others to adopt their faction's "line" (whatever it may

---

[13] This is a main theme of my Zen-Marxism series, to explore the social psychology of how and why people take on a "cause", and the role of those who are already active towards helping to create conditions that make that more likely and powerful.

be). Engaging in that "strategy" belies any understanding of "how people learn". Their "recruiter mentality" — and I should really write "our" mentality, as I am guilty of viewing my own role in that way on occasion, though I try to stop acting in that way the moment I become aware of it — gets in the way. It short-circuits the time needed to develop liberated zones through which participants come up with new forms and approaches to age-old political questions.

The women's liberation movement learned how to *reframe* what had previously been considered apolitical "personal" concerns (emotions, psychology, subjectivity, desires, sexuality, ways of relating) and made them central to radical organizing. Long-time Marxist activist Bettina Aptheker, for one, vividly described the consequences of failing to treat subjective experiences as part of one's revolutionary mission.[14] Left parties shoot themselves in the foot by constructing "programs" (really, in most cases, just a compilation of "correct lines" on every issue under the sun) to advertize their "position" to captive audiences in Occupy and other social movements, as though selling deodorant. "Buy our brand, not their brand!" At root, the Party conceives of its programmatic demands as *doing something to or for others:* raising their consciousness, organizing them, winning them

---

[14] Bettina Aptheker, *Intimate Politics: How I Grew Up Red, Fought for Free Speech, and Became a Feminist Rebel.* Seal Press: 2006.

as recruits to this or that group or line — even *empowering* them. It remains an ongoing battle to incorporate the political dimensions of what we used to call the "personal". We must be willing to march to the barricades *within* with as much commitment and ardor as we exhibit in challenging what's going on *out there* in the world. Left parties' sordid history of fighting with each other over which words and positions to promulgate keeps them from building and involving people in revolutionary institutions, liberated zones and direct action projects. They scavenge the garbage dumps of rhetoric for that one elusive phrase — the key, they presume, to unlocking the workers' bolted (or "false") consciousness![15]

Words, words alone, the correct combination of words! Does anyone really believe that exhortations and guilt trips could convince anyone to change the way they perceive and experience the world and shoehorn consciousness into the squeaky new shoes of revolt? Words! Exposés! Find the magic words, and *Shazzam!*, the working class will open up to them, they think, legs spread wide and steamy on the bedspread of history. *Abracadabra!* They have nothing to change in their own lives, no physical attacks to make on any institutions, no risks to take. *Aufhebung!* Wordy programs, maximum programs, minimum programs, transition-

---

[15] See, especially, Mitchel Cohen, "The Shortcomings of Traditional Leftist Strategy," (Part Seven of *Zen-Marxism*).

al programs — not deeds! Is it any wonder that today's Marxists wander ratlike through the mazes of their discontent admonishing the *working class* to hurry-up and find its way, dammit!, to its predestined cheese of socialism?

If only, they think, they could convince enough workers of the need for communist revolution and the establishment of the dictatorship of the proletariat. So, leaflet those workers to "raise their consciousness"! Support movements by twisting in "Marxist" lessons and slogans like bits of lemon at the end of every leaflet. Cajole workers to vote for the Democrat of their choice or, if they are really militant, for a socialist or Green candidate. The primary activity of the organization: to "raise consciousness" by, as V.I. Lenin put it, continually exposing abuses of the capitalist system on a nationwide scale. *And then what?* Lenin offered one answer, for conditions that existed in Russia back in 1917 — the party's armed seizure of state power in the name of the working class. But today? We Marxists have little to say about that strategy's applicability to conditions in the U.S. nor about how socialist transformation would take place in so-called "advanced" capitalist countries. Often, we don't have a clue but can't admit it, and so bluster our way through whatever movements we're involved in. The underlying assumption? If enough people come to believe in the need for socialism, then it would (Magically? Spontaneously?) come about. And if we all applaud loudly enough Tinkerbell won't die!

Exactly how does "raising consciousness" lead to revolution in industrial capitalist countries? No one says. Confused? Join the party. And here's the problem: Even when a person comes to see the ways in which that "recruiting mentality" has historically impaired the Left, they nevertheless can't get their organizations to stop doing it!

And so we're told: "Don't re-invent the wheel" by going back to basics and trying to find new ways forward, as though that admonition is some sort of truism. I beg to differ. *There is much to be gained in re-inventing the wheel.* Same with "preaching to the choir," as though speaking with people who already are, say, against the war in Afghanistan is somehow a waste of one's time. I prefer to think of it not as "preaching" but as working together and *harmonizing* the choir, *tuning-up the orchestra* to achieve some sort of musical and political concordance and impact.

Much of the Left's old ways (such as issuing demands, programs, and engaging in *pro forma* protests) is formulaic and — at least in the U.S. — already integrated into the system. *New Rule: Learn to bite your tongue.* Think, first, about learning from and supporting others, no matter how desperately a "demand" may be rattling in your teeth clanging to get out!

"Another world is possible" is not just an idealistic slogan; we need to take it to heart and embed it in new, non-

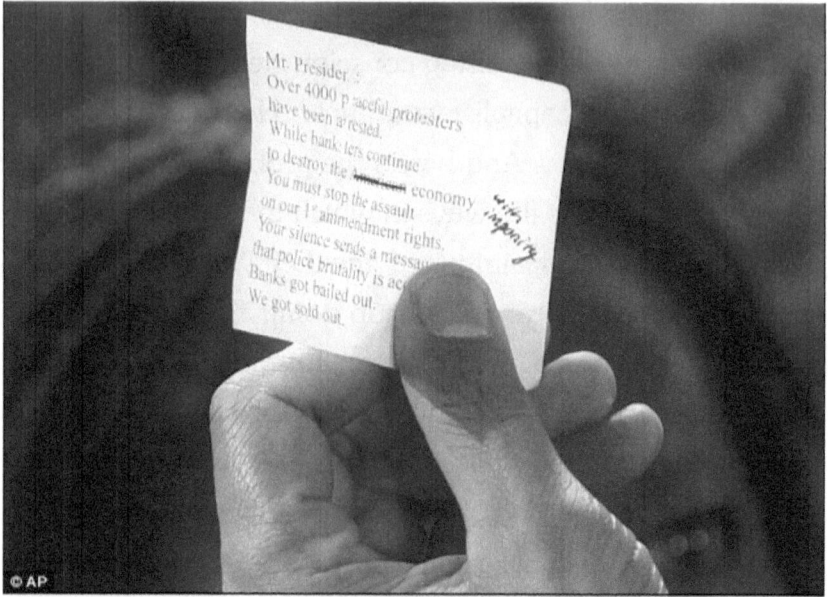

photo: Charles Dharapak/AP

Some malign Occupy Wall Street by arguing that they have no demands. But Occupy's framework has been clear from the start. Here, President Obama holds a note handed to him by an Occupyer after a speaking engagement in New Hampshire. (Nov. 2011)

hierarchal institutions. Which is exactly what people throughout the world are actually doing, and in very different and difficult circumstances. In the U.S., direct action is incorrectly viewed as any tactic that falls outside the more-or-less official "march & rally" protests. As movements appear to wane, liberals — including many in Left parties and journals — hammer at direct action movements like Occupy. They accuse them of "adventurism" and try to stuff them back into the "let's at least try to win some reforms or raise consciousness" box, thus pushing those movements to accept the authority if not the legitimacy of the existing system. As a result, those involved in the self-transformation, new relationships and long-term resistance that direct action communities make possible are confronted with intense opportunistic pressures by liberals and some leftists, as well as repression by the State and corporatocracy. In the face of the need for immediate reforms, how can we sustain direct action communities so that they can bring into existence new social structures *and* new ways of being?

When one gets stuck, it's necessary to remind oneself: **"It wasn't always this way, it isn't this way everywhere, and it doesn't have to be this way."** In fact, that should be emblazoned as subtext on every radical banner.

Storming the Pentagon

IN OCTOBER 1967, I was 18 years old and beginning my third year at the State University of New York at Stony Brook, organizing students to participate in the first militant demonstration on the East Coast against the Vietnam war, at the Pentagon.

Singer-songwriter Phil Ochs — my hero, and a major artistic force within the antiwar movement — was scheduled to perform at Stony Brook the night of the big march. Many students were saying they wouldn't go on the march because they wanted to stay and hear Phil's concert. I and other members of the campus chapter of Students for a Democratic Society wrote letters asking Phil to change the date. No answer. In desperation — oh, how it cut my heart out — we organized a boycott of his records.

Then, of course, his manager (his brother, Michael) was quick to respond. "Go ahead, attack the heavies in the movement if it makes you feel better," he wrote in an open letter printed in *Statesman*, the official student paper. But they did move up the date to October 20th, the evening before the march. Phil was interviewed on WUSB radio, Kenny Bromberg's show. "Who's this creep Mitchel Cohen who's telling everyone to boycott my records?" Phil raged.

October 21st. The huge anti-war demonstration in Washington D.C. swept past the Lincoln Memorial and over the Memorial bridge into Virginia, wave after wave of anti-war warriors crashing against the steps of the Pentagon. Abbie Hoffman and dozens of anti-warriors dressed in sackcloths played trumpets and encircled the world's biggest "edifice complex" trying to raze Jericho's walls and levitate the building. One-hundred-thousand people — some carrying signs depicting their town's opposition to the war against Vietnam, their union's, church's, campus's — inched up to the line of soldiers standing shoulder to shoulder pointing their rifles at our chests, their unsheathed bayonets glinting like a thousand points of fright in the afternoon sun.

I remember it as vividly as the infamous sunrises over the Woodstock music festival in 1969, the Bread and Puppet festivals in Vermont years later, and the incredible sunsets in New York City the week following 9-11: I remember the man carrying the hand-made sign: *"Lyndon Johnson pull out, like your father should have."* The chants, *"Hey hey LBJ, how many kids did you kill today?"* The young woman who in a moment of artistry danced in-and-out of the line of soldiers as thousands of voices sang *"Join us,"* inserting flowers into the barrels of their rifles. Soon, a dozen people joined her. "Flower Power," East Coast style!

As the afternoon wore on, word of a "sit-in" spread like wildfire through the enormous crowd, and dozens began climbing ropes tied to a parapet overlooking a set of huge doors, just beyond the soldiers' reach. The sit-in was blocking one of the entrances. The Pentagon was no longer unassailable! Yea, and in high school gym I couldn't climb the ropes to save my life. Oh well. Try anyway. I'd managed to drag myself up a few yards when a hand grabbed one of my legs. I panicked, tried to kick it away without losing my grip, but it wouldn't let go.

"Uh-oh, this is it, they're going to arrest me," I thought, my first arrest. I kicked frantically, tried to get away. Finally, in panic, I looked down and saw *my father* yanking me back and my mother screaming: "Where do you think you're going?"

"What are you doing here?"

They came to protest too. "How did you find me? I've gotta join the sit-in, all my friends are up there."

Indeed, my friends from Stony Brook SDS were already up on the ledge. Even a professor from Stony Brook, Mike Zweig, was sitting-in. "You have to let me go. I helped organize the buses!" I shouted, as though that compelling point would clinch the argument. The frustrated and embarrassed tears already'd begun spilling down my cheeks.

"No way. You're exhausted, get down right now."

My parents were right about one thing: I *was* exhausted, racing around on an adrenaline high having not slept for three days. SDS and the Organization for Progressive Thought had been selling bus tickets around the clock door-to-door in the dormitories, cafeterias and TV lounges at Stony Brook. We brought seven bus-loads of protesters to the Pentagon — around 300 people. My brother Robert, who had just entered Stony Brook a month before, and I were among the handful responsible for selling tickets, planning bus arrangements and making sure the drivers wouldn't strand us *en route* as happened to busloads from other campuses. There would be time enough later for sleep. I simply had to be up there! And now my parents (how did they ever find me?) were yanking me back.

My father was a Corporal in the Marine Corps in the South Pacific in World War 2, and was awarded the Navy and Marine Corps medal for heroism by Franklin Delano Roosevelt. A plane had crashed on the Philippine island where he was stationed. The plane was on fire and dad was the only one to run *towards* the plane after hearing cries from inside it. He grabbed two 50-pound fire extinguishers, strapped them to his back, sprayed the gas tank and wings, ripped the door off its hinges and carried out to safety half-a-dozen people.

Dad always spoke out against the atom bomb and the Vietnam war. "You'll go over my dead body," he famously exploded one night at supper at our apartment in the Marlboro Projects in Gravesend, Brooklyn — as though I had any thoughts at all to go into the military. (In fact, I was in the process of resisting the draft at the time.) Now, at the Pentagon, he offered a compromise: "You're not going up there, understand? But they're going to need food and blankets. Let's start making a collection."

Those were in the days before the anti-nuclear movement introduced a structure built upon affinity groups, in which one person who is not to get arrested would be designated as doing "support," and would be responsible for the group's logistical needs such as food, medical support, bail, and . . . blankets. We spent the next few hours collecting

Abraham (Sonny) Cohen & Ruth Hope Sunshine's wedding, Aug. 12, 1945. Sonny (20 years old, seated on left) wears Marine Corps dress blues and 19-year-old Ruth (an only child) sits to his left, with other members of their immediate family. Ruth's mom, Gertrude K. Sunshine, was a member of the Industrial Workers of the World and sits directly to her left, and Ruth's father, Jack, who emigrated from Poland, where he was arrested for selling condoms on the street and went on to become the owner of the Certified Aspirin company in New Jersey, sits directly across from Gertrude (3rd from right). As with all people, there's a story that goes along with each one, especially dad's older brothers Dave (standing, 2nd from right, who was a bookie), Harry (who counterfeited stamps), and older sister Dora (who refused to sit at the same table with them). Dad's sister Mary had fled from home a few years earlier to be with Trotsky in Mexico and was never seen again. That may have had something to do with my dad's antipathy to Trotskyists. (If some here look pretty shady, you'd be absolutely right.)

dozens of blankets and warm clothing for those sitting-in. Afterward, my parents dragged me to the bus back to Stony Brook and made sure I didn't hop off. They waved goodbye as it pulled away. I crashed out in someone's (whose?) arms. Vaguely I remember someone kissing me.

Forty-five years ago! Che Guevara had been murdered by the CIA in Bolivia just two weeks before. We — yes, that expansive "we", meaning *moi* and another troublemaker at Stony Brook, Spencer Black, who would much later become a noted ecology-minded state legislator in Wisconsin — phoned-in Che's obituary to the NY Times and billed it to the student government. They were at a loss to account for it when the university administration, which still ran student government's finances, reviewed the bills.

A month later, New York City would be rocked by a police riot against antiwar protesters. Thousands of students descended on a dinner at the Waldorf for the war-makers. Some had gotten jobs in the kitchen. When the country's elite lifted the lids of their dishes they found pigs' heads staring back at them, and dozens of naked waiters and waitresses chanting: "U.S. out of Vietnam!"

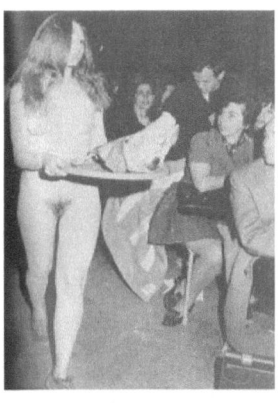

Naked anti-war protesters serving pigs heads to the elite in NYC, 1967.

Outside, all hell was breaking loose. This was the anti-war movement's first "street action" on the East Coast. Hundreds of people would begin crossing Park Avenue at the green light, very slowly. We'd be stretched fully across when the light turned red. Everyone linked arms and faced the traffic terrified, intending to block the cars. I closed my eyes, heard the gut-wrenching Screeeeech! When I dared open them I saw an Oldsmobile had skidded to a stop just inches from my thighs.

The police moved in. We snake-danced the wrong way down one-way streets, tying up traffic and making it hard for police cars to chase us.

We were kids, and we were as brazen as we were scared shitless. Leaving the dinner, Secretary of State Dean Rusk's car was hit by a molotov cocktail. The cops cracked heads. Willa Kay grabbed my hand — *Kay, where are you now?* — tearful, gasping for breath: "Mitchel, let's get out of here!" We raced across Manhattan in search of the bus back to Stony Brook and were amazed to find that everyone was arriving at the same time, unscathed. A few weeks later I would be one of several Stony Brookers rejecting my draft card at the Smithtown Draft Board. We faced five years in jail. My parents learned about that from WINS radio news. ("Give us 22 minutes, we'll tell you what your progeny is up to.")

The anti-war movement was erupting everywhere. Draft

resisters blockaded induction centers, burned draft cards, chased military recruiters from campus after campus, and exposed war research and "defense" contractors' ties to the university. On the West coast, thousands blocked troop trains and munitions factories. Even Bill Clinton, in the one good thing he ever did, took part in anti-war protests (although now it appears that he was informing on those movements in Europe for the CIA).

At Stony Brook, I was speaking publicly for the first time against the war when construction workers attacked our anti-war rally because they thought we had taken down the American flag. (Maintenance workers had lowered it when it began to rain.) One punched me in the stomach, keeling me over. Another worker punched Neal Frumkin, the head of SDS at Stony Brook, and broke his tooth. We went with the Suffolk County police through the construction site looking for them, but they were nowhere to be found.

Fifteen years later, the same worker by coincidence picked me up hitchhiking. He laughed about that incident, which to me had been so traumatic — "Yea, I was an ass," he said, "glad to see you're still at it!" As if to make it up to me, he fed me an inside scoop: construction supervisors were submitting falsified reports that covered-up a crack in the main beam in the new Graduate Biology building. "Of course the administration knows about it," he snarled, "but someone's getting a kickback. That building could collapse!"

Time accelerates and compacts. Whole lifetimes are shoe-horned into the space of a few months. The Tet Offensive, LBJ's abdication, Martin Luther King's assassination, Paris, Columbia University, Robert Kennedy's assassination, Czechoslovakia, Chicago, Eugene McCarthy's anti-war presidential campaign, the farm workers' boycott — all crammed into that semester, 1968.

The world was spinning madly out of their control, revolutionary movements being born. We lived "emergency lives" filled with meaning, fear, excitement and desperation. World War 2 was our parents' war and had shaped their world; to us it was ancient history, having ended 23 years earlier. An eternity! And yet double that "eternity" from '68 to today!

I am old. Young folks today *thank me* for coming to *their* protests. So respectful, these young whippersnap ... er, Occupyers! My daughter — all grown up and living on the West Coast — can't believe I was ever young, the things we did.

The decades drop like precious petals, paths to follow. I wend my way back in my mind to that New Year's Eve when Kay kissed me and brought me back to her parents' apartment in Stuyvesant Town. Her father woke up and caught us rolling on the living room carpet, our hands with minds of their own feverishly trying to disentangle from the twists of cotton and rayon underwear.

Stony Brook students were always organizing. We had huge contingents at every anti-war and civil rights demonstration, and had built the largest SDS chapter on the East Coast, even bigger than Columbia's, a fact curiously omitted from books on the New Left. Today's authors seem to find import only in what went on at elite Ivy League schools — just as they did in the old days — and care not a whit for state universities or community colleges.

The Independent Caucus of SDS was everywhere at SUNY Stony Brook in 1969. Red Balloon emerged from the caucus the following year, the most politically volatile in Stony Brook's history. I was 20 years old by then and still a sophomore after four years in and out of college, coordinating the United Farm Workers grape boycott on Long Island. My girlfriend that year, Fran B., had a summer job interning at the White House. I feared she might be an FBI agent even though she was still a teenager, which on the one hand shows our levels of paranoia, and on the other our super sensitivity to the possibilities of infiltration, which were very real as we later learned (and sort of already knew). Fran took off from work to come with me to Woodstock ... and broke up with me there as Joan Baez sang "Sweet Sir Galahad." The rains camouflaged my tears — I thought they'd never stop.

Each new September brought new romances, and with them new possibilities. When school resumed, I stared across professor Jonah Raskin's English class and fell like Alice into the rabbit-hole eyes of a 19-year-old transfer student from Oberlin. Those eyes! They could see everything, know everything! Nothing else existed. Roberta brought an exciting acid-tongued feminism into our emerging collective, as well as a more studious anarchism.

Along with Roberta and me, Jack B. made up the third member of the Red Balloon Collective's founding triumvirate. We held meetings on the bed Roberta and I shared in a suite in the new dorms named "Kelly Quad," a suite built for six but soon to hold 15. We lived there illegally. The Jefferson Airplane, Janis Joplin, Jimi Hendrix, Phil Ochs, Crosby-Stills-Nash & Young, the Moody Blues, Donovan and of course Dylan blasted from the speakers in our room 24/7. We put out underground papers with others in SDS; but we finally decided to start our own paper. After two days of wrangling over names: "Vanguard" this, "Proletarian" that, "Worker" the other thing, Roberta was ready to jump ship. Already, 18, 19 and 20-year-olds were jaded by the "Old Left" verbiage and sterility. We didn't want any part of the boring, lecturing style of *The Militant* (Socialist Workers Party), *Challenge* (Progressive Labor Party) or other papers sold regularly on the campus. (A few years later we helped the NY Black Panther Party write and publish the first issue of *Right On!* and we arranged for them to move into our suite in the official "Experimental College" — a result of an extended campaign to abolish grades — but that will have to be another story.)

I had just finished a poem, which I read to the crew squatting in the suite. One line went: "The cat leapt out of the tree last night, through the air like a red balloon." Frustrated, Jack said, "Hey, let's just call the paper 'Red Balloon'. We can change it next week." Forty-plus years later I still meet folks who tell me that Red Balloon changed their lives and they are surprised to learn that the collective lasted in one form or another into the mid-'90s.

Our first official action as a collective was a commemoration of the opening of the then state-of-the-art computer center with an action against the University's ties to the Department of Defense, followed by the "DOD Jamboree," which exposed secret war research on campus. Allard Lowenstein was scheduled to speak on campus the afternoon of the Jamboree. Lowenstein, a politician from New York City, was a stalwart opponent of the war but also a Democratic Party wheeler-dealer. Like many, Lowenstein had previously participated in the Student Non-Violent Coordinating Committee in Mississippi. The mainstream media credited him with having "single-handedly" mounted the pressure inside the Democratic Party in 1968 that forced Lyndon Johnson to declare that he wouldn't run for re-election as President. (After being exposed as a conduit for CIA funds into the National Student Association, Lowenstein was murdered by a disgruntled former protégé in 1980 who thought that Lowenstein was hounding him via messages sent through a radio capacitor secretly implanted in his teeth by the CIA.) As he often did in speeches across the country and contrary to the positive way many remember that liberal bastion of American politics, Lowenstein always targeted *the Left*. Like many liberals of those times, he took special delight in denouncing our attempts to drive military recruiters and war-related research from the campus.

Four hundred people in the newly-opened Student Union building, never shy over letting their opinions be known, alternately hooted and cheered Lowenstein. Amidst the tumult, Lowenstein got popped by a water balloon left over from the Defense Department Jamboree attack on the Administration Building, courtesy of a member of our new collective that had in just a few days grown to a couple of dozen. No harm done, at least not physically. Instead of laughing it off, though, Lowenstein — ever the drama queen — treated it as though he'd been shot! He launched into a vicious red-baiting tirade, and pandemonium erupted. That act marked the Red Balloon Collective's birth on campus and permanently sealed our "militant" reputation. It also highlighted our low tolerance for liberal demagogues. Our theme song, for a time, was Phil Ochs' "Love Me I'm a Liberal." It could have been written with Lowenstein in mind.

The Red Balloon Collective, like many other small groups, strove to upset the ideological apple carts without physically hurting anyone, in order to expose the government's and corporations' hypocrisy, and the university's complicity with the war machine. At one protest, when we didn't have enough people to fully shut down the Administration building over the University's complicity with the war, we had would-be protesters sit on every toilet in every bathroom in the building. As the morning dragged on, dozens of workers had to flee the building in search of bathrooms. The rest of our small group rallied out front. In a few hours the administrators, unaware of our "tactic", had no choice but to shut down the building. When Hunter College banned the posting of flyers except in several brown bulletin-board sized rectangles, instead of arguing over free speech (as though the administrators didn't know what they were doing) students affiliated with our collective painted brown rectangles at key places, and posted flyers in them, the administration never the wiser. Over the years, we involved thousands of people in actions. In contrast to the "old left" Communist organizations and their "official organs" (newspapers) that blanketed the campus trying to recruit cadre to their party's line, the Balloonistas — similar to the Wall Street Occupyers today — tried consciously not to waste time arguing over the "correct line". In fact, although we had an obvious direct action orientation, *we had a line against lines.* There are many paths to truth, to living meaningfully, to changing the world. In fact, if there is only one answer, the *question* is wrong.

Nicaraguan Poet Ernesto Cardenal put it well: "Nothing ever comes to the sleeper but a dream." We believed in *action*. While we all make mistakes (and some of ours were doozies), the biggest mistake in the face of mass murder by the U.S. military in Vietnam and the repression of the Black Liberation movement here at home would be to do nothing. Nothing changes without people willing to take action and risks. So, in a sense, *that* was our "line". Yes, we studied, intensively — as a guide to Action. Leave no turn unstoned.

I wish I could go back and "fix" some of the things we did wrong. How could you trust someone who says "I wouldn't change a thing"? I wish I could go back and change hundreds of things I'd done, some of them embarrassing, inept, stupid, sometimes racist, sometimes sexist, or simply wrong. I once asked the former Weather Underground leader Bernardine Dohrn what she would have done differently. "I would have paid much more attention to the women's liberation movement, treated it as the important movement it was instead of just giving it lip-service, and brought it into SDS." I was floored when she added, "You know Mitchel, no one's ever asked me that before." Yikes!

Debates in the New Left

> The materialist doctrine that people are products of circumstances and upbringing, and that, therefore, changed people are products of changed circumstances and changed upbringing, forgets that it is people who change circumstances and that the educator must him or herself be educated.[16]

Fredy Perlman's 1969 essay, "The Reproduction of Daily Life," flew out of the mimeo machine at the State University of NY at Stony Brook and changed our lives. To mass print articles at the time — there being no affordable Xerox technology — we would type onto blue-film stencils. Every typo became an adventure, filling in the mistyped letter or word with gooey correction-fluid (I still remember those numbing fumes!) filling in the holes in the stencil, waiting for it to dry, realigning the stencil and typing over it, and then anchoring it onto the AB Dick mimeograph machine to print thousands of copies. Every night we'd pick the lock to the basement room in South Hall in G-Quad, which housed student government's new Gestetener stencil-cutter and AB Dick mimeograph. A few hours later, teams of SDSers would fan out distributing copies of that essay and other radical literature under the door of every one of the thousands of dorm rooms on campus.

Although most of us had barely turned 20 or 21 — or

---
[16] Karl Marx, *Theses on Feuerbach*, number 3.

maybe *because* of that — we were already engrossed in trying to understand the many ways human beings reproduce the oppressive and alienated circumstances of capitalist society even as we seek to change them. The power of capital resides not just in institutions of corporate investment and high finance, but in our own daily activities. Fredy Perlman's essay helped us appreciate just how deeply the tendrils of capitalism curl into our souls. Simply in the course of "functioning" in capitalism, we expand the apparatus and availability of commodity production (things which have the potential to make life easier) and, at the same time, increase the power of the social and economic relations aligned against us, narrowing the possibilities for freedom. Yet what choice do we have but to sell our labor-time for a wage? Capitalism provides opportunities to change the world and at the same time undermines our ability to actually do so.

That conundrum pervades the later writings of at least one key New Left theorist, Herbert Marcuse who, unbeknownst to us, had been mentoring the still not widely known Angela Davis. Marcuse had studied the writings of both Hegel and Marx; he was a leading figure of the Frankfurt School whose academic luminaries fled Germany in the 1930s and established the International Institute for Social Research at Columbia University in New York City. By the 1960s, Marcuse, who had by then moved to California, had come to hold the

extremely pessimistic view that the self-reflection essential for radical transformation was impossible in advanced capitalist societies like the U.S.

According to Marcuse, the real domination by capital had come to so penetrate daily life that it not only shaped but *defined* and *regimented* everyone's needs and desires. It then fed those manufactured desires with commodities which we buy, hoping to fulfill those false needs,[17] averting and wholly undermining the potential for revolutionary consciousness to emerge. While the New Left as a whole agreed with the first part of that critique (that the system manufactures and manipulates false needs and desires), it is the last part of that equation that divided the New Left. A sector of the New Left that later became associated with the Weather Underground, for one, accepted the main tenets of Marcuse's pessimistic argument

---

[17] See, for example, John Berger, *Ways of Seeing,* the British Broadcasting Company and Penguin Books, 1992, where Berger examines the way art reflects bourgeois norms but also shapes consciousness, made more obvious with the advent of advertising and the juxtaposition of images. *Ways of Seeing* was the first text I used in the underground Marxism for Beginners class I taught for almost 2 decades at Stony Brook.

about the non-revolutionary character of the working class in the U.S. and Europe, and wrote it off as part of an "aristocracy of labor" benefiting from its "privileged" exploitation (not capitalism's, but the working class') of the rest of the world. Detroit activist and New Left theorist Fredy Perlman, on the other hand, while appreciating the deep penetration of capitalist relations and ways of seeing into everyday life, disagreed with Marcuse's one-dimensional conclusion. Perlman observed that no system is *mono*, having only one vector. The logic of the system as a whole, Perlman wrote, contradicts its parts at every turn. In fact, it is because capitalism is built on inherent contradictions that *within every oppressive circumstance there also lies opportunity.*[18]

I hitched into New York City from Stony Brook to hear Marcuse speak near the end of the '60s, at an event at the Fillmore East on the Lower East Side. Marcuse reiterated the themes of his most pessimistic book, *One-Dimensional Man,* arguing that bourgeois ideology had come to so dominate all aspects of everyday life in advanced capitalism that the resistance of the working class had become nothing but ritual — when it occurred at all. The working class can thus

---

[18] John Gerassi, who died last summer, recounted a wonderful vignette wherein Marcuse repeatedly asked him to set up a meeting with Gerassi's godfather, Jean-Paul Sartre. The author of *Being and Nothingess* responded that he'd reluctantly meet with Marcuse on the condition that if the latter said anything about *reification,* Gerassi was to interrupt him and get him out of there.

only act through mechanisms mediated and promulgated by capitalism, bolstering the existing system.

Three decades later while visiting Berlin, I had cause to remember that youthful "voyage" to see Marcuse at the Fillmore East, which I recounted in the lead poem in my book, *The Permanent Carnival*:

> In Berlin I have a guide. Lars takes me
> to the Canal at Landwehr where Rosa Luxemburg
> and Karl Liebnecht were murdered by
> so-called socialists in 1919. Lars and his friends
> are building an archive on student movements.
> Adorno and Marcuse are their idols.
> I'd once heard Herbert Marcuse speak —
> they are ecstatic. For three hours they grill me
> about the movement in the U.S., the Situationists
> and, of course, Marcuse. I tell them
> it was long ago 1968 when I was 19
> at the Fillmore East between sets
> by the Jefferson Airplane and Phil Ochs.
> Sorry, he was bor-i-i-i-i-ng. Half the audience walked out.
> He was very depressing. No matter,
> they want every detail. I tell them how
> we'd hitched from Stony Brook in blizzard
> the last ride in a Lincoln Continental
> dropped us right in front of the Fillmore.

Everyone stared, thought we were famous,
signed a few autographs.
"That's it?," they said.
"No, then there was the time we slept together."
"What?!!!"
"Hey, dya think old Herbert
was so one-dimensional?"
"Is that true?"
My New York sarcasm did not translate.

Thus, it became one of those lovely ironies of history when some student radicals in the '60s hurled copies of Marcuse's book at corporate offices and bank windows, sometimes attached to bricks. Many had inexplicably latched onto *One-Dimensional Man*, of all things, as their battle cry for action!

NYPD pepper sprays young women doing absolutely nothing, while trapped inside orange netting, September 2011.

🎵 *It was twenty years ago today*
Sgt. Pepper taught the man to spray
It's never really out of style
When used against the rank and file
So may I introduce to you
The act you've known for all these years

Sgt. Pepper Spray and Heads Clubbed Band 🎵

Lt. John Pike, UC Davis, pepper-spraying protesters peacefully sitting on the ground.

In the American Fall, 2011, actions targeting the apparatus of capitalism and globalization began sweeping the country, picking up the rhythms of the Arab Spring and Wisconsin, and turning them into Occupy Wall Street. In most places, the Occupyers were brutalized by police, arrested *en masse* and sadistically sprayed with chemical weapons.

No longer, vowed the Occupyers (some of them disillusioned Obama voters), shall we allow the pundits, politicians, corporate (and even 'progressive') media, police forces and governments to sidetrack movements for social, economic and environmental justice into the electoral arena, where our votes are bottled, bought, sold and outright stolen, rendering us complicit in reproducing and consuming our own alienation.

A message of solidarity issued by a collective of Cairo-based Occupyers declared: "We are now in many ways involved in the same struggle," adding: "What most pundits call 'The Arab Spring' has its roots in the demonstrations, riots, strikes and occupations taking place all around the world."

Critics of the Occupy movement have dismissed suggestions that they share many similarities with protests in the Middle East, arguing that the latter have been about libera-

PORTLAND, OREGON PEPPER-SPRAY, 2011

ZUCCOTTI PARK, NYC 2011

tion from tyranny while those in the U.S. are focused on economic reform. But the solidarity statement explicitly rejects that division, claiming that the Egyptian struggle is against "systems of repression, disenfranchisement and the unchecked ravages of global capitalism"; it highlights the social and economic damage caused by the implementation of neoliberal free market policies under the Mubarak regime.

"As the interests of government increasingly cater to the interests and comforts of private, transnational capital, our cities and homes have become progressively more abstract and violent places, subject to the casual ravages of the next economic development or urban renewal scheme," reads the statement. "An entire generation across the globe has grown up realizing, rationally and emotionally, that we have no future in the current order of things."

OAKLAND, CA 2011

We're Sgt. Pepper Spray and Heads Clubbed Band
We hope our torture doesn't show

Sgt. Pepper Spray and Heads Club Band
Protect and serve the status quo

SEATTLE PEPPER SPRAY, 2011

♪ *We're Sgt. Pepper Spray and*
Sgt. Pepper Spray and
Sgt. Pepper Spray and Heads Clubbed Band

OAKLAND, CA - OCT. 25, 2011
Tear gas fills downtown Oakland streets as police attack Occupyers late into the night.

♪ It's wonderful to club you
It's certainly a thrill
You're such a peaceful group of kids
We love to spray your face and throat
We love to break your ribs

NEW YORK CITY 2011

Lt. Anthony Bologna walked up to young women peacefully gathered and pepper-sprayed them in the face for no legitimate reason, earning him the nickname "Tony Baloney". He was transferred to a Staten Island precinct, but thus far has not been prosecuted.

AS AMERICAN AS OCCU-PIE | 73

NEW YORK CITY 2011

 *I don't really want to stop the show*
But I thought you might like to know

♫ *That the people want to occupy*
Without pepper spray in their eye

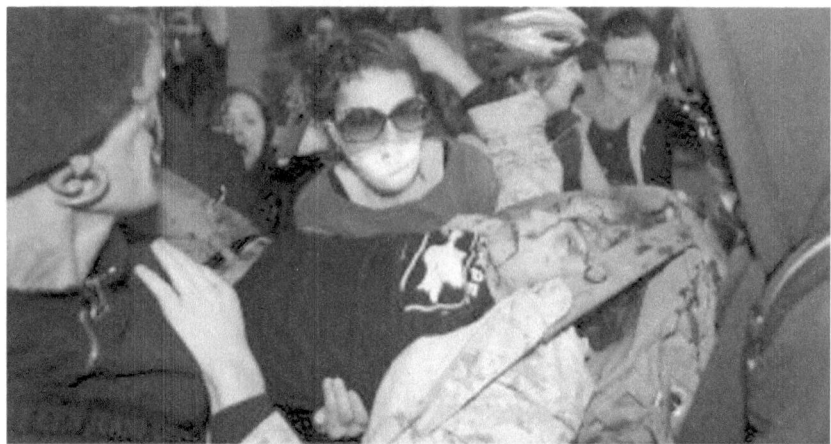

Former Iraq War Veteran Scott Olsen, attended to by the people's medics after being shot in the head with tear gas cannister fired by Oakland police from a high-powered rifle.

photo from Socialist Worker

SANTA MONICA COLLEGE, CA. Police pepper spray students outside a Board of Trustees meeting, April 3, 2012.

So let me introduce to you
The one that everybody fears
Sgt. Pepper Spray and Heads Clubbed Band*

*Words by Dave Lippman

Photo: James Fassinger/Guardian [London]

Protesters march on Port of Oakland, Nov. 2, 2011 in response to call by Occupy Oakland for "general strike" over brutal police attack the previous week. Earlier in the day, workers crippled the port by refusing work.

NEW YORK CITY 2011

25,000 Wall Street Occupyers and union supporters reclaimed the Brooklyn Bridge on November 17, 2011. The crowd roared as a giant "bat-signal" — "99%" — and the following stencils were laser-projected onto the ugly Verizon Building. Below are all the stencils used in sequence that night. (The entire manual for how to make and use such equipment is reprinted here, in the *Appendix*, from interoccupy.org)

Satiric graphics of the UC Davis cop pepper-spraying Occupyers soon went viral over the internet.

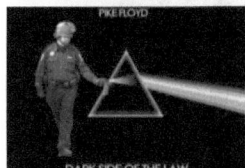
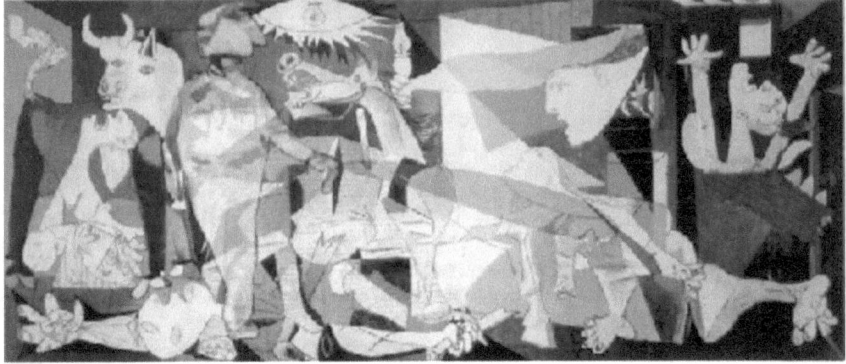

With Occupy Wall Street, Americans are learning to revolt like an Egyptian.

For the first time in recent memory, Occupy has succeeded in placing the idea of **challenging the rule of capitalism** onto the historical agenda. While some critique Occupy Wall Street for refusing to issue demands, they ignore the fact that no reformist demands could rectify the *system* we're living in:

- Wall Street bankers and brokerage firms received $14 *trillion* in bailouts, according to economist Michael Hudson, while homeowners, farmers and renters received no assistance at all. Wall Street got bailed out, and we got sold out! Predatory "lenders" have foreclosed on more than ten million homes since 2008, and some 12 million more households have mortgage payments that far exceed the value of their property.

Ironically, had even a fraction of those funds been made available to homeowners, farmers and renters, most of the recipients would have been able to pay off their mortgages. The banks would still have ended up with the loot but people would have been able to keep their homes. Coincidence, or capitalism as usual?

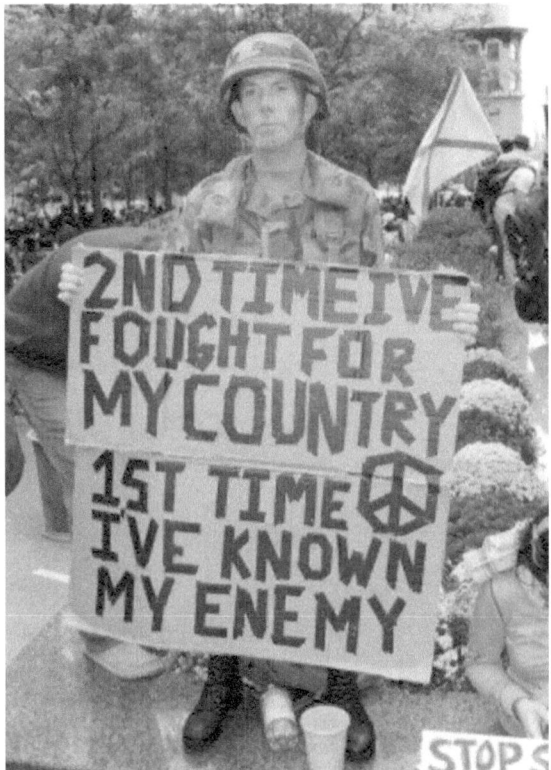

- U.S. wars in Iraq, Afghanistan and Libya (and "spillovers" in Pakistan, Yemen, the Congo and Syria) continue to destroy the lives of hundreds of thousands of people, while those profiting from those wars are rewarded with lucrative government contracts, tax abatements and U.S. military protection.

- Politicians are afforded the finest publicly funded health care and retirement packages, but they vote to privatize health care for the rest of us, with an eye towards sacking Social Security.

- The government cuts taxes for the rich and increases taxes and the cost of social services (hidden taxes) on the 99 percent.

- It also reduces services for lower and middle-income people to pay for the bailouts to the bankers.

- Students are up to their ears in debt, while supposedly "non-profit educational institutions" like NYU and Columbia U. tear up the local communities in expansions paid for by tuition increases. The total student debt now exceeds $1 trillion, surpassing the total consumer debt.

- Instead of increasing wages and providing meaningful jobs, for the last 30 years the corporate and financial institutions — through the government they control — have forced people to go into debt (at exorbitant interest rates), mortgage their homes and run up their credit cards just to pay for basic necessities like health care, housing, child care, transportation, education and food.

- Oil, natural gas, and nuclear power corporations are creating the greatest man-made environmental catastrophe in history; the government subsidizes *them* while thousands of working class people lose their jobs, homes, land, clean air and water. Entire ecosystems are destroyed, as species are poisoned and rendered extinct at the highest rate since the Cretaceous-Tertiary mass extinction (some 65 million years ago in which 50 percent of the species alive at that time were wiped out).

- The planet is being ravaged in an orgy of accumulation and plunder by a few, while the rest of us are crushed by economic, environmental and imperialist ventures over which we have no say.

Appeals to the morality or conscience of those in power are futile. They know exactly what they are doing and whose interests they serve. And the basic unfairness of it all, which propels Occupyers across the country, is more and more recognized as not simply caused by personal greed (although that abounds) but by "a *system* that runs on greed, exploitation, plunder. Greedy bankers are a symptom, not the root cause of economic collapse."[19]

COUNTRY	RATIO OF PAY CEO VS. AVG WORKER
JAPAN	11:1
GERMANY	12:1
FRANCE	15:1
ITALY	20:1
CANADA	20:1
SOUTH AFRICA	21:1
BRITAIN	22:1
MEXICO	47:1
VENEZUELA	50:1
UNITED STATES	475:1

The truth will set you free.

---

[19] Pete Dolack, "It's not about personal greed, it's about a system that runs on greed," flyer, 2012.

The cost to the American people of the 2008 Wall Street bailout has been enormous. The giant banks and brokerage houses — those bastions of free-market capitalism, opponents of government hand-outs to the working class and the poor, and qualm-free when it comes to foreclosing on millions of homes and farms — went crying to the government for handouts: "Save us! We're too big to be allowed to fail!"

At the very least, the government and the Federal Reserve *could have* said to Wall Street: "We'll bail you out, give you the $14 trillion, but here's what you have to do for it: Cancel all mortgages on family homes and farms. No foreclosures. Return people to their homes." Other stipulations could have required a cancellation of all student and healthcare-related debts, and public apologies by the CEOs in exchange for shortening their future prison sentences. But neither Bush, Obama, Congress nor the Fed took that route, and not a single banker or corporate polluter went to jail.

The funds handed over to Wall Street were taken from schools, libraries, hospitals and firehouses, environmental protection and mass-transit. Meanwhile, prices were sent skyrocketing for basic goods and services like college educations and tolls on bridges. When NYC subway fares go up again next year, remember that these are hidden taxes on the working class and poor, and are due to the massive Wall Street bailouts and huge defense budgets, needed by capital but paid for by the working class. Capitalist ideologues preach "laissez-faire", but they always beg for government intervention when working class people at home or abroad threaten their exploitation, profits, policies and plunder.

GLOBAL REVOLT TAKES MANY FORMS

Across the world, new forms of action are taking place specific to each of those geographical areas, and they are unmasking the injustice inherent in the global capitalist system. In **China**, facing great personal danger from the authoritarian state, some have used the internet to brand all the disparate protests there part of the "Jasmine Revolution," making them seem coordinated and part of something larger. Thus, when a recent strike by truck drivers in Shanghai was tagged online as part of the Jasmine revolt, the government yielded to the demands of the drivers within three days, reducing working hours, increasing wages and inspiring further actions.

The "protests" rely on the new "social media technologies". People text friends to take part in weekly 'strolls' for human rights. "The strolling announcements consist of a round-up and analysis of the latest protest incidents in the country, supplemented by pictures and videos, along with the designation of a 'strolling' site. ... When a strolling announcement is branded as part of the Jasmine Revolution, the government sends police units to the designated location to suppress it."[20] What they find, however, is a crowd of people wandering around a marketplace or a square minding their own busi-

---

[20] Ayushman Jamwal, "Chinese dissidents 'strolling' toward democracy, online and off," *Waging NonViolence,* July 14, 2011.

ness — no visible signs, no speeches, no outward indication that they are part of a protest, and thus no police harassment. Afterward, reports are circulated on the web. Such deployments make the regime look foolish, and have become part of daily conversation in China, dissolving people's fears and inspiring similar stroll-protests.

In some countries, where demonstrations are banned by the authorities (as they were under apartheid in South Africa), *funerals* become a place where large numbers of people gather. And there's no shortage of funerals. With no rally speakers or protest signs, the music and procession convey the political message. (At the 1975 funeral of famed singer Oum Kalthoum in **Egypt**, for example, although not formally a "protest", 4 million mourners hijacked the deceased "people's singer's" casket and paraded with it through the working class streets of Cairo.)

One of the more famous protests occurred in December 2008 when **Iraqi** reporter Muntadhar al-Zaidi took off his shoe, held its sole facing U.S. President George W. Bush and threw it at him, shouting in Arabic (according to the BBC), "This is a farewell kiss from the Iraqi people, you dog." With his second shoe he yelled, "This is for the widows and orphans and all those killed in Iraq." President Bush ducked twice, avoiding being hit. In much of the world, holding up the sole of a shoe is roughly the equivalent of giving someone the finger.[21]

---

[21] The Turkish company that made the shoes thrown at Bush, Ramazan Baydan,

Al-Zaidi inspired similar shoe tosses all over the world, including the **Ukraine**, **Toronto**, **Washington D.C.**, and in **Calgary**, where protesters took things from the realm of the symbolic into more of a direct action by creating a "shoe cannon".

In 2011, a new form of protest sprang up in **Belarus**, after the government devalued its currency. Participants gathered in agreed locations without any banners and stood silently (or sometimes clapped in unison). The silent protests proved to be so unnerving that parliament passed a law  declaring it illegal to gather in a public place to express political views or protest through "mass silence", reminiscent of **South Vietnam**'s futile ban on the manufacture or import of cloth dyed red or blue.[22] Online parodies hit the blogosphere. In the face of rigid and oppressive authority, ridicule becomes an effective weapon — and creates an "impressive display of farce," as exemplified by the repression in **Russia** against the all-women musical performance group "Pussy Riot".

The much maligned pirates of **Somalia** introduced another form of direct action, to prevent the dumping of nuclear wastes into their waters and poisoning the fish that the 9

---

received orders for 300,000 pairs in just 1 week following al-Zaidi's action.

[22] In 1974, the U.S.-installed Thieu regime in S. Vietnam was desperately attempting to deprive the populace of the ability to make National Liberation Front flags (red & blue, with a yellow star). The government ordered any existing red or blue cloth to be dyed a different color immediately.

million people of Somalia depend on to keep from starving. Mysterious European ships started appearing off the coast of Somalia, writes Johann Hari in the British-based *Independent,* "dumping vast barrels into the ocean. The coastal population began to sicken. At first they suffered strange rashes, nausea and malformed babies. Then, after the 2004 tsunami, hundreds of the dumped and leaking barrels washed up on shore. People began to suffer from radiation sickness, and more than 300 died. ...

by Rejin Leys

"Somalian fishermen took speedboats to try to dissuade the dumpers and trawlers, or at least levy a 'tax' on them. They call themselves the Volunteer Coastguard of Somalia — and ordinary Somalis agree [with their actions]. The independent Somalian news site WardheerNews found 70 per cent 'strongly supported the piracy as a form of national defence'.

94 | INTRODUCTION

"No, this doesn't make hostage-taking justifiable," Johann Hari continues, "and yes, some are clearly just gangsters — especially those who have held up World Food Programme supplies. But in a telephone interview, one of the pirate leaders, Sugule Ali, said: "We don't consider ourselves sea bandits. We consider sea bandits [to be] those who illegally fish and dump in our seas."[23] The Somali pirates — many just teenagers — seized control of a number of ships and kidnapped personnel, holding them for ecological as well as financial ransom.[24]

And in **Egypt**, for months *before* the Occupation of Tahrir Square that toppled the U.S.-backed Mubarak dictatorship, workers — most of them women — led strikes and riots against the state's expropriation of thousands of hectares of cropland needed for growing food that had been replaced by export zones of genetically engineered cotton.[25]

---

[23] Johann Hari, "You are being lied to about pirates," *The Independent,* Jan. 5, 2009.

[24] David Rovics' song, "Here's to the Pirates of Somalia," can be downloaded for free from his website at www.DavidRovics.com.

[25] See, for instance, Amar, Paul. "Uprising in Egypt: A Two-Hour Special on the Revolt Against the U.S.-Backed Mubarak Regime." *Democracy Now, Feb. 5, 2011.* "In 2008 in Egypt, women textile workers of the state-owned monopoly complex in Mahallah al-Kubra stopped production to demand a 30-fold increase in wages. The textile factory workers spun Monsanto grown cotton. This cotton had displaced thousands of hectares of wheat and food crops on precious and scarce irrigated farmland. This action disrupted the male deal between agro-industry and the Egyptian government to grow cash crops for export.

"In 2011 the women textile workers struck again. The women and their male allies sparked the millions strong Egyptian uprising and the Arab Revolution." Also, see Terisa Turner, in "African farms in corporate

OCCUPY DID NOT COME OUT OF NOWHERE

In the U.S., upsweeps in mass resistance to the structural adjustment programs of neoliberalism followed on the heels of the successful anti-apartheid struggles of the mid-1980s, the women's liberation, ACT UP and ecology movements, each contributing new tactics and opening new possibilities.

At century's turn, mass direct actions followed the "leaders" of the world capitalist economy wherever they met: **Seattle** (November 1999), Davos **Switzerland** (Feb. 2000 and again in 2003), **Boston** (anti-genetic engineering mass uprising in March, 2000), **Washington DC** (April, 2000), **Prague**, **Czechoslovakia** (September, 2000), the Republican and Democratic Party national conventions in **Philadelphia** and **Los Angeles** (Summer, 2000), **Gotenberg** (**Sweden**), and **Canada** at the Organization of American States meeting, the Oil Congress in **Calgary**, against the G-8 meeting in **Quebec City**, and in **Victoria**, where activists forced NATO to move the venue for their big meeting in October 2001.

But the "anti-globalization" movement (and when I use the word "globalization," I mean "globalization *of capital*,"

---

cross hairs," UPI, November 22, 2011: "Huge tracts of land are being sold or leased to sovereign wealth funds, hedge funds, government agencies, notably the Chinese government land-buying agencies, large corporations in the agro-industrial sector, [and] very wealthy oil-rich and otherwise rich individuals."

also known as "neoliberalism") did not start in Seattle. The fights against the IMF and World Bank's structural adjustment policies took their earliest and most consistent shapes in the form of mass rebellions in **Africa**, **Latin America** and **Southern Asia** beginning in the late 1970s. Seattle was a continuation of that movement, a bringing of that war into the urban centers of the empire.

The world's police forces use social protest movements as opportunities to update their mechanisms of repression. Activists are trapped in a death tango with the police state — our increasing numbers, the state's increasingly devastating technology. Our movements provide the State apparatus with a giant laboratory of human guinea pigs for testing the latest weapons of war, police configurations, nerve gasses and more effective and gruesome methods of repression.

During the Seattle protests in 1999 against the World Trade Organization, I saw police beaming high-intensity lights (lasers?) to destabilize people and knock them off balance. (Would pocket mirrors and reflective Mylar sheets protect us from those beams, and reflect the new weapons back on the forces using them?) The military mixed neurotoxins into teargas and mace — the same Malathion-like gasses sprayed indiscriminately over **New York** and, indeed, the entire Eastern seaboard to kill mosquitoes said to be carrying the West Nile virus a few months earlier.[26]

How can we minimize the State's power despite its sophisticated technologies of torture, and provide our movements with the greatest advantage? How do we structure our actions and our organizations to bring about basic social and economic transformation despite the State's bent on repressing such movements — and do so without betraying our moral principles?

Our movements help to create living alternatives to the globalization of capital and the exploitation and expropriation that comes in its wake. If there's one thing that the participants in the new left of the 1960s agreed on, it was that we — that great, inclusive, tiny 2-letter word "we," meaning all of humanity, or at least the 99 percent! — could, through direct action, change the circumstances in which we find ourselves.

In the face of the cruelest oppression and horrendous wars, the new left believed that *we could* organize and *change things.* But left unanswered is *How* should we organize to change things? *What form* might those changes take, and how do those forms change depending on the way we go about trying to achieve them? Many have recorded their stories of the '60s, but few have outlined the New Left's un-

---

[26] See Mitchel Cohen, *West Nile Story: Orchestrating Hysteria in the Run-Up to 9/11*, NoSpray Coalition, 2011.

derlying political, social-psychological and revolutionary *theory* which did address those questions, and over which the Left split into a million pieces. The idea that a new world was and still is possible and that it could be brought into being by sufficient numbers of people throwing our bodies one way or another against the wheels of empire and into radical direct action efforts — *that* is the hallmark, the quintessential philosophy that drove the actions of the new left, just as it does Occupy Wall Street. I hope to explain here some of what we learned and draw lessons from it, and to integrate it with learnings from new movements today.

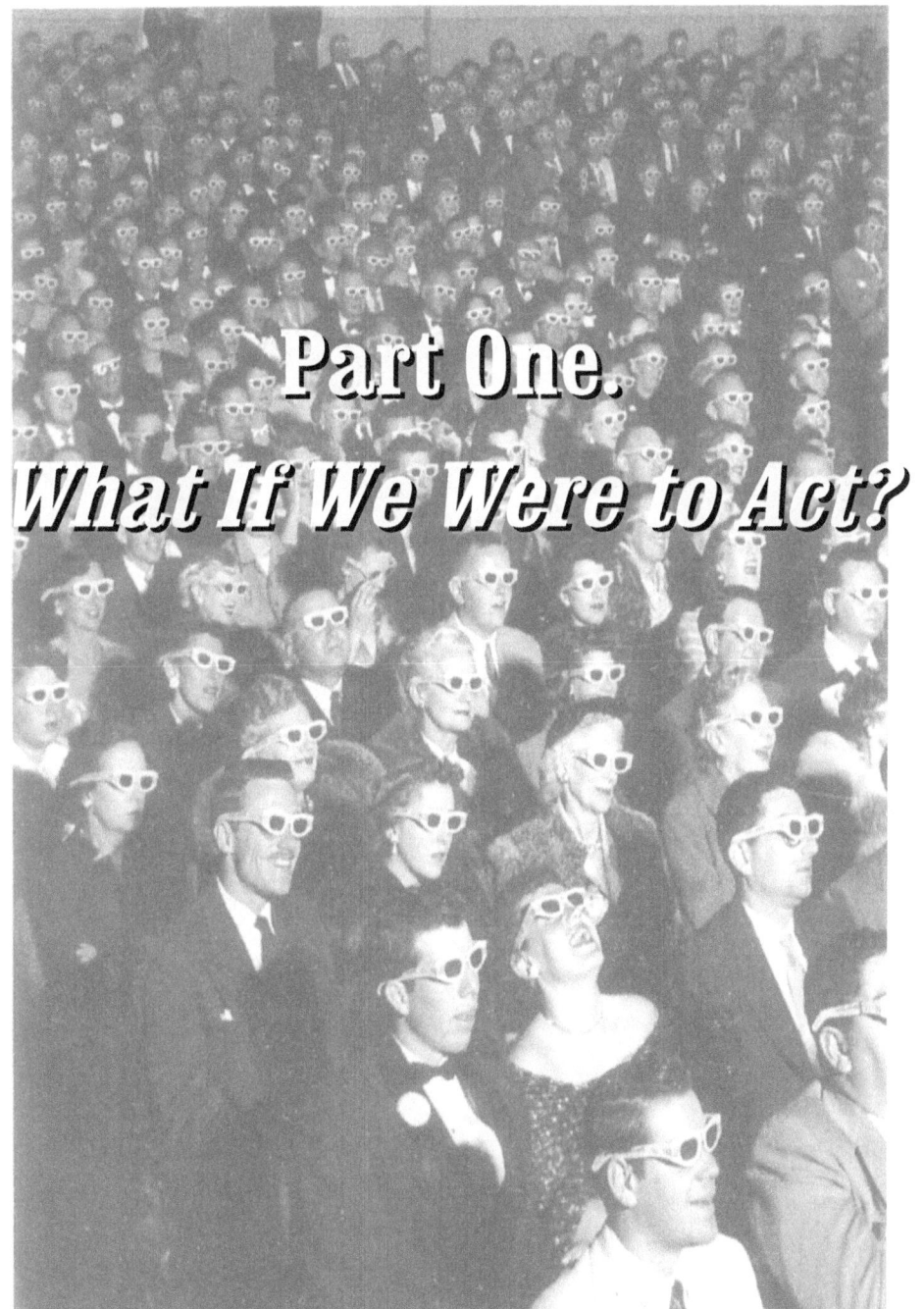

OCCUPYER AT ZUCCOTI PARK, NEW YORK CITY, SEPTEMBER 2011

photo by Joshua Trujillo

"GET YOUR EYES OFF MY PEPPER-SPRAY!" 84 year-old Dorli Rainey pepper-sprayed by Seattle police while observing the Occupy Seattle protests in November, 2011.

In 1984, dock workers in San Francisco refused to unload a ship carrying goods from South Africa. They didn't wait for Congress to pass a law that said "No, don't unload those ships." They didn't even wait for their own national union officials' approval. They acted *directly,* even though to do so violated the Taft-Hartley Act, with major fines and jail sentences imposed. The goods from South Africa rotted in the hold, and the capitalist collaborators with apartheid lost their money.

What if the same thing had happened to ships laden with arms for the death squad government of El Salvador? *Someone* had to load them. What if anti-intervention groups had focused on blockading shipments of attack helicopters and machine guns instead of lobbying congress to change government policy? What if CISPES — the Coalition in Solidarity with the People of El Salvador — and other groups stopped trying to get millionaire psychopaths in the halls of Congress not to support mass murderers, and focused on organizing workers on the docks and airstrips?[27]

Many activists grow disgusted with spending our lives pushing the boulder of electoral politics up the eternal incline of "raising consciousness" — call it "The Myth of CISPES".

---

[27] Many dedicated and stalwart activists organized with CISPES and other groups over the years, and they did very valuable work raising issues pertaining to U.S. imperialism in Latin America. My intent is to point out the futility of trying to "change things" via the strategies such groups employed, and in no way to besmirch the character or commitment of many involved.

Like the recent Occupy Wall Street protests, we refuse to accept the legitimacy of the one percent claiming for themselves the right to rule the world, or that we, the 99 percent, are politically impotent to do anything about it. We act, as we did in the '80s to directly block funding to the death squads in El Salvador and Nicaragua, and opposing those holding the world hostage in their game of nuclear chicken.

In 1982, the Red Balloon Collective published a semi-satirical newspaper, *Freeze & Scream,* that presaged the "Yes Men." It claimed to be the official newspaper of the tepid Nuclear Freeze campaign, and called for escalating direct actions against nuclear madness and the arms manufacturers — one day of actions the first month, two days the next, and so on. We distributed bundles of the 16-page paper at the giant one-million strong anti-nuke march to Central Park on June 12, 1982. We'd stashed 50,000 copies the night before along the route of the march and distributed bundle after bundle to students and activists from across the country. A few months later we learned of scores of small actions everywhere, in response to our call. Our affinity group in New York City targeted General Electric's office tower (we flyered the workers for weeks, and succeeded in shutting down the whole building) and the next month occupied Raytheon. The cops said, "you're not allowed here." I pointed to a sign on the door that read "Raytheon Demonstration Room" and said to the cops, "that's what this room is set aside for, and that's what we're doing — *demonstrating*." The cops were confused; we took advantage of the moment to exit, stage left, no arrests. People took up the call and did actions designed to impede the war machine and its profiteers at dozens of corporate headquarters all over the country.

The following year, the Disarm Now Action group (DNA) blockaded Northrup Aviation in Rolling Meadow IL, an hour west of Chicago, which manufactured guidance systems for MX missiles, and followed it up in conjunction with the Sojourner Truth Organization by blockading bridges leading to the Rock Island Arsenal in the Mississippi River, to prevent the manufacture and deployment of artillery and attack helicopters to El Salvador.[28]

In those same years students and many unions throughout the world rose in uproar to free Nelson Mandela, imprisoned in the South African dungeon on Robben Island for 27 years, and end Apartheid in South Africa. We targeted corporations doing business with the Apartheid regime, block-

---

[28] See Mitchel Cohen, "Report from the Barricades," in *Stony Brook Press*, June 1983. Our purpose was not arrest but to blockade, impede, and disrupt military business as usual. In one action against the Northrup corporation outside Chicago we attempted to use locks on corporate doors, chains across the roadways, cement blocks and fallen trees as well as our bodies. It was at that action that a loaf of Wonder Bread first became useful as a blockading device. Not having sufficient numbers to block all the entrances, I scattered slices of bread in the driveway with a sign reading: "Danger: Bread in road. Please use next entrance," where 150 blockaders waited. Not a single Northrup worker used that breaded driveway.

aded South African Airways offices in Manhattan and at Kennedy Airport, "took out" their computers (Coca Cola has many appropriate uses!), and put our bodies into supporting the valiant struggles in South Africa against apartheid. The defeat of the white supremacist regime was a tremendous victory, not only for the people living there but for the idea of freedom and equality, setting the stage for a new round of contradictions in the fight for real democracy (as victories *always* do).

At the Concord Naval Weapons Station in northern California in 1987, Vietnam Veterans Against the War blockaded trains moving weapons to the docks and airfields, from where they'd be shipped to the contras in Nicaragua, via a storage supply house in El Salvador. One of the Navy trains refused to stop and as some people dove out of the way the train picked up speed and ran over U.S. military veteran and antiwar activist Brian Willson, cutting off his legs.[29] Shortly thereafter, tens of thousands of outraged antiwarriors descended on the Naval Weapons Station and physically tore up the tracks.[30]

In 1989 and 1990, Neighbor to Neighbor organized a consumer boycott of Folger's Coffee, which was picked by

---

[29] S. Brian Willson, *Blood on the Tracks* (introduction by Daniel Ellsberg), PM Press: 2011.

[30] Billy Nessen, *Uneasy Alliances: Radicals, Progressives, and Racial Division in the 1984-1986 Berkeley Anti-Apartheid Movement,* an unpublished manuscript.

slave labor, enforced by death squads in El Salvador and funded by the U.S. government.[31] Taking a lesson from the anti-apartheid actions four years before, they consulted with dock workers in the International Longshore Workers Union and set up picket lines that the workers would refuse to cross, at every major West Coast port from San Diego to Vancouver, costing Proctor & Gamble (Folgers' parent company) a pretty penny.[32]

By *not* setting out to influence votes in Congress (even though any change in U.S. policy would surely have been welcome), and instead by organizing resistance directly, the anti-corporate campaigns attacked the sources of funding of the U.S.-backed death squad regimes and energized new strata.

Those direct actions set the tone. Dock workers in the Bay Area of California — particularly in Oakland — went on to engage in targeted political shutdowns in support of freedom for political prisoner Mumia Abu-Jamal, against the U.S. war in Iraq, and most recently in opposition to the suppression of the Occupy Oakland encampment.

---

[31] Fred Ross, Jr., Forward to Jacques Levy, *Cesar Chavez – Autobiography of La Causa,* Univ. of Minnesota Press: 2007

[32] WHDH in Boston was the only mainstream media outlet that ran Neighbor to Neighbor's ads narrated by actor Ed Asner, which showed an upside-down coffee cup oozing blood. Proctor & Gamble pulled a million dollars in advertising from WHDH, which only ignited the flames and caused the *New York Times* to run a front page story on it. Neighbor to Neighbor set up picket lines at the docks. By now they included many CISPES and stalwart activists in other groups. The longshore workers' refused to cross them, breaking Folger's support for the Contras.

Direct Action as strategy did not begin in the '80s. Nor in the '70s or even the '60s. People have always sought to gain control over various parts of their lives and against those forces preventing them from doing so. Two centuries ago in 1811, the Luddites spurred a mass movement across Great Britain against the installation and central corporate control of the new giant mechanical looms that were displacing tens of thousands of workers and subjecting the rest to the "needs" of the machine and the unnatural rhythms of what would soon become the assembly line. From the mass organizing campaigns of the Wobblies a century later, to affinity groups in the Spanish Civil War in the 1930s (affinity groups began as "sniper nests" in Spain in the fight against fascism), to the very large antiwar, anti-nuke, animal rights, Earth First! defenders of the last remaining old-growth forests in the U.S., and the anti-genetic engineering movements; to the heroism of the Sea Shepherd and Greenpeace activists in blocking the slaughter of thousands of whales, dolphins, baby seals and other marine life, direct action has served as counterpoint to those who portray themselves as "the loyal opposition" and who accept the system as is (requiring just a little tweaking here and there to reduce the "abuses"). In addition to putting their bodies on the line, New Left participants theorized (and put into practice) direct action *as a form of revolutionary strategy.*

With a more developed critique of capitalism came new

strategies probing for the system's weak points, at which smaller applications of leverage could have greater impact. Keep in mind that the needs of the whole often conflict with the interests of individual components (in this context, government policies govern the whole system and sometimes clash with the immediate interests of individual corporations). There is also fierce competition between individual corporations seeking to maximize profits, at each other's expense. Can radical democracy flourish by taking advantage of the interstices opened through such "inherent contradictions of capital," allowing us to directly accomplish our goal, rather than by wasting our time and energy in appealing to those in power to do so *for* us?[33]

Occupyers at Wall Street in 2011 were able to gain traction by inhabiting that ambiguous line between City-owned and privately owned property. They ended up occupying the privately owned (but quasi-public) Zuccotti cement rectangle, which in New York City passes for a "park". In the time it took the powers-that-be to resolve whose jurisdiction that sunless cement square fell under, the Occupyers had already established and reinforced a beachhead in the capital of capital. When City officials and the police department overreacted, as they inevitably do, the widely broadcast images of hein-

---

[33] See Mitchel Cohen, *Tips for Activists in the Anti-Apartheid Movement*, Red Balloon Collective, 1985. Also, Mitchel Cohen, "They only Followed Orders," in *Red Balloon Magazine*, Winter/Spring 1992.

ous police brutality against young female marchers struck a protective chord among the good people of New York City, and Occupy Wall Street won broad public support.

The kind of focus provided by the direct action context differs from what one might expect in customary issue-oriented organizing. A key frame of direct action is that with every "demand" we raise we need to ask: *"How might we begin fulfilling the demand we're making for ourselves, here and now?"* That approach shapes the demand; it differs significantly from the way unions, Leftist parties and coalitions have historically seen their mission and approached their work.

We need new strategies and organizational formations for slowing down — and preventing — the wave of cutbacks, privatization, layoffs, housing and farm foreclosures, bank bailouts and huge consumer and student debts, to say nothing of the massive destruction of the planet's biosphere and imperialist wars. Empire has no conscience; *neither the system nor those running it can be shamed into ending exploitation of labor and domination (expropriation) of nature* — the twin sources of capitalism's profits, which drive the economic system and propel it to expand, at the planet's expense.

Direct action, on the other hand, interferes with the system (including capitalism's integration of customary modes of protest); it sets the conditions for activities, demands, and new kinds of organization. Witness the power and creativity unleashed by the sustained direct action campaigns in Tunisia and Egypt (the Arab Spring), followed quickly by Wisconsin, and now Occupy Wall Street. These so reinterpreted social reality that, looking back on 2011, it becomes absolutely stunning that the "demand" to democratize economic and social institutions has, all of a sudden, caught fire and articulated with exceptional clarity the undemocratic class rule to which we all are subject.

Photo by Michael Mertz

SEABROOK, NEW HAMPHSIRE 1980

> This photo was taken at the battle to prevent construction of the Seabrook nuclear power plant, 1979-80, in southern New Hampshire. The Red Balloon Collective organized three affinity groups

from Stony Brook and Brooklyn, part of a cluster of around 120 people, within the 1,500 people taking part. We had purchased giant bolt-cutters on Canal Street in Manhattan; in fact, when some of us walked into the hardware store and asked for the cutters, the clerk winked and said, "Going to Seabrook, eh?" and sold them to us at half price.

We cut through fences at Seabrook as though they were made of butter and had torn down a section, when suddenly a military helicopter hovered over the road about 20 feet away. We took off through the woods as the helicopter gave chase. Eventually we shook it by scattering off the trail, and, after a mile or so, ran into others being chased, from another direction, by three cops — who turned and fled when they saw the large angry group converging and preparing for battle. We ran another mile, and emerged from the forest ... only to be confronted by an abrasive salesperson from the Revolutionary Communist Party hawking his newspaper shouting: "Buy the *Revolutionary Worker*. Find out what the revolution's *really* about." He was standing on the path at the tree-line having taken no part in the action, trying to sell us the correct line as we darted past.

photo by Michael Mertz

Nuclear Liberation Front cluster of affinity groups, at action called by the Coalition for Direct Action at Seabrook to prevent the construction of the Seabrook, New Hampshire, nuclear power plant, 1980.

Breaking out of the old ways and looking at our own actions in a new way. "Loyal opposition" no longer.

Take the Pledge: Refuse the Debt

What if students organized a national campaign to renounce the trillion-dollar total debt and vowed not to pay it?[34] What if groups bought up the debt for pennies on the dollar, as StrikeDebt.org recently did, and tore them up?

What if they took over their campus newspapers and produced them themselves, no longer accepting advertising from companies on strike and systematically rejecting ads from the armed forces, CIA and the Department of Defense, and gave voice to the creativity of our movements? Many student papers began to do just that in the late 80s, organizing themselves into the Network of Alternative Student Press.

And what if instead of shutting down buildings to protest tuition hikes and cutbacks in services, students began "opening them up" — building by building, libraries, gymnasiums, study areas — keeping them open all night for people to use, putting the goals of open admissions and free tuition — once standard operating procedure in New York City and

---

[34] Check out the "Occupy the Student Debt Campaign" at http://www.occupystudentdebtcampaign.org and StrikeDebt.org — debt resistance for the 99%.

state-run California colleges — into immediate practice?

Framing the issue in that way forces *the university administration* to shut down the buildings in the face of people acting directly to *keep them open*. That permits us, as Karl Marx put it, to "retain the moral ascendancy" by exposing and directly doing something about the university's complicity with the austerity budgets, larger scandals and crimes. Then, when government or university bureaucrats try to close buildings claiming the need to lay off workers and cut back services (or, in the new euphemism of the day, "to downsize"), we'd say, "No, we're not going to let you. We're going to keep them open so people could use them to study." The tactical advantages are obvious; we would enjoy overwhelming popular support, putting our vision of the type of society we'd like to live in directly into effect. We'd be breaking out of symbolic forms of "protest" that, though once powerful, have largely been co-opted and integrated into the system.

Had these sit-ins *opened up* the facilities instead of closing them down, to all appearances the snapshot would have looked the same: the administration would have called in the police; parodies of the "bureaucratic mind" would begin appearing on campus walls; printing presses would be pounding out our messages. So we began to try it out. One evening, members of the Red Balloon Collective — influenced no doubt by Breton's "Surrealist Manifesto" which the collective had just read — sat down in the library and announced a sit-in. We'd done similar 'non-actions' periodically for years to chart the police and administration response, but on this occasion a few of the more nonlinear artistic types decided to sit peaceably out in the hall just before closing time.

"It's time to clear out, the building is closing in five minutes," we were told. Until that point we were just seven people sitting in the library.

"Well, we can only leave if the administration meets our demands," someone mumbled, carefully concealing the joint being passed around.

"What are they?"

"Well, we're just demanding *amnesty,*" someone ad-libbed.

"Hey," one cop said, "we got a *conjunction* against that!"

"Oh yea, *and, but,* or *or*?"

The cop took a step back, clearly confused. He conferred on his walkie-talkie and then glared at us. "The university won't negotiate demands for amnesty. You have to leave."

"Well, we refuse until we're granted amnesty. We're not leaving." Actually, we'd done nothing yet that was illegal. The library was still open. We just sat.

The cop called for reinforcements. "Gotta situation here," he squawked into the walkie-talkie, which crackled in indignation. "Unless you leave right now you'll be placed under arrest."

"Just give us amnesty and we'll leave right now" we pleaded, our stoned laughter sweeping the lobby.

"Can't do that. Against policy." Aha! Gotcha! Catch-22.

"We won't leave home without it."

This went on for half an hour. More police were called, administrators were awakened from their slumbers, more students gravitated to the library to see what was going on. "What're the demands?" someone shouted through the doorway, magic marker in hand.

"No demands. Just amnesty."

"For what?"

"For sitting here, and wearing this wooden spoon in my lapel." (Mayakovski's long reach, too, reclaimed its grasp!)

"What lapel? But, hey, no demands? Finally a demonstration I can agree with!" Within an hour over 300 students had joined the "protest." A reporter from *Newsday* asked:

"What are you protesting?"

Some wise-ass who'd just seen "The Wild One" answered in his best Marlon Brando impression: "What've you got?" Another said: "They won't give us amnesty."

"Amnesty for what?"

"For sitting here." The reporter couldn't figure out the self-referential twists and recursive turns. Neither could the administration. Neither could Public Safety. (Neither could *we!*) It was two in the morning. An administrator whined:

"Why don't you all just leave?"

Cop says: "They can't. I gotta fill out reports."

We say: "We'll leave if you give us amnesty."

"Amnesty? For what?"

"For sitting here."

"Hell no. The university has a policy against amnesty. We're gonna bring you all up on charges."

"Then we can't leave."

By six in the morning, with half the campus outside the library watching the absurd denouement, a negotiating team announced they'd succeeded in winning some reforms in exchange for our promise to leave then and there. If we did, no charges would be brought against us.

"What? No charges? And we've won some reforms?" We looked at each other in disbelief. "Maybe we should hold out for more reforms," some suggested.

We'd been officially denied "amnesty" — it was against university policy. So the administration negotiated a settlement. "With whom? Who negotiated for us? Oh, Student Government. Who the fuck asked *them*?" The liberals always butt in, just when things are going well. They, of course, faced no charges themselves, never took the risk. All the administrators were very happy at having earned their salaries that night. Good thing they hadn't offered us amnesty from the start or we might never have won the reforms that we

weren't even demanding! Abbie Hoffman had taught us well: "Who says you can't yell *theater* in a crowded fire?"

During the wave of student protests against budget cuts in 1975, the Red Balloon Collective at the Stony Brook campus of the State University of New York organized a two-week-long series of actions. Scores of students divided into four clusters designated by the color of the armband each person was given. Each group trundled off in a different direction through the bowels of the campus. One squad marched up to the administration building (a diversion to keep Public Safety bottled up inside). Another headed for the computer center. The remaining two groups circuitously made their way to the gym and set up camp inside.

Instead of shutting it down — the main tactic of previous sit-ins — this time our goal was to fight austerity and budget cuts by opening it up for public use, and to prevent the university from curtailing access. We started by occupying the gym, re-naming it the "Che Guevara Memorial Gymnasium." We kept it open all night and it became our base for expanding into other buildings. The gym takeover turned out to have been a stroke of genius. Many students came out of the dorms to join the occupation in the middle of the night, and we won over a lot of the jocks. Basketball games at 4 in the morning, 60 people on a side and 5 basketballs down the main court, proved to be a great way to relieve some of the sectarian tensions that built up during endless meetings. "Well," said one wizened participant, "this sure beats faction fights."

Thus, we avoided "friendly fire," and launched sorties at other areas of the campus. We established a forward bunker in the "Emma Goldman Reference Room" in the library. Night after night we occupied the study areas. Public Safety — known not as "pigs" but as "mooses" (they weren't smart enough to be pigs, Marja said) — massed in the reference room. Each night, the head of Public Safety recited the Rules of Public Order. "Oh, bedtime stories," Marja'd chuckle. Folks curled into their sleeping bags, and feigned sleepy yawns.

Some nights there were 150 of us; other times as few as twelve, plus all those studying students who'd stayed at their study carrels throughout wondering what would happen next. Because we were not preventing other students from using the facilities, we had enormous student support. Steve Wishnia, later to form the seminal punk group *False Prophets*, had off his shoes, socks, shirt, and sometimes his jeans and underwear by the time Public Safety approached him on their sweep through the large room. Each time, Steve slowly drawled: "Give me a minute to get dressed, it's cold out." He'd begin getting dressed — in slow motion. It's a fine art to accurately weigh just how much you could get away with in a given situation. While Security tried to hurry people along, others were hiding under the card catalogs and desks, or were making love upstairs behind the microfilm cabinets. Every night it took the police hours to get us out of the library. One night, Public Safety came with cameras to document our identities. But we'd been tipped off. (We had supporters everywhere, including secretaries in the administration offices.) They were surprised to find all of us wearing Groucho Marx masks, identities preserved.

When we named our home base the "Che Guevara Memorial Gymnasium" and flew the red and black flag out

front, the *NY Daily News* ran the story. We proudly promoted ourselves "Cuban-backed students" to counter the anti-Cuban hysteria being whipped up at the time. When the police mobilized to arrest us we actually telegrammed Fidel Castro requesting that he send Cuban troops to Stony Brook to protect us — and of course we sent a copy of the telegram to the papers, which ran that story too. When the University administration sent us a bill for $640 for Stony Brook's police overtime costs and threatened to cut off our student government funding unless we paid it, we forwarded the bill to the Cuban Mission and again to the press. We ended one press release by demanding "the entire wealth of the North Amerikan continent, except for the Hackensack McDonalds." Why we chose to exempt that particular culinary establishment we didn't know ourselves, but our *Yippie!* instincts paid off. The university received a ton of calls from newspapers wanting to know why we'd specifically excluded that industrial burger joint, and the publicity, in turn, helped stave off arrests.

What if the demand "Open'm up!" instead of "Shut it down!" became the rallying cry on every campus, library, train station, hospital, day care center, public park slated for privatization or "structural adjustment" cutback? [Note to college students: You can do this on every campus today: Open up and extend the hours of libraries and other services we need. Don't ask, take a lesson from Nike, which ripped off *Yippie!* Jerry Rubin's motto: Just *Do It!*]

As news of our Stony Brook "open-ups" spread, members of our collective began johnny-appleseeding the State University system. We distributed our newspaper everywhere; the well-researched lead articles "Why You Should Cheat on Your Exams ... And How to Do It!" and "Who Rules Our Schools?" exposed the corporate, banking and government connections of the Board of Trustees. The

Chancellor, after all, had worked for USAID and the CIA, and was a member of the ominous Trilateral Commission. Campus papers across the state reprinted our story. We helped organize and joined takeovers on a dozen campuses, generating excitement wherever we went. At Stony Brook we were just your everyday meshugennah radicals; on other campuses, we were invited to address gatherings, plan protests, share skills and leap contradictions in a single bound. No one is a prophet in their own land.

We, of course, had no desire to be prophets anywhere. Our mission (should we choose to accept it) was to help shape a movement across New York State through which people could devise for themselves new ways to fight based on their collective initiative, creativity and commitment, not on begging the government or other third parties to do it for them.

One Red Ballooner was involved in a campaign at SUNY Buffalo to organize the first nucleus of the statewide Graduate Students Employees Union. Another was doing likewise in State College, Pennsylvania. Similar collectives at Binghamton, Oneonta, Albany, Cortland, Purchase, New Paltz, Cornell and Hostos Community College — our regular stops on the Red Balloon Magical Mystery Tour — launched sit-ins to *keep things open* and to make the banks, not workers, pay for it. "Stop the cutbacks! Cancel the debt! Make the rich pay!" became the battle cry across the state.

At Hostos Community College in the Bronx, students took over the whole school and opened it to all. They worked with the Young Lords, and invited teachers from all over the city to teach classes. For a *month* the college became a truly free university. Stony Brookers taught and took courses, found teachers and defended the magnificent liberated zone against the cops. In all the excitement, the state of New York seemed much smaller than today; dozens of Stony Brook-trained organizers turned up all over the place as though campuses hundreds of miles apart were just subway stations on the D train.

At one stop, SUNY Albany, we participated in an inspiring event. Albany was a-blizzard the day of a statewide rally against the budget cuts. Speaker after speaker called on us to be nice to the bankers who were foreclosing on our futures, the better to lobby them effectively. A radical core managed to gather representatives from the different campuses. The snow piled up and the winds whipped the banners.

All of a sudden, a few comrades from Binghamton carrying black anarchist flags began to "charge" the Capitol building. They were quickly joined by Marxist students carrying red flags, who could not allow themselves to be outdone by anarchists. Someone blew a plastic trumpet (da da da *dum* da da!) and, to the dismay of the rally organizers — young bureaucrats-in-training who droned on and on about protesting "responsibly" and warned against causing ourselves be "marginalized" — hundreds of students swooped down on the Capitol pelting it with snowballs and war whoops, red and black flags flapping against the blizzard. Thousands turned away from the speakers to watch the slippery "charge" up the Odessa steps. The next day, the front page of the *New York Daily News* screamed in a two-inch headline: "10,000 Storm State Capitol." This was terrifically inspiring to read (though completely untrue). Back on our separate campuses, all who'd stood around spectating now swore they'd been in the thick of the action. True, only around 300 radicals raced through the blizzard (fantasies of storming the Russian winter palace propelling us on), slipping into the state Capitol building through a few windows and an open door while 9,700 watched, but then our press coverage — thank you, Abbie — always exceeded our actual capacity.

PROPOSAL FOR OCCUPY WALL STREET

Submitted, Fall 2011

What if, *in addition* to occupying parks and public spaces across the country, Occupy Wall Street would begin to reclaim the more than ten million homes and farms that the banks foreclosed on in the last few years, and return them to those evicted from them? What if we begin occupying *and directly opening up* those schools, libraries, hospitals, firehouses, subway stations and post offices that the government has shut down? It's time to reclaim, occupy, and "open up" property stolen from us, the 99 percent!

Imagine occupying and re-opening St. Vincent's Hospital in Greenwich Village. The Bloomberg administration shuttered this essential hospital — with the support of the Democrats. Christine Quinn, a Democrat politician and chair of the NYC City Council, received large campaign contributions from "developer" Scott Rudin, who feted her at banquets. It was Quinn's approval, along with the Mayor's, that gave Rudin the go-ahead to close the hospital and turn it into luxury condos.

Imagine: Occupy Wall Street reclaims that hospital, re-opens it, and invites health care providers from around the world to come and treat people — as is happening right now in Greece and, as we go to press, in Chicago! Or, to start with something smaller, occupy a library whose hours have been cut, keep it open

> 24/7 and move the People's Library into it.
>
> **"Occupy and Open-Up"** is a direct response to the cutbacks forced on us by those owning and administering wealth in this country. It's the kind of action that we "99 percenters" (and maybe even some of the 1 percent) could get behind and participate in, involving wider sectors of society.

I distributed that proposal as a flyer every day at Occupy for a few weeks, but in keeping with the spirit of Occupy and appalled at the arrogant behavior of a number of Left parties, was careful not to frame it as a "demand". Other suggestions were similarly blowing in the wind. In a wonderful example of synchronicity, Occupyers began moving families back into their foreclosed homes and effectively disrupted a number of foreclosure sales in NY State Supreme Court, setting the tone for disruption of foreclosure sales that swept the country (though hidden in the corporate media). In the summer of 2012, Occupy Oakland took over a beautiful old library building that had been donated by Andrew Carnegie but which had been shuttered for years. They cleaned it, fixed it up and moved hundreds of books from the People's Library into that space, re-opening it for the community to use. Oakland police, under orders of the City government, evicted the Occupyers; but Occupy Oakland set up the People's Library right in front, on the sidewalk. Neighborhood residents were excited to learn that they could take any book they liked, no papers to fill out, no card to show. Just "bring it back when you're done, so others could have the same opportunity to read it." The City found that so threatening that they ordered the Oakland PD to evict the people's *library* from a previously shuttered library building.

What if the Transportation Workers Union — now to its credit heavily supporting Occupy — worked with Greens to devise a comprehensive transportation program based on renewable energy, slowing the destruction of the ozone layer and reducing society's dependence on Exxon-Mobil, BP and Shell? And what if the workers also exposed the nefarious role of General Motors, DuPont and Firestone Rubber in tearing up ecologically friendly electric trolley systems in dozens of cities across the country in the 1930s, '40s and '50s? That conspiracy — *and aren't all corporate decisions conspiracies by their boards of directors to rip as much labor as possible out of workers, sell products to consumers, and maximize profits?* — was rewarded by local and federal governments with billions of dollars in write-offs, subsidies and tax-breaks. It forced ground transit to switch to more costly and environmentally destructive gasoline-fueled diesel buses that poisoned the air for 60 years.

PapaDoc Duvalier & Nelson Rockefeller planning Haitian workers' enslavement to the billionaire's corporate interests.

What if, instead of limiting ourselves to petitioning the government to stop financing the junta in Haiti and cracking down on the popular movement there, we in the U.S. targeted those corporations (Disney, Sears, J.C. Penney, WalMart, Texaco, Wilson Sporting Goods, Halliburton and MacGregor, among others) that outsource to sweatshops to produce their goods and break the unions, oppose attempts to raise the minimum wage, fund the death squads and rake in millions off the earthquake in Haiti and slave labor there?

What if striking telephone workers not only marched against cutbacks in health benefits but occupied, *en masse,* the telephone exchanges — can you hear me now? — blocking the

Bullets Hit Missile

A Peacekeeper missile was hit by random gunfire while being shipped from Wyoming to California, and the $70-million weapon will have to be destroyed, the Air Force said yesterday.

Bullets caused $11 million in damage to the first and second stages of the four-stage intercontinental ballistic missile, also called the MX.

The damage was discovered during a routine inspection.

NY Newsday, July 30, 1994

state's surveillance of our movements, reaching out and touching AT&T and Verizon where it hurts?

What if workers at the Schenectady General Electric

plant fought to end G.E.'s spewing of PCBs and other deadly chemicals into the Hudson River *as part of their contract negotiations?* What if they said, "We will not allow the company to dump this crap into *our* Hudson river," and took direct action to stop it? Maybe student actions could inspire the G.E. workers to buck their own union's inaction as well as the company's! What a difference organized workers could make in the fight to save that river, let alone the planet.

Lackeys, Sellouts & Hacks, O My!

Why have unions concentrated only on wage demands and bettering working conditions, but not on the production end: products, pollution and power? In 1935, the federal government finally agreed to recognize the legal right of workers to organize (but, as a compromise with southern representatives in Congress, agricultural workers and waitresses were excluded from the final legislation — a decision that was not corrected until Cesar Chavez and Delores Huerta organized the United Farmworkers Union in the 1960s, mobilizing national indignation over the workers' plight into mass consumer boycotts of non-union grapes, wine and lettuce). But the 1935 social contract that became the law of the land came with a price: it dramatically limited the purview of unions and worker organizations to certain kinds of negotiations over wage levels, health and safety problems on the shop floor, grievance procedures and working conditions and excluded political action.

In other words, workers were (and remain) allowed to organize into unions, but only in exchange for accepting capital's authority over the kinds of issues they're allowed to raise and "legitimate" ways to fight for them. The government uses threats to repeal automatic dues check-offs and an array of prohibitive fines as leverage to keep unions in line.

Already critical of corporate unions, the Red Balloon Collective attended a talk by Leonard Woodcock, then head of the United Auto Workers. Chairing the meeting was a professor who was a member of the Democratic Socialist Organizing Committee, now the Democratic Socialists of America (some of us taunted that DSA meant "Deny Socialism Altogether"). Woodcock addressed the question, "Are blue collar workers intelligent and capable of running production or are they mostly mindless manual laborers?"

Of course you don't have to be a flaming radical to know that workers aren't stupid; most of us are workers ourselves! Woodcock took a foolish (but telling!) tack, trying to prove his point by arguing that "his" workers knew all along that the Ford Pinto would explode when hit from the rear, long before *Mother Jones* published its now famous exposé. "They're not stupid. They knew."

All right, point taken. But at what cost? "Mr. Woodcock,"

I asked, "if you all knew the Pinto would explode, then why didn't the union warn the public and stop its production? You're telling us that workers aren't stupid, by now arguing that they're immoral!"

Woodcock was taken aback by the way I'd unexpectedly *reframed* his point. His answer came as no surprise to those of us who've had experience with corporate union hacks: "That's not what unions are for; that's a management decision. Our domain is to fight to improve wages, benefits, and work conditions." Woodcock didn't see it as within his union's jurisdiction to say, "No, we will not build this death trap."

How could anyone knowingly build death traps? Would Woodcock have had UAW workers manufacture gas chambers for Hitler, claiming "We need jobs"? We expect that sort of immorality from capital, from corporate bosses. But unions are supposed to be different. Why should workers accept the rules preventing us from having a say over what we produce?

Unlike the popular organizations in, say, Haiti — where they take on all sorts of important social, economic and ecological issues[35] — unions in the U.S. are hamstering the

---

[35] See, for example the work of the rural Haitian workers and peasants who have organized themselves into the MPP, headed by Chavannes Jean-Baptiste, and who have been opposing the introduction of genetically engineered trees and crops into the countryside. Also, NY-based organizer David Wilson traveled to Haiti just prior to the 2010 earthquake, and observed that in the countryside many small towns were running on solar panels jerry-rigged by locals from spare parts. Hear Mitchel Cohen's in-

same old tread wheel, going nowhere fast. That 1935 social contract — now being sundered everywhere by a triumphalist globalization of capital (*aka* "neoliberalism") — has been taken by unions today as inviolate, a law of nature. As a result, we, as workers, hardly think to raise the environmental, aesthetic or political demands of our communities — so crucial to our lives when we get off work — as part of our on-the-job struggle through the union machinery and other formations we ourselves built and defended over the years. "Those are for consumers to deal with," we're told — as though our interests as workers can be separated from those of environmental activists, urban "inner city" poor, even "consumers" — in other words, the 99% — when we get home from work!

What would it take for unions to stop accepting the rigid constraints imposed by capital and government on working class organizations, and instead *reframe* the production of commodities — and not just wages — as a continuously re-negotiated struggle between big capital and labor?

It is that false separation of "workers" (producers of value) and "consumers" (users of value) that has locked us into an increasingly untenable situation, and has kept unions from:

- refusing to build Pintos that explode upon impact;

---

terview with Wilson on "Steal This Radio #100," at http://tribecaradio.net/wpradioblog/stealthisradio/steal-this-radio-with-mitchel-cohen-100/.

- forcing Exxon to double-hull their tankers;
- shutting down factories that dump wastes into the Hudson River;
- boycotting non-organic California strawberries to stop the methyl-bromide and other pesticide poisoning of workers and consumers;
- deciding, as workers, what happens with what we produce, including the manufacturing of anti-personnel and so-called 'depleted' uranium weapons used by the U.S. military against civilian populations in Iraq, Yugoslavia, Panama, Afghanistan and Libya — and increasingly by police forces here at home.
- negotiating the percentage of profits that may go to the boss vs. the amount that would be plowed into social programs to benefit workers and the environment.

The wave of protests that came together in Seattle, 1999, marked a "new beginning." For the first time in ages, workers' organizations in the US began to break out of the "wages only" box and mobilized against NAFTA, GATT, and the WTO as instruments of global capital and international trade.

When You're a Hammer, All Your Problems Look Like Nails

"If you don't accept our cutbacks," GM president Wilson informed UAW head Walter Reuther in the 1950s, "we'll automate our plants and lay off half the work force. Who'll pay your union dues then?"

"And if half the work force is unemployed, who's going to buy all your cars and make you rich?" Reuther reportedly shot back.

Capital works hard at maintaining the illusory wall between "workers" and "consumers" — a pitiful and disempowering way to describe workers when we're not at work, in order to drive a wedge between an alleged "middle class" and blue collar workers (portrayed, in the still-dominant paradigm, as mostly beer-consuming blue-overalled men, although significant alterations of that always-wrong image have been gaining acceptance, lately). With the assistance of trade unions and mass media, most workers have internalized this split; it keeps us from taking action where capital is most vulnerable and where we have the most leverage — on the job.

In an open letter to the first Left Green Network gathering at Hampshire College in Massachusetts in 1987, I outlined the need to reject that framework and proposed ways for our burgeoning environmental movement to overcome that false divide. What has come to pass since then is that capital has expended enormous sums — part of its overall cost of production — to maintain the acquiescence of worker organizations to its labor/management rules. Unions, where they have not been demolished outright by neoliberalism, have been instrumental in actually assisting the imposition of capital's "structural adjustment programs" at home as well as abroad. Such agencies as the AFL-CIO's "Solidarity Center" and National Endowment for Democracy serve as cops (AFL-CIA?) for the system against union members' wider interests, solidarity, and direct action impulses.[36]

Most leftist parties also have accepted the worker/consumer distinction; they proselytize workers to vote for candidates who would better tend to their interests but often at the expense of workers elsewhere. This came through quite

---

[36] See the website IEFD.org, set up by Professor Bertell Ollman, originating as a spoof of the National Endowment for Democracy. The IEFD website houses a very good library of readings and reference material on the question of "democracy".

clearly in the Green Party campaigns of consumer advocate Ralph Nader for President of the U.S. Ralph presented the primary clash in our society as between "consumers" and "irresponsible corporations," therein upholding (at least in theory) "responsible" ones, and ignoring the exploitation and expropriation on which capitalism as a system is built.[37]

Even organizations arguing for a different social-economic system altogether (most Leftist parties) see job actions in terms of leverage to win demands within the 1935 framework. Rarely are we encouraged to take action, on the job as well as off, to put into effect portions of the new society we'd want to live in. To the official left, implementation of a socialist program is to occur only *after* socialists come into control of the state — a major squabble between the old and new lefts of the 1960s, and still remaining to be resolved.

So I resume my 1987 appeal for radicals to find ways to break down that false dichotomy between "consumers" and workers. We need to create new organizational forms that go beyond the traditional trade union *and* vanguard party models, which are based on acceptance of that duality. We need to expand what is seen as legitimate to fight for on the job, and

---

[37] To the U.S. Green Party's credit, however, it has maintained a very strong opposition to imperialist wars. Unlike some of their European sister parties, the U.S. Green Party has repeatedly mobilized its membership for every antiwar movement — a huge step, given the pro-imperialist history of the erstwhile socialist factions that had dominated the U.S. electoral Left for the last century.

Under the Thumb. August 19, 1871

merge those fights with what we need in our communities.

All of this entails *reframing the question* — challenging what we take for granted today, what is perceived as "natural" or "legitimate" — so that in all areas of our lives we take direct responsibility for the world around us instead of ceding it to others exalted as "experts": politicians, bankers, priests, corporate execs, scientists, media moguls, union managers, or even professional activists.

But as a 22-year-old at Stony Brook, none of this was consciously worked out. Impulsively, I crashed my next question against the great union leader's fortress of solipsism: "How come, Mr. Woodcock, you and the rest of the UAW's executive board crossed the picket-line of the secretaries who work for the United Auto Workers but who are part of a different union? Is that your idea of class solidarity?" What does it mean for labor that the UAW's leaders turn out to be bosses and scabs?

All hell broke loose. The DSA professor — his name was Hugh Cleland — branded me "anti-union." Me! Who was at that very moment organizing cafeteria and bookstore workers into independent unions linked by a workers council! "That's a lie!" I shouted.

"Next question!" he hollered.

Such are the devious ways apologists seek to cover their bloody tracks. But the question still lingers: Why didn't auto workers, knowing the Ford Pinto would explode upon being hit from the rear, collectively refuse to manufacture such death machines, expose the company's plans and save dozens of lives?

Raise Less Consciousness and More Hell

The challenge for any radical organization of a new type is not so much to proselytize around political questions or exhort the exhausted to hustle back to the barricades, but to enable us all — particularly workers (who are, after all, *us*) — to dramatically expand our organizations' purview to include *what* is produced, and *how*.

In accepting the false dichotomy between workers and consumers, we allow invisible constraints to strap us to the gears of capital, the periodic bluster of trade union hacks and "minimum common-denominator coalitionites." We need to bust them open.

One way to do that is by revealing the hidden environmental, political, racial, sexual, class and cultural dimensions within *every* economic issue. And, second, we must make it possible to organize and fight for so-called "consumer" demands on the job as well as in the community, by taking direct action on the job and forcing the company or government to comply with whatever we are demanding in our communities. In that way, we can begin the process of taking political, ecological and social responsibility for the world around us.

In Australia in the late 1970s, worker and community organizing pressured unions to issue "Green Bans". In what would have been developer and power-broker Robert Moses' worst nightmare, the workers refused to construct highways and malls unless they were first approved at public meetings by the communities impacted by such "development." They would not build *anything* unless both the workers and the community approved it.[38]

There is a wealth of similar but not widely known direct action collaborations between workers on the job and the communities they serve — an alliance previously seen as outside the purview of labor organizing. In the last decade, for example, the California Nurses Association heroically took the lead in mobilizing its membership to oppose attempts to make Swine Flu and smallpox vaccinations mandatory.[39] What if nurses in the U.S. took it a step further, and decided to challenge the patriarchal and denigrating hospitals? What if they set up

---

[38] The Communist-led unions enacting Green Bans were finally broken up when the government hired Maoist thugs in "alternative" unions to assassinate the leadership, with the support of the Australian government.

[39] Mitchel Cohen, *West Nile Story: op cit.*

their own community-based worker- and client-run clinics? And what if they combined with AIDS activists, midwives, holistic and herbal healers, acupuncturists, chiropractors and nutritionists to create underground buyers' cooperatives and a qualitatively better complementary health care system, not the same old medical meat-market mauling us with industrial medicine at the beck and call of pharmaceutical corporate profits and the insurance racket that too many current health care proposals, including Obamacare, are bent on preserving? *That* would be a health plan worth investing in!

What if newspaper workers in San Francisco kept publishing their strike newspaper even after the strike ended, as the "voice of labor, community & environment" in the region?

What if mass-transit workers fought against fare hikes, and demanded — as part of their union negotiations — that transportation *be free*? What if they'd "look the other way" when people walk through the gates, instead of calling the police?

What if homeless people began squatting the thousands of abandoned housing units, and community groups and unions rallied to defend them and hold back the police?

What if construction unions stopped treating jobs as private fiefdoms, and accepted the homeless, squatters and homesteaders as apprentices, teaching skills and fixing up their buildings? Anti-community and ecologically destructive "development" projects (hydro-fracking, tar-sands pipeline,

142 | WHAT IF WE WERE TO ACT?

nuclear power plant construction) pit workers who need jobs (especially as so many are outsourced) against the neighborhoods they'll be destroying, setting up a downward spiral of competition between people who should be allies.

Photo from Red Balloon #10, Winter 1975-76

Jumping subway turnstiles during the last great wave of resistance to austerity and cutbacks, 1975. Computer graphics and collaboration between transit workers and Occupyers made resistance a lot more effective this time around. (See next page.)

WHAT IS DIRECT ACTION? | 143

On March 28, 2012, hundreds of commuters went through the NYC subway gates for free when Occupy Wall Street and transit workers teamed up to post official-looking "advisories" declaring "Free Entry" and propped open the gates at two dozen stations. "Despite the fact that buses and subways are supposed to be a public service, the government and the MTA have turned the system backwards — into a virtual ATM for the super-rich," Occupy wrote on its website. "This fare strike is a means for workers and riders to fight for shared interests together." (See Communiqué on next page.)

COMMUNIQUE
from the Rank-and-File Initiative

This morning before rush hour, teams of activists, many from Occupy Wall Street, in conjunction with rank and file workers from the Transport Workers Union Local 100 and the Amalgamated Transit Union, opened up more than 20 stations across the city for free entry. As of 10:30 AM, the majority remain open. No property was damaged. **Teams have chained open service gates and taped up turnstiles in a coordinated response to escalating service cuts, fare hikes, racist policing, assaults on transit workers' working conditions and livelihoods — and the profiteering of the super-rich by way of a system they've rigged in their favor.**

For the last several years, riders of public transit have been under attack. The cost of our MetroCards has been increasing, while train and bus service has been steadily reduced. Budget cuts have precipitated station closings and staff/safety reductions. Police routinely single out young black and Latino men for searches at the turnstile. Layoffs and attrition means cutting staff levels to the bare minimum, reducing services for seniors and disabled riders. At the same time, MTA workers have been laid off and have had their benefits drastically reduced. Contract negotiations are completely stalled.

Working people of all occupations, colors and backgrounds are expected to sacrifice to cover the budget cut by paying more for less service. **But here's the real cause of the problem: the rich are massively profiting from our transit system.** Despite the fact that buses and subways are supposed to be a public service, the government and the MTA have turned the system backwards—into a virtual ATM for the super-rich. Instead of using our tax money to properly fund transit, Albany and City Hall have intentionally starved transit of public funds for over twenty years; the MTA must resort to bonds (loans from Wall Street) to pay for projects and costs. The MTA is legally required to funnel tax dollars and fares away from transportation costs and towards interest on these bonds, called "debt service." This means Wall Street bondholders receive a huge share of what we put into the system through the MetroCards we buy and the taxes we pay: more than $2 billion a year goes to debt service, and this number is expected to rise every year. If trends continue, by 2018 more than one out of every five dollars of MTA revenue will head to a banker's pockets.

This much is clear: the MTA's priorities are all out of whack. This fare strike is a means for workers and riders to fight for shared interests together — but this is just a first step. All of us — the 99% — have an interest in a full-service public transportation system that treats its ridership and employees with dignity.

- **The MTA is a shared, public service — fund it with tax revenues.**
- **Eliminate free money for bondholders at the expense of taxpayers.**
- **End the assault on worker's livelihoods.**

What if progressive scientists and ecologists circumvented the U.S.-imposed embargo on Cuba and worked with their counterparts there to develop and learn from Cuba's organic agriculture and alternative energy programs, relieving it of its dependence on foreign oil, domestic nuclear power plants, one-crop sugar economy and petroleum-based fertilizer? What if we, acting in solidarity with the Cuban revolution, helped make that island a beacon for ecologically-sound planning and alternative health care?

Turning Motion into Movement

All of these "What Ifs" embody a radical vision that is fundamentally democratic (with a small "d"); they are based upon direct community participation through which people take charge over the decisions that affect their lives on every level and minimize *relying upon* those in power to make the changes they seek. While the kinds of direct action projects imagined here have roots in the "self help" movements of everyone from Marcus Garvey to Barry Goldwater, they differ in that they presuppose a radical critique of and antagonism to the capitalist system that dominates our society and which is expanding throughout the world.

That doesn't mean we should never petition those in power; it means we don't rely on it. Instead, we focus on putting the world we want directly into effect, and create in the here-and-now some tiny sliver of a future society worth living in. These will hopefully inspire others, and become bases — liberated zones — from which to launch further sorties against the system. Direct Action/Participatory Democracy serves as both means and ends at the same time.

Clearly, direct action as conceived here is not simply a more militant form of protest, as some portray it, but a total reconceptualization of how societal transformation comes about and the role of conscious activists in organizing themselves to achieve it. That is, direct action is a *strategy* for achieving a new society and not just a tactic used in attempts to attack the policies of the old one.

The strategy of direct action explicitly draws out connections between what to demand, how to achieve it and what forms of organization we'd need. It seeks to bring everything that impacts on our lives within our control. Direct action as strategy, therefore — even over the most mundane and seemingly non-political aspects of daily life — is inherently political; it has no need to bring in "the political" from the outside, but — in this new way of seeing our "mission" — uncoils the politics *already present and wound up in everything*. As a result, it necessarily expands our conception of what to consider valid political work.

Direct action is, most of all, a *way* — a Tao. It is a strategy of dual power based on participatory grassroots democracy, of building up the embryo of liberated or autonomous zones (often quite temporary ones; sometimes they are not even geographical but based on affinities around subverted norms), which serve as communities of resistance and nurturance within the shell of the old. They create in effect a parallel socialist universe; but these differ from utopian communes in that they are continuously *engaged,* they can't withdraw from the effects and pressures of the system even if they want to. The more successfully they build outward from the base of participatory grassroots democracy the more inevitably the capitalist system tries to co-opt and absorb them, or comes to clash with them directly. Participants then fight to defend them and to expand their reach.

Steffen A. Kaplan/New York Times, Nov. 21, 2002

Students Against War walk-out from LaGuardia High School and other schools in unsanctioned antiwar march in NYC, Nov. 2002, led by 16-year old Monica Ross, a founding member of the Brooklyn Greens.

Part Two.
Beyond Symbolic Politics

> From the moment of my birth to the instant of my death
> There are patterns I must follow just as I must take each breath
> Like a rat in a maze the path before me lies
> And the pattern never alters until the rat dies.
> — Simon & Garfunkel

You can always tell something about the culture of a country by the way it honors its poets. The giant shopping mall on Long Island is named after Walt Whitman; a toilet in a gas station on the New Jersey Turnpike memorializes Joyce Kilmer; here, a shopping center on a soon-to-be-paved-over stretch of beautiful desert in New Mexico, is named after Henry David Thoreau, the man who argued for doing Civil Disobedience against "development" and for the preservation of the forests, deserts and the natural habitat.

DESPERATELY SEEKING STRATEGY

From the moment we begin to think about what to include in our programs of action, demands and slogans — that is, from the moment we begin to act *consciously* — we must be guided by one overriding question: "How do we begin immediately to implement this (and every) demand for ourselves?" That approach would influence the kinds of demands we'd make and the way we'd present them.

Unfortunately, radical organizations seldom ask that. To do so would signify a huge "paradigm shift." Most progressive groups would rather prepare position papers on every issue under the sun and agitate for all sorts of reforms, but rarely examine the hidden assumptions underlying *how* they expect the more profound changes they proselytize for to actually come about, let alone ways to structure their organizations to further that new kind of work. Instead, they jump from issue to issue, an army of "consciousness raisers," verbally demanding changes in government policy but unable to develop any long-term strategy for what to do when the government doesn't meet their demands. How might people successfully bring about the changes they seek?[40]

---

[40] I address the theoretical and historical underpinnings of this question in "The Shortcomings of Traditional Leftist Strategy," pamphlet #7 in the *Zen-Marxism* series available from the author.

It is only through honestly posing such questions — *"How do we begin immediately to implement our demands for ourselves?"* — that the traditional division between reform and revolution can be bridged; it is only through the process of direct implementation of any given demand by the people raising it that a fight for a particular reform takes on a radical and potentially revolutionary character.

Organizations using this approach look very different from the hierarchal vanguards or "consciousness raising" coalitions to which most activists today are accustomed. They are built around doing, defending, expanding and coordinating concrete projects which embody the self-help/direct action efforts of communities in resistance, through which people attempt to meet their own needs while never letting-up pressure on the state do so throughout society.

Real pressure on government comes about as a consequence of direct action, although in itself pressuring government is a *tactical* consideration and only one of the reasons we engage in it. Direct action is also necessary to purge *our-*

selves of the detritus of capital and patriarchy, counter the mutilated and scrubbed memory of our own histories and reconnect us to the multitude of people who continue to fight back under the most difficult circumstances. Those who do not participate in direct action efforts with their communities risk internalizing and perpetuating the values and *ways of being* inculcated in us without ever thinking about them or becoming aware of the possibility that **things could be different**.

The system hammers all such excursions back into line, at every turn attempting to limit the vast stirrings of human beings reaching for their humanity, their empowerment, to the most narrow self-interest demands, stripping them of their political and human potential. "Legitimate" working class struggles today are reduced to improving wages, health benefits and working conditions. This is true for liberals as well as conservatives. During the Gulf War the only acceptable protesters, according to the dominant ideologues of the National Peace Campaign, were those who supported sanctions and wrapped themselves in American flags. The anti-war movement honchos, like their partners in the trade unions, strove heroically to accommodate themselves to the needs of capital.

Unlike the anti-globalization rank-and-file in Seattle, November 1999, the trade union bureaucracy did not protest the World Trade Organization *per se,* but their exclusion from it. Teamster president James Hoffa Jr. stated repeatedly that he wanted a "seat at the table."

Our task, as radical activists, as trade union rank-and-filers, is neither to lead people to a seat at the table nor to even *desire* to do so, but to turn that "table" into sawdust, and to nurture eruptions of the new society within the belly of the old. We then fight to sustain those moments, those communities, that bite of the apple, that shocking experience of connection suddenly made tangible. Our strategies must, unlike those of the old left, compel the formation of *communities of resistance and nurturance* through which people act directly and without mediation to express their subversive relationship to the existing capitalist aesthetic, ways of relating, exploitation, alienation and all that is oppressive, authoritarian, ecologically destructive, anti-democratic and stupid, and not merely "deconstruct" the theory explaining why we don't do so. We need to *live the revolution* and not merely talk about the *need* for us to live it. Revolution is not a future event somewhere over the rainbow but a process in which we are involved, right here, right now.

Only through direct action communities can revolutionary ideology truly become a material force. It breathes through our consistent involvement in entities that directly attack capital and embody our vision of the future. Those entities include: Abuse centers, hotlines, AIDS buyers' and healers' collectives, women's (and other's) alternative health clinics, food co-ops and regular give-aways, anti-foreclosure (and, for that matter, re-expropriational) squads, squatters' movements, workers' councils, CSAs, and many other formations covering the breadth of everyday life, nurturing the parts of ourselves suppressed by capitalism and patriarchy. Through them, participants directly empower themselves over the conditions affecting their lives, striving to meet their own needs (and redefining what those "needs" are and where they came from) in ways antagonistic to the relations of capital — although they are not always conscious of it.

Building these forms of mutual aid and empowerment, where needed; solidifying them (where they arise through other means); linking them together — which does not mean creating a centralized decision-making apparatus *over* them — and protecting them, that is what turns motion into movement. That is the content of revolutionary activity, the answer to the question: "What should revolutionaries *do*?"

Revolutionaries call up, unleash and unify the hidden longings of people *that are already inside them* (as opposed to "teaching," "conveying," mechanically "leading," "raising the consciousness of," "bringing in from the outside," "lobbying," "sending a message to" and all the rest of the drivel that passes for "organizing" by the Left in the U.S.), and embody those longings in ongoing forms, communities or *entities*. That is what constitutes "conscious political work."

Not just for the sake of *others* — the hallmark of liberalism, no matter how militant — but for ourselves. Direct action, as strategy, is necessary *for our own* development, our own "self-help," to begin reclaiming bits and pieces of our lives that we often don't even know are missing until we experience in a new way the things we take for granted, through communities of resistance and nurturance. Direct action, as strategy, guides us in how to go about doing *everything:* How we grow healthy food and feed each other, raise children, produce goods, attack the system, select issues to fight around, set up guerrilla clinics to provide alternative health care and reproductive rights, take over abandoned buildings, fix them up and move in, train to protect ourselves from rapists, muggers and violent police attacks and against imperialist forays abroad. provide for our common defense, produce and circulate underground newspapers and videos, and communicate and network.

In Every Moment a Dual Potential

Communities of resistance and nurturance spring up and die out continuously, as people are thrown into motion by the contradictions of daily life structured by and under the real domination of capital. They are the formations that most encourage individual self-development within the larger collectivity.

Jay Kinney and Adam Cornford

Every moment, every fraction of every moment under capitalism, contains within it the germ of its own negation; the breakers of consciousness rise like huddled armies wrestling with the ocean. Every struggle generates nodal points during which direct action communities of resistance and nurturance can, potentially, blossom, combine and vie with existing institutions and social relations to create new ways and conditions through which *everyday* life is re-organized — that is, *Whose rhythms control the space?* Widespread dislocation generates fertile conditions (or, in more epochal terms, "revolutionary periods") for mass communalist movements. Our problem is to figure out how to extract such moments of "dual power" from the tangle of capitalist relations and strengthen them.

However, all moments of social upheaval also contain the potential to explode in fascistic movements and accelerate the ability of capital and patriarchy to reproduce oppressive forms and ways of seeing in ever more virulent strains. Thus, every moment of mass dislocation is doubly edged. It is a tug-of-war, as Rosa Luxemburg put it, between socialism and barbarism — not as some future event but as contained within every moment of the present. And it goes on continuously. Radicals are not only keepers of some future flame, but they are trans-temporal social acupuncturists, needles in hand, incising and re-orienting the energy flows within every moment.

The unconscious psychological dynamics of people in motion are propelled by a thirst for liberation, connection, empowerment, disalienation, and for meaning in their lives — even when they are joining fascist groups, or when they are members of so-called "gangs" or "militias". However distorted a form dislocation may take, a small group can re-orient the flow to enhance the potential — in moments of social upheaval — of eruptions in revolutionary direct actions and away from fascist ones. Which way they'll go depends on what *we* do and what we had been doing all along, ahead of time. Within every danger there also resides opportunity, if only we learn to look for it and nurture it.

That dual potential is a feature of all social motion, even the most repressed and debilitating. *All* motion carries within it liberatory as well as oppressive (or disempowering) seeds. Even vicious movements that are all-too-frighteningly reminiscent of the brownshirts of the 1930s, like the Tea Party or even David Duke's, grow only by finding and manipulating the unconscious liberatory longings as well as the fears of their mass base. Radicals must develop the discipline and insight, which can take many years, to find and nourish those potentially liberatory seeds that lay buried in every moment, even those most controlled by capital, and learn how to wrest them free of capital's hegemony. In the process, we learn to reframe the situations before us, enabling us to generate new and meaningful choices in whose soil direct action communities of resistance and nurturance can blossom.

Such is the *art* of Revolution. Preparing ourselves emotionally, psychologically, creatively, lovingly becomes an increasingly important part of our *political* work.

In sum, the primary task of revolutionaries in the United States today is to:

1) Look for and solid-up the tiny slivers of resistance — embryonic "liberated zones" — wherever they develop, wherever people are acting directly to accomplish the tiniest seemingly non-political thing for themselves;

2) Where necessary (and that decision depends upon the accuracy of our overall analysis), create resistance where it doesn't arise on its own (which *could* border on "vanguardism," an all-too-prevalent trap, so watch out!); and,

3) Work within them to encourage and facilitate working groups, networks, cooperation and councils — in some ways, more an artistic project than a traditionally-conceived "political" one.

There is an art to insurrection, an aesthetic to deflecting the crushing blows of capital and amplifying its dissonance until it fractures as a result of its own vibrations. Direct action communities of resistance and nurturance are crystals of collective self-development and empowerment through which the new world hums.

Strategy & Organizational Form

The most propitious organizational form for this new kind of organizing is the radical collective, or "affinity group". Affinity groups are "action teams," ranging anywhere from four to twelve or thirteen people who *feel* an affinity towards each other and who decide, for themselves, their own approach to what they want to do, in whatever way they come to make decisions. They initiate projects, and they also involve themselves in activities initiated by others, which they work to strengthen. They don't try to recruit people away from other groups and into their own, but help participants form *their own* affinity groups.

People join affinity groups through their actual work on projects, not by abstractly debating the ideological merits of the *kind* of demands to raise — transitional, maximum/minimum, trade union, or any other kind. That "actual work" entails *many* types of activity, as discussed throughout this book — from guerrilla war to guerrilla theater on subways, spraypainting slogans, or even collectively baking bread for Occupy. The point is that participants themselves decide what their groups will do; individuals may belong to more than one affinity group.

As they develop, radical collectives aspire to link with other collectives and affinity groups. A network of radical collectives and underground press:

- finds ways to link those potentially liberatory moments in people's ordinary lives and activities;
- explores their hidden potential so that the participants themselves become conscious of the significance of their own actions; and,
- helps small collective projects blossom into comprehensive, powerful movements.

Sometimes all of that is in the mind of participants from the start; they develop their collectives as an essential piece in a larger direct action strategy. Other times, they form around a particular issue or locale but may come to feel the need for a larger network. And creating that new level of organization — however loosely or tightly structured it might be — always raises, and cannot help but raise, problems as well as opportunities. (Marxists call such built-in and inevitable clashes "inherent contradictions.")

How have networks built in this way actually functioned? One way has each affinity group select a "spoke" — a reference to two things: the spoke of a wheel (leading to the hub), and a temporary spokesperson — who meets with spokes from all the other affinity groups and collectives in a "SpokesCouncil." The powers and responsibilities of that council are defined by the affinity groups. In some forms, the spokes have no power; they simply transmit information back and forth across the different levels of organization. In other forms, they may be acceded power by the members of participating affinity groups to represent them, with carefully enumerated decision-making responsibilities or coordinating authority. In all forms, the role of the SpokesCouncil (or co-ordinating committee) is primarily to facilitate the work of the participating affinity groups and collectives, to strengthen what those groups themselves have decided to do.

Regardless of the overall form, all networks have one thing in common (which they share with Leninist parties) — *individuals* cannot join the network (although they can support it in various ways); to be part of the larger organization they must be active members of an organized affinity group, collective, cell, chapter (local) which is already part of the network, and participate regularly in its projects; or, they can form a new one. In this way, the affinity group or radical direct action collective — not the individual — becomes the "atom," the basic unit upon which everything else is built.

Organizations built upon affinity group and radical collective models better facilitate the dual power direct action strategy enumerated here than do those based on the vanguard party/social democrat "consciousness raising" construct. The kinds of demands direct action collectives make, the ways in which they are arrived at and presented, and the lateral organizing that takes place around them have a very different feel to them — the texture of empowerment — than those made by policy-oriented coalitions or party organizations .

Organizations carrying out this new formulation of strategy would have, built-in to them, the legitimation of the fight for collective and individual empowerment over our own lives — that is, a built-in ethical and moral imperative missing from the exhortations of social democrat and vanguard parties. And that participatory democratic dimension would resonate through every moment of organizational life.

Consequently, the debate over organizational form is not only about former party cadre feeling the need for more internal democracy — the main plaint of those leaving Communist parties and other vanguardist formations. Organizational structure is, first and foremost, a question of how members of radical groups see their "mission".

Strategic and Prefigurative Politics

Even while it engaged in extremely important activities intending to stop a war or guarantee civil rights for all, the

New Left of the 1960s also based itself on what has been best described as "prefigurative politics," in which one's oppression and alienation were just as important as the fight to assist others. According to *Uneasy Alliances: Radicals, Progressives, and Racial Division in the 1984-1986 Berkeley Anti-Apartheid Movement,* an unpublished manuscript written by radical activist Billy Nessen, "prefigurative politics wanted to establish in the current movement the values, personal relations, types of decision-making and organization envisioned in the future society. It emphasized the importance of means in addition to goals, in part because goals are shaped to a degree by how they are arrived at and because means may become goals themselves."

Prefigurative politics also recognized and affirmed that the movement "was about participants' deeper hopes and visions, and the 'necessity of revolt,' about 'more sweeping, profound issues and impulses.' Prefigurative politics was concerned with the changes in people and their relations to one another; participation would make people more caring and their lives more meaningful. Prefigurative politics also sought to avoid a power gap between participants in the movement, which was expressed in a wariness of hierarchy, entrenched leadership and power."[41]

---

[41] Billy Nessen, *Uneasy Alliances: Radicals, Progressives, and Racial Division in the 1984-1986 Berkeley Anti-Apartheid Movement.* Unpublished manuscript. All quotes in this section are from that remarkable extended essay.

All of this, on a theoretical level, comes out of the New Left's focus on the many dimensions of "alienation" and the notion that we are not just fighting for *others* but for a nonalienated future for ourselves, an orientation missing from much of the old left analyses and a main theoretical contribution of the New Left.

Nessen adds his own experiences to those recorded by historian Wini Breines, *Community and Organization in the New Left: 1962-1968: The Great Refusal.* Because his insights are so apropos to the underpinnings of direct action as strategy, I continue quoting from him at length: "Individual and mass defiance, disruption of business-as-usual, not formal and long term organization, was a key to a successful movement. Improvisation, interpersonal relations and communications were most important in the making of a powerful action. Moreover, actions were not simply occasions to protest or challenge the system, but moments that could positively affect, even transform, participants.

"Prefigurative politics affirmed the importance of community, the desire for which was a longing for wholeness, connection, and communication in social relationships, an overcoming of the isolation of individuals and their lack of control.

"Mass meetings/popular assemblies were central elements, not by-products, of the movement. Like actions — in which they often arose spontaneously — they were a place both to further explicit goals and to transform people through participation." These sorts of meetings and actions tried to embody and express the future in the present.

"Lastly, prefigurative politics wanted directly democratic rather than representative, top-down, or centralized decision making. Direct democracy was a means to encourage and sustain movement participation, to create community. It could convert 'powerlessness into shared competence and responsibility.' Whatever the original or societal meaning of 'participatory democracy,' within the movement direct democracy was how it was often expressed. Participatory democracy was also a goal: the form of democracy sought for the future society, even a name for that society.

"Strategic politics was more goal-oriented, focusing on winning specific demands. It was not concerned with means or with changes taking place in participants.

"Strategic politics emphasized 'strategic thinking': programs, clear political positions, and analyses — how to get from here to there. Planning and correct leadership made for strong actions.

"Strategic politics saw building lasting organizations as essential to a successful movement. Representative structures were needed to sustain democracy for other than small or homogeneous groups. Centralized organization was [seen as] necessary to help focus and direct the energies of a movement. Such organization would help pass on accumulated experience, foster internal education, allocate movement resources, increase links and communication between different parts of the movement. For example, efficient organizing of students and linking with other constituencies to overcome the isolation and insularity of students requires a strong organizational structure.

"Strategic politics stressed formalized leadership. Leadership always exists whether recognized or not; ... such leadership [it is claimed] also promotes political coherence.

"Breines' description of prefigurative and strategic politics was an analysis of Students for a Democratic Society (SDS), the most important organization of the white New Left. But she and others clearly acknowledge the influence of the black movement and, in particular, of the Student Non-Violent Coordinating Committee (SNCC, pronounced snick) on SDS. Other writers have portrayed early SNCC as the founder of prefigurative politics, without necessarily using the term, and have essentially narrated the evolution of SNCC as the abandonment of prefigurative politics and the adoption of strategic politics."

As is currently the case with Occupy Wall Street, activists who start from a prefigurative approach will generally end up structuring their organizations differently than those who see their mission primarily as one of lobbying government, passing legislation to win reforms, or raising consciousness. The latter organize themselves as a cadre of "consciousness raisers" to "inform the masses" about how bad things are and harangue them to write letters to congress, or follow their tedious annual exhortations to subsidize Washington-bound bus companies to be a body in yet another futile protest. They see themselves as dumpers of "important facts" down the coal chutes of "consciousness" into the empty bins of people's heads, hoping they will overcome their "false consciousness". The smoke of their organizational structures — elitist, vanguardist, anti-democratic — and the nothingness of their strategy for transforming society pollutes the ideological atmosphere almost as badly as *The New York Times*.

Direct action, on the other hand, rejects the existence of false consciousness and therefore the primary strategy for societal transformation based on it: the accumulation and dissemination of information in order to raise consciousness.

The real issue is not *how much* we know, but *how we process and experience* what we know. That is much harder to get at. In general, it is not "lack of political information" that keeps people in the U.S. from taking action to remedy their situation, but fragmentation, isolation, impotence, inaction and fear — internalized in each of us, reproduced in every moment of daily life — a bombardment of emotions, feelings and a sense of futility *in spite of* — and maybe even *because of* — the huge amount of information we have of the issues, of how bad things really are. The situation is made even more overwhelming with the vast amount of instant information available on the internet. Too many leftists spend their hours propounding the Truth about issue after issue in the abstract; they invent boring slogans and even more boring rallies that can only serve to reinforce dependence on policy-makers even when calling for their overthrowal, and thereby their own (and all of our own) impotence.

One of the main innovative ideas of *Zen-Marxism* has been to articulate the following: As people are thrown into motion by objective conditions (unemployment, wars, foreclosures, debt, racial attacks, the breaking up of relationships due to added stress), they are also thrown into psychological turmoil. Their security blankets dissolve; if there are no socialist-oriented direct action mass-based groups already existing for them to join, some of them may become fodder for fascism. But in acknowledging that — and thereby the crucial need for the Left to bolster horizontal, participatory mass-forms — where are *our* alternatives, presence, organized opposition, articulation of a revolutionary vision as manifested in gentle, non-competitive, loving — at any rate, different — social relations that could grip the imagination of large numbers of people? Where is the Left's focus on pulling the creative but isolated radical voices of so many different struggles into a larger context? Where is the humility to learn from them, so that then and only then may we add our own sensibilities, put our vision immediately into practice through direct action and help move the politics in this country dramatically to the Left? Otherwise, the calamities that shake people up leave them with no place to go and render them susceptible to right-wing militias and proto-fascist cults.

Those movements that address the psychological and emotional crises people are experiencing — their "subjectivity" — have a greater chance of lasting and thus succeeding. It is part of the reason for why Occupy Wall Street took root, and generates questions the Left needs desperately to answer: How do we create a climate that values people sharing very personal experiences and converts them into radical progressive political action? How do we create the spaces and time in which to gather, and encourage those thrown into motion by crises in their everyday lives to explore the roots of their emotions, childhood abuse, sexuality, powerlessness, victimization, friendships, strengths, love and the search for meaning, *as an integral part of what we mean by "political work"*? "Alienation" is an objective condition manufactured by capitalism and it has a very subjective component. Will Left groups ever learn to validate subjectivity with the same intense scrutiny as it does the objective conditions, or will they continue to covertly undermine it by locking it all away as a "private" or depoliticized "personal" matter and throw away the key? The problem is not quantitative; it is a fallacy to think that people "are not oppressed enough at the present time to cause them to rebel." These are areas that data, ever more data, cannot reach.

Seize the Time!

Too often, we forget that *time* is needed to build *anything*, and so we sabotage our own efforts. We need *time* to work on projects so that we become able to ask the right questions (let alone answer them!) and to give internal relations the chance to evolve. Yet we preempt that much-needed "time" constantly in responding to the emergencies of the moment.

There must be time and space (liberated zones, communities of resistance and nurturance, temporary autonomous zones, occupations) through which participants can develop and experience the freedom that can erupt from communities established in response to the volcanic contradictions of capitalism. Those experiences allow us to develop the creativity, security and emotional flexibility to sidestep or overcome the fears conditioned into us, but that all takes time. Without it, they are debilitated by emergencies of every sort, and preclude the chance to actually taste that apple.

It takes time to apprehend and learn to experience the world in new ways.

It takes time to develop the honest and self-critical sensibility needed to overcome automatic, conditioned and self-sabotaging patterns of thought and behavior. How much easier to just issue a press release denouncing this or that policy!

Further, it takes time to overcome *our own* panic — concealed though it may be, under layer after layer of social conditioning useful to the reproduction of capitalism and patriarchy — and be able to "ruthlessly critique everything existing," including (especially) oneself. Marx spoke of the importance of working class struggles not only in achieving political victories in the larger society but on the formation of communist consciousness within the working class itself. This transformative capacity of even economic struggles (depending on how they were framed and fought) was, for Marx, paramount. For instance, as early as the The German Ideology (1845), Marx and Engels had written:

> For the creation on a mass scale of communist consciousness, as well as for the success of the cause itself, it is necessary for individuals themselves to be

> changed on a large scale, and this change can only occur in a practical movement, in a revolution. Revolution is necessary not only because the ruling class cannot be overthrown in any other way, but also because only in a revolution can the class which overthrows it rid itself of the accumulated rubbish of the past and become capable of reconstructing society.[42]

It takes time to learn how to participate effectively in radical movements in a non-arrogant way, and help to strengthen them. (That's what I love about the Zapatistas, philosophically. They spent years, even decades, preparing decision-making processes that allowed them to move much more quickly later.)

It takes time to re-unite in ourselves the fragments of what capitalism has forcibly separated: the political and economic, "consumer" and "worker," "subjective" and "objective," what we fight for as revolutionaries in our communities and what is seen as legitimate to fight for on the job.

It takes time to develop the capacity to *unask* the hidden assumptions of our lives and *reframe* them, as standard operating procedure.

It takes time to transform our lives so that we begin to bring about, as Che Guevara put it, a new socialist human being

---

[42] Karl Marx and Frederick Engels, *The German Ideology*. The full text, translated slightly differently, can be found in Easton and Guddat, *Writings of the Young Marx on Philosophy and Society*, Anchor Books, 1967, p.431, and in David McLellan, *The Thought of Karl Marx*, p.87. The quoted paragraph was noticeably edited out of Tucker's *Marx-Engels Reader*, and also from International Publishers' *The German Ideology*.

within all the harrowing competition and insanity of the old.

It requires nurturing each other even when we disagree, defending our liberated spaces — *but who has the time?* coughs the rabbit, scurrying down the rabbit hole to Wonderland, there's another emergency, "I'm late, I'm late, for a very important date!" And yet without that precious Time we are lost.

We must learn to guard that vital "Time," protect it from intrusion by the emissaries of Truth who come to raid our collectives, recruit us or impose their undemocratic processes on us (in the name of "socialism," no less), yet who find one reason after another to keep from committing themselves to open, collective *and loving* processes.

Capitalism has, in the course of its "development," destroyed or co-opted nearly all pre-existing communities which could have served as bases for "liberated zones." But "the Left" has been complicit in that destruction. It has considered communities of resistance and nurturance — and the time needed to pull them together — to be "luxuries", to be thwarted by the next "must do now" crisis. Who will be our Tecumseh, that valiant and wise Native American organizer who, against all odds, pulled together wide and revolutionary coalitions against the colonizers?

Most important, the Left in the U.S. has to keep itself from undermining the consolidation of forms through which individuals can develop new ways of experiencing their lives, and consequently new relationships, which would lead to a much stronger and more vibrant revolutionary movement. That is why the counterculture of the 1960s, in spite of all its problems, was so important. Participants in the New Left were fighting not only for "others," but for our own liberation as well.

But throughout the '60s and persisting to this day, Left groups continue to thwart attempts to address the psychological and social conditions through which participants could collectively empower ourselves. Instead, they exploit people's residual guilt feelings: "You don't deserve to fight to end your own alienation, there are others so much worse off than you. You must sacrifice yourself for them." We are run ragged around some capitalist-provided "emergency" or "demand," one emergency after the next, quick to become a permanent condition, reinforced by guilt-trips, baiting and all sorts of pressures — some of which we're seeing in the Occupy struggles. Despite many worthy efforts of individual activists (I hate the word "activists." When did we start accepting it? That demarcation separates we, the self-selected vanguard — the "Chosen People" — from the unwashed masses as though they aren't actually "us"), many left groups employ quick-fix lines and ever-present crises to exploit and over-run our openness, democratic spirit, exploration of and engagement with complex issues. Instead of helping to build, they undermine and recruit. Their main goal is to recruit newcomers to their style of counterproductive bickering over the correct demand or line, trying to re-mold our activities in their image, around their agenda.

Just as imperialism squeezes every attempt at liberated space outside its home borders, so too do left parties short-circuit that space within them. This is a terrible tragedy. It prevents leftists once again from developing the ability to *unask* questions (which is what allows us to transcend such false dualities as consumer vs. worker, economics vs. ecology, and the like), *reframe* the possibilities (so that we can experience our lives in a different way), and *strengthen and link direct action communities of resistance and nurturance* (which would enable the Left to become a force to reckon with). All of that requires time and secure spaces in which to develop.

Participants in those spaces need that time to explore how to go about consolidating and linking communities of resistance and nurturance based on direct action. What threads do we weave them from? Can this even be done? What's holding us back? Who are our friends, who are enemies? Who will be making up the generic "we" that decides any or all of this? And how will those decisions be reached? Different choices and modes of acting are possibilized in different periods. How do we understand the transition from one period to another so that we know how to shift gears, strategize differently? Yesterday's revolutionary demands inevitably become today's apologia for capital. How can we tell ahead of time when we're in a period of transition — eras that require new kinds of organization and strategy? What are the assumptions that left parties have been unable to challenge that keep them impotent — worse, embolden fascism?

And how do we keep ourselves from falling into that pit time and again?

When Che said, "At the risk of seeming ridiculous, let me say that a true revolutionary is guided by great feelings of love," he was stating the obvious, but it really was not obvious until he put it out there. How come we never think of the first part of that sentence? Why is being guided by great feelings of love seen as risking ridicule, and why are so many afraid to be seen that way?

Do our fears destroy our ability to love as well as to organize? Can those seeking to change society succeed in overcoming or bypassing those fears? Is our job really to organize ourselves around "getting out the Truth to the masses" — "consciousness raisers of the world, unite?" — or is that our need for validation talking? We strive to subvert the corporatized ways people *experience* "the news," politics, and their own lives and relationships. We clearly need to help build direct action movements and institutions through which we can collectively empower ourselves and act meaningfully, directly. But how? Political organizations of-a-new-type are needed that begin not with the question, "How do we get our message onto the internet or national media?" but, "How does revolutionary change occur and what is our role in helping to bring it about?"

The concept of "direct action as strategy" that I am developing here — ideologically, historically, philosophically, practically *and* organizationally — of course strives to win reforms in the short run; but it primarily attempts to synthesize the strategic and prefigurative politics of the earlier period. Can we develop prefigurative direct action politics as part of a conscious, organized strategy of participatory democracy and dual power more quickly than the system absorbs it? That is the task before us. Only in that way can we transcend the prefigurative/strategic false duality and re-invent revolutionary socialism and feminism as freedom movements, not as yet another appeal to the authoritarian state to meet this or that demand, enabling it to further consolidate its power over us.

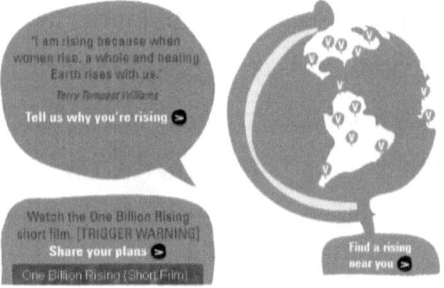

Part Three.
Learning How to Re-Frame Issues

photo by Marc Ribaud/Magnum

"And yet everybody wants to breathe and nobody can breathe and a lot of people say 'we'll be able to breathe later'. And most people don't die because they're already dead." - *Grafitti, Nanterre, 1968*

The question of organizational form grows out of the way members see their "mission" and cannot be separated from it. Vastly different organizational forms emerge from different orientations to political work, some more appropriate than others for accomplishing direct action strategies, others more appropriate for administering the raising of consciousness. Attempts to "structure away" these strategy-based differences, even by those striving to increase organizational democracy, will only exasperate participants and frustrate attempts to form truly democratic groupings.

In order to successfully shape demands through the lens of direct action/participatory democracy right from the start we need to engage in a process I call "Reframing the Question." "Reframing" applies as much to how organizations are structured as it does to what those organizations do. Every political generation needs to explore the relationship between consciousness, mission, structure, activity and strategy anew. Only by teaching ourselves how to reframe the question as a matter of course can we have any hope of undermining the logic and damage of capitalism *in us* and in our organizations. Otherwise, we reproduce that damage and ways of relating in everything we do even as we strive to transform ourselves and overthrow the system.

Take the attacks on welfare recipients spearheaded by that deadbeat dad, Newt Gingrich. In response, most Leftists ask: "We oppose Gingrich's position on Welfare. How can we persuade the government to increase payments?" That's all well and good, but it leaves us forever fighting a defensive battle over a shrinking pie against other workers with equally valid concerns. How can we reframe that issue so that it opens up new windows for the Left and undermines the assumptions that prop up the system? How can we keep it from being turned into just one more stagnant *position* on another futile list of demands?

Welfare for the Rich

All successful reframings start with the process of "Unasking the Question," through which we examine *the history of the question itself* — in this case, the hidden assumptions embedded in attacks on welfare — in order to find the essential lynch-pin around which the whole question spins.

As in most sociological debates within capitalism, behind every view stands an economic relationship that usually goes unseen. The question, *"What are the assumptions hidden in this question?"* doesn't ordinarily come up. No one thinks there are assumptions hidden behind what they take to be "natural" or "normal". Unasking — the first step in Reframing — helps to reveal all that. One way to reframe the issue of Welfare, for example, is to ask:

- Should the working class and the poor continue to provide welfare to the bankers and the rich?

- Should we subsidize giant corporations by offering them enormous tax abatements, exemptions and bailouts at the public expense?

- Should we continue to assess corporate holdings and large private properties below their actual value, while taxing workers to make up the difference?

- Should we allow wealthy Wall Street brokerage firms to pay reduced utility rates, which increases the rates for everyone else?

- Should we allow millionaires to continue paying taxes at lower rates than everyone else?

- Should huge corporate holding companies get away with paying no taxes at all? and,

- For that matter, should we, as workers continue to allow the bosses to pay us less than the full value of our labor, while they pocket the difference?

All of these constitute welfare for the rich. At our expense. They scapegoat poor women struggling to feed their kids for the miserable pittance they're grudgingly allocated, barely enough to pay the rent, while the government hardly blinks an eye as corporations and banks stuff their fat faces at the public trough. For corporations, every day is Christmas! Huge corporate incomes go untaxed or under-taxed. Capital gains taxes? Here's the chart of how much wealthy people pay in taxes on their capital gains (that is, profits they've made on the stock market):

1977	40%		1986	28%
1978	28%		1997	20%
1981	20%		2003	15%

The same with transfer taxes — they're virtually non-existent. In most states, workers and poor people pay sales taxes on every item they buy, but the rich pay absolutely zero on stocks they purchase or sell. And yet a few cents per trade would wipe out New York's entire budget deficit and plow billions into subways, schools, hospitals and infrastructure. What an unseemly sight — the rich lining up, begging billion-dollar handouts from Congress! AIG, Goldman Sachs, Citibank, Morgan-Chase, Bank of America, Exxon, BP and the rest will gladly take a trillion dollars in public funds to cover their risky business deals while paying their execs enormous salaries and retirement packages (golden parachutes) in the tens of millions of dollars each, chanting their mantra: "Break up the 'culture of poverty'" — all the way to the bank! Meanwhile, their corporations provide no jobs. They rake in obscene profits, pay their officers seven-figure salaries, and then "downsize" — the new euphemism for throwing tens of thousands of people out of work. So when we hear calls to *Privatize Social Security,* or to *Restructure Welfare,* flip the terms of debate, and say: *Of course!* Throw the corporations and the rich off the public dole! Don't reward them with public funds for their terrible decisions. And make them pay taxes they've avoided all these years at the expense of the middle class, working class and poor.

What we have in capitalism is a mass transfer of wealth from the working class to corporations and their owners.

It's not hard to imagine many ways of targeting particular corporations within that framework. We need to learn how to reframe every issue in a similar way so that they yield creative options through which people can empower themselves and from which the Left as a whole comes out stronger. We do that by developing the ability to turn the motion of our opponents against them — a sort of political jiu-jitsu. When they scream "Fingerprint welfare recipients," we should march into Chase Manhattan to fingerprint the bankers! When they cry out for "capital punishment," we can shoot right back: "No, start punishing capital! Give us back our homes! Give us the jobs you promised!, the resources you've stolen!"

To reframe issues effectively takes practice. It won't happen without preparing. Capitalism's "logic" is too embedded, Patriarchy's power relations too hegemonic. We need to train ourselves

to *Un-Ask, Reframe* and *Direct Act* as a matter of course, and that creativity only happens when we're not paralyzed by fears and insecurities that have been inculcated into us. There are specific organizational forms that help us to do that. Creating conditions in which participants can side-step

WHAT IS DIRECT ACTION? | 189

FRED WRIGHT

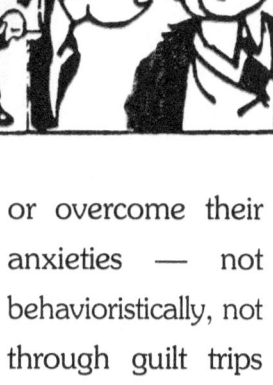

or overcome their anxieties — not behavioristically, not through guilt trips and manipulation — is a fundamental *political* task.[43]

Our publications should provide forums on how to prepare ourselves to take advantage of the moment and act creatively through direct action in *everything* we do, as a way of life. The Left rarely addresses this "subjective problem" as a necessary component of its political

---

[43] I discuss this aspect of our work in much more detail in "Fear and the Art of Neurosis Maintenance," "Turning Motion Into Movement: Tips for Anti-Apartheid and Other Activists," and "A Headful of Ideas that are Driving Me Insane," three other booklets in my *Zen Marxism* series.

work, relying instead, ironically on urging greater individual effort to overcome "petty bourgeois individualism."

Riding the Subway

Let me give one example here of what I mean by "reframing a situation": I was riding the D Train to Manhattan around 7 pm one summer evening. Diagonally across from me a young Italian man and woman were making out. Further down the car, a Black man was smoking a joint, reading some advertisements aloud, and laughing at his own parodies of them. Across from him two Puerto Rican teenage girls were chattering away in Spanish. Aside from the six of us the car was empty, yet it was filled with life. I was engrossed in reading when a burly Irish cop strode into the car smacking his nightstick into the palm of his free hand, eyeing up and down each of the passengers. The man at the other end of the car had already disposed of his joint at the first sight of the uniform; the two lovers stopped kissing as the cop leered at them. The young girls stopped their animated discussion and repeatedly glanced at the cop, as though they'd done something wrong. All the joy fled from that train car like air from a punctured balloon. The cop walked over to me and tapped his stick against the shiny stainless steel pole and, without saying a word, pointed it at my new Converse high-tops which were leaning against the pole where it joined the floor.

"What?" I said, insolently staring back at him, trying to keep a steady gaze without jerking my eyes away as I felt the adrenalin course through my body and my heart really start to pump. "Get your feet off the pole." Do I want to make an issue of this?, I thought. I needed to get to a Save the Audubon meeting in Manhattan. Is this a good time, and is this the right issue? Besides, this cop is itching to smack someone. So, like a good little boy, I decided to slide my feet back a couple of inches and felt like I'd just sold out everything I believe in.

At that moment the train came screeching to an unexpected halt. Either the engineer had thrown the brakes full force, or someone in another car had pulled the emergency cord. We all went sliding down our seats and the cop, because he was standing, went flying, grabbing onto a handle at the last minute to steady himself.

In a few seconds the train started up again and limped into the station, but not before a remarkable thing happened. Although none of us were hurt when the train braked abruptly, the two lovers across from me looked at each other and then daintily sat themselves on the floor of the car and the man began moaning: "Oh, my head. I think I fractured my head." The woman giggled, and cried out: "My hand, I think it's broken." And they looked across to me.

It's funny how instantaneously connections are created. Without giving it a thought I grabbed my knee and yowled: "Oh, my knee. Ohhhh. Ohhhhh." The fellow who'd been smoking the reefer began laughing, and said: "Yea, man, my toe. I think I stubbed my toe-o-o-o." And the two girls began shoving each other and took turns chortling in Spanish while the other one called out in English: "She says her shoulder's broken," and the other would say, when her turn came, "And she says it's her lips, she'll never kiss again!" All the playful mayhem occurred within three or four seconds. As the train stopped at the station and the doors opened, the cop took one final look at us rolling all over the seats and floor in hysteria and fled, no doubt panicking at the thought of all the accident reports he'd have to fill out. Our newfound community laughed all the way to Manhattan, and when the train began filling up with newcomers, the genial atmosphere was infectious.

What had been going on, in political terms, was a battle over turf: Whose "ways of being" controlled that space? Not only the literal space of that train car, but the "space" of mind. Which would dominate: Fear of Authority (and the self-repression that always makes us cringe before it), or empowerment?

An axiom of zen-marxism is that both possibilities are present at the same time and at all times, and they fight it out with each other for hegemony; different conditions allow one or the other mode to prevail. This two-sided war within the mind of *every* individual is the gist of a dynamic perspective known as "dual consciousness," which was first postulated by the Sojourner Truth Organization, although I'm taking it to a new level here. These include circumstances leftists don't normally consider, like nutrition, which causes hormonal imbalances and, in turn, severe mood fluctuations that play havoc with political work as well as personal relationships. The peacefulness I'd enjoyed on entering that train had been overwhelmed by the adrenalin rush brought on by the cop. Why should anyone have the right or authority to command one's inner space in that way?

While some cops riding the trains at night may not act in such an authoritarian manner — and, indeed, a lot of passengers welcome them, authoritarian or not, because they keep away the hooligans and muggers — the atmosphere *always* changes when a police officer enters, regardless of the cop's intentions. It happens in little ways: You notice their hands covering their gun to prevent someone from lifting it out of the holster in a crowd, and your eyes bounce around the train, suspicious of everyone. It takes a lot of mental energy to concentrate on peacefulness, in that type of situation. If you wear, as I often do, a "Remember Michael Stewart" pin, in memory of the graffiti artist murdered by eleven transit cops while handcuffed and in their custody, you get strange glances from the cops — not always hostile ones; sometimes they just want to talk about it. But they've still got the gun and club during that discussion, and the law stands behind them whatever they do, so you'd better know your place and keep on your toes.

Such palpable self-repression is the way most New Yorkers respond to implied and pervasive threats. The potential geniality and shared control of the space around us becomes warped; even the way we hold our body changes, and our creative abilities — so necessary to reframe situations and generate new and unanticipated options — are overrun by the fearful, unconscious cringing before authority. Just when we most need to act creatively, we are least capable of doing so. Instead, we dredge up (yet again!) all the emotional baggage, fears and animosities that lurk in the back alleys of disempowerment.

Photo by Jennifer Jager

Roman Gladiator and *The History of Debt* author David Graeber and Green Party Presidential candidate Jill Stein hold sign commemorating the total student debt passing the $1 trillion mark at rally in Washington Square Park, NYC, April 2012.

The ability to act creatively, reframe situations and seize back one's space, as we did on that unforgettable subway ride, depends, to a large extent, on disruption of the "normal" routine and self-control or an overriding of one's fears. That enables one to make lightning-like connections that could never have even occurred at that moment to an isolated, fearful person.

Let me be careful here, so as not to be misinterpreted as proposing an elite vanguard of Platonic "Fear-overcomers" or Nietzschean übermensch. The challenge to overcome our fears does not neatly divide between those who are fearful and those who have overcome them; that is not the paradigm I am proposing. Rather, both tendencies — a) to see the world through the lens of one's conditioned fears, and b) collectively empowering ourselves and our communities by overcoming or side-stepping our anxieties — wage a war in all of us at all times, and at the same time. Sometimes the one, sometimes the other, will dominate. We need to understand how this process works if we are to bolster those conditions that will allow us to creatively reframing the way we see the world around us, and our own actions within it.

What enabled the D-train passengers to seize back our space if we were so full of fears? *It was a disruption of the repressed norm, made possible by contradictions in the system itself.* The train suddenly screeched to a halt and created new possibilities; people reacted creatively and playfully to their disorientation in that circumstance, instead of with fear. What can we learn from that? First, being able to respond creatively in this incident had nothing to do with "raising consciousness." No politically "astute" individuals tried to deliver "the Truth" to the ignorant masses about the historical nature of the role of the police in capitalist society. No one exhorted the others to overthrow the cop's tyranny. Nor did a self-proclaimed vanguard issue the correct revolutionary program as a means to enlist people in their cause. In fact, it was those considered non-political by the Left who, in that moment, initiated and won what a zen-marxist would consider an effective *political* battle.

Second, a community of resistance formed, for however short a period, inserting itself in a space where people had previously been isolated. (In that regard, it is no coincidence that it was people already in some sort of positive relationship to each other — the "lovers" — who first broke through the fear.)

Third, people acted through what we'd been taught — we had a *right* to that public space — and directly claimed it without arguing about whether or not we had such a right.

Of course one such battle, if we can call it that, doth not a revolution make. Nevertheless, when refusal to be cowed by authority becomes widespread it expresses itself in many seemingly insignificant battles over the full range of daily life, piling up into a climate of disalienation. It develops an extensive "counterculture" through which dramatically different interpretations of social reality become legitimized and adopted by large numbers of people.[44]

True, at the present time in America such refusal is not widespread; and, true again, the general feeling of hostility to authority is not enough to override people's fears and allow them to challenge it. Some who do are ending up in right-wing, proto-fascist militias — an outcome in part made possible by the Left's failure to organize truly empowering communities of resistance and, instead, its feeding of rebellious impulses into boring, sterile and ultimately self-defeating petitioning efforts to change government policy instead of organizing direct attacks on the institutions exploiting and oppressing us.

The Left needs to consolidate such feelings in sustained communities of resistance and nurturance that can foster ever-greater struggles over long periods of time. That climate is exactly what the Left must nurture, for only at a time when people *en masse* are engaged daily in dis-alienated, non-fearful activity can moments of individual and occasional rebellion hold the potential to blossom into serious revolutionary challenges to capitalism, patriarchy, and all systems of domination.

---

[44] See, especially, Dan Foss and Ralph Larkin, *Beyond Revolution: A New Theory of Social Movements,* Bergin & Garvey Publishers, Inc., 1986, for a brilliant dissection of social movements, which parallels much of what I've written here.

A Question of Property

The dominant capitalist ideology frames the concept of "welfare" as, at best, a question of unequal or unfair advantages, to which one could take a liberal ("pro") approach or a conservative ("anti") one without it making much of a difference in the long run. Reframe it? How? *By keeping focus on the property question,* as Marx recommended. What does that mean?

Ah, ye olde 'Property Question'. Who gets to own and decide what's produced and how it's allocated? Workers and poor people pay increased taxes out of our pockets and suffer cutbacks in essential services *to pay for* the privileges enjoyed by the ruling class but denied everyone else. That's the fundamental exploitation inherent in this "mixed economy": socialism for the rich and cutthroat capitalism for the rest of us. Reframing the concept of "property" means *to question who gets to do what* with what we produce.

At the same time, we have to avoid the old maximalist ways of framing demands, such as: "Workers should seize the boss's property and expropriate the capitalists." Sounds good? Think again.

Framed in that way, workers are proselytized to seize *someone else's* property. The fact that it's the hated boss' is of little solace. In the way the demand is phrased it's still someone else's. The Protestant Ethic runs as entrenched as ever, and workers will generally react with a sense of guilt and inhibition. We must learn to frame demands to avoid reflecting our own conditioned thinking.

One of the lessons in studying histories of our movements is the discovery that in a short time we'll be fighting against today's victories. Recognizing that, one should always strive to hold the moral high ground while nailing the ruling class ideology to the cross of its illusions. There's no point in even raising a demand if we are not developing the means to address it effectively and retain control over the outcome. The form of organization required to actually carry out any demand reflects all that "subjectivity" that went into formulating it. We're encumbered by it. Guilt has long fingers, a strange way of squirming through ancient dust.

A "community of resistance/direct action" perspective would frame the demand differently: "Join us. We are taking back *our* property, which we as a class produced, it's rightfully ours and had been stolen from us." Reframed in that way, we retain the moral high ground. Even though we are talking about the same physical property in both cases, this second formulation feeds directly off of the socially accepted belief that an individual's property is sacrosanct and should not be taken by the corporation, state or anyone — a "normal" sensibility. It is easily extended to the right of the working class to own its own labor. What could be more natural? The bourgeois formulation of property that has plagued human kind since the inception of capitalism 600 years ago becomes an alien set of social, cultural and economic relations. Through unasking, reframing and direct action the bourgeois view of the "sacred" belief in private property — and customary behaviors that go along with it — loses its power.

Saving Private Property

Indeed, it is this way of reframing the "property question" that ultimately separates a Marxist analysis from that of liberals and other "progressives." Sociology courses in U.S. colleges are filled with paternalistic descriptions of oppression, which they define in terms of "strata" or "identity" demarcated by a quantitative *lack* of something. In that framework, homeless people are homeless *because* they don't have enough money; workers are oppressed *because* they can't afford to buy enough goods or pay the rent; women are oppressed *because* their wages are not equal to men's, etc. In contrast, a Marxist analysis sees class, and thus exploitation, oppression and alienation, as *socio-economic power relationships* and not categories defined by levels of income, hierarchy of affluence, poverty or privilege. In other words, what class you are part of is not a quantifiable category demarcated by differences in income (one's unequal purchasing power as consumer) but one's relationship to the system of production and reproduction, regardless of one's salary.

> **The division into classes in capitalism in not just a problem of some accumulating more goods, privileges, power and services *than* others, but *over* others. People are not "homeless," they're *made* homeless.**

"As soon as a person sells their labor to a capitalist and accepts only a part of the product as payment for that labor, they create conditions for the purchase and exploitation of other people. No one would willingly give their arm or their child in exchange for money; yet when a person deliberately and consciously sells their working life in order to acquire the necessities for life, one not only reproduces the conditions which continue to make the sale of their life a necessity for its preservation; one also creates conditions which make the sale of life a necessity for other people.

"Later generations may of course refuse to sell their working lives for the same reason that a person refuses to sell their arm; however each failure to refuse alienated and forced labor enlarges the stock of stored labor with which Capital can buy working lives."

- Fredy Perlman
The Reproduction of Daily Life, 1969
reprinted 1972, Black & Red

The sheer power of a Marxist class analysis in explaining the pushes, pulls, tensions and contradictions in capitalism cannot be reached via the liberal route, nor through that of its cousin, "identity politics." **The division into classes in capitalism is not just a problem of some accumulating more goods, privileges, power and services *than* oth-**

ers, but *over* others. That exploitative (rather than simply uneven or unfair) relationship defines the system; but it is concealed. People are not "homeless"; we're *made* homeless. Someone, or some force, or some system, is materially benefiting from the exploitation/oppression/alienation of the working class. Fighting for homeless people does not mean fighting for some sociologically underprivileged *strata*, but against the system based, by definition, on a small wealthy class profiting — i.e., receiving *welfare* — from the exploitation and impoverishment of the vast majority.

EXCERPT

THE TWILIGHT OF CAPITALISM

BY MICHAEL HARRINGTON

The very categories in which capitalism thinks of itself will become absurd as the system disappears. They will then seem to the everyday consciousness as superstitious as the divine right of kings appears to the mind of modern capitalist human beings.

Under one form of feudalism, serfs are required to work a certain period of time on the lord's property; in return they get the right to work their own property the rest of the time. This relationship is not predicated on an exchange of money, and it does not take place on a free market. It is imposed by tradition, sanctified by religion, and enforced by political power. The serf is personally dependent on the lord and owes him fealty. Therefore s/he must work for him for nothing. The fact that their labor time is divided up into paid and unpaid portions is right there for everyone to see — except they would not see it, for the very distinction between paid and unpaid labor time requires a commercial society where such a distinction already existed in reality — and that this obvious relationship doesn't enter into the general consciousness until capitalism emerges. What the serf and the lord saw in their relationship was the will of God.

In capitalism, on the contrary, the economic reality must appear other than it is. Feudalism and all other pre-capitalist forms *present the economic in a non-economic guise*. Since exploitation is the will of God and not of humans, the unjust relationship between lord and serf can seem to be what it is. Its sanction is, after all, divine. But capitalism is a secular society of supposedly free agents making contracts on the basis of *quid pro quo*. If the workers were told that they were going to get paid for two thirds of their time, but that they would be required to make a gift of the remaining third to the capitalist, they would reply that they were being cheated precisely according to the bourgeois law of the market. This society has to hide its true character. But note that this fraud is sincere — that is, Marx says that it fools the capitalists (who are sober and upright men, believing in an hour's work for an hour's pay), as well as the workers.

So wage labor is not only a historically specific form of work that becomes general under capitalism. It is also the very secret of the capitalist mode of production, for it is here that the surplus is concealed, that precondition for the accumulation of capital and the growth of the system as a whole.

Capitalist society, then, is based on an illusion peculiar to it: that workers are paid for the value of their work. But this deception has an enormous "objectivity," for it rationalizes the functioning of a gigantic system which has revolutionized the very face of the earth. It is a lie, but a lie that informs the most substantial social reality humankind has ever known. And yet, the power of this fraud is provisional; for ultimately, it is a fraud. The very categories in which capitalism thinks of itself will become absurd as the system disappears. They will then seem to the everyday consciousness as superstitious as the divine right of kings appears to the mind of modern capitalist human beings.

In precapitalist societies, where there is no widespread production for the market, the drive for surplus labor is limited by the needs it has to satisfy. For that mat-

> ter, in the earlier modes of production, the accumulation of great wealth signaled a decadence, not a progress. Moses well understood that the worship of the Golden Calf would corrupt his people.[45] Capitalism, on the contrary, has an insatiable appetite for surplus labor and riches, for if the system does not produce more this year than last, it faces a crisis. This capitalist crisis is itself unprecedented, for it normally breaks out at the high point of a boom and is characterized not by a scarcity of goods as in precapitalist famines, but by an overabundance of goods that cannot find a buyer.
>
> Marx's central theoretical critique of the classical political economy was that it was not aware of its historical assumptions, that its categories were presented as timeless.[46]

Capital could not exist, let alone be embodied in a ruling class, without economic, political, social, cultural and ideological enforcement on every level, nor without our own complicity with and reproduction of the web of exploitative relationships, institutions and privi-

---

[45] Haideen Anderson interprets this same event as the defeat of matriarchal cultures, in which the golden calf — translated within a capitalist framework to be a symbol of greed and false idolatry — meant something completely different in women-centered societies. She rightly criticizes Marxism for narrowly seeing that event only within the parameters of political economy and not also within the framework of the transition to Patriarchy.

[46] Michael Harrington, *The Twilight of Capitalism*. I've neutered the pronouns where the use of the male "he" was used to mean women as well as men but otherwise served no distinctive purpose.

leges that pass for "normality." Maintaining and further hammering our complicity into place — what Noam Chomsky calls "manufacturing consent" — is the main function of bourgeois ideology which, today, is not sufficiently undermined by analytical presentations of Truth. Truth will *not* necessarily set you free. Speaking Truth to Power is *not* sufficient to physically shutdown the death-ships, corporations, polluters and police. Some sort of action is needed that puts those truths into practice. Neither capital nor its state give a damn about our protests and exposés — *unless they in some way threaten their interests.* New forms of organization are emerging that indeed threaten their interests — at least in the long-run — by prefiguring, in our everyday lives and activities, the kind of society we want to live in, one in which *direct democracy* — the will of the needy, not the profits of the greedy — prevails.

"Reframing" an issue enables us to wrench it free of its capitalist presuppositions and integuments and make it serve *us*, instead of one wing or another of the ruling class. It is what allows us to develop direct action as strategy for changing the world.

Academic Marxism: Opium of the Intelligentsia

What passes for a Left in the U.S. generally suffers from constricted vision and constipated imagination. Take the ubiquitous pre-Occupy demand: "Money for Jobs, not for War". Is that the only way an organization can mobilize anti-war sentiment, by arguing that the funds are needed elsewhere, there-in losing the sense of outrage over the war itself regardless of the quantifiable costs? Compare it to the U.S. New Left and liberation movement slogans: "Let the people decide," "Power to the people," "By any means necessary," "Bring the War Home," "Hell no we won't go," "Self-Determination," "If the government won't stop the war, we'll stop the government," "The personal is political," and "Work, Study, Get ahead, Kill!" Most are "anti-demands," i.e., demands addressed to ourselves, our movements, and not to any other authority. They indict the system, rather than trying to reform it. And some of them reject the rule of capital altogether.

So to with the exuberant slogans from Paris '68: "Beneath the paving stones, the beach!" "Humanity will not be satisfied until the last capitalist is strung up by the guts of the last bureaucrat"; "Most people don't die; they're already dead."

Marx observed, every time a worker reproduces her labor power, every minute s/he devotes to the assigned task, s/he enlarges the material and social apparatus that dehumanizes her, expands capital's reach geographically, and enables capital to exploit her and other workers more intensively. In other words, liberal demands help to expand capital's domination, not confront it. Revolutionaries don't seek to *manage* the system better; they strive to overthrow it and transform all social and property relations on which capitalism is based.

True communism — and by that I am not referring to the state capitalism that existed in the Soviet Union or China — is *not* capitalist liberalism with a human face. It's a movement towards a society in which exploitation and the wage system are eliminated once and for all. True, so long as we remain a capitalist society Leftists may *need* meaningless jobs in order to survive, but we certainly don't *want* them. As the saying goes, the only thing worse than having a job under capitalism is *not* having one! The Marxist-Leninist groups comprising the Old Left demanded better terms for alienated labor; the New Left wanted to abolish it altogether.

For too long — and I am speaking here to others within the Occupy movement who see themselves, like me, as part of the Left — we have allowed those who dominate the forms of "dissent" — the loyal opposition — to frame the issues, bestow their blessings on certain kinds of organization they deem valid, and dictate the means to organize around those issues. Even some Occupy sympathizers take that same arrogant approach and make demands on our movements *without participating in them*. The old left, unions, churches, student governments, politicians, liberal feminists, mainstream environmental groups, minimum common denominator coalitions, academic Marxists and solidarity groups have rejected — and even opposed — the direct action strategy outlined here for one reason or another. They have repeatedly boxed us into a pseudo-democracy, selecting one or the other of equally meaningless choices — environment or jobs, consumer or worker, "voting" or "protest," march on Washington or symbolic civil disobedience, objective "facts" or subjective emotions, Democrats or Republicans, syphilis or gonorrhea — keeping us impotent.

The kinds of demands issuing from the official left today all concern pressuring for changes in government or corporate policy. That is, they accept the legitimacy of those in power and thereby the underlying assumptions of the system, whose social expression they deplore. They require us to squander our time and resources in futile protests, lobbying Congress to make the changes *for* us — measures which, were we to live in a revolutionary society, we wouldn't want anyway.

Occasionally, they offer the illusion of power; sometimes we even take over the steps of the Capitol or Federal Hall and scream: "No more money to the contras / to the death squads / to apartheid / to the oil companies / to the banks," before we're whisked away in pre-arranged arrests to which the protesters have graciously acquiesced, in time for the evening news. (I much prefer the Red Balloon Collective's "Whiners' Contingent" which at various demonstrations orchestrated mass whining: "But why-y-y-y can't we have pea-ea-eace?," while marching behind banners that read:

"Whiners & Beggars & Liberals, O My! Sheep for Social Responsibility, Democratic Party slaughterhouse chapter."[47]) Liberals whine and whimper so plaintively, visit Congressional offices and try to explain why rape, torture and murder by the death squads they're funding are bad. They ultimately end up with: "It's bad for business!" — their ace in the hole, their coup de grâce.

Take the 2009 elections in California (please!). The state committee for single payer health care strategized away whatever moral position it might have hoped for by adopting a not-too-hidden racist approach, appealing (it thought) to the immediate self-interest of the voters: "Proposition 186 won't cost you a cent because it calls for free health care just for *legal residents,* not illegal aliens," the liberal appeal advertised (choking on the corpse in their mouths), "so go ahead and vote for it." Might as well have demanded: "Money for *us,* not for *them!*" The same holds for those who

---

[47] At one march in Washington against Apartheid and U.S. aggression in Central America in April 1985, as people marched past our Whiners' Contingent banner, the Red Balloon Collective stirred up militant whining: "But why can't we have peace? *Pleeeez* abolish apartheid. *Come onnn!*" Some of the more "serious" folks, usually in Official Left contingents, couldn't understand the commentary on our own movement from within and spit on us, thinking we were Moonies. But thousands of people — especially the student contingent, understood exactly what we were critiquing and whined along in extremely annoying, irritating snivels! A few dozen yards down the block another large banner from the "Whiners' Contingent" read: "Pleeeeze Abolish Apartheid — We simply abhor it (over there)!!" Signed: Rich corporate liberals against apartheid. (See Red Balloon Magazine, Spring 1988)

opposed the Gulf War and the current wars in Iraq and Afghanistan by arguing that "we can't afford to squander critical resources, we need the money for jobs at home." It's okay that they allow their tax dollars to pay for the slaughter of people around the world, but only if it doesn't cost too much. This "Lowest Common Denominator" orientation to political work, like the "lesser evil" candidates they offer every couple of years, presents two sides to the same electoral nightmare, two mouths on the same face, two worn shoelaces on the same worn sneakers, the Scylla and Charybdis of our revolutionary odyssey.

For Each & Every Warrior Whose Strength is Not to Fight

The weakness of strategies based on Lowest Common Denominatorism was in full evidentiary blossom during the 1991 bombardment of Iraq, repackaged as "the Gulf war." "Support Our Troops, Not the War!" insisted the National Campaign for Peace in the Middle East, which grew out of the old National Mobilization Committee to End the War in Vietnam and later would morph into United for Peace and Justice — the same politics, the same dependence on lowest-common-denominator Coalition-building, the same loyal opposition to the 2-party system, and, in fact, *the same people*. The underlying assumption: Support "our" troops for imperialism but not *theirs* (note the shift: we're no longer talking about "people," now, but "troops"). And whatever you do, don't say *anything* about Palestine or Israel!

Across the country — indeed, throughout the world — independent, enraged antiwar protesters, including a number of AWOL soldiers and seafarers from other countries, acted directly to resist the war. They blocked or sabotaged shipments of munitions to the Gulf. In one incident, a German-owned container vessel, the *Eagle Nova,* staffed by German officers and crew members from the Philippines, refused to deliver military goods to the Saudi Arabian port of Dammam on the Gulf.[48] In another case, 27 Moslem crew members on the *Banglar Mamata,* a Bangladesh vessel, jumped ship in Oakland, California, rather than continue on to deliver their cargo of ammunition to U.S. troops.[49] Unionized Japanese officers and crewmen on container ships and tankers chartered by the U.S. also refused to transport U.S. military cargo to the war zone. International working class direct actions against the war build-up were, in fact, so widespread that officials worried that "supply disruptions could become frequent enough

---

[48] American Maritime Officers Service, *News Briefs,* March 1991. The ship had been hired by American President Line for commercial feeder service between the United Arab Emirates and India.

[49] *ibid.* Once the crew jumped ship, the U.S. Navy's Military Sealift Command canceled its charter for non-performance, and the vessel's owner suddenly came to the conclusion that the ship was "unseaworthy."

to affect U.S. front-line fighting ability in a long war."[50]

Between Aug. 2, 1990 and March of the following year, more than 13,000 U.S. soldiers resisted the war's drumbeat directly. Hundreds were imprisoned, and tens of thousands of others went AWOL — many of them Black or Latino — a far greater proportion than during the Vietnam War. In one incident, 67 National Guard members from Louisiana went AWOL *as a group* from Fort Hood, Texas, in early February to protest inadequate training, unfair leave policies and racism, in the shadow of the war. Tod Ensign, a staff person for Citizen Soldier, termed it "the largest known act of mass military resistance" during the Gulf war.[51]

On Dec. 9, 1990, a Vietnam veteran, Tim Brown — described by the Associated Press as "a genial, upbeat person who lived alone on a houseboat and rarely discussed politics" — died after setting fire to himself in Isleton, California, to protest the US military build-up in the Gulf. In leaflets he'd placed on nearby car windshields, he'd written: "I, Tim Brown, Vietnam veteran, declare that my act of self-immolation is a direct protest of American war policy in the Middle

---

[50] *ibid.*

[51] Mitchel Cohen, "For Each and Every Warrior Whose Strength is Not to Fight," *Guardian*, May 1991 and also in *Fifth Estate*. Also, Mitchel Cohen: "Pentagon Ups Penalties for Military Resisters," *The Guardian,* Feb. 6, 1991; "Gulf War is Not Over for Military Resisters," *The Guardian,* May 29, 1991; "They Didn't Follow Orders," *Fifth Estate;* and, "The Real Heroes Series," produced by *Storm Warning,* Vietnam Veterans Against the War Anti-Imperialist, 915 East Pine, #408, Seattle, WA 98122.

East. America, do not go to war. America, do not repeat the mistake of Vietnam. Don't wait for the war to start and then protest. Protest now while there is still time." On February 17, 1991, at the height of the U.S. bombing of Iraq, Gregory Levey, a former UMASS student and special education teacher, set himself on fire while carrying a peace sign. He died on the Amherst Commons in Massachusetts, in protest of the US bombardment and the murder of innocent civilians there. "No Blood for Oil!" and "Hell no, we won't go, we won't die for Texaco!" became the battle cries of the burgeoning anti-war movement.

Unlike the self-immolation of Buddhist monks during the Vietnam war, these courageous and heart-wrenching acts received virtually no publicity in the mainstream media. Only one or two papers picked up the AP story on Tim Brown's act. But our own media, including WBAI radio in NYC and the Pacifica network across the U.S., *The Guardian*, and newly formed groups like *Hands Off!* (see below) got the word out and helped to stir an already growing unrest within the military. Military resisters began appearing everywhere, in and out of uniform, speaking out against the war despite threats of court-martial and imprisonment.

While held captive in Iraq as a prisoner of war after his plane was shot down, Lt. Jeffrey Zaun of New Jersey was a media hero, much like Jessica Lynch a decade later. TV and newspapers plastered his picture all over their pages. But that hero worship lasted only until he got back, and Zaun offered his views on his experiences in the Gulf: "This country didn't see the cost of the war. I did. People think we went in there and kicked ass; but they didn't see the Iraqi mothers get killed. I don't want to kill anybody again." The press buried his statement, as the U.S. military used bulldozers to bury alive tens of thousands of poorly armed Iraqi working class conscripts in the desert sands.

Those who tried to persuade their fellow National Guard members to resist were deemed "ringleaders" and court-martialed. Sgt. Robert Pete received a six-year prison sentence while Dwayne Black and Derrick Guidry received a year each. All three additionally received dishonorable discharges.[52] And many of the approximately 2,500 U.S. soldiers who filed for conscientious objector status during that time were held on serious "desertion" charges; they faced long prison terms for their *public* anti-war stance.

In addition to those court-martialed here at home, over a hundred anti-war GIs in Germany were still being held by military authorities as late as March, 1991, or were forced to go into hiding. Soldiers returning from Saudi Arabia reported hundreds more GIs being held there.[53]

---

[52] *Guardian,* June 5, 1991.
[53] Ruth Turner, Military Counseling Network.

In a steaming packed courtroom on the Marine Corps base at Camp Lejeune, North Carolina, court-martial proceedings against dozens of Marines who resisted the Gulf War went on all through the summer, with nary a word in the corporate press.

Captain Yolanda Huet-Vaughn, an Army doctor, refused orders to be shipped to the Gulf. When Huet-Vaughn denounced the war on the nationally-syndicated Sally Jessy Raphael TV show and remarked that some of Saddam Hussein's chemical weapons were made by U.S. companies, Sally Jessy lost it. She came storming up to the doctor, got her face about seven inches from her and screamed: "Get out! Get off my show!," reported WBAI's Amy Goodman, who was also a guest at the taping. Huet-Vaughn claimed that, as a doctor, her training was to heal people, not to murder them. At Fort Leonard Wood in Missouri, Capt. Huet-Vaughn, a Mexican-American, was confined to the base 24 hours a day, forced to call-in her whereabouts every 4 hours, and prevented from seeing her children in private (they had to remain outside at all times when they visited her). Fifty to 60 supporters packed all of her hearings, refusing to allow the government's machinations to be hidden behind closed doors.

Sam Lwin was a student at the New School for Social Research in New York City. Just twenty-one years old, he faced seven years in jail for organizing his Marine Corps reserve unit, Fox Company, at Fort Schuyler in the Bronx to resist. He had filed for Conscientious Objector status before the unit was activated in November, 1990. Lwin, along with seven other COs from his unit, refused the call-up. Sam faced 7 years in jail, a dishonorable discharge, and loss of all benefits including health care and pension for refusing to kill. His fellow students at the New School formed the group *Hands Off Sam!*, which soon took on the cases of other resisters, went national, and became, simply, *Hands Off!* (Lwin ended up serving 4 months in prison, a reduced sentence thanks largely to the widespread support organized by his fellow students.)

Ronald Jean-Baptiste was one of the first of the Gulf war resisters. He spoke publicly at the first anti-war rallies as a Haitian-American, saying: "They won't let me donate my blood to help people because I'm Haitian, but they want me to shed it for them and to kill people. I won't do it."

Stephanie Atkinson of Illinois was court-martialed out of the Army Reserve for refusing to fight in the Gulf. Upon leaving the military, she became an outspoken critic and went to work with the War Resisters League defending other resisters.

Why don't we remember their names, these resisters, these direct action heroes of humanity, who faced such terrible personal consequences and yet still refused to kill for

U.S. imperialism? Why have their actions been written out of the accounts of the resistance within the military to the Gulf War? These were resisters who refused to be pawns killing other poor people for oil, profits and empire. They acted with great moral courage, saying: "This is what's right, this is what's not, no power on earth can move me from this spot." Nor should we forget what they were up against, these kids — for that's what most of them were. They were thrown out of the military and into jail, lost their scholarships, their jobs, sometimes their families and friends. We often hear how much we owe to veterans who fought in this country's wars. But we owe far more to those who *refused* to fight, our anti-war veterans, for putting their bodies against the wheel of the war machine and causing it to slow down, and sometimes to stop.

Remember Kevin Sparrock, a student at New York City's School of Visual Arts; Erik Larsen, a student at Chabot Community College in California; and, Tahan Jones. They were among the most visible of the resisters because they helped organize anti-war demonstrations across the country. They were accused of desertion during a time of war. The government filed briefs against them *calling for the death penalty.*

Remember Eric Hayes. He was the president of the Black Students Association at Southern Illinois University, and a Marine Corps reservist. Eric was dragged out of his dormitory room in the middle of the night in December, 1990, handcuffed by military police and hauled off to the brig at Camp Lejeune a thousand miles away for failing to report when his Illinois unit was activated. (Eric was eventually sentenced to 8 months in jail.)

Remember Marine Corps Cpl. Jeff Paterson. On Aug. 29, 1990, he refused orders to board a military transport plane for deployment to Saudi Arabia. When his staff sergeants attempted to push him onto the aircraft, Jeff sat down in the hangar and refused to move. (Jeff became a leader of the anti-war movement, and worked with *Refuse and Resist!*)

Remember Demetrio Perez and James Summers, both students at Santa Fe Community College in Florida, and John Isaac III, a student at City College of New York. They were charged with "Desertion with Intent to Shirk Hazardous Duty" and "Missing Movement" for resisting orders to ship off to the Gulf; they were court-martialed and found guilty. (Perez was sentenced to 15 months, Summers to 14 months, and Isaac to 8 months at hard labor.)

As it became evident that more and more military personnel were none too eager to fight for the Emirocracy and the expansion of the American oil empire, the U.S. military began kidnapping resisters and forcing them onto planes headed to the Gulf. In one case, Sgt. Derrick Jones, a medic, filed an application as a conscientious objector and left his unit for several days. Through his lawyer, he negotiated with his commander, Capt. Cloy, to return to his unit, and was promised that he would not be charged with missing movement as he waited for his CO claim to be processed. But when Jones returned to his unit in Germany, he was immediately taken into custody, handcuffed, dragged onto a plane and flown to Saudi Arabia against his will.

The same thing happened to David Owen Carson, Robert Chandler and dozens of other military resisters. Bryan Centa, a medic stationed at Lee Barracks in Mainz, Germany, had also filed an application for a conscientious objector discharge. Centa was handcuffed and put in leg irons and "dispatched" to Saudi Arabia. The U.S. Attorney General failed to file a single complaint against the military in any of the dozens of kidnappings, or acknowledge the racism involved in many of those incidents.

This being America, how could racism *not* have played a very prominent part in the government's attitude towards the resisters? Sometimes it came out in stupid but relatively innocuous ways, such as a military superior's explosion when a white French reporter, Judith Weiner, embraced and kissed Sam Lwin, a native of Burma, during a recess at one of his hearings. Sergeant Richmond, a white man and Lwin's platoon troop-handler, ordered Sam into the hall and screamed at him: "You're not supposed to show affection while in uniform." Since all across the country troops were seen on nationwide TV coming home hugging and kissing while in uniform, Richmond's explosion was clearly triggered by the fact that Lwin, an Asian, was kissing a white woman.

Or, take the case of Danny Gillis. Gillis, a Black man from Baltimore, was court-martialed on charges stemming from a racial attack on him. He faced seven years. Along with Jimmy Summers, another of the resisters, Gillis had been held in solitary confinement in a cell measuring six feet by eight feet.

Gillis became a Moslem after he had enlisted in the military; he filed for conscientious objector status in November 1990. On December 17, Gillis' unit was ordered to Saudi Arabia, and he refused to go.

As the rest of the unit boarded the bus, Gillis sat down on the concrete and refused to get on. Staff Sgt. Schillumeit, who is white, ordered him onto the bus. Gillis again refused. Unable to get him onto the bus, the sergeant called four white Marines to tie Gillis' hands behind his back and beat him up.

Meanwhile, two Black Marines, passing by, saw four whites punching and kicking a tied-up Black man and came to Gillis' defense. Officers as well as enlisted men standing-by entered the fray on both sides according to their race. The fight continued until a colonel ordered everyone to "clean it up." At that point, Schillumeit called for a van with wider doors, and Gillis was thrown into it. A minute later, however, he managed to jump out, run about ten feet, and collapsed, screaming: "You're prejudiced. I'm going to get all of you...on grievances." Gillis was arrested and thrown into the brig for 41 days. In addition to "missing movement," Gillis was charged with disrespect of a superior officer for saying "You're prejudiced," willfully disobeying a lawful [sic!] command, disorderly conduct, and wrongfully communicating a threat for saying "I will get all of you."

Facing seven years in prison before Judge Oulette, Gillis, like many of the others, felt he had no choice but to accept a plea bargain arrangement; the prosecutor consolidated all the charges into one offense, and asked for a 12-month sentence. Oulette, in a vicious act, rejected the agreement between Gillis and the prosecution and sentenced Danny Gillis to an additional half-a-year in jail on top of the 12-month agreement.

Gillis required an operation on his shoulder due to injuries received during that fight. Meanwhile, one of the Marines who came to Danny's defense during the fight, Jody Anderson, *did* go with his unit to Saudi Arabia. Jody, like virtually all the Marines, never saw combat despite all the hoopla; but the Marine Corps did wait for the war to be over before arresting Jody on charges of mutiny, inciting to riot, three counts of assaulting an officer, threatening officers, and disobeying a direct order. All told, Jody faced life imprisonment plus 44 years.

"This was clearly a political decision on the part of the military," said Melissa Ennen, of the New York City-based *Hands Off!*, who organized support for the resisters at Camp Lejeune and who now runs a movement space in Brooklyn known as *The Commons*. "The government," she asserted, "was trying to conceal the extent of anti-war activity within the military, isolate those it considered the ringleaders and crush those who had the courage to resist." More soldiers deserted or went AWOL for political reasons during the build-up and course of the Gulf war than in any similar period this century, including the Vietnam years. No wonder President George H. W. Bush felt such a need to "finally overcome the Vietnam syndrome."[54]

And yet, most of the non-governmental organizations that made up the *Campaign for Peace in the Middle East* — one of the two nationwide anti-war hierarchies — deserted the deserters. Was it because of the challenge to national chauvinism, not wanting to appear unpatriotic? Or perhaps it was because unlike the majority of visible resisters in the 1960s, most of the Gulf war resisters were African-Ameri-

---

[54] This only touches the surface of the massive resistance within the military and outside of it to the Gulf War. So much has been forgotten or covered up. At the time, I and others at *The Guardian* newspaper in New York City carved out articles week after week while at the same time participating in the direct action arm of the resistance movement. See "Read My Apoca-Lypse: The Gulf War and the Mass Psychology of Fascism," for much more on this subject.

cans, Latinos and Asian-Americans? At any rate, *The Campaign* went AWOL on this issue.

Small grassroots organizations like *Hands Off!* did heroic work in defense of the resisters, filling the void as best they could. Due to shortage of funds, military resister Jody Anderson was forced to retain one of the non-movement lawyer sharks, who totally botched his case. Where was the National Conference of Black Lawyers? How about the National Lawyers Guild? For the period of the Gulf war these two erstwhile progressive formations didn't lift a finger for the military resisters! The National Lawyers Guild feigned involvement by putting up stickers around military bases with a "hot line" for resisters to call, and hired their own secretarial staff at $10 an hour to answer the phones. But when soldiers called, they were told the NLG had no trained lawyers available and that they should call *Hands Off!* or the *War Resisters League*.

As a result of lawyer incompetence, Jody Anderson was sentenced to two years in jail. Anti-war resisters rallied to Jody's cause; his trial and sentencing created a real bond between many of the soldiers who went to the Gulf and those who resisted, which allowed them to organize in the brig.

In a similar travesty of justice, the army reneged on a plea-bargain deal with Sgt. John Pruner at Fort Riley, Kansas, that would have limited his incarceration to 6 months. According to Tod Ensign of *Citizen Soldier*, "Pruner was one of two soldiers who exposed the Army's changed policy on COs. The policy made it more difficult for Saudi-bound GIs to win conscientious objector status." Pruner faced 6 years in prison. As Pruner's court-martial began the army, foreshadowing what would be applied to all defense lawyers a decade later, denied security clearance to his lawyer and prevented him from reviewing documents needed for his defense. Nothing in the corporate press!

Even full-scale race riots went unreported. One soldier, returning to New York from the Gulf, told *The Guardian* that race battles within the U.S. military in Saudi Arabia were common. "White commanding officers regularly gave 'on site' promotions to white Marines; when Black Marines complained, wholesale battles between whites and Blacks took place," he said. The military simply covered it up. Some racial "incidents" in the military did make it into the press. But, in general, they have been "whitewashed."

Take the case of Cpl. Anthony Stewart, a Black soldier who at first was reported to have committed suicide. Under pressure from Stewart's family and others, the military revised its version to say he had "accidentally" killed himself. As more and more pressure was put on the military, including charges of racism and cover-up, the Marine Corps again altered its version, and put on trial Lance Cpl. Steven

Quiles, a white soldier in Stewart's platoon, for "accidentally" killing Stewart while cleaning his M-16. Quiles was sentenced to 15 months at hard labor, even as others reported that Stewart's death was intentional and racially motivated. Quiles didn't serve a single day in prison for the murder. In addition, his bad conduct discharge was revoked, and he returned to the good graces of the military. Stewart's parents, meanwhile, are *still* demanding a full investigation.

The military's fabrication of the events around Stewart's case is eerily reminiscent of its "spin", to put it nicely, around football star Pat Tillman's death in Afghanistan 12 years later. Although not racial, Tillman was killed "accidentally" by soldiers in his own platoon. Sports writer Dave Zirin fills in the blanks: "Pat Tillman is the only NFL player — or professional athlete — to die in the theater of war since September 11th, 2001. He walked away from millions of dollars to join the U.S. Army because of the way 9/11 shook his system. On 9/12/01, Tillman gave an interview where he said, "My great-grandfather was at Pearl Harbor and a lot of my family has gone and fought in wars, and I really haven't done a damn thing."

> Twenty-two months after enlisting, Pat Tillman was dead. His memorial service was aired on national television. The Army awarded him a Silver Star for his "gallantry in action against an armed enemy." They said Tillman's convoy had been ambushed in Afghanistan. They said Tillman charged up a hill to

protect his men but was shot down by the Taliban. Responding to this heroic story, the National Football League, as they are quick to mention, created statues and memorials in his honor.

... [But] the Pentagon's official story, the very story the NFL initially embraced, is an awful lie. Tillman actually died in friendly fire, a fact that was criminally hidden from his family, his fans, and to the greater public. Tillman also began to turn against the war before his death, telling friends in the Rangers that he believed the war in Iraq was "illegal." A voracious reader, he started reading anti-war authors in an attempt to wrap his head around how he had become the most famous solider in an endless conflict.

After the Bush administration finally revealed the truth, Tillman's shocked family and friends did the only thing they could do: fight to find out the real facts of his death. They went public with the narrative of a Pat Tillman that was inconsistent with the Bush administration and NFL's. They put forth a Pat Tillman that was an intensely iconoclastic atheist, turning against war.

The misrepresentation of Pat Tillman's death speaks to the lies used to sell war, and to the way people's rage and grief was exploited in the wake of 9/11. But thanks to the tireless work of his family, and the creators of the documentary *The Tillman Story*, his true story is now public knowledge. As Pat's mother Mary said in *The Tillman Story*, "I think they just thought, if they spun the story and we found out ... we'd just keep it quiet because we wouldn't want to diminish ... his heroism or anything like that ... but, you know, nobody questions Pat's heroics. He was always heroic. What they said happened, didn't happen. They made up a story, and so you have to set the record straight."⁵⁵

The Gulf War military resisters' depositions are filled with reports of abuses, many of them racial, that began once they applied for CO status. They were subjected to endless harassment. One of the most common complaints was that they were regularly ordered to perform extra night-time duty, which meant they could sleep no longer than three hours in a row, night after night. Florida native Doug De-Boer testified that he had been intentionally deprived of sleep by being forced to stand excessive night watches. "I have had night watches virtually every night of the week for three weeks in a row … During the day I am like a zombie, and have become sick because of sleep deprivation," De-Boer said, as he received a 15-month sentence.

Thirty-three Catholic bishops, from 23 states, called on President Bush to "stop the military's prosecution of conscientious objectors" and to grant them amnesty and honorable discharges (although as a group they said nothing about the war itself). Many French Green Party delegates to the European Parliament expressed their indignation at the treatment of the resisters in letters to the U.S. military, citing "deprivation of sleep, isolat[ion] in special cells, [and] censure of mail." And the Canadian branch of Amnesty International sent an observ-

---

[55] Dave Zirin, "Where was the Pat Tillman story on NFL Sunday?," *The Nation,* September 12, 2011.

er to the trials of Demetrio Perez and Jimmy Summers, and adopted several resisters as prisoners of conscience.

One resister who attempted to apply for Conscientious Objector status was told by his white commanding officer: "Blacks can't apply for CO."

"Why not?" his mother asked.

"Because of their culture." His mother sought clarification. "Because Blacks are from a violent culture."

Such stories of racism in the military are not isolated instances, any more than they are in civilian life. On one occasion a North Carolina judge intoned: "I'll have none of this talk about Black or white in my court. It's irrelevant whether the officers are Black or white. There is no racial prejudice in North Carolina." The spectators could only laugh. "He apparently could not understand what we found so pathetically funny," one said.

Sam Lwin reported being called "Chinaman" and "gook" throughout bootcamp. "I was ordered to count from one to ten in Burmese and to sing in Burmese by my sergeant, in front of other drill instructors," he told me. During his conscientious objector hearing, Lwin was stereotypically asked if he knew kung-foo or karate. One drill instructor told Lwin directly, "I don't like you because you're oriental."

Lwin was the first resister to come to trial at Lejeune. At his court martial the government's star witness, Cpl. David

Patrick Conley, admitted under cross-examination that he had bragged: "The last good deed I do for the Marines [before being discharged next month] is to send Sam Lwin to jail for 20 years." Lwin's commanding officer, Capt. Gaspar, admitted that he had berated Lwin for applying to be a conscientious objector and gave him a rough time, but considered his harassment "advice".

Marquis Leacock, an African-American resident of New York City, said that the resisters were "the only ones who have eight platoon sergeants to take care of 14 of us. We are called names such as 'communist pig,' 'traitors' and degrading references to our race and culture." Leacock received a 1-year sentence.

One of the sergeants "enjoyed ordering us to line up and chant 'I am shit' over and over," said one. In the brig, they were not allowed to read political literature. Authorities monitored diaries and artwork, and censored outgoing and incoming mail. Resister Demetrio Perez reported that military officers tried to force them to sign documents against their will and without approval of their attorneys.

James Summers recounted, "When I arrived at the brig, the guards immediately started making fun of me and my CO status. They put me in leg irons, handcuffs and chains around my waist, and locked me in my cell for five days. I was taken out once a day for five minutes to take a shower."

Enrique Gonzalez, a student at Nova University School of Law in Fort Lauderdale, Florida, told of being denied transportation and of being forced to walk up to 12 miles a day back and forth to work, unlike the other soldiers.

The resisters' supporters packed the courtroom every day and set up a "peace camp" around 20 miles away. Their presence made a crucial difference in the trials. Before packed courts the resisters began to win important pretrial motions against the Marine Corps, challenging the overwhelming mistreatment and harassment. One judge ruled that their confinement to barracks was illegal and permitted them to leave the base. Most importantly, he recognized that the harassment they underwent was not made up of isolated incidents but was systematic and illegal, opening the way for class action suits against the military.

Many of the resisters wrote movingly in their Conscientious Objector applications about the development of their anti-war beliefs while in the military. Why did they, whose backgrounds are really not very different from other soldiers, choose to buck the military's ideological stampede and retain a semblance of humanity in the face of jackboot patriotism and brutal, murderous authority?

Marcus Blackwell, of Brooklyn, N.Y., a student at the Boro of Manhattan Community College when he resisted the call-up, wrote: "Universal love should be the basis of man's action and this should be apparent in his deeds. I respect other people and live by that rule. War destroys more than just property or landscape. It also destroys human beings and the human soul.

"When I joined the military, fighting a war was the farthest thing from my mind. Some people may say that my thinking was very muddled. As a matter of fact, I couldn't even picture myself being on the front line in a war. Well, my thinking *was* muddled. I looked at joining the military as a job. I thought that being in the military was one way to be a successful person.

"But when I was sent to the School of Infantry in Camp Lejeune, my eyes were really opened. I was exposed to various types of weapons that can be used against a person, like the .50 calibre machine gun, the M249 Squad Automatic Weapon and the AT-4 Rocket Launcher. Learning how to invade enemy grounds and throwing hand grenades made me wonder, 'Is this really me that is doing this?'

"So now I was able to shoot and kill a person from 500 yards, destroy whole families and villages and kill people through the air. But who was I really harming? I was harming myself. I was harming my spirit, disrupting that inner peace and harmony that holds me together.... The job I was doing may have been good for the Marine Corps, but it was not for the good of man."

WHAT IS DIRECT ACTION? | 235

Blackwell was sentenced to 17 months at hard labor in a military prison.

Sgt. David Bobbitt, of Staten Island, New York, also believed that his experiences in the Marine Corps prompted him to examine his beliefs on war. During infantry training, he wrote, "I saw a man fall from a helicopter to his death. It was very hard for me to accept that he had died, and even harder still to comprehend the casual attitude toward his tragic death by the other Marines. Are we really the superior beings on earth? And if so, is it because we can destroy and maim everything on this planet?

"My military occupational skill is 0311; what that comes down to is rifle man. My job was to learn all about weapons and how to use them effectively. It sounded very intriguing at first; after all, I enjoyed hunting for animals. After boot camp, I found out what my job really was; it was no longer so intriguing. For that matter, neither was hunting for animals."

Bobbitt was sentenced to 14 months in jail; along with Blackwell, he received a dishonorable discharge.

Meanwhile Dick Cheney, Stephen Solarz, Dan Quayle, Newt Gingrich, William Bennett, Rush Limbaugh and a host of feverish warmongers all somehow managed to avoid having to troop off to the Vietnam or Gulf war themselves, but they had no compunction about sending others, economically poorer and powerless, to kill and to die in the

Gulf — or to send resisters to wither away the best years of their lives crushing rocks in prison.

For most of the resisters, their experiences upon joining the military were far different than what they'd been taught to expect. As one of the resisters, (former) Lance Corporal Colin Bootman, explained: "I was born in Trinidad, West Indies, and immigrated to New York when I was seven. After receiving my green card and education in America [I joined] the military during my second year at the School for Visual Arts. I immediately felt alienated from the military mentality expected of me. I felt like I was supposed to be proud, but I wasn't. I kept denying this, thinking maybe I could grow to like it. Every drill I saw guys walking around with knives tied to their breast or hip and I thought, How come I don't feel like they feel?

"After serving two years in the Marine Corps my feelings toward training began to consciously change. An important influence on my thinking were the enlightening conversations I had with members of my family who were involved in Grenada. My aunt Jacqueline Creft was the former Minister of Education in Grenada and a leader of the New Jewel Movement. She was assassinated as a result of the political turmoil. In addition, one of my cousins lost his leg trying to escape the full impact of a blast. My family told me that no one knows exactly how damaging and cruel war can be until it happens. Aside from losing lives and limbs, many people lost their homes and land. My family encouraged me to leave the military because they saw no future in waging wars." Bootman served a 2-year jail term for refusing to kill.

For (former) Lance Corporal Keith Jones, the "poverty draft" was also very real. He was born on Hunter Air Force Base in Savannah, Georgia, and moved to New York City when he was four. His father served in the Air Force for twenty years, including in Vietnam. When Keith began attending City College of New York, the Marine Reservist recruiter offered him a steady paycheck of $140 a month for three years, special college loans, as well as the less tangible but equally important emotion-bolsters of honor and pride.

At first, Keith said, he felt proud of his achievements at boot camp. He was "close-minded" to anti-war organizations on campus. But a little bit later, after acting in a play written by Vietnam veterans, he decided that the abstract language of Infantry Training School, such as "You will take many casualties," served to hide the real physical mutilation of young men's bodies in war. Keith was, at that time, studying advanced weaponry; he was learning what it was capable of doing. He refused to fight, and joined a Buddhist temple committed to world peace. Keith was sentenced to 16 months in prison, where he hammered out license plates.

The paths by which each individual came to reject the military were varied and multi-faceted. They don't fit neatly into behaviorist Skinner boxes; resistance to oppression takes many forms, and contrary to some, greater oppression does not necessarily imply greater resistance as though human beings are rats in a maze pressing the bar at the end for cheese. We do not fall comfortably into "politically correct" niches, coming to consciousness only in ways approved by the bastions of moral rectitude. But there *are* certain common elements that provide the soil that nurtures resistance and fosters the courage to take enormous risks. Especially important are strong community ties which encourage and support their humane sentiments, and serve as counterweights to the false "community" offered by the military.

Still, many in the peace movement refused to take up the cause of the resisters. "What did they expect? That's what the military is for. It's not a jobs program" was a common sentiment. Many in the peace movement accepted the

U.S. government's demonization of the Iraqi "enemy". They wrapped themselves in yellow ribbons and American flags, pretending that they did so in order to "reach" the American people and not out of their own desires to be accepted by the country they criticized. Such opportunism tied liberals in moral knots; they were unable to "reach" even their own checkbooks to defend those in the military who refused to kill for big oil and the exigencies of U.S. imperialism, or to understand why so many people, particularly Blacks and Latinos, felt compelled to join the military.

"Few people thought they'd be sent off to kill people and die when they joined the military, or to bomb the hell out of civilians and have none of that reported on the news; in fact, the military's advertisements hardly made mention of war or killing at all," *Hands Off!* coordinator Melissa Ennen argued. "Although there was no compulsory legal draft, there was, in effect, an economic one. Working class kids saw no jobs and no future for them in civilian life. The military presented itself as a 'way out' of the cycle of poverty."

The "false advertizing" of the military lured working class and poor youngsters to enlist. The glamor of Hollywood's popular "clean war" macho films like Rambo, and a desire to "be all you can be" and "serve your community," played a significant part in the resisters' defense during their court-martials. It is no coincidence, they argued, that over 30 percent of the U.S. troops deployed to Saudi Arabia were people of color, double the percentage of the U.S. population as a whole. 46 percent of the women stationed there were Black, while only 6.7 percent of the officers in the military are Black or Hispanic. And, as many Black and Latino people have been finding out, in the military racial polarization is not overcome in the face of a "common enemy" but is dramatically intensified ... and the horrible results covered up.

Some of the resisters were undoubtedly confused. They had not thought out all the ins and outs of imperialism. They did not issue long tracts on political economy — they were not guerrillas of "thesis warfare protracted," firing wordy salvos from their tenured ivory tower perches (although many of them *were* students). But many of those refusing to support the military resisters also tended to reduce youngsters' motives for joining the military solely to economic needs and a "poverty draft" — again, rats in a maze. They missed a fundamental point about youngsters' desperate socio-psychological need in this society for community and to be meaningful. Thus, they led the anti-war movement in pursuit of false strategies. Prior to the Gulf war, high school students who used the subway station near my apartment told me of their disgust with the "me-first-ism" they felt all around them, the lust for gold chains and material greed. They wanted something more *communal,* more *artistic* from life. Many said they would volunteer for the military (the so-called "economic draft") "to serve their country," *not*, as most liberals believe, primarily to get out of desperate economic straits but to find some higher purpose, some *philosophy* of collectivity and idealism. They often quoted John Kennedy's "Ask not what your country can do for you, ask what you can do for your country" to explain their feelings. (Hard to believe that many of us once upheld such liberal notions as a virtue!) They tragically believed they could find such higher purpose and community in the military.

Where was the peace movement for these kids? Why didn't it help them develop true alternative communities to the one they wrongly believe existed in the military? Each night, I ripped down recruiting posters on the train station near my apartment and tried to talk high school students out of joining the military. But there was little to offer in its place. Where were the anti-war movement's sports teams, political clubs, alternative discussion groups, community centers, draft counseling? It was not until high school students themselves organized groups like *Students Against War*, *Students for Social Justice* and *Food Not Bombs* that kids were able to find some alternative to the pseudo-community they expected from the military — a crucial component and overlooked function of *Occupy Wall Street*. Those kids 20 years later "got it".

War Resisters League organizer Michael Marsh observed the same frustrations: "During the Gulf War, countless soldiers told me how they had joined the military because they felt out of control of their lives and needed discipline. Others enlisted seeking to replace feelings of hopelessness with meaning. Still others joined in search of self and community. As shocking as it is to think that someone might join an institution based on killing to find community, it shouldn't be all that surprising either. Our country is being filled by a moral vacuum and increasingly younger children are finding themselves alone in this space."[56]

The government's response in countering the power of community was and continues to be to try to isolate and stampede the individual, making the price of anti-war resistance so high economically, psychologically and physically that resisters would be driven to plea to lesser charges for things they didn't do and forego their political and moral stances in exchange for "getting it over with" and lighter sentences.

In spite of feelings of despair, frustration and sadness that all of us in the anti-war movement fall into (not surprising given the never-ending stream of murderers running the country), in actuality there is an enormous source of hope here: In the courage of the resisters who, against all odds and with no liberals trying to "raise their consciousness,"

---

[56] *Nonviolent Activist,* Jan.-Feb. 1994.

found ways to resist; in the new, creative tactics invented by affinity groups during the war, and the emergence of new communities of support when the larger, more established umbrella organizations failed; in the new alternative press networks and dynamic high school groups; and, in the realization that, no matter how sad and desperate the situation, people *always* find ways to refuse to "only follow orders."

Groups like *Hands Off!*, *Citizen Soldier*, the *War Resisters League*, the *Central Committee for Conscientious Objectors*, *Storm Warning!*, *Vietnam Veterans Against the War* and many local activists become mainstays of support for resisters; and, indeed, the communities of local resistance that sprang up around them made all the difference in the world. New groupings took responsibility for each other and began projecting a different, healthier and more revolutionary vision than the organizations they supplanted. That organizing became a factor in the early release of many of the resisters who had applied for conscientious objector status.

Yet, at the time, the war's liberal opponents refused to support resisters in the military. With the exception of notable work done by the *War Resisters League* and such groups as *Hands Off!* and *Citizen Soldier*, the "Campaign" — striving to keep its mainstream membership organizations in fold — supported "our" troops but, beyond token efforts, failed to support our resisters.

Well I don't agree with Hitler's policies, but I still believe that we should "support our troops"

Iraqi draftees and civilians were not deemed worthy of even that consideration. They were treated as demons sent by the "insane" and "worse than Hitler" Saddam Hussein to "destroy our way of life." "We should support sanctions and a trade embargo against Iraq," said one leader of the Socialist Party at that time (a member of the Campaign),[57] a theme echoed by many of the Campaign's leadership; in fact, that was its official position. It was as though the people of Iraq, whose lives were being devastated by the trade embargo as well as the bombing, needed to be punished and it was our

---

[57] Currently, the Socialist Party, at least in New York City, has become much more radical under new, youthful working class leadership.

moral responsibility to do so — with much the same sanctimony as those who have taken it upon themselves to finger someone throwing a rock at a demonstration to the police.

Solidarity groups like the *Committee in Solidarity with the People of El Salvador* forgot to express their solidarity with the people of Iraq. The anti-war *Military Families Support Network*, made up of the relatives of those sent to the front, waved U.S. flags at every opportunity and never put a human face on those whom their children were being sent to murder.

Many in the anti-war movement failed to challenge Bush's demonization of Saddam Hussein, the Iraqi people, and Arab people in general. They rarely said a word about the tens of thousands of civilian casualties. Those were merely "collateral damage." But when Saddam's Scud missile attacks killed several Israeli civilians,[58] the mainstream peace movement's visible leadership launched diatribe after diatribe against Iraq — as though Iraqi citizens were responsible for their dictator's war crimes and should be forced to pay the terrible price — providing political cover for the U.S. government's murder of a quarter-of-a-million Iraqi people outright, and 500,000 more — many of them children — over the next decade (the Clinton/Gore years), a result of the embargo and ongoing bombardments. To quote Clin-

---

[58] Scud warheads weighed in at one-quarter of a ton in explosive power, compared with the tens of thousands of tons of explosives rained on Iraq daily by B-52 carpet-bombing.

ton's Secretary of State, Madeleine Albright: "Yes, we think the price is worth it."

As it turned out many of the Israeli civilians said to have been killed by Saddam's Scuds were in actuality killed or injured by Israel's use of defective U.S. Patriot surface-to-air missiles manufactured by the Raytheon Corporation. (Saying that does not excuse Saddam's targeting of civilians in any way, but it does reveal the extent of the U.S. over-the-top propaganda effort.) The media echoed military officials and called those deaths "collateral damage" — when they chose to report them at all. Despite company officials' prior knowledge of such defects, to this day no Raytheon executive has been indicted nor Raytheon factory bombed by B-52 airplanes.

"Peace activists who focused solely on the prospect of American deaths gave credence to the bombing strategy, resulting in a larger civilian death toll, but fewer casualties among American soldiers," wrote then-Wisconsin activist Zoltán Grossman, referring to the Campaign's strategy. "Either we accept Iraqi civilians — and soldiers, who are drafted involuntarily into service — as human beings, or we don't. Either we defend them as we would our own families, or we acquiesce in their slaughter."

But this the Campaign was unwilling to do. Mostly, the resisters in the military were people of color; they provided leadership and inspiration to the radical antiwar movement, which scared the hell out of the Democratic Party-oriented liberal donors — the "loyal opposition" — accustomed to calling the shots. The resisters' shadows loomed large between the evil and the whitewash. Thousands of working class kids in the military courageously resisted the war. They dared to reclaim their humanity, in a season of robots. Only rarely did the Campaign's marches confront the war-makers on the basis that the mass slaughter of Iraqis was wrong in and of itself. In the minds of many, Iraqis *deserved* to be starved by sanctions or bled by bullets.[59]

The Campaign certainly didn't want to see radical fingers pointing at U.S. imperialism; it offered patriotic support for the U.S. government, pressing only to curtail some of the excesses of what its member organizations saw as a "democratic and just" government whose policies were a little bit too extreme. The Campaign condemned the policy decisions of both sides equally ("on the one hand / on the other") as if the giant and the gnat are identical, or that the U.S. government's murder of a quarter-of-a-million Iraqis, mostly civilians, was but an unfortunate and perhaps overzealous (but justified!) act, and that the reports in corporate media could be trusted. Imperialism? "Don't use such terms," we were told. "It'll just 'alienate' people."

---

[59] See, Mitchel Cohen, "Read My Apocalypse: The Gulf War and the Mass Psychology of Fascism," Red Balloon Books, 1998.

Yellow-Ribboning the Lies: How George H.W. Bush Sold the 1991 Bombing of Iraq to America

"The U.S. has a new credibility. What we say goes."
- President George H.W. Bush
NBC Nightly News, Feb. 2, 1991

On October 10, 1990, a 15-year-old Kuwaiti girl, identified only as Nayirah, appeared in Washington before the Congressional Human Rights Caucus. She was presented as a Kuwaiti war refugee, and testified that she had been a volunteer worker in the al-Adan hospital in Kuwait City and had seen Iraqi soldiers, who had invaded Kuwait on August 2nd, tear fifteen babies from hospital incubators and "leave them on the cold floor to die."

Television flashed her testimony around the world. It electrified opposition to Iraq's president, Saddam Hussein, who was now portrayed by U.S. president George Bush not only as "the Butcher of Baghdad" but — so much for old friends — "a tyrant worse than Hitler."

Bush quoted Nayirah at every opportunity. Six times in one month he referred to "312 premature babies at Kuwait City's maternity hospital who died after Iraqi soldiers stole their incubators and left the infants on the floor,"[60] and of "babies pulled from incubators and scattered like firewood across the floor." Bush used Nayirah's testimony to lambaste Senate Democrats still supporting "only" sanctions against Iraq — the blockade of trade which alone would cause hundreds of thousands of Iraqis to die of hunger and disease — but who waffled on endorsing the policy Bush wanted to implement: outright bombardment. Republicans and pro-war Democrats used Nayirah's tale to hammer their fellow politicians into line behind Bush's war in the Persian Gulf.[61]

---

[60] Doug Ireland, Village Voice, March 26, 1991.

[61] The use of the Big Lie to manipulate public opinion and neutralize opposition to a particular war was not invented by Bush. See, for instance, James Laxer, "Iraq: US has match, seeks kindle: American leaders have often falsified reasons to attack other countries," (ActionGreens, Mar. 31, 2001). Laxer is a Political Science Professor at York University, Toronto.

But Nayirah was no impartial eyewitness, a fact carefully concealed by her handlers. She was the daughter of Saud Nasir Al-Sabah, Kuwait's ambassador to the United States. A few key Congressional leaders and reporters — including the co-chairs of the congressional committee sponsoring her testimony, Tom Lantos (D., California) and John Edward Porter (R., Illinois) — explained that Nayirah's identity would be kept secret to protect her family from reprisals in occupied Kuwait. (Lantos is still in Congress; Porter decided not to run for reelection in 2002.)

The pro-war crowd in Congress did not share that minor detail with Congress, let alone the American people. As *Harpers* publisher John R. MacArthur wrote in the *Times* after the war had ended, "Such a pertinent fact might have led to impertinent demands for proof of Nayirah's whereabouts in August and September of 1990, when she said she witnessed the atrocities, as well as corroboration of her charges."[62]

Everything Nayirah said, as it turned out, was a lie. There were, in actuality, only a handful of incubators in all of Kuwait, certainly not the "hundreds" she claimed. According to Dr. Mohammed Matar, director of Kuwait's primary care system, and his wife, Dr. Fayeza Youssef, who ran the obstetrics unit at the maternity hospital, there were few if any babies in the incubators at the time of the Iraqi in-

---

[62] *Ibid.*

vasion. Nayirah's charges, they said, were totally false. "I think it was just something for propaganda," Dr. Matar said. In an *ABC-TV News* account after the war, John Martin reported that although "patients, including premature babies, did die," this occurred "when many of Kuwait's nurses and doctors stopped working or fled the country" — a far cry from Bush's original assertion that hundreds of babies were murdered by Iraqi troops.[63]

It is likely that Nayirah was not even in Kuwait, let alone at the hospital, at that time; the Kuwaiti aristocracy and their families had fled the country weeks before the anticipated invasion. Some defended their country at the gaming tables in Monte Carlo, where at least one member of the ruling family was reported to have gambled away more than $10 million, even as his fellow rulers called for economic and military assistance from abroad.

"Before the war," writes John R. MacArthur, in the *New York Times*, "the incubator story seriously distorted the American debate about whether to support military action. *Amnesty International* believed the tale, and its ill-considered validation of the charges likely influenced the seven Senators who cited the story in speeches backing the Jan. 12 resolution authorizing war. Since the resolution passed the Senate by only five votes, the question of how the incubator story escaped

---

[63] *ABC World News Tonight*, 3/15/91.

scrutiny — when it really mattered — is all the more important."⁶⁴ Subsequent investigations found no evidence for the incubator claims. *Amnesty International* later retracted its support of the story and apologized for having publicized it.

How did Nayirah first come to the attention of the Congressional Human Rights Caucus, which put her before the world's cameras? It had all been arranged behind the scenes by Hill & Knowlton, a public relations firm hired to rally the U.S. populace behind Bush's policy of going to war.

On the heels of their orchestration of Nayirah's phony "incubator" testimony (which became the pretext for sending thousands of U.S. soldiers into battle), Hill & Knowlton invented the infamous yellow ribbon campaign, to whip up support for "our" troops. In pure advertising terms, the war campaign was a public relations masterpiece. First Nayirah's unchallenged testimony, then the yellow ribbon campaign, and then the claim that satellite photos revealed that Iraq had troops poised to strike Saudi Arabia — all fabricated by the PR firm, with the support of the U.S. government.⁶⁵

---

[64] John R. MacArthur, *The NY Times,* Op-Ed, January 6, 1992.

[65] Despite the heart-rending testimonies TV viewers in the U.S. were subjected to night after night, in actuality fewer than 200 Kuwaitis were killed in Iraq's invasion of Kuwait. Compare that to such "peaceful" ventures as the U.S. invasion of Panama the year before, which killed an estimated 7,000 Panamanians; or, a year after the first Gulf war, the 10,000 Somalis killed by U.S./U.N. troops in what was portrayed as a "peace mission" to bring food aid to the allegedly starving region. (In actuality, people in only certain areas of Somalia were starving — those that had been subjected to IMF structural adjustment programs. See, Mitchel Cohen, "Somalia &

Hill & Knowlton was paid between $12 million (as reported two years later on *60 Minutes*) and $20 million (as reported on *20/20*) for "services rendered." The group fronting the money? Citizens for a Free Kuwait, a phony "human rights agency" set up and funded entirely by Kuwait's emirocracy to promote the war in the U.S.

Yet, even though these facts are now well-known, the myths persist, and are reinforced in order to continue the perpetual drumbeat of war against Iraq. A 2003 HBO "behind-the-scenes true story" of the Gulf War "never makes clear that the incubator story was fraudulent, and in fact had been managed by an American PR firm, not Iraq. Curiously, however, the truth seems to have been clear to Robert Wiener, the former CNN producer who co-wrote 'Live from Baghdad.' As he explained to CNN's Wolf Blitzer, 'that story turned out to be false because those accusations were made by the daughter of the Kuwaiti minister of information and were never proven.' Unfortunately, HBO viewers won't know that when they see the film."[66]

"When Hill & Knowlton masterminded the Kuwaiti campaign to sell the Gulf War to the American public, the owners of this highly effective propaganda machine were residing in another country" — the United Kingdom — writes

---

the Cynical Manipulation of Hunger," Red Balloon Collective, 1994.)

[66] Fairness and Accuracy in Reporting, "HBO Recycling Gulf War Hoax?" December 4, 2002.

254 | REFRAMING

Sharon Beder and Richard Gosden in *PR Watch*. "Should this give pause for thought? Does it demonstrate a certain potential for the future exercise of global political power — the power to manipulate democratic political processes through managing public opinion?"[67] Hill and Knowlton demonstrated that when it comes to facts, the truth can be bought and sold to the highest bidder regardless of the consequences for U.S. soldiers and Iraqi civilians. It also raises the question, Can real democracy exist under such manipulative circumstances?

Unlike HBO and the corporate media, John A. MacArthur set out to examine those questions. Here's what he found:

- Both congressmen who chaired the Congressional committee sponsoring the hearings had a close relationship with Hill and Knowlton, the public relations firm hired by Citizens for a Free Kuwait, the Kuwaiti-financed group that lobbied Congress for military intervention.

- A Hill and Knowlton vice president, Gary Hymel, helped organize the Congressional Human Rights Caucus hearing in meetings

---
[67] Sharon Beder and Richard Gosden, *PR Watch*, Volume 8, No. 2, 2nd Quarter 2001.Hill & Knowlton has since been working at the behest of the pharmaceutical industry to ban over-the-counter vitamin and nutritional supplement sales in Europe.

with Mr. Lantos and Mr. Porter and the chairman of Citizens for a Free Kuwait, Hassan al-Ebraheem. Mr. Hymel presented the witnesses, including Nayirah. (He later told MacArthur that he knew who she was at the time.)

- Until he started working on the Kuwait account, Mr. Hymel was best known to the caucus for defending the human rights record of Turkey, another Hill and Knowlton client criticized for jailing people without due process and torturing and killing them.

- This Hill & Knowlton exec (Hymel) was also one of the firm's lobbyists for the Indonesian Government, which had killed at least 100,000 inhabitants of East Timor since 1975. Mr. Lantos's spokesman says that "Hill and Knowlton's client list doesn't concern the Congressman."

- Hill and Knowlton's political action committee contributed $500 to Lantos's election campaign in 1988.

- Mr. Lantos and Mr. Porter chose to house their Congressional Human Rights Foundation, a group they founded in 1985, in Hill and Knowlton's Washington headquarters! The PR firm provides a contribution to the foundation in the form of a $3,000 annual rent reduction, and the Hill and Knowlton switchboard delivers messages to the foundation's executive director, David Phillips.

- Hill and Knowlton's client, *Citizens for a Free Kuwait*, donated $50,000 to the foundation, after Iraq's invasion of Kuwait on Aug. 2, 1990. (The foundation's main supporter is the U.S. Government-financed National Endowment for Democracy.)

As MacArthur writes: "Since the gulf war, Hill and Knowlton's collaboration with the Lantos-Porter human rights enterprise has been strengthened by the naming of the firm's vice chairman, Frank Mankiewicz, to the foundation's board in October 1991. Perhaps the Congressmen and directors were impressed by the recent addition of China to Hill and Knowlton's prestigious portfolio of clients. (The firm's clients, Indonesia and Turkey, were notably absent from the foundation's 1990-91 list of human rights 'activities'.)"[68]

In 1998, Hill and Knowlton found a new client — then-President William Jefferson Clinton — who hired the PR

---

[68] MacArthur, *op cit.*

firm to advise him and to polish his image.

The last time the PR firm was involved, by the time their lies were exposed TV newscasters were waxing ecstatic over the rockets' red glare, computerized "smart-bombs" bursting in air, tens of thousands of U.S. soldiers were suffering from Gulf War Syndrome and 250,000 Iraqi people were dead.

A few weeks after the HBO-drama had aired in December 2002, HBO felt compelled to respond to the intense criticism of its distortions offered by Fairness and Accuracy in Reporting, among other activist groups. As FAIR reports, "HBO recently added a message to the end of its movie 'Live From Baghdad,' clarifying the scenes that seemingly endorsed the fraudulent stories about Iraqi soldiers removing Kuwaiti babies from incubators. The film, a fictionalized account of CNN's coverage of the Persian Gulf War, leaves viewers with the impression that these events actually happened. HBO's message, which appears after the end of the credits, reads:

'While the allegations of Iraqi soldiers taking babies from incubators were widely circulated during the run-up to the Gulf War (the time frame of the drama of our film), these allegations were never substantiated.'"

FAIR concluded: "Since most TV viewers don't watch the entire end credits, it is doubtful that many people will ever see the clarification. And while it's helpful that HBO has acknowledged a problem in its film, to say that the claims were 'never substantiated' is an understatement. It would be more accurate to note that attempts to confirm the story after the Gulf War uncovered evidence that it was a fabrication."[69]

The masterful manipulation of propaganda and the lies of the first Gulf War set the stage for many events of the last 20 years.

---

[69] *Fairness and Accuracy in Reporting (FAIR)*, "ACTIVISM UPDATE: HBO Adds Disclaimer to Gulf War Movie," January 3, 2003.

READ MY APOCA-LYPSE: The Gulf War and the Mass Psychology of Fascism

In the movie "Rosewood" — a true story, based in 1923 Florida — the white sheriff joins a lynch mob. He, and many others in the mob, know full well (but refuse to admit it out loud) that a white woman's claim that she was beaten and raped by a Black man was a lie. The white mob besieges the Black community, raping, lynching and mur-

Trade unionists chain themselves to the Lincoln Memorial, 1951, to protest the execution of Willie McGee, a black man arrested six years earlier in Laurel, Mississippi, for raping a white woman. A 26-year-old Abe Cohen — Mitchel's dad — is furthest to the right facing camera. The photo was taken the day before McGee's execution. Also published in "The Eyes of Willie McGee" by Alex Heard, 2010.

dering at will. How easy it was to whip up that white mob into anxiety-ridden frenzy and mass hysteria, despite their knowing of the truth.

That, too, is a form of direct action — albeit racist, fascist, sexist; the Left does not have a copyright on direct action stipulating that it can only be used for the public good. The idea of the fanatical crowd acting beyond rationality is a staple of capitalist ideology. One of the key exponents of this view, Gustav Le Bon, whose views went on to influence Adolf Hitler as well as sociologists in the United States, wrote in an extremely influential essay in the late 1800s that the state's function is to protect the interests of the individual against the "tyranny of the crowd". "At public meetings the slightest contradiction on the part of an orator is immediately received with howls of fury and violent invective, soon followed by blows and expulsion should the orator stick to the point," Le Bon wrote. "Without the restraining presence of representatives of authority the contradictor, indeed, would often be done to death."[70]

The state, for Le Bon, thus exists for the good of all individuals regardless of class; it has no history. It stands above and apart from the struggle between classes. Like most liberal ideological categories, it simply is and has always been the product of individual rational minds protecting themselves from the irrational rage of the great unwashed. Its motto: "I think, therefore I rule."

Le Bon's assumptions blind him to the obvious: joining some crowds — or should I say "reconnecting" with other human beings alienated from each other by the conditions of liberal capitalism, contrary to all previous history — is a supremely rational act. Yet, deny it as he will, Le Bon's own argument is the best possible brief for the rationality of join-

---

[70] Gustav Le Bon, *La psychologie des foules* (1895; English translation *The Crowd: A Study of the Popular Mind*, 1896), as excerpted in *The Hidden Injuries of Class* by Richard Sennett and Jonathan Cobb, New York: Alfred A. Knopf, 1972. See also Mitchel Cohen, "Liberalism and Fascism vs. Marxism: A Critique of Le Bon's *The Crowd* and It's Irrationality vs. Class Consciousness," Red Balloon, 1984.

ing crowds:

> An isolated individual knows well enough that alone he cannot set fire to a palace or loot a shop, and should he be tempted to do so, he will easily resist the temptation. Making part of a crowd, he is conscious of the power given him by number, and it is sufficient to suggest to him ideas of murder or pillage for him to yield immediately to temptation. [71]

But earlier, the same crowds are seen as capable of grand and compassionate acts:

> Such heroism [on the part of crowds] is without doubt somewhat unconscious, but it is of such heroism that history is made.

Thus, if you want to affect history — that is, even according to the most reactionary capitalist social psychology, if you want to alter your condition — you have to be part of the crowd: "Were peoples only to be credited with the great actions performed in cold blood [that is, as rational individuals], the annals of the world would register but few of them." It is only because of his class position that Le Bon sees looting a shop, for instance, as "irrational." Wilhelm Reich challenged the irrationality of what we take to be "normal": "The question is not why hungry people steal food, it's why they don't," Reich observed, reframing the question. Same with Anatole France, who drolly wrote, "The law, in its ma-

---

[71] *Sennett & Cobb, ibid.,* p.55.

jestic equality, forbids the rich as well as the poor to sleep under bridges, to beg in the streets, to steal bread."

It is true that "the crowd" formed fascism's mass base in Nazi Germany, and Reich had a good deal to say about this in *The Mass Psychology of Fascism, Sex-Pol,* and other works. But it is equally true that a crowd, shaped by other conditions, defeated Hitler and the Nazis. Even as far back as 1896, the newly developing field of sociology should have proffered a more insightful analysis, one that examined the conditions that propelled different crowds to act in different ways. Le Bon, unfortunately, constructed his Bureau of Abstractions and Generalities, in which all crowds unpack their underwear in the same manner, from the same unconscious impulses — and this was in a time of great working class ferment and agitation. To speak of revolutionary "crowds" such as the Industrial Workers of the World consciously struggling against exploitation in the same breath as white supremacist fascist crowds stampeded by manipulation of their unconscious repressed sexuality, is to deny the reality of class warfare and the sacrifices of so many people; it is to speak with a corpse in your mouth.

The role of a Marxist social psychology, therefore, is to explore the particularities of, for instance, white supremacist or fascist mobs and discern how that mentality was able to take hold in working class minds and overrun their consciousness of their own class interests.

One does not have to go back 110 years or even 80 years to do that. The January 1991 Gulf War involved an orchestration of anxieties and emotions on an even grander scale than the incident in 1923 at Rosewood. Just one year after the invasion of Panama, in which 7,000 Panamanians were killed by U.S. forces, George Bush, Sr., brought the full military air power of the U.S. to bear against Iraq.

The day before the U.S. Air Force began bombarding Iraq (prefiguring Donald Rumsfeld's "shock and awe" bombardment 12 years later), over 70 percent of the American people opposed the coming war. A few days after the U.S. terror campaign had begun the figures were reversed. In one sense, it is a tribute to the U.S. public that government officials felt the need to orchestrate an elaborate if discordant symphony of lies to rally the American people behind the government's war. On the other hand, it is tragic that so many believed them.[72]

The U.S. military murdered hundreds of thousands of Iraqi teenage draftees, civilians and children who had done nothing to threaten people living in the United States. The U.S. media reported barely a word of those casualties. Nor did the press report on the millions of people who took to

---

[72] See Mitchel Cohen, "How George Bush Sold the 1991 Bombardment of Iraq to the American People." Also, "Read My Apocalypse," in *Red Balloon* #22 (also known as *"Dysentery"*), Winter 1992.

the streets across the country and throughout the world to protest what can only be called a "holocaust."

From the start of the "crisis" we were lied to by the government and corporate media. They carefully planned their deceptions to rouse the breast-beaters and militarize the public mind. One lie after another, just as they did in whipping up support on behalf of death squads in El Salvador, the contras in Nicaragua, the invasion of Grenada, the bombing of Libya, and the invasions of Panama, Somalia and Haiti. The U.S. bombed Iraq with impunity. PR firms like Hill & Knowlton counseled Bush to dub the deadly missiles "smart bombs." As incredible explosions rocked Iraq, they were sanitized as "surgical strikes," making them more palatable to the American people. The Pentagon assured us that the missiles were "90 percent accurate" — even though, as it turned out, they actually hit their intended targets less than 30 percent of the time.

And what were their "intended military targets"? Iraq's sanitation and water-purification plants, infant formula factories, dams, houses, nuclear reactors and laboratories, agricultural and chemical plants, biological facilities, and shelters — in other words, the entire Iraqi infrastructure. Beginning on Jan. 17, 1991, the U.S. military dropped the equivalent tonnage of "one Hiroshima per day" on Iraq. Massive "surgical strikes" and carpet bombings decimated the civilian

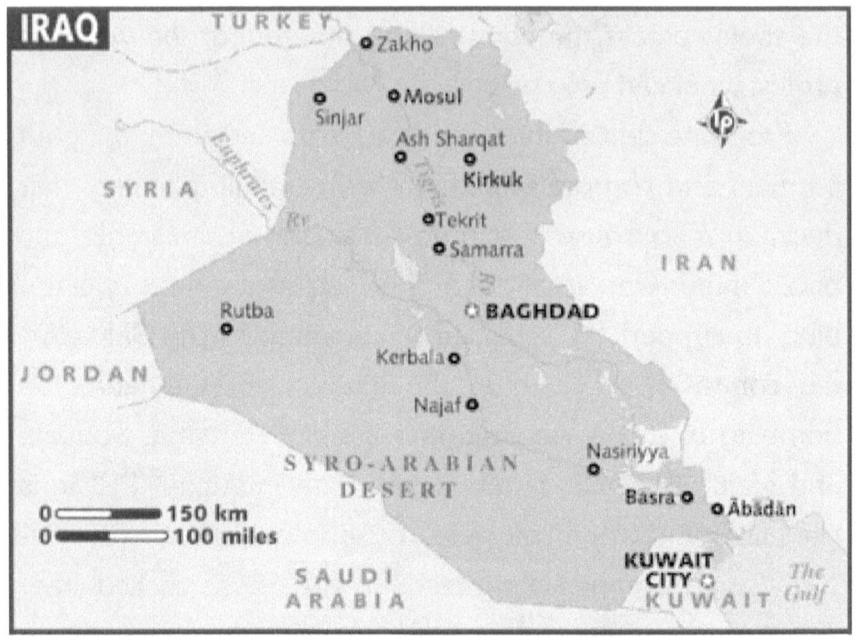

water supply. The entire water purification system in Iraq's major cities was destroyed; drinking water was rendered fully contaminated with germs, chemicals and radiation.[73]

Civilians who managed to escape direct hits from the bombs died in enormous numbers from mass starvation. Thousands of children died from diseases such as dysentery and diarrhea after drinking the newly polluted water.

At least 28 Iraqi sites were bombed in the first few weeks; the U.S. claimed the sites might be useful in producing bio-chemical warfare agents, even though most of those

---

[73] Zoltán Grossman, "Collateral Damage," Red Balloon Collective anti-war packet, 1991.

facilities were simply civilian agricultural and chemical plants. Among the targeted "bio-chemical" facilities was a fertilizer plant in Basra (Iraq's second-largest city, with a population of 371,000); the Qaim phosphate mine near Syria; an ethylene plant in Musayyab (pop. 16,000) and a facility in Fallujah (pop. 36,000), both along the Euphrates river; and, along the Tigris river, a chemical plant in Samara (pop. 25,000); the Salman Pak facility which was said to be making biological warfare agents — another lie; and a chemical facility in Bayji (pop. 7,000). A reporter for CNN — which broadcast much more sanitized reports to the U.S. than its international arm did to the rest of the world — described one of the burning chemical plants as sending off "green flames." All told, at least 600,000 Iraqis lived in towns (not including Baghdad) that may have been covered by toxic gases or germ clouds from the U.S. bombings.[74]

The U.S. Air Force also blew up two nuclear reactors at the Tuwaitha nuclear complex which utilized enriched uranium, releasing the nuclear fuel into the environment. The reactors had been recently inspected by the U.N.'s International Atomic Energy Agency, which determined that, U.S. propaganda to the contrary, no nuclear material had been diverted for military use. The U.S. also bombed the SAAD-16 centrifugal uranium enrichment plant near Mosul, Iraq's

---

[74] *ibid.*

third-largest city, and a nearby nuclear plant in Erbil. All of these caused huge numbers of civilian casualties — "collateral damage," the military called it — and enormous destruction of the environment.

U.S. soldiers in Apache helicopters swept down over the desert and shot Iraqi soldiers in the back as they fled unarmed, many carrying white flags of surrender. A "turkey shoot," one U.S. general called it, and "a target-rich environment." Apache helicopters swarmed like locusts, cutting down their victims all through the day, and then night, and then day again. It was all too easy. Between the Tigris and Euphrates rivers — the cradle of civilization where, we're told, human life probably began; and at their nexus, the site of the biblical Garden of Eden — the B-52 serpents carpet-bombed the Garden with the apples of the New World Order, killing at least 250,000 people over those six weeks of bombardment and unleashing a plague of cholera, dysentery and typhoid that, according to a Harvard University medical team report, likely killed 170,000 more children the next year.[75] An investigating team of the U.N.'s Food and Agriculture Organization now estimates that 800,000 people, mostly children, have died since the end of the war due solely to the U.S./U.N. sanctions, environmental devasta-

---

[75] "170,000 Kids to Die in Postwar Iraq: Study," *New York Newsday,* May 22, 1991, reprinted from the *Los Angeles Times.*

tion, and embargo of Iraq.

In response to anti-war protests, President George H.W. Bush took to the tubes to reminisce about the moment when he ordered the world's most powerful Air Force to pound Iraq's cities. He actually pointed to his eye and gloated: "See, see, there's a tear there right now just thinking about it. See it? See it?" All sense of humility went out the window. The Pentagon threw all its new toys of mass destruction into the slaughter, trying out new weapons, finding new justification (as the Cold War was winding down) for its enormous "defense" budget.

After the war, Maj. Gen. William Keys, commander of the Marine 2nd Division, discussed the psychological effects of the U.S. propaganda barrage: "U.S. intelligence so vastly overrated the strength of the Iraqi army," he said, "that they built these guys to be a monster. ... I [actually] thought they were bigger people."[76] Because of the exaggerated claims of U.S. officials, military personnel in the field said they were surprised to find that no Iraqi chemical weapons of any sort had been deployed; it was the U.S., not the Iraqis, who used cluster bombs, anti-personnel weapons, oxygen-igniting air-fuel bombs, and napalm, which burns the skin off of people — all in the name of "civilization" fighting the "barbarians."

---

[76] Molly Moore, "Porous Minefields, Dispirited Troops," *Washington Post*, March 17, 1991.

Meanwhile, for the first time ever, the U.S. encased artillery shells and tanks in so-called 'depleted' uranium, irradiating the countryside, its "first use," while feigning perplexity over why some symptoms of Gulf War Syndrome resembled radiation sickness. The war in the Gulf was, in fact, the world's first "low-intensity" nuclear war.[77]

When asked what would be the limits of the U.S. slaughter, Brigadier General Richard Neal — who would later go on to administer justice, U.S.-style, to Haitian refugees imprisoned by the U.S. at its naval base at Guantanamo Bay, Cuba — invoked the ghost of one of his illustrious predecessors, Gen. George Custer, explaining: "It's right in the middle of Indian territory"[78] — as if to avenge that singular Anglo-American defeat at the hands of this continent's original anti-imperialists.

A quarter-of-a-million killed! At least in the British press one could find *glimpses* of "the enemy" as human beings. The *London Guardian* portrayed the U.S.-led attack for what it really was — a slaughter.

"Through the powerful night-vision gunsights, the Iraqi soldiers looked like ghostly sheep flushed from a pen — bewildered and terrified, jarred from sleep and fleeing their bunkers under a hellish fire.

---

[77] See Mitchel Cohen, "Glowing in the Gulf: Radiation, Genetically-Engineered Drugs and Gulf War Syndrome," in *Fifth Estate*, Fall 1997.

[78] *New York Newsday*, Feb. 6, 1991.

"One by one, they were cut down by attackers they could not see. Some were blown to bits by bursts of 30mm exploding cannon shells.

"One man dropped, writhed on the ground, then struggled to his feet; another burst of fire tore him apart.

"The men and women of the Army 18th Airborne Corps are carrying the war to the enemy in the blackness of night, at 50 feet above the sand, with the U.S. Army's longest punch: the fast, deadly and controversial AH-64 Apache attack helicopter.

"When they return to forward attack bases ... the evidence is displayed in startling, sharp, intensely violent videotapes from gun cameras.

"The $10 million-plus Apaches are night fighters and tank killers. Their pilots are guided by an infrared optical system that turns blackness into a bright phosphorescent daylight in which you can all but read the expressions of shock on the faces of the Iraqi soldiers as they are hit by cannon rounds and rockets.

"For those who try to stay in bunkers, laser-guided Hellfire missiles are launched to an altitude of a half-mile, where they then arc almost straight down onto the target.

"In the briefing tent, the officers play the tapes and a hush falls. Even hardened soldiers hold their breath as Iraqi soldiers, as big as football players on the television screens, run with nowhere to hide.

"These are not bridges exploding or airplane hangars. These are men."[79]

Troops in the field were shown the gruesome videotapes of Iraq's teenage soldiers gasping for breath and then burning up beneath the U.S.'s new air-fuel bombs, which ignite the oxygen in the air and suffocate all life in the vicinity, but the corporate media showed none of that at home. British reporters covered the soldiers' reactions, but in the U.S. press — except for the story I wrote in the *Guardian* — not a word. The American people were kept from seeing the slaughter. Dan Rather and Tom Brokaw were shown the videotapes "shot by the U.S. military of Iraqi soldiers being mowed down by Apache helicopters" but, according to Rather, "It has not yet been cleared for the American public to see."[80] It never was.

Guidance systems for the Apache attack helicopters were built by General Electric, which owned NBC-TV (until it was recently sold to Comcast). G.E. remains one of the nation's largest war contractors, making guidance systems and other parts for virtually every missile, the Stealth bomber, the F-18 Hornet Fighter, the Trident submarine and the MX and Cruise missiles. In June, 1990, NBC censored a program on

---

[79] John Balzar, "Video horror of Apache victim's deaths," *London Guardian*, Feb. 25, 1991.

[80] *Washington Post*, Feb. 25, 1991.

nation-wide boycotts, removing any mention of the international boycott of General Electric and its products.

G.E. board member David C. Jones is a retired U.S.A.F. General and a former Chairman of the U.S. Joint Chiefs of Staff, 1978-1982. Also on the board is Julian B. Goodman, a director of McDonnell Douglas, which received $9 billion in government military contracts in 1989. Goodman is the former chair and CEO at NBC. Ronald Reagan was host of G.E. Theater from 1954-1962. During Reagan's term as president, G.E.'s prime military contracts leapt from $2.2 billion in 1980 to $6.8 billion in 1986. And workers at NBC created quite a stir when they confronted network president Robert Wright, appointed by G.E., for pressuring them to contribute to G.E.'s Political Action Committee which targets members of Congress to support G.E.'s military operations.

The same analysis can be done for each of the networks and print media. Henry Kissinger and former Secretary of Defense Harold Brown (a director of IBM, which received $1.3 billion in U.S. contracts in 1989) sat on the Board of Directors of CBS. Two other IBM directors, Thomas S. Murphy (who was also Chair and CEO of Capital Cities) and Frank Cary (former IBM chair) ran ABC. Cyrus Vance, who was a director of General Dynamics, which received $7.3 billion in U.S. government contracts in 1989, and Charles Price II (a director of Texaco) sat on the board of the *New*

York Times. Is it any wonder why, in the entire war, they never showed images of a single soldier being blown to bits?

Only Bill Moyers, long after the war's end, used a small portion of the Apache tapes in his public television analysis. To this day not a single network has shown those horrendous tapes, nor has there been a single Congressperson brave enough to subpoena them so that this country, with its vaunted free press, could determine just how much stomach for slaughter its people would stand when allowed to see human beings — prevented from complying with the U.N. resolution to retreat — chopped to raw meat by U.S. troops before their eyes.

Squadron commander Lt. Col. Tieszen "rides in the front seat of the Apache, working an arcade of weaponry and directing his squadron attack. Behind him, peering over his helmet, sits the pilot, Chief Warrant Officer Ron Balak. ... 'We're out there to kill their tanks and trucks, to harass and demoralize their troops,' said Tieszen. 'We've been here since August. We've waited a long time for this. ...'

"W.O. Balak described his first combat mission in a 20-year flying career: 'You always envision some scenario of how combat will be. But I just didn't envision going up there and shooting the hell out of everything in the dark and have them not know what the hell hit them.'

" 'A truck blows up to the right, the ground blows up to

the Left,' he said. 'They had no idea where we were or what was hitting them. When we got back, I sat there on the wing, and I was laughing. I wasn't laughing at the Iraqis. I was thinking of the training and the anticipation ... I was probably laughing at myself.'"[81]

The extent of the massacre at least got an airing in the British press. The *London Sunday Times* estimated that "as many as 200,000 Iraqis may have died in the Gulf war, according to senior Pentagon officials. Preliminary reports suggest that allied bombing was much deadlier than previously thought and that thousands of Iraqi troops may be buried in bunkers and trenches."[82] Later, *New York Newsday* reported that tanks, outfitted as bulldozers, swept tons of desert sand over the Iraqi trenches, burying alive thousands of soldiers.[83] The *Cologne Daily Express,* a German paper, quoted a former Air Force general that, after one week of bombardment, there were already 300,000 casualties, including 100,000 in Baghdad alone. *The Frankfurter Rundschau,* a mainstream German daily newspaper, quoted a representative of the European parliament, who reported "tens of thousands of deaths in Baghdad."[84]

---

[81] Balzar, *London Guardian,* Feb. 25, 1991, *op cit.*

[82] James Adams, "Go after Saddam, Iraqi toll could be 200,000 dead," *London Sunday Times,* March 3, 1991.

[83] Patrick Sloyan, "Buried Alive: U.S. Tanks Used Plows to Kill Thousands in Gulf War Trenches," *New York Newsday,* Sept. 12, 1991.

[84] *The Frankfurter Rundschau,* Jan. 23, 1991.

"No official figures on Iraqi dead and injured have been released by the allies and no formal study to produce the figures has been ordered," *New York Newsday* continued. "Instead, the allies intend to keep the statistics as vague as possible, in part because the true picture is so horrifying.

"As the reports flowed in [in late February], the Pentagon realized that their initial assessments of the damage caused by more than four weeks of bombing had to be revised." At the end of February, "Brig. Gen. Richard Neal of the U.S. Marines refused to put a figure on the casualties. 'I am not prepared to tell you what the casualty rate is for the Iraqis. I think it's going to turn out to be enormous,' he said."

That there are mass graves seems certain. A Palestinian in Kuwait City said he had helped bury many Iraqis killed in bombing raids. The authorities were trying to keep the deaths secret to avoid lowering morale.[85] A *London Observer* Pentagon source added: "Like the Japanese in the South Pacific, we will still be discovering bunkers filled with bodies in 40 years' time."

The American press was too busy writing puff stories to actually go out there and interview American soldiers. The job of putting a human face back on the Iraqi "enemy" was left to The *London Observer*:

---

[85] Colin Smith, "Pathetic Children of the Mother of Battles," *London Sunday Observer,* March 3, 1991.

"Scattered about were the kind of personal mementoes carried by homesick soldiers everywhere. One snapshot, near the body of a man lying face down with a terrible wound in his right leg, was of what appeared to be a children's birthday party. The children, three girls and a boy in party hats, sat around a table laden with food and dominated by a heart-shaped cake. ... What occurred here and elsewhere was undoubtedly one of the most terrible harassments of a retreating army from the air in the history of warfare. 'I wouldn't even call this a mopping-up operation,' said one bewildered captain of the first battalion, 5th Marine Division.

"'We used to say that we wouldn't take no prisoners unless they came out bare-butt and wavin' a white flag,' said Lance-Corporal George Cadiente, 'but, oh man, some of them were crying. One guy, you know, he defecated [on] himself, when they heard we were marines they were certain we were goin' to kill em. ... Some of them wouldn't come out of their bunkers. They were curled up in there and wouldn't come out. We'd throw stones in, pretending they were grenades, and they still wouldn't come out. They'd just curl up some more. And the place was full of guns, grenades, RPGs. They could have fought us. When we tied their hands with the plastic strip some of them were saying, "We love you, we love you." I had one kid who couldn't have been more than 16. He just sat there on the ground and started crying. He was convinced I was going to kill him. He hadn't eaten for days, you could see it. Just a kid.'

" 'Poor bastards. You can't even dislike them. All you can do is feel sad for them,' "[86] said Capt. Kurt Snyder, from Seattle. Twenty-year-old Marine Pfc. Martin Santos, of Palm Beach, Florida, 'recognized the same fear in the faces of hundreds of Iraqi prisoners he was tasked with policing' as he experienced himself. 'The first ones I saw were afraid,' said Santos. 'They had pictures of their kids. You would see a tear coming out of their eyes. They make motions like they were washing their hands of war and say, 'I'm done.' "[87]

Surprising to U.S. officers, many Iraqi soldiers captured by the U.S. army "expressed little or no resentment toward their comrades who deserted." Said one veteran career officer: "I did not blame them for deserting. But we had to stay and try to save our honor."[88]

Those were the "demons" U.S. troops were sent to exorcise. But instead, U.S. troops became haunted by their own demons. Ignoring the growing consciousness exhibited by U.S. soldiers, the U.S. corporate media propagated more and more blatantly racist caricatures. In a page one *New*

---

[86] *ibid.*

[87] Molly Moore, "1st Day of War: 'As Scary As You Can Get,' " The *Washington Post,* March 17, 1991.

[88] Bob Woodward, "100,000 Iraqi Troops May Have Deserted," *Washington Post,* March 17, 1991.

York Times "news" story, Andrew Rosenthal chastised Iraqis, whom he likened to children, for having the audacity to watch "a program of cartoons" instead of a speech by George Bush, Sr., which was broadcast live on Baghdad television.[89] CNN's Brian Jenkins commented "objectively" that captured Iraqi soldiers looked like a "fearsome ... warlike people." The Saudis, on the other hand, were said to be "gentle, mild-mannered." Brokaw, Koppel, Rather and the rest of the liberal white male cheerleaders for genocide paraded their coterie of withered white colonels and assorted war criminals and mass-murderers on TV night after night, dusted them off and propped them up as "experts," assuring us of the missiles' unerring accuracy, aimed "only at military targets." While foreign TV carried live footage of the devastation wreaked by the bombing, most American reporters cowered in their hotel bars polishing off martinis, claiming that the fighting was too fierce to venture outside. Instead, they cast poetic eyes on the "beauty," as one anchorman disgracefully put it, of U.S. "smart-bombs" crashing into Baghdad.

NBC Anchor Tom Brokaw sprays hair before going on camera reporting on devastating earthquake killing hundreds.

---

[89] *NY Times,* Sept. 17, 1990. Harlem Minister Calvin Butts pointed out that none of Saddam Hussein's speeches were broadcast here by our allegedly free press, and proceeded to term Bush "the embodiment of Satan."

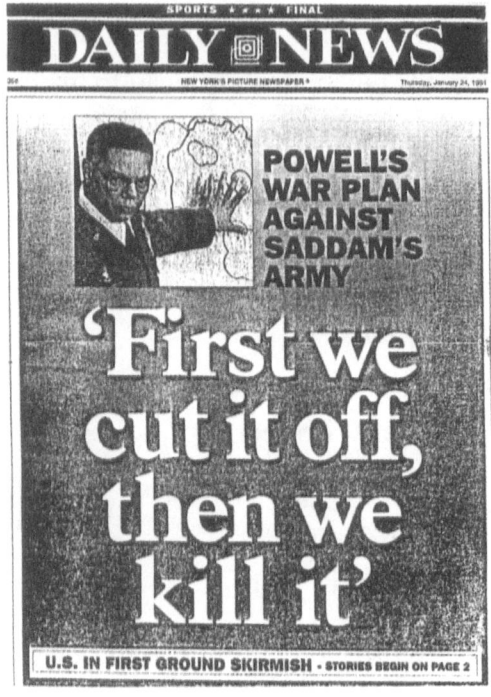

As the military bombardment blasted Iraq, the U.S. government's propaganda blitz bulldozed into full gear. The network media cast a "silent curtain" around the vast anti-war resistance. To counteract the corporate media's white-out of the anti-war movement, agitators wheat-pasted posters outside every media headquarters in New York listing all the demonstrations the networks refused to cover.[90] Fairness and Accuracy in Reporting and Paper Tiger TV organized an important early demonstration that targeted the media's complicity with the war effort. A thousand protesters marched past all of the networks' headquarters, many wearing xeroxed Brokaw, Koppel, Rather and Jennings masks, ending at ABC in a face-to-mask confrontation with Peter

---

[90] "From Koppel to Kuwait: U.S. Media Covers-Up Mass Anti-War Movement Around the World and Lies About Civilian Deaths in Bombardment of Iraq," was one such wallposter pasted all over New York City, signed by "The Terra-ist International Media Awareness Fund".

Jennings himself. Others managed to slip into the studios at Channel 13 in New York and disrupted the live McNeil-Lehrer NewsHour with anti-war statements and banners. "No Blood For Oil!" and "Hell no, we won't go, we won't die for Texaco!" became the battle cries of the burgeoning anti-war movement.

But, over the years, so effective has the corporate media been in re-writing history that most Americans either never knew about or forgot the vast extent of resistance to the war. For four months in late 1990 and early 1991 many, *many* nontraditional, uncompromising and vibrant anti-war actions swept from coast to coast day and night. And to document all the worldwide resistance in those pre-Internet days, our own news services, New Liberation News Service and the weekly New York-based *Guardian* newspaper, kept the movement informed of what was going on. Hindered by a lack of significant financial resources which in the past had funded large anti-war coalitions, new forms of struggle were forced — and enabled — to emerge. Affinity group networks sprang up everywhere, spraypainting city walls and sidewalks with information as well as slogans to break the media-imposed silence. In New York City, anti-war demonstrators gathered and burned the wood police barricades in the middle of busy streets — the last time they were used. They were soon supplanted by steel interlinking barricades

— and 5,000 people cheered. Marshals from the two national anti-war organizations — the *Coalition Against U.S. Intervention* (today, *A.N.S.W.E.R.*), and the *Campaign for Peace in the Middle East* (today, *United for Peace and Justice* — "Peace Police," we called them on the East Coast, and "Karma Patrol" in the West) — tried to stop them from burning the barricades, but ended up looking on helplessly. Not a word in the *Times*. In San Francisco, tens of thousands of anti-war people blockaded bridges and main thoroughfares day after day — still not a word in the *Times*. In Seattle, 15,000 marched, in Portland 15,000 more, riots in Minneapolis, San Antonio, Chicago — not a word in the *Times*. Protesters carried anti-war banners onto the floor of televised basketball games in Montana and Wisconsin and refused to leave; in Montana, the players stood on the sidelines and applauded. In a wonderful and remarkable moment, then-Chicago Bulls coach Phil Jackson challenged members of his World Championship basketball team to think about what effect the bombardment was having on people in Iraq and asked Michael Jordan, Scotty Pippen, Horace Grant and all to take a stand against it.[91] One high-

---

[91] Jackson's effort — like Bill Walton's courageous stance against the U.S. invasion and bombardment of Vietnam — was one of the few instances of a major sports figure acting responsibly, and it won me as a Bulls fan. Detroit Pistons star Polynais has also taken heroic (and unpopular) positions in support of Haitian refugees. Contrast them to baseball's première idiot, outfielder Vince Coleman (formerly of the NY Mets), who, when asked his thoughts on Jackie Robinson, answered: "Jackie *who?*"

ranking U.S. Treasury Department economist, Anthony Lawrence, found his career in jeopardy after he unexpectedly denounced the war on CNN as "an imperialist attempt to wrest the oil resources."[92]

Radical anti-war activists organized safe houses for deserters and resisters, shut down freeways, federal buildings and recruiting stations, and began generating a tangible climate of sustained resistance. In New York City, protesters flooded past the "peace police" and marched on Wall Street time and again, to "take the war to the real war-makers," as participants put it. The night the U.S. began its terrible bombardment of Iraq, eight demonstrators were severely injured by a car that plowed into them as they, along with hundreds of others — the residue of a much larger gathering earlier in the evening — marched across the Brooklyn Bridge at 1 a.m. At least one young woman was knocked off the bridge 40 feet to the pavement below, and suffered massive injuries. Anti-war demonstrators had to fend off blows from New York City's finest in order to assist their severely injured comrades.

Actors Woody Harrelson, Sylvester Stallone and Martin Sheen joined the protests against the war. Model Cindy Crawford and singer Kris Kristofferson added their voices to the anti-war chorus. In New Orleans, Harrelson's public

---

[92] *The Guardian (UK)*, Feb. 4, 1991. That was the last time Lawrence was invited to participate on a major TV outlet.

anti-war stance caused him to be ousted as Grand Marshal of the Mardi Gras carnival parade, provoking an uproar.[93] Sylvester Stallone turned down an invitation from Marine Commandant Alfred Gray Jr. to entertain the troops in the Gulf. Said the actor who'd played Rambo: "No, I won't go. ... I don't think what's going on over there is right. So why go over there and support it? Is the fact that we're going to pay more for gas a situation that justifies sending 500,000 men over there to put their lives in jeopardy? Because Exxon is feeling the pinch?"[94] And Sheen participated in protests with thousands of others and was arrested a number of times at the Nevada nuclear testing site.

Yet, despite the huge anti-war resistance in the U.S. and around the world, once the bombing ended it was as if the movement had never existed. After the quick conquest, the ruling class triumphantly paraded its war machine down the Wall Streets and Constitution Avenues of every town between New York and Nuremberg, firing all its ideological

---

[93] On Feb. 9, two dozen Louisiana high schoolers formed the "Woody Harrelson Fan Club" and paraded in full costume in front of the Endymion Carnival parade which had ousted Woody, as spectators cheered and shouted "Wo-oody!, Wo-oody!" and "Cancel the War for Mardi Gras!," according to the anti-war zine *Dialogue* (March 1991), Besides the Woody Harrelson Fan Club parade, other organized anti-war expressions during Carnival were organized by the Church of the Great Green Frog on Fat Tuesday, and from several members of the Krewe du Vieux Carré parade, held January 26. Generally deriding wealth and authority, the parading subgroup Seeds of Decline held erect its theme of "Genitals of the Rich and Famous," by mocking U.S. officials and their weapons.

[94] *The Star,* supermarket tabloid.

cannons in an epic attempt to blast away whatever truth remained beneath the hundreds of tons of confetti and ticker-tape. Many Americans seized the chance to don the brownshirts of the new world order, announced by President George H.W. Bush on September 11, 1990. Even though "victory" parades across the country were greeted with surprisingly small turnouts and widespread anti-war opposition, in New York City — the exception to the rule — several hundred thousand spectators jammed the 12-block Wall Street area.[95] While the troops themselves remained disciplined, even somber, the largely male crowd — who themselves did not serve in Iraq — swaggered through the streets, yellow ribbons wrapped around their dicks and stars and stripes streaming in the empty sockets of their eyes. They let it all hang loose in a catharsis of violence. The number of rapes and murders in the U.S. skyrocketed, to the highest number in U.S. history,[96] along with increased incidence of

---

[95] NYC Mayor, David Dinkins inflated those numbers by a factor of ten. That was too much for even the normally exaggerative *New York Times,* which felt obliged to call his bluff and bring the figures back into the realm of the possible.

[96] 106,590 rapes reported in the U.S. in 1991, 109,060 in 1992; 24,700 murders in 1991, 23,760 in 1992, according to http://www.disastercenter.com/crime/uscrime.htm. In 1991, there were 1,911,770 acts of violence reported, and slightly higher figures for the next two years, after which the number of violent crimes reported dropped precipitously nationwide. According to data provided by the Undersecretary of Defense in an unpublished report, rapes in the Navy jumped from 240 investigated cases in 1990 to 422 in 1992, a nearly 100 percent increase. (T.S. Nelson, "For Love of Country: Confronting Rape and Sexual Harassment in the U.S. Military.") And, according to 1992 testimony before the Senate Veterans Affairs Committee, an estimated 60,000 to 200,000 women veterans were sexually assaulted

gay-bashing,[97] wife-beating and assault. Police became even more brazen in their brutality; the beating of Rodney King by cops in L.A. after being stopped for a traffic infraction a few months after the end of the Gulf war capped the "we can get away with anything" mood that swept the country. Over the next few years as the atrocities and scope of death leaked into public consciousness, the Germanic strains of "We didn't know!" rang out, and, even more, "We don't *care.*" Once victory was assured and the vast anti-war and G.I. resistance movements were whitewashed out of public memory and suppressed, most Americans were every bit as indifferent to the slaughter as were the good citizens of Nazi Germany.

The Campaign tried to wrap the anti-war movement in the flag and waved it proudly to make the movement less threatening to the Campaign's caricature of the "average American". So long as it was Iraqis and not U.S. troops who were dying, the slogan "Support our troops" fueled an unconscious racism and played right into Bush's hands. Progressives' yellow-ribboned, flag-waving liberalism co-signed the blank check Bush needed to kill a quarter-of-a-million

---

while on active duty (Pardue and Moniz, 1996), with 1991 and 1992 containing the greatest number of rapes and sexual assaults.

[97] Gay-bashing was up 31 percent in 1991, according to the National Gay and Lesbian Task Force. In a survey of five cities, the National Gay and Lesbian Task Force Policy Institute found that anti-homosexual violence increased between 1989 and 1990 by over 40% and from 1990 to 1991 by over 30% on top of that. The number of documented anti-gay murders in the U.S. increased from 3 to 8 in the 1990-1991 period.

people (while calling *the other side* barbarians) and bomb Iraq back to the stone age.

Today, the great reforms of yesteryear, having been stripped of their surrounding movements and their threat to capital's interests, are used to indoctrinate, medicate and regulate. Indeed, in some sense *our most important struggles are not only against capitalism today but against our own prior victories.* Our papers and websites should report struggles that are making *our* institutions and ways of thinking the new socially-accepted and hegemonic reality. We need to think about how a *socialist* society would deal with this issue (whatever the issue may be). Doing this effectively entails:

1) busting open the shell of false choices presented to us, such as "Sanctions vs. War," and "Worker vs. Consumer";

2) reframing the issues to expose the historical traps and offer up new options that had previously been hidden by the way the questions were posed;

3) Publicizing the current resisters as well as the histories of resistance and providing them with material support.

4) legitimating new forms of struggle, both within and outside of existing formations;

5) breaking the official silence on all that our communities are doing, the many small resistances and creative actions;

6) making us all "experts" by involving ourselves in alternative health care research and other "how to do it" projects

that allow us to survive as much as possible beyond reach of the system's fangs;

7) finding ways to link all our communities and providing each other with mutual aid;

8) remaining focused at all times on "the property question" — that is, on the class enemy behind the specific policies; and,

Rev. Billy Talen leads the "Church of Stop-Shopping" and full choir against billionaire "developers" in New York City.

9) engaging in activities that undermine reliance on official forms of protest, and instead create direct action communities of resistance and nurturance.

Part Four.
Truths & Consequences

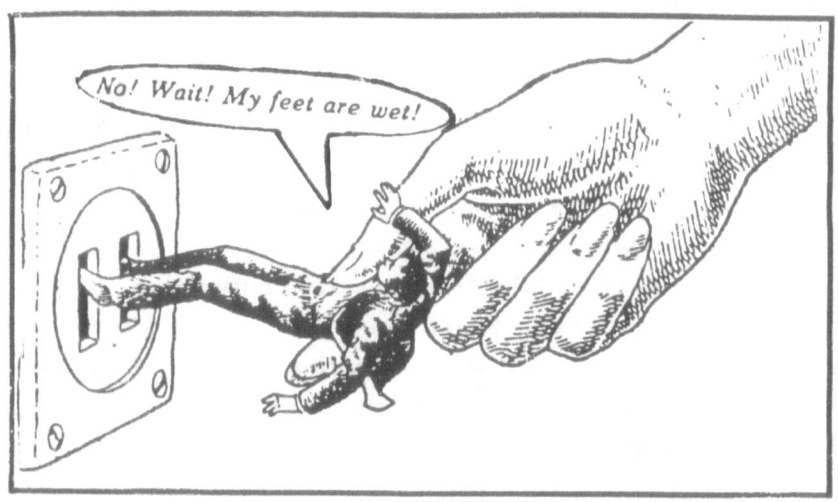

Graphic by Lucius Cabins

AP Photo/Michael Probst

Blockupy Frankfurt, May 19, 2012 — The German police take off their helmets as a sign of support for the protesters and march with them, clearing the way for them (but not officially participating). Frankfurt German police officers escort an anti-capitalism protest march with some 20,000 people. Protesters peacefully filled the city center of continental Europe's biggest financial hub in their protest against the dominance of banks and what they perceive to be untamed capitalism, Frankfurt police spokesman Ruediger Regis said. The protest group calling itself **Blockupy** has called for blocking the access to the European Central Bank, which is located in Frankfurt's business district.

IT'S THIS WAY

I stand in the advancing light
my hands hungry, the world beautiful.
My eyes can't get enough of the trees --
they're so hopeful, so green.
A sunny road runs through the mulberries,
I'm at the window of the prison infirmary.
I can't smell the medicines —
carnations must be blooming nearby.
It's this way:
being captured is beside the point,
the point is not to surrender.

- Nazim Hikmet, Turkey

Every moment of danger also affords opportunity. How can we learn to find it and prepare ourselves for it? You don't have to be a Nazim Hikmet or even T.S. Eliot to uncover the hollowness, the desperation, the hidden longing just beyond reach that the system converts into commodities to sell us to stuff into that void. You know, "don't let the terrorists win. Go shopping," said Bush and Giuliani. Shop against fascism; shop against loneliness. We end up turning to the market, the system, *the government* to save us from desperate situations that emerge mainly because we as a Left failed to make necessary preparations all along.

Recent history offers a cascade of such blown opportunities. In the mid-1980s, a Georgian farmer's land was foreclosed and about to be confiscated by the sheriff. Did the Left organize to defend that Black farmer? No. True, the NAACP issued a belated protest to the government — but that came only after others had already taken action. Those others, as it turned out, were — believe it or not — the Ku Klux Klan and Nazis. Violently racist farmers and assorted goons came to the aid of that Black farmer, barricaded the farm against the sheriff and bankers' goons and sent a hundred armed troops to protect the farm from confiscation. The local sheriff was forced to back down due to the strength of the organized, armed resistance.

The fascist right, unlike straightforward "conservatives," has always had an explicit anti-monopoly-capitalist plank in its program. And its adherents are well-armed. Unlike the 1930s, when organized leftists in the Midwest *did* arm themselves to prevent the auctioning off of family farms,[98] today such direct and organized resistances — with or without weapons — are few and far between. So, for example, when the Branch Davidian compound was under siege by federal agents at Waco, Texas (Feb. 26 thru April 19, 1993), in bla-

---

[98] These were called Penny-auctions. As banks foreclosed on farms and put them up for sale, armed farmers and their supporters let it be known that no one was to bid on them under penalty of death (literally). The original owner would then buy back their farm for one penny with no one willing to risk a higher bid against him/her with a gun barrel jabbing them in the back.

tant disregard for the rights and well-being of the people assembled there, the Left was left strategyless and, even worse, stampeded into supporting the slaughter rationalized by liberal Congressional representative Pat Schroeder (Dem., Colorado) and U.S. Attorney General Janet Reno, who approved the bloodbath and then conducted the official investigation of her own actions. One does not have to approve of the religious beliefs of the Branch Davidians to defend their right to practice their religion, to assemble, to create their own intentional community and to recognize and recoil in horror from the federal government's massacre there.

But most left parties — showing little interest in supporting resisters in the military or direct action communities of resistance and nurturance, and preferring, instead, to develop intellectual *positions* on every issue under the sun (as hysterically but accurately parodied in the Monty Python film "Life of Brian") — remained silent about Waco, just as it did over the Philadelphia police bombing of MOVE eight years earlier.[99] Once again, the hypocrisy of liberals masquerading as leftists astounds. Even in those instances where what I call the "official Left" did take a stand, the manner in which it did so rendered it increasingly irrelevant. How often we've seen left-

---

[99] On May 13, 1985, Wilson Goode, Philadelphia's first Black mayor, approved a bombing by police helicopter of a large building housing the MOVE extended family. The fires that ensued burned down 61 wood-frame houses on nearby blocks and killed 6 adults and 5 children in he MOVE house, portrayed as "collateral damage".

ists debate how to denounce some horrible event, only to rend its readers and listeners, with stirred up emotions but nowhere to go with them, helpless before the system's onslaught and fascism's twisted *appeal.* Successful opposition requires more than verbal exhor-

tations, electoral maneuvering and sloganistic condemnation. Our every demand, every analysis must break with the system's hegemony by containing within it the means for people to act collectively to *empower themselves* over the conditions of their lives, as opposed to appeals to authority to act on their behalf. Otherwise, we betray our own rank-and-file's initial enthusiastic clamor for changing things, exposing our own impotence and feeding the climate giving rise to fascism.

This means that we must stop playing "loyal opposition" and stop falling for the twisted reach of nationalism, especially among those who, within the Left, censor the more radical movements so that they could more readily appeal for "regulation" of some of capitalism's abuses. During the 1991 Gulf War, we heard the following: "We cannot afford to squander critical resources seeking to police the world" (*Committees of Correspondence*) and "Money for Jobs, Not for War" (*Work-*

ers World Party). Such cost-benefit assessments relinquish the moral high ground, as though the reasons for unemployment, housing foreclosures, health care costs and the like are due in any way to the capitalist State's financial shortages and not to the fundamental premises of capitalism itself. And if there was no financial shortfall due to imperialist wars, then the wars would be all right? Now, most leftists themselves don't believe that, but those slogans persist. And not merely opportunistically (bad enough!), but as a result of a complete misreading of the public's morality and consciousness, at that! Such manipulations always come back to haunt. Such slogans didn't (and still don't) trust the people; they offer them a *bribe*. Does anyone who understands how capitalism works really believe that had the U.S. government stopped "squandering critical resources" those funds would be put to use (along with the non-existent "Peace Dividend" projected by some with the end of the cold war) to meet public needs instead of being used to enhance corporate profits and provide windfall stock dividends for the wealthy?

A century ago, Rosa Luxemburg sharply criticized those on the Left who pitched for a "cleaner capitalism," one without imperialism:

> The essence of this position is the attempt to persuade the bourgeoisie that imperialism and militarism are damaging to itself even from the point of view of their own capitalist interests. It is hoped that by this ma-

> neuver the alleged handful of people who profit from imperialism will be isolated and that it will be possible to form a bloc consisting of the proletariat together with large sections of the bourgeoisie. This bloc will then be able to 'tame' imperialism and 'remove its sting.' Liberalism in decline directs its appeal away from the badly informed monarchy and towards a monarchy that is to be better informed. In the same way the 'Marxist Center' appeals over the heads of a misguided bourgeoisie to one which is to be better constructed.[100]

For too long the Left has depended upon a "civility," an "exception" for America when it comes to understanding how their own state functions. "If only government officials could be made to see the terrible effects of their policies," the hands wring over and over again — as if that would make a difference.

Indeed, as Gore Vidal (followed by Lawrence Ferlinghetti) sharply put it, America has become a one party bird with two right wings. The imperialist state, capitalism, and patriarchy are *the enemy*. All the exposés in the world of capitalism's abuses, imperialist wars, empire, genocide, alienation, white supremacy, conditioning, extraction of surplus value, sexism, homophobia, racism, nationalisms, violence, provincial ways of seeing mean nothing to the system; *it can't be shamed into transforming itself.* We expose those manifestations and abuses by capitalism as means to mobi-

---

[100] Rosa Luxemburg, *Anti-Kritik,* Chapter 6.

lize each other to take action, not to lobby the state. Our commentaries — all of the words written here, as well as other analyses — mean nothing if they do not help to rescue and nourish the liberatory moments that allow people to empower themselves directly, in whatever they collectively decide to do, and to hell with the government, corporate, religious or other "aliens." (A novel twist, eh?, seeing *capital's* agents as "aliens," "special interests" and "outside agitators!")

Networks of affinity groups and radical collectives can become communities of resistance and nurturance that take direct action to transform every aspect of daily life, every way of relating, every assumption shaped by capitalism and patriarchy (which we, without thinking, take for granted and externalize as "normal"). They can embark on, as Rudy Deutschke put it, "the long march through all the institutions of society" (or, as the current Occupy Wall Street slogan goes, "Occupy Everywhere!"). They are generally more expeditious than hierarchal organizations in fomenting the kinds of creative explorations and de-centralized, self-motivated projects that can lead to new forms of social movements. On the other hand, the more rigidly structured the organization, the more it needs to *impose* discipline on members, reproducing all the worst power relations of this society. Hierarchal organizations work in ways that invalidate de-centralized creative projects, displacing the "burden" onto "experts" who, even if they don't mean to, wield information as power, frustrating transformation of the ways people *experience* the world around them and thus their ability to act upon it.

Nowhere is this more evident than in the aftermath of Hurricane Sandy. Where hierarchal government agencies like FEMA and the Red Cross were either unable to or not interested in providing support to working class and poor communities, Occupy Wall Street's lateral networks of young activists immediately mobilized support for those communities under "Occupy Sandy," and worked *with* people on-the-ground to provide material assistance and professional medical care. (See Chapter Six)

Radicals must never allow ourselves to become reconciled to institutionalized religion, private ownership of production, the state, privileges based on race, sex, or sexual orientation, the nuclear family, or all the other institutions and attitudes that dominate the corporate media's advertisements for what is "respectable" — especially when it comes to our forms of action! The Left has often acceded or deferred to basically liberal welfare-state Keynesianism; too often we find ourselves trying to do what the Democrats and liberals ought to be doing — defending the welfare system, the public school system, the butchery that passes for a health care system, and other institutions that previous generations fought so hard to win. These are all horrible and degrading pittances of what people deserve; they're capitalism's safety-valves, stop-gap monuments to the failures, immorality and irrationality of capitalism — a system that should never have existed and which deserves to be consigned to the proverbial dustbin of history. We need to reframe the question!

Stop defending welfare capitalism as if it is ours, as though we're only seeking to curtail capital's excesses, make its imperialism a little less bloody, its widespread hunger and poverty a little less visible. *We don't want* schools — "factories of despair," Phil Ochs called them — at least not in their current form. Despite having to fight tooth and nail a century ago for a network of free public schools, they have now become part of the mechanism of stupefication and drugging. Their primary mission, more and more, has become policing kids, training the wage-workers and soldiers of the not-too-distant future, and conditioning students to be rigid, obedient to authority and competitive, instead of promoting sharing and cooperation. *We don't want* their version of city hospitals, if their function is primarily to medicate children, workers, the elderly and the poor — even if those treatments are covered by the insurance or the State. And welfare? Is that what we really want, that miserable pittance, that fraction of what we really need? We're made to seem like greedy ingrates for going on food stamps and struggling to meet the rent, while those in power dole out $14 trillion —

welfare for the rich! — to bail out the banks. They send us to war to protect corporate investments and make the world safe for corporate democracy, extraction of oil, and Genetically Modified Organisms. We need to create radical alternatives to the education, welfare and health care systems, and not get caught up defining our positions within capital's framework.

Come the revolution all the institutions we take for granted today will be overhauled to serve the needs of the people, not profits, or swept onto the used-condom pile of history. As they exist today, they are not part of our radical vision, but are concessions wrung from the system by past generations; to the extent they're granted, the ruling class does so only to stave off revolutionary movements. As those movements recede or are militarily crushed, capital co-opts and re-absorbs their gains, institutionalizing the shell of reforms as mechanisms to contain and re-integrate all rebellion back unto itself.

Better Latent Than Never

It is only after the Left fails to consolidate direct action communities of resistance and nurturance, or when such empowering forms have been broken up, that many people begin looking elsewhere for amelioration of the dissatisfaction they feel.[101] The problem keeps reappearing in

---

[101] See Leon Trotsky, *Fascism: What it is and How to Fight it.*

new guises: Why, for example, did so many working-class women throughout the '80s join rightwing anti-abortion groups instead of the Left, which should have been their natural constituency? What was the Left doing wrong?[102]

One bold leftist and women's liberationist, Eleanor Bader, went underground into the National Right to Life convention in 1989 to try to find some answers. Her story was bound to upset many on the Left who portrayed women in groups such as the National Right to Life Committee solely as victimized dupes (and their needs dismissed) or as fascists, to be screamed at and spit on.[103]

The fact of the matter, as Bader reported, is that many working class women turned to right-wing groups like the NRTL to address needs omitted from the agendas of liberal women's organizations such as the National Organization for Women which, having organized themselves around women's equivalent of trade-union-type issues, appealed to the lowest common denominator in order to influence legislation. Fascists, on the other hand, organize in ways that liberals in general ignore or trivialize, nor is that dismissiveness

---

[102] The 1992 pro-choice clinic defenses in Buffalo and New York City, in which radicals mobilized to physically stop the right-wing Christian fundamentalists from imposing their morality by force on everyone else, was a notable and hopeful exception to the liberalism and timidity of the Left, and of middle-class liberal feminism in particular. So too were the highly creative disruptors of business as usual organized by ACT UP, the foremost exponent of direct action throughout the late '80s and '90s.

[103] *Red Balloon Magazine*, Winter/Spring 1992.

limited solely to the issue of abortion. To its detriment, the Left approaches the working class rank-and-file of other right-wing movements in the same patronizing way.

While fascist organizations are attempting to recruit small farmers in the Midwest (who are being driven off their farms by agribusiness conglomerates and the big banks), the Left *preaches* against fascism while providing no coherent framework for activities that could cut into fascism's appeal.

Clearly, small farmers — like all disempowered small property owners thrown into motion — comprise a potential mass-base for right-wing movements. To win them over, these movements take advantage of the Left's disempowering strategies, which are geared around attempting to influence government policy instead of mobilizing the working class to fight in its own interest and gain victories through its own direct action. The left cannot afford to keep squandering such opportunities; we have to "seize the time," as Bobby Seale used to put it. When the Left offers no concrete revolutionary way for people to deal with their lives other than by appealing to the existing government to "intervene," the Tea Party and David Duke do.

The same conditions hold for organizing loggers cutting down redwoods; the milieu giving rise to Nazi skinheads; women in right-wing groups; and in general, for much of the working-class. How should the Left deal with the working-

Jesus Died for Somebody's Sins— But not Mine!

The basis of irreligious criticism is:
Men and women make religion—
Religion does not make them.
This state, and this society,
produce religion, which is
an inverted consciousness of the world
because this is an inverted world.
Religion is the generalized theory of this world,
its encyclopediac compendium,
its logic in popular form,
its spiritualistic point d'honneur,
its enthusiasm,
its moral sanction,
its solemn component,
its general ground of consolation
and justification.
It is the fantastic realization
of the human essence, in as much
as the human essence possesses
no true reality. The struggle
against religion is therefore indirectly
the struggle against that kind of world
whose spiritual aroma
is religion.

Religious suffering is the expression
of real suffering, and at the same time
the protest against real suffering.
Religion is the sigh
of the oppressed creature,
the heart of a heartless world; it is
the spirit of spiritless conditions; it is
the opium of the people.

The abolition of people's illusory happiness
is the demand for their real happiness.
The demand to abandon illusions about our
conditions
is a demand to abandon conditions
which require illusions.
Religion is only the illusory sun
that revolves around human beings
so long as they don't
revolve around themselves.

Karl Marx

Patti Smith, as photographed by Robert Mapplethorpe, may he forever kick up the dust as he rests in peace.

The most successful right-wing demagogues, like fundamentalist Christian preachers, realize this and frame their program around romantic portrayals of the nuclear family. They provide an illusion of collectivity and empowerment; they polemicize against the big banks, big government, nuclear power, monopoly corporations and even (sometimes) imperialist war with as much fervor as the Left. And they integrate people into direct action (or "survivalist") communities, with their militias substituting for the now-broken down family and other fragmented community structures. Today's left, on the other hand, spins its wheels and burns itself out straining to mobilize large protest demonstrations, lobbying the government to step in and save us, disempowering us further.

What the Right does not and cannot do — even with the billions of public dollars in handouts to the rich rubbed in our faces with every hospital or post office being shuttered — is to *attack capitalism* for failing to provide the working class and farmers with the same kind of relief it provides Wall Street and giant corporations. Nor has it built alternative institutions to accomplish that, except as token gestures. That is why Occupy Wall Street has been so successful; it offers people across the political spectrum a model through which they can join the fight. Occupy seeks to address the underlying fragmentation of community from which fascist movements otherwise spawn. By maintaining itself as participatory and democratic in its practice and not only in word, Occupy becomes the movement of choice, when just a few months before the Tea Party controlled not only the national political debate but the Right's romanticization of the "family," "nation" and "community."

Radical Psychoanalysis and Action

Wilhelm Reich began countering the rigid, stultified personalities that he found to be the rule in the Communist Party leadership as well as Nazi groups, under conditions that existed in Austria and Germany the late 1920s and early 1930s. Reich decided that the workers revolting in Germany were doomed when a million attended a rally and all carefully observed the signs saying "keep off the grass" — and, no, that was not an indication of ecological consciousness, but of their internalization of the authoritarian state even as they moved to oppose it. Reich found extreme and sexually repressed rigidity in what he called the "character armor" of the members and leadership of the Communist Party that became ensconced in Party structures and prevented creative ideas from blossoming. His studies with Freud and in his own practice as a psychotherapist and a member of the Communist Party led him to conclude that repression of human sexuality was an essential component in molding mass psychology in Germany. His answer was to involve young people in what he called Sex-Pol clinics, loosely under the auspices of the Communist Party. By 1931, he had organized more than 50,000 working class kids and young adults into collectives that confronted the rigid puritanical and repressive atmosphere of both the Communist and Nazi parties. The Communist Party leadership expelled Reich precisely because of his effectiveness in this sort of organizing, which the apparatchiks running the party rightly perceived as a threat to their patriarchal and rigidly sectarian ways.  As such, the Communists organized no effective counter to Hitler's movement until it was much too late. Hitler understood this only too well. He said:

> "Only one thing could have stopped our movement -- if our adversaries had understood its principle and, from the very first day, had smashed with the utmost brutality the nucleus of our new movement."

We, as leftists and feminists in America today have not fully drawn the lessons of that historic and ultimately genocidal failure. We need desperately to create conditions through which people can address and resolve their needs directly in today's new and contradictory conditions (which constitute, in Marxist terms, the transformation of the "formal" domination of capital to the "real"). Too many leftists do little more than *moralize,* and tragically fail to learn to organize in new ways which would enable them to generate circumstances that provide other options.

Direct Action vs. Macho Individualism, or "Heavy Revvies, Call Home!"

That said, please note that in this framework for developing long term strategy, direct action is not a matter of militancy or machismo. Too many anarchists, as with right-wing Tea Partyites, say: "We are 'free individuals.' We want the state off our backs," by which they give themselves permission to act without a sense of responsibility to any community other than that of their fellow cadre. They distort direct action, reducing it to a tactical "style" employed within demonstrations. Others hold paper memberships in organizations, including ones that profess to be Marxist, without taking part in the daily efforts through which they could transform *themselves*, as well as the "objective conditions." They are, in actuality, merely using politics to vomit back, act out and provide cover for their capitalist conditioning. All of that is antithetical to the concept I'm putting forth. In fact, a true understanding of "Direct Action" rips that self-glorifying framework to shreds.

To the extent that such actions, involving varying levels of personal risk (1) help break us free of subservience to the sanctity of corporate property and the long arm of the law as we've internalized it ("cop–in–the–head," revolutionary theater director Augusto Boal called it); (2) directly attack selected targets; or, (3) create an overall climate of resistance that prevents the rationalized massacre of people by the forces of the State, such *tactical* direct actions are important components of any larger strategy.

But proponents of "trashing tactics" and "fucking shit up" for the hell of it rarely develop direct action beyond a more militant-than-thou image. As such, "direct action" is a misnomer when ascribed to the breaking of windows or spray-painting of slogans. At the same time and ironically, the moralistic denunciations such actions frequently provoke reveal as much obsession with corporate property as those who are smashing windows. To quote the Jefferson Airplane: "All your private property is target for your enemy, and your enemy is *we*."

There is a deeper question begging here, obscured by the sometimes vehemently self-righteous frameworks (on both ends): *What are the advocates of either position trying to achieve, and are they striving for the same goals?* Often (not always), the Condemnators (to coin a term) do not oppose those tactics as revolutionaries trying to build something greater, but from the perspective that breaking windows is counterproductive to exacting more leverage on liberals and winning particular demands. The same progressives refused to support resistance in the military and for the same reason.

The implied question — *Which tactics are most effective for achieving reforms?* — presupposes that one's goal is, for starters, to win demands within the existing system. How to build or cohere truly revolutionary movements doesn't enter into their considerations. Better to conceive of direct action as its own strategy, based on a fundamentally different consideration of the question we are addressing, in this case: *How does revolutionary change takes place?* Direct Action is falsely portrayed as an expression of rage or "acting out". But let's reframe it, instead, as one answer to the question: *How are we going to do more than use our actions as a means to pressure those in authority to make reforms?* Direct Action, in other words, is a long term strategy for making revolution by building, defending and expanding democratic institutions of "dual power" (more on that in a moment), and the freeing up of consciousness from the comfortable habits of thought that enable such actions. These *become* the new society. It is a non-macho, anti-vanguardist and horizontal way of organizing ourselves.

There have been innumerable creative actions over the decades that have about them the "aura" of direct action.

Many of them involve guerrilla theater, and great gobs of sarcasm and humor. The Yes Men, Billionaires for Bush & Gore, Missile Dick Chicks, Hexterminators, Firesign Theatre, Bionic Baking Brigade, Rev. Billy and the Church of Stop Shopping, and  perhaps thousands of small collectives have taken aim at the stupefying TV "brainwashing" of Americans.

Back in the late '80s, a group called the Danish Underground Consortium carried out a series of public stunts meant to disturb both society's daily routine and some routine ways of thinking. In one action, the Consortium's forebears kidnapped an education minister's bicycle and held it for ransom. The kidnappers mailed pictures of the

missing bicycle flanked by masked guards. When the demands were not met, every few days a new picture was sent to the media showing another part that had been removed — first the bell, next the light, and so forth — a clear warning of the victim's ultimate fate if workers at the education department were denied pay bonuses. In light of a wave of political kidnappings in Europe at that time, this spoof caught the wave of the nation's jittery imagination, and all of Denmark became engulfed in following the denouement as if it was a soap opera. (It ended with the education minister quitting his job.)

That is the sort of satirical action of which *Yippie!* founder Abbie Hoffman was master. In 1968, Abbie was subpoenaed by the House UnAmerican Activities Committee. Instead of being cowed by fear of loss of job, charges of homosexuality or being an agent of the Soviet Union — charges that had cowed many members and fellow travelers of the Communist Party the previous decade — Abbie came dressed as Uncle Sam and fellow *Yippie!* founder Jerry Rubin as a Hollywood fantasy of a Latin American guerrilla.

In the U.S., this form of consciousness-explosion became known as "*Yippie* tactics," which came to the fore most dramatically during the Conspiracy trial of the Chicago 8. There, Abbie Hoffman dressed as a judge. When the presiding Judge, Julius Hoffman (no relation), ordered Abbie to take off his robes and stop mocking the Court, Abbie was all too pleased to oblige, for under it he was wearing a Chicago policeman's uniform. Successful actions skillfully undermined expectations and the conformist rituals of everyday life. They were successful because they reversed the fear of

Jerry Rubin demanded his own subpoena (he called it "subpoenas envy"), at HUAC hearings in Washington, D.C., October 3, 1968. He carried a toy M-16 and wore a bandolero of live bullets. Imagine how far he'd get today!

being labeled, and wore those charges as a badge of honor instead of shame. The Jefferson Airplane — more than Karl Marx or anyone else — summed it up best for an entire generation: "We are all outlaws in the eyes of Amerika. ... We are forces of Chaos and Anarchy. Everything you say we are, we are! And we're very proud of ourselves."

Grace Slick, lead singer of the Jefferson Airplane, and Janis Joplin. Ah, we were so much older then, we're younger than that now.

Taking part in creative disruptions clears out the cobwebs in one's brain and allows one to build institutions of dual power. The planning group itself becomes a "community" of sorts with the power to change conditions for participants and, consequently, the way they experience the world around them. A direct action approach helps to create nurturing conditions through which participants collectively empower themselves.

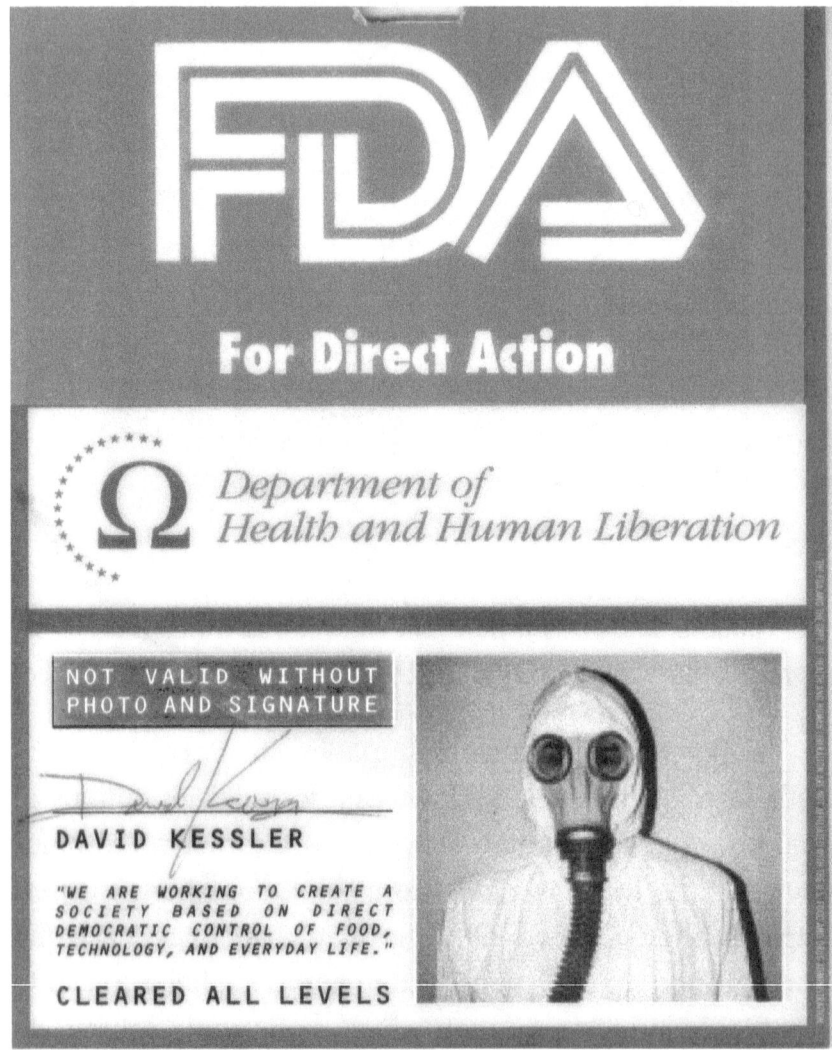

← On the previous page

Badge worn by anti-Genetic Engineering activists in Northampton, MA, as they entered supermarkets, pointed Geiger Counters they rigged to click wildly at food containing "Genetically Modified Organisms," and "officially" ordered the items removed from the shelves under threat of closing the store. In all cases, they were treated as officials from the government — must have been the exact-match photos! — and, to the surprise of all, the stores complied with their instructions.

Similarly in Tennessee, where anti-GMO activists wrote their own Laws banning genetic engineering, printed a few pages and pasted them into a McKinney's law book, dressed to appear "official" and visited market after market ordering the removal of genetically engineered foods from the shelves. When managers questioned them, they whipped out the law book, pointed to the exact law and wrote out summonses. It took a while before anyone caught on, at which point they had to flee the state.

Often, we wear the TV images supplied by commercial advertising, instead of asking ourselves where our conception of, for example, the "rebel" as heroic individual or bandito, is coming from. It's a capitalist theme running through our heads. Example: Helmets and Masks. An anarchist demonstration in Berkeley, 1989, was the first I'm aware of in which a large group of people wore bandannas over their faces, doing their best bad-guy impersonations as they ran through the streets battling police over the right of homeless people to move into a building the University wanted to turn into a luxury hotel. Certainly it is sometimes necessary to wear masks to avoid identification. But one's motivation is important, here. Is this kind of mask necessary, or is it being worn to intentionally look scary — and to cultivate a bravado image, not in preparation for any real circumstance? And even when masks are needed, are we intending to frighten people on the streets?

NOTICE:

DUE TO CIRCUMSTANCES BEYOND OUR CONTROL, THE SECOND COMING OF JESUS CHRIST DID NOT OCCUR AS PLANNED ON SEPTEMBER 30, 1988, AS YOU MAY OR MAY NOT HAVE NOTICED.

THE SECOND COMING HAS BEEN RESCHEDULED FOR SEPTEMBER 16, 1998.

WE HEARTILY REGRET ANY INCONVENIENCE THIS ERROR MAY HAVE CAUSED.
-THE MGT.

In the anti-austerity action at Stony Brook mentioned earlier, when we occupied and opened up the library the police threatened to take our pictures in order to identify us after the fact. So we decided to wear masks. But because of our concern about scaring people away and because we held intentionally irreverent views of ourselves, we decided that all demonstrators would wear Groucho Marx masks, not bandannas. As Groucho Marxists, even though our faces were hidden we re-framed and demystified the whole situation and turned people's fears into laughter. The cops looked like idiots chasing dozens of Groucho Marx look-alikes through the library.

At a Free Mumia march in the East Village, six of us carrying one of the lead banners wore square pieces of yellow cloth as masks on which we'd drawn smiley faces. Behind our masks, we could see each other exploding in anger as the cops clubbed and arrested our friends. But all anyone in front of us could see was Smile Smile Smile! It unnerved the cops so much that we were able to float rather ethereally through their police lines unscathed, as they were chasing down others!

A very different approach was taken at the anti-Operation Rescue demonstration at Dobbs Ferry New York. Participants wore bandannas, and also relatively useless helmets — useless, in that they were mostly for show and macho self-image, not sturdy motorcycle helmets that would actually protect one's head against police nightsticks. It's hard to take seriously claims that they were needed "for protection" when they surely antagonized the police without being able to protect from the blows.

When Rosa Parks refused to give up her seat on that famed bus, she thoughtfully had a professional photographer on-board near her. She was taking direct action. She didn't go home and write a letter to her legislator. She refused to move, to be treated as a second-class citizen, *at the point of injustice.*

Contrary to popular mythology, Rosa Parks had learned and *practiced* her history-making action at the Highlander School for organizers in Tennessee. Similarly, the students in Greensboro, North Carolina, who sat at segregated lunch counters demanding to be served, had trained to withstand the abuse they knew they would face, and to respond (in this situation) non-violently. They didn't go in cold. Both Parks and the Greensboro lunch counter activists indeed demanded that the government pass legislation outlawing discrimination. But they also acted directly, putting their bodies on-the-line. They took over those lunch counters and forced open those establishments to all.

The Student Nonviolent Coordinating Committee set up freedom schools; the Black Panthers established health clinics, free breakfast-for-children programs and community "cop watch" patrols against police brutality; women's reproductive rights organizers set up family planning and safer abortion clinics. All of these are examples of collective direct action.

While many raised the issues of civil rights, Jim Crow

laws, and voting rights as demands upon the government, the people actually doing the actions framed the general issues in ways that enabled the participants to begin implementing them immediately, for themselves. Submitting registration forms to vote (when it was banned for Black people or made extremely difficult) became a form of direct action. So did drinking from segregated water fountains, shutting down bus lines by engaging in the Montgomery bus boycott, and attempting to walk into segregated schools. Symbolic civil disobedience would be one, or two, or three steps removed from the immediate; people would sit down, for example, as a form of petitioning the government or other authority to take the desired action or change some law. Through direct action, on the other hand, we create liberated zones from which to fight and deepen, inwardly, to include more and more facets of our lives, and to expand, outwardly, into more and more communities.

In 1969, Stony Brook students from the Independent Caucus of SDS set up a free breakfast-for-children program in Riverhead, Long Island, with members of the Black Panther Party. As a result of poor nutrition kids were flunking out of school and vastly increasing their chances of becoming permanent riders on the merry-go-round of poverty and hunger. You'd think the government would say, "You're doing a good job. You're being peaceful. We'll help you out."

No! As soon as we began feeding kids the government tried to shut us down, using one ridiculous pretext after another. The final one was that we only had two sinks and we were supposed to have, by law, three sinks! (This, in an area where children were starving to death before our "intervention".) We organized the whole Riverhead community to fight to re-open the free breakfast program, to defend our liberated zone, and *then* marched on Town Hall demanding that the *government* feed those kids — *while we continued to do so!*

It's the same today with Food-Not-Bombs, which is feeding people who are starving to death, living in the streets and eating out of garbage cans. Instead of assisting them, the government of San Francisco had them beaten and arrested — for "feeding people without a permit." In the mid-1990s, more than a thousand people were arrested in San Francisco for feeding people! Some faced long sentences on trumped up charges for refusing to "cease and desist." Keith McHenry, one of the key organizers of Food Not Bombs, faced *life imprisonment* under the draconian "three strikes and you're out" laws — again, for feeding people! And the Left — *Where's the Left?* — had no way of responding because it kept boxing itself into the "protest mode," petitioning to change this or that policy where a campaign of, say, liberating supermarkets and distributing free food by the ton would seem more appropriate; at the very least, join in the cooking and get out there and staff those food tables! Such projects put our vision of the new society directly into practice while performing an immediate and necessary service. This is what Occupy Wall Street had been doing, feeding thousands of people every day as part of the Occupation. They were met with similar harassment ordered by the Mayor and enforced by the police.[105]

What Occupy does, in the best direct action fashion, is to appropriate unto ourselves the power to act directly over more and more of the conditions that affect our lives, to challenge the ideological hegemony of the 1% and the framework it imposes for examining social issues, and to take direct responsibility for what is happening in our world. Its beauty rests in part in the fact that participants may, through working groups and other forms they set up, organize around "demands," but the movement as a whole does not verbalize a "line" or compilation of lines (a "program"). It refuses to

---

[105] Near the end of 2011, it was revealed that the NYPD had received millions of dollars in donations from Wall Street firms. J.P. Morgan-Chase gave $4.6 million; Goldman Sachs, Barclays Capital, investment bank Jeffries and Co., investor Carl Icahn, Rupert Murdoch's News Corp., and investment firm The Renco Group each gave over $100,000; Bank of America gave over $75,000 — all in 2010-2011. The funds went to the NYC Police Foundation, which is the private fundraising arm of the NYPD. Commissioner Ray Kelly sent JPMorgan CEO Jamie Dimon a note expressing his "profound gratitude" for the donation, and described the gift as "unprecedented" in size. These donations were completed by the Spring of 2011, before the start of Occupy Wall Street. They allowed the NYPD to upgrade many of the weapons and gadgetry used in the surveillance and suppression of Occupy Wall Street.

Photo by Paul Kniesel

Tipper Gore [Haideen Anderson], being interviewed by Dan-I'd-Rather-Not [Mitchel Cohen] as others in the Red Balloon Collective run interference with the cops, at Penn Station on Clinton's Coronation Day, January 20, 1993, just prior to being dragged out of the station by police. Say a few words into the magic marker!

pawn off onto others the responsibility for building the new society in the here-and-now, in what we used to call "the belly of the beast." For the most part, we are not trained to think or act in that way, and many left groups — unable to generate the kind of excitement and participation that Occupy Wall Street has succeeded in generating — have resorted to trying to force OWS to change the entire character of its successful effort in order to make reformist demands on the State. Thus far the movement has rejected those demands on Occupy and has developed novel ways to expand, reframing and legitimating direct actions on the job, docks, campuses, and in the family, wherever we are, as part of our daily struggle. The personal *is* political; Occupy has thus far wisely kept its actions from being pigeonholed, enabling workers as well as consumers to find their common interest. After all, consumers are simply workers when we get home from work.

'Outlaw' Emotions

We all struggle over environmental, political, social, aesthetic, sexual, racial, economic, cultural and class-based power-relations within our movements and organizations. These do not spontaneously disappear in the course of direct action campaigns. Direct action communities of resistance and nurturance, however, create conditions that enable us to challenge and overcome assumptions and customary ways of doing things that hold back our movements.

In the 1956 edition of *The Rebel*, which was widely influential on the New Left, Albert Camus asks: *"A slave who has taken orders all his life suddenly decides that he cannot obey some new command. What does he mean by saying 'no'?"* Camus explores the psychological and philosophical meaning of an individual's act of rebellion. But Fredy Perlman, like Jean-Paul Sartre, reframed the question more interactively, as a dialectic between an individual and his or her society. How is it that, in the face of generalized conditions of oppression, Perlman asked, people *sometimes* rebel and, more often, they don't? *What are the conditions that foster rebellion? What are the conditions that hold it back?* And, let me add, *Will we recognize new forms of rebellion when we see them?* and, *What is the role of people who think about these things in advance, including those who are reading this book right now, in helping to advance favorable conditions and restraining those holding them back?*

Although revolutionaries can and must generalize about how people will respond to oppression, we must resist the temptation to draw cause and effect links between the level of oppression and willingness to rebel (as if those can be quantified, anyway). People learn *different* things within the same set of "objective" circumstances and react to them in different and often contradictory ways. They might learn from the history of pogroms to resist the power of the State, or they might conclude that they have to flee from it. They may internalize the blame for exploitation and oppression, and accommodate themselves to it. One might even become a pogromist oneself! — a possibility that Fredy Perlman poignantly explored in his 1982 essay, *Anti-Semitism and the Beirut Pogrom.*

> The idea that an understanding of the genocide, that a memory of the holocausts, can only lead people to want to dismantle the system, is erroneous. The continuing appeal of nationalism suggests that the opposite is truer, namely that an understanding of genocides has led people to mobilize genocidal armies, that the memo-

ry of holocausts has led people to perpetrate holocausts.

Unfortunately, many who identify with the New Left of the '60s took the behaviorist path, claiming "the more people are oppressed, the more they'll rebel." Others prioritized the need to wait for the "ripening of objective conditions" or "subjective factors" (such as an increase in the level of revolutionary consciousness), failing to understand Antonio Gramsci's observation of almost a century ago (written from inside an Italian fascist jail): *The objective conditions in capitalism are always ripe for revolution.* Lack of news-like information about the government's latest outrage is never the main factor keeping people from rising up. Contrary to Marcuse's thesis in *One Dimensional Man*, there is *always* the possibility of a life-affirming response to oppression because the objective conditions are always present, and they contrast sharply with the images of justice and "democracy" that Americans are taught to floss their teeth with. Conditioned patterns of subservience and domination can be overcome (or at least side-stepped), but only in certain conditions made possible in liberated moments, within which revolutionary movements are launched and *sustained.*

In the course of every struggle for *freedom* — not simply justice; not "law" (whether "international" or otherwise); not "equal rights" — there emerge communities of resistance and nurturance that redefine cultural "norms," for however fleeting a moment, and validate "outlaw emotions" (in Alison Jaggar's apt term), which undermine the system's hegemony over us and are reflected in our psyches. We may not notice them because they often fall outside the boundaries of what we've come to accept as "the political." In such moments, people may suddenly "feel satisfaction rather than embarrassment when their leaders make fools of themselves. They may feel resentment rather than gratitude for welfare payments and hand-me-downs. They may be attracted to forbidden modes of sexual expression. They may feel revulsion for socially sanctioned ways of treating children or animals. In other words, the hegemony that our society exercises over people's emotional constitution is not total."[106] In fact, over time the society undermines itself, its own inculcations and teachings. A new radical self-awareness rooted in the growing mass movement is what makes revolutionary change *possible*. As Marx put it in *The German Ideology*, "Mankind thus inevitably sets itself only such tasks as it is able to solve, since closer examination will always show that the problem itself arises only when the material conditions for its solution are already present or at least in the course of formation." Awareness and possibility emerge simultaneously, not sequentially. And with them comes the potential for

---

[106] Alison Jaggar, "Love and Knowledge: Emotion in Feminist Epistemology." In Alison Jaggar & Susan Bordo, *Gender, Body, Knowledge: Feminist Reconstructions of Being and Knowing,* Rutgers University Press, 1989, p. 160.

people to envision and momentarily embody a completely different way of living through eruptions of new, human-centered (as opposed to capital-centered) socio-economic relations within the belly of the old.

The pre-eminent responsibility of conscious revolutionaries today, it seems to me, is not to "recruit" activists to spout the "correct" demands via the selected vanguard Communist party or Anarchist coven; nor is it to raise their consciousness — a failed strategy that continues to plague the Left to this day. Our job is to find ways to nurture impulses toward direct action and democracy and enable them to erupt into one, two, many moments of freedom.

Conclusion

Direct Action is about doing things — not to or for *others*, but in ways that break down the category of "other" altogether, by expanding the conditions for freedom. Such moments erupt as "bubbles of potentiality." They emerge in *all* aspects of daily life, even those that seem the most tangential, apolitical and vapid. Our task is to link those unmediated free-spaces — those liberated zones — and find ways to nurture them over long periods of time, despite our differences on particular issues.

"Raising consciousness" about oppression — without first cohering those direct action communities of resistance and nurturance through which people come to experience their lives in new ways, enabling them to challenge the hegemony of capitalism and transform society — will not "cause" people to rebel. It will at best succeed only in disarming, demobilizing and despairing them.[107]

Why? Because our memories echo the fragmentation of capitalist and patriarchal rule. They guide us, and they also hold us back. They give us courage, and they also dredge up fear. They connect us to that long train of heroes with purposeful lives — transtemporal communities of resistance and nurturance — and they separate us from them as exceptions, mutants, saints we could never hope to emulate. They divide our immediate individual needs from those of the community's long-term vision and sacrifice. They tell us, "This is the greatest democracy in the world" and, as undercurrent in that same moment, "You can't fight City Hall." One minute they fire us up with rage and a desire to tear the system to shreds — "Those who hesitate are lost"; "A stitch in time saves nine"; "The early bird catches the worm" — and the next they render us fragmented, scattered, unfocused and impotent — "Haste makes waste"; "Look before you leap"; "Don't rock the boat."

We *all* want a different world — but what do we do in the

---

[107] See, especially, Dan Foss and Ralph Larkin, *Beyond Revolution: A New Theory of Social Movements*, for a brilliant investigation into the circumstances in which large numbers of people are able to overcome the dominance of the existing society and their alienation within it, and rebel vs. the circumstances in which the system re-establishes itself over the psyches and rebellious institutions, reclaiming them for the furthering of capitalism.

mean-time? Memory has long fingers, unexpected ways of creeping through ancient dust. It ties us to the constraints of our histories and at the same time it has the potential to free us from them.

How can we reframe the nationalisms we face today? How can we understand them in terms of race, racism in terms of nation, and their relationship to the intersection of capitalism and the nation state — circles within overlapping circles? At a time when some large environmental groups in the U.S. wrangle over whether to endorse policies that forbid immigration of dark-skinned people, all the once-separate issues now express themselves as multi-layered dimensions of the same issue: What does it mean to be human in a time of Robots?

The problem is not lack of consciousness; it's lack of organized forms through which people can express all this and act directly on what's keeping them down, using the knowledge that they already have to empower themselves by means of their participation. In other words, disempowerment is not based on lack of knowledge but on a lack of radical organization.

Disempowerment is a tool used to keep us in our place. And collective direct action busts us out. Radicals need to keep reminding ourselves that *we* don't empower others; *people empower themselves* by engaging in direct actions through which communities of resistance and nurturance can cohere. Our task then shifts from exhorting people to adopt our program or to join our organization in the abstract, to participating with others in creating and sustaining new organizational forms (like "Occupy"), through which people come to organize and explore their *own* consciousness, creating new possibilities. That's a far different approach to social mobilization, political change and organization than the way leftists conceptualize them, and consequently their role. And that difference in "vision of our mission" resonates in the organizational forms we create.

We must make it as American as the Trident ("the only nuclear sub my mom lets me chew!") to take direct responsibility for the nature of our society and the survival and well-being of our planet and not cede that power to "experts," managers, government officials and technocrats. Be realistic — demand the impossible! All power to the imagination! Steve Biko — the leader of the Black Consciousness student movement in South Africa who was tortured with electric cattle prods sold to the apartheid regime (let us not forget!) by the U.S. and then murdered in his dungeon cell — said it best: "The most potent weapon in the hands of the oppressor is the mind of the oppressed." Through our direct action strategy, we aim to deny the system that weapon. ✎

	1	2	3	4	5	6	7	8	9	TOTAL
IDEALISTS	0	0	0	0	0	0	0	0	0	1
REALISTS	7	5	2	9	4	6	1	2	3	0

THE GNAWING OF THE MICE

The Socialist Scholars Conference, Left Forum & Grad School Theses

O where do they find all that time to sink
Into minute review of Marx's life? —
Ev'ry belch and fart, scat inf'rence — I think
Forever could they tender fine distinc-
Tions and forego the living for dead trif-
Les, explore glum trails of contradiction
With deep dialectical incision,
Finely tune the fuzzy mental axis
To camouflage the graveyard their praxis
Details: Every split, bleak feud or faction
To "prove" the futility of action!

O paralysis of analysis,
Seductive ivory-tower palaces,
Guerrillas of thesis-war protracted,
Emerging biographers contracted
In tenure's sterile wonderland, all hail
Your People's Delegate from Bloomingdale's!
Providing gossip, letters, notes unbound
Into which, when all life dries up, to turn
And thrive in muck no prole needs ever learn —
Consume names, dates, debates, their lives affirmed
Till human voices wake them, and they drown.

STEVE BIKO, as drawn by Sanford Lee, in *Red Balloon Magazine*, Spring 1988. "The most potent weapon in the hands of the oppressor is the mind of the oppressed."

Part Five.

*Ring the bells that still can ring, Forget your perfect offering.
There is a crack, a crack in everything,
That's how the light gets in.
~ Leonard Cohen*

As the U.S. government prepared to invade Iraq in 2003, large protests took place all over the world, including in NYC (on land) outside the United Nations. At the same time, a team of Greenpeace and other activists passed by boat down the East River in front of the U.N. and used large helium-filled balloons to hold up the banner shown here, held together by light-weight netting.

Tips for the Movement

How to Raise Issues & Write Letters

1) **Clearly define the opponent, enemy, policy or argument you're challenging.** Paint the picture, draw the reader in with specific images.

2) **Always retain the moral ascendancy.** This allows you to take the offensive. Here's how:

   a) **establish your own credibility, sincerity, concern.** Extend that to include the entire audience or community to whom you are speaking or writing. One way — *concisely* tell your own story so that your motives and where you are coming from are clear, listeners do not feel threatened by you and in fact can identify with you and what you are saying.

   b) **protest the injustice inherent in a policy or action,** such as military aid to Indonesia, the bombing of innocent people in Afghanistan, the state's support for Monsanto and refusal to even *label* genetically engineered foods that you and your audience all eat, or the City's attempt to implant a waste transfer station in a residential or ecologically sensitive area.

3) Note that the other side sometimes tries to do this too. Jimmy Carter tries to hide being a mouthpiece for Monsanto and making profits for investors by couching genetic engineering in terms of "feeding the world." How to deal with this effectively?

CEREAL KILLER

a) Use humor, satire and ridicule. But,

b) do not "call names," exaggerate, ascribe personal motivations or what's in their head, or falsely characterize the opposition — doing so risks losing the moral ascendancy, which is more important to hold onto than short-term benefit. This is a tricky balancing act between satire (good) and snottyness (bad).

4) Once an injustice is established, **reframe the argument.** Don't unconsciously accept or be boxed into their language or definitions: People aren't "homeless," they're <u>made</u> homeless; Is the crop really "Weed resistant" or is it "herbicide saturated"? Are people with breast cancer "genetically predisposed" or are they subjected to a toxic environment? Were Manuel Noriega and Saddam Hussein really "Worse than Hitler" (thus obscuring or minimizing the crimes of the Nazis) or were they "CIA-installed allies" acting at the behest of the U.S.?

5) **Debunk their experts** (and, sometimes, the need for experts). How? Make a list of the ways to debunk their experts on each issue. For instance, show their biases, hidden investments, lies, additional evidence they're concealing, their behind-the-scenes funders, their previous actions, interlocking corporate boards they sit on, etc.). **Spell it out — truth rarely is self-evident,** although a picture of Donald Rumsfeld shaking hands with his good friend Saddam Hussein in 1983 goes a long way to dispelling their lies and credibility.

And **be specific in every one of your charges;** never say "some" scientist said this, or "they" are doing that, etc. or you will sound paranoid and lose credibility. It adds to your own credibility to be specific and to correctly attribute whatever you are claiming.

6) **Establish the complicity of a local institution with the unjust policy you are protesting** (it could be a university, government, corporation, bank, food co-op, court, police, military, CIA, etc.). Demand that the institution you are challenging recognize and take a stand against its own complicity with the specific injustice, even though you are convinced that it won't. Find and expose the linkups, the interlocks, to pressure local institutions to disassociate from or to stop assisting in any way that odious or unjust policy. **This is not simply for research purposes but to enable people to undertake specific actions on their own.**

7) **Put a face on the enemy.** There are always *people* behind such institutions (although it's hard to believe that a real person would actually *do* such unjust things) — members of boards of trustees or directors, investors, bureaucrats, university officials, police — the usual suspects. In general (but not always) we're not

Peter Sellers as Dr. Strangelove, modeled on Henry Kissinger

out to convince the enemy that he or she is wrong — they will not be moved by rational argument that goes against their class- or self-interest (unlike those in our own movements); we're trying to move a policy-maker to change his or her position whether s/he likes it or not, by building a force sufficiently powerful to exact a price from those s/he represents — one they do not want to pay — should they refuse to change their position. **Speak or write towards building this force,** do not to worry about rationally trying to convince the enemy. Think of tactics you can use to accomplish this and whether they are appropriate for the issue at hand (picketing the Board of Directors *at their homes*, leafleting professors' classes if they have military contracts, for example) — think outside the box!

8) **Make the enemy the object of ridicule and**

Pix Americanus? Unretouched photos of Kissinger picking his nose and then eating it.

scorn so that no one wants to be associated with them. Quote from their own words. (Henry Kissinger's quotes are usually very good for this sort of thing: "To give food to people just because they are starving is a pretty weak reason." Or this from Lyndon Johnson: "Without sufficient air power America is a bound and throttled giant, impotent and easy prey for any *yellow dwarf with a pocketknife.*") The point: Most people immediately try to disassociate themselves from such an outrageous statement or person lest it implicate them — even their own supporters! Satirize their hidden assumptions — without coming across as crass or malicious! Sometimes a pie in the face does this better than arguing, as *Yippie!* Pie-Man Aron Kay decided, and the Bionic Baking Brigade. **Be careful, though, *not* to ridicule those who are not really the enemy but who just have a different opinion.**

9) **Punch *with* the best instincts of people, not *at* them**. Don't moralize against those you are trying to influence. Abolish the word *should* (and the condescending tone embedded in it); talk inclusively as "we" rather than the more lecturing style "you" (as in "*you* should feel differently than you do") when addressing friends and supporters. Get rid of the sense that you're lecturing others, and turn it into a sense of "how do *we* move forward together."

10) **Give examples of what positive things the insti-

tution should be doing instead. We know that these institutions won't act in the way we'd like, but delineate them anyway to show those we're trying to convince how things could be different if the institution changed course and did the right thing (which you are advocating) or was truly a democratic entity run by the people. This allows us to make connections, to show how the particular issue is an expression of other and more systemic forces.

11) **Always give others on your side credit, don't hoard it for yourself. Share knowledge!** And at the same time, **don't stretch the truth. Don't exaggerate,** however tempting it may be to embellish your point. Show where people can find more information. **Always provide a contact number.** Respect the work of others. Give example of the specific actions they have taken. Inspire commitment and creativity.

12) Once complicity is established, **resist in an organized, disciplined manner. Take direct action against the institution.** It's most effective when resistance exposes to all the institutional hypocrisy, the double-standards that invariably come about as a result of the institution's complicity with injustice. (Think: *What do we mean by "organized manner"? Why is that important?* This does not mean "rigidity" or too many rules!)

13) Once you've established your own base, **link up with others,** without compromising principles. Compromise on *tactics,* not principles. Watch out for those who try to establish coalitions on the basis of "the least common denominator." At the same time, balance that against the importance of not being sectarian.

14) Respect the intelligence of those with whom you're trying to communicate. **People change by changing themselves, not by you (or anyone) changing them.** We can help facilitate that, but it takes an active effort on the part of a person, not a passive flip-flop. (If people can be talked into holding a position, they can just as readily be talked out of it.) People change by actively participating in struggles that change conditions around them. This enables them to experience the world (and their own lives) in a different way. It enables them to learn new things on their own. It is the job of organizers to change the conditions (in all the ways cited above) through which people can take action and experience (and not necessarily "see") the world in a different way. This is what allows them to join movements *and* to change themselves, at the same time.

- Mitchel Cohen

How to Make a Bat-Signal
Guerrilla Projections

Guerrilla projections have become a popular, practical, and sometimes spectacular way to put forward a political message. Whether it be virtually reinstalling a labor mural in Maine, tagging a state capitol building with a "For Sale" sign in Wisconsin, or throwing up a "Bat Signal" on the Verizon building in New York City, projections have proven to be an effective and often inexpensive way to broadcast inspirational ideas and enhance planned actions.

This guide provides some basic information about projections and projectors, and links to online resources that will be helpful for research.

As the #occupy movement moves forward we hope that projections will be used to spark new dialogue and spread important ideas for how to challenge and transform entrenched power.

Projector Facts

A projector's brightness is measured in lumens. The more lumens, the brighter the projector. Typically for outdoor projection, a projector should have at least 3000 lumens. The brightness of a projection will be diminished by ambient light on the projection surface. The 99% "bat signal" was projected using a 12,000 lumen projector, but less powerful projectors can still have a terrific impact under the right conditions.

The brightness and also the size of a projection depends on the projector's distance from the projection surface, and the projector's "lens throw ratio." Useful information on projectors including lumens and lens throw ratio can be found on the following website: www.projectorcentral.com.

Projection Content

Content for projection can be provided by a laptop, camera, dvd player, or anything else that can be plugged into a projector. Many kinds of software can be used to create content for projection including but not limited to PowerPoint, MSPaint, iMovie, Final Cut Pro, and After Effects. High Contrast imagery is ideal for projection. http://interoccupy.org/occupy-bat-signal/

Legal Questions

Laws vary from state to state, and even city to city, so we can't tell you what may get you in trouble under what circumstances. We also strongly suggest that you give a local lawyer a call if you have concerns or questions. We are not lawyers.

If you're legally in an apartment projecting onto a building, the authorities should need either a warrant or knowledge of a crime in progress to enter the apartment.

In New York City, there is a statute that prohibits against advertising on someone else's property, but other than that projecting is not illegal. If you're on the street with a generator, there may be laws about flammable material, or about using generators, or noise statutes (but you should use a quite generator anyway).

If you're on a roof without permission you could be charged with trespassing.

If someone asks you to turn of the projector, cooperation is the best way to avoid confiscation of equipment or legal repercussions.

Power Options/Requirements

A projector can be powered by a plug in power source, a car, a generator, or a big battery. Using a generator is certainly simpler, and just about anyone can figure that out, but considering the noise and exhaust that a generator creates, as well as iffy legal issues regarding public use of generators, we think that battery power is a favorable option.

Different projectors draw different levels of power, so make sure to check that your power source can support the power requirements of your projector. Older projectors tend to draw more power for less lumens.

Battery Power Requirements

- Pure sine wave inverter (we used the Power Bright APS600-12 Pure Sine Wave Power for about $180)
- A deep cycle ("marine") battery
- voltmeter
- drip-charger

Battery Calculation

100AH batteries, can power a ~4-600 watt load safely for just under 2 hours.

Most deep cycle batteries come with an AH (amp hour) rating. To calculate the appropriate size battery for your setup check out:

http://www.powerstream.com/Amps-Watts.htm

http://overlandresource.com/what-is-an-amp-hour-and-how-to-calculate-batterycapacity.

Pure Sine Inverter

We used 600w pure sine inverters.

You need an inverter that's strong enough to start the projector, but not one that's so big it'll drain the battery just by running. When the inverter is not supplying power, it draws low amperage from the battery and may be left connected to the battery for up to three hours. However, we recommend the inverter always be disconnected when not in use

Projector Hand Carts

Projectors can be propped up in various ways. The OWS street projection crew built easily maneuverable, battery powered projection setups using used hand carts. Each handcart was outfitted with a projector shelf made from 3/4" plywood and vertical plank for weighting the projector shelf and mounting the inverter. The battery is ratchet strapped to the base of the cart.

Checklist
do's and don'ts

- Test everything before going out.
- Keep the battery charging as much as possible. The drip-chargers aren't capable of over-charging the battery.
- Take care not to knock or bump a projector while it's on (non-LED projectors, which is most) is the easiest way to kill a bulb. The filament inside the projector is very very hot, and fragile. Jarring movement can easi-

ly break the filament, be careful.
- Use the voltmeter to test the battery. If the battery drops below 11.2 volts (roughly), it's probably time to use the remaining power to cool the projector. Turn it off, let it cool down.
- Recharge your batteries ASAP once drained.
- Recycle dead batteries. Lead acid batteries die pretty quickly, especially when not used regularly or left uncharged for long.

Direct Action in New Orleans

People of the Dome

by Mitchel Cohen

I'm sick and tired of hearing things
from uptight, short-sighted, narrow-minded hypocrites.
All I want is the truth. Just gimme some truth.
I've had enough of reading things
by neurotic, psychotic, pig-headed politicians.
All I want is the truth. Just gimme some truth.
- *John Lennon*

As Hurricane Katrina ravaged the Gulf states, many organizations kicked into high gear to send relief to local groups in Mississippi and Louisiana, with no help from the government or formal relief agencies. Among them was the Malcolm X Grassroots movement, with whom the Brooklyn Greens shared an office. Tons of donated supplies poured into the office and were trucked to Jackson Mississippi, where they were distributed through community-based direct efforts.

I spoke daily with Les Evenchick, a Green who lives in the French Quarter of New Orleans. I was also in touch with New Orleans residents Malik Rahim and Mike Howell; the areas in which they live were dry and they were holding out as long as they could. The story they tell is shocking: **U.S. and local government officials ordered the local drinking water**

turned off and refused to allow water or food relief into New Orleans. Hundreds of people died unnecessarily as a result.

And yet, there was no shortage of water or food being sent — it was just not allowed into the City! When Green Party activists tried to donate a large amount of water for the people in the SuperDome a few days after the levees broke, armed soldiers pointed rifles at them and prevented them from delivering supplies. Even three WalMart trucks loaded with drinking water were denied entry and turned away. No water was allowed into New Orleans. Evenchick says that "this was a brazen attempt to starve people out."

There was no health reason to turn off the drinking water at the time, as the water is drawn into a separate system from the Mississippi River, not the polluted lake, and filtered through self-powered purification plants separate from the main electric grid. If necessary, people could have boiled their water — strangely, the municipal natural gas used in stoves was still functioning properly as of Thursday night of that first week! I emailed Governor Kathleen Blanco (a Democrat) asking, "Who ordered the turn-off of the drinking water?" I received no response.

A commanding officer of a police squad complained that his 120 cops were provided with only 70 small bottles of water. Hospitals were supplied with nothing. Could FEMA,

Homeland Security and local officials have *forgotten* to store bottles of drinking water in the SuperDome, Convention Center and hospitals?

The only FEMA official on the scene in the early stages, Marty Bahamonde, testified to Congress that he begged FEMA director Michael Brown for water, food, toilet paper and oxygen, saying that "many will die within hours." Brown's press secretary, Sharon Worthy, responded that the FEMA director needed more time to eat dinner at a Baton Rouge restaurant that evening. "He needs much more that [sic] 20 or 30 minutes," Worthy wrote. "Restaurants are getting busy," she said. "We now have traffic to encounter to go to and from a location of his choise [sic], followed by wait service from the restaurant staff, eating, etc." Let them eat gumbo.

Green activist and former Black Panther Malik Rahim, who lives in the Algiers section — which, like the French Quarter and several other areas above sea-level, remained dry — points out that the government could have and should have provided water and food to residents of New Orleans but did not do so intentionally, to force people to evacuate by starving them out.

French Quarter resident Mike Howell adds that the capability had been there from the start to drive water and food right up to the convention center, as those roads were clear. "It's how the National Guard drove into the city," he said.

The evidence is overwhelming that the government intentionally did not allow food or water into New Orleans.

These were the people who had twice voted in huge numbers against the candidacy of George Bush, the only area in the state to have done so. In recent years they also fought off attempts to privatize the drinking water supply, battled Shell Oil's attempt to build a Liquefied Natural Gas facility, and tried to prevent the teardown of public housing — battles in which then-Mayor Ray Nagin sided with the oil companies and millionaire developers. Nagin had surprisingly contributed funds to George W. Bush's presidential campaign and was a registered Republican until just prior to the Mayoral election in 2002.

Who gave the order to block water and food from entering New Orleans? Who ordered the drinking water inside the city to be turned off? No one has yet answered those questions.

Attempts to starve civilians into leaving an area is a war crime under the Geneva Conventions.

On Thursday of that first week, volunteers — who had rescued over 1,000 people in boats — were ordered to stop, under the pretext that it was too dangerous. The volunteers wanted to continue rescue operations. They said there was little risk, and that desperate people had been welcoming them with open arms. The military "convinced" the volunteer rescuers at gunpoint to "cease and desist." They did the same to a state senator who had led a flotilla of hundreds of boats and rafts all the way from Mississippi to rescue people.

Who gave the order to block the volunteer rescue teams in New Orleans? No one has yet answered that question.

In a play to counter their horrific image in national media, officials claimed that people were standing on roofs trying to shoot down the rescue helicopters. In actuality, there were a couple of people shooting into the air as a signal to helicopters to pick them up. Yet officials repeated the lies about people shooting at helicopters to justify shutting down voluntary rescue operations and for sending in thousands of fully armed military troops, along with private Blackwater mercenaries fresh from Iraq, under orders to "shoot to kill."[107]

Two U.S. military helicopters spent a few days plucking 110 people from the roofs of their flooded houses. We saw them on T.V. and cheered. At last! This is what the military should be doing! When they returned to base they were called into the commander's office. They thought they were going to be given medals. Instead, as reported in *the NY Times*, their commanding officers reprimanded them and re-

---

[107] Blackwater billed the federal government $950 per man, per day — at one point raking in more than $240,000 a day. At its peak the company had about 600 contractors deployed from Texas to Mississippi, reports Jeremy Scahill in his pathbreaking book, *Blackwater: The Rise of the World's Most Powerful Mercenary Army*, published by Nation Books.

moved them from helicopter duty for "violating orders."

Who gave the order *not* to rescue people? No one has answered that question.

For more than two weeks, hundreds of volunteer doctors and fire personnel — including a squad from New York City — were denied entry to New Orleans. They were dispatched, instead, to provide backdrop for President Bush's photo-ops in other areas. The medical personnel were kept twiddling their thumbs, as people were dying.

Who gave the order not to allow rescue workers into New Orleans? No one has answered that question.

In an interview with WWL-TV, Mayor Ray Nagin complained vociferously that Louisiana National Guard Blackhawk helicopters were being stopped from dropping sandbags to plug the levees soon after the breech and before the flooding. No repairs were allowed on the levees until long after the poor areas of New Orleans were totally flooded!

Who gave the order to block National Guard helicopters from dropping sandbags to plug the levees? No one has answered that question.

Venezuela's president, Hugo Chavez and Cuba's President Fidel Castro offered millions of dollars and hundreds of doctors to help save lives in New Orleans. They were turned down.

Who gave the order to turn down the aid offered by Venezuela and Cuba? No one has answered that question.

Millions of concerned citizens wanted to send assistance as well. FEMA recommended that they send contributions to "Operation Blessing," a front group for rightwing evangelist Pat Robertson. Robertson had recently televised a speech calling for the assassination of Venezuela's president Hugo Chavez.

Who gave the order to divert tens of millions of dollars in contributions sent to help the people of New Orleans by outraged American citizens, to rightwing Christian zealots? No one has yet answered that question.

Numerous New Orleans residents were billed $500-$1,000 for gas and electricity by Entergy (the same company that operates the Indian Point nuclear power plants in New York) during the months following Katrina, *while the electricity and gas were turned off and the meters were not even read.* Only after Entergy received millions of dollars in subsidies did the company start adjusting some peoples' bills, and even then only if the customer challenged the charges. **Who allowed Entergy to get away with this greed, harass poor and suffering people, and blackmail the state and city into giving it hundreds of millions in grants and subsidies?** No one has yet answered that question.

The Saudization of New Orleans

Les Evenchick is an independent Green activist who lives in the French Quarter of New Orleans in a 3-story walk-up. He points out that people were told to go to the bus depot to evacuate, but the bus station had closed down the night before. Unless you owned a car, Les told me, FEMA and state police would not let you leave.

Hundreds attempted to walk out of New Orleans; they were forced off the road and ordered back to the Coliseum or SuperDome, where no water or food was available.

As a consequence, some resorted to looting, mostly water, food, diapers and medicine. "It's only because of the so-called "looters" that old people, sick people, and small children were able to survive," Les says. "But the 'anti-looting' hype was really just an excuse to militarize the area, place it under martial law and evict the population, mostly Black people, mostly the poor."

On August 30, a front-page Yahoo news story showed two pictures of people wading in water carrying supplies. The caption under the picture of the Black person, taken by an *Associated Press* photographer, read: "A young man walks through chest-deep flood water after **looting** a grocery store in New Orleans." The caption under the picture of a White couple wading through the water pulling supplies, taken by a photographer for *Agence France Presse* read: "Two residents wade through chest-deep water after **finding** bread and soda from a local grocery store." Got that? Whites "find," Blacks "loot."

MSNBC interviewed dozens of people who had managed

Dave Martin / Associated Press

A young man walks through chest deep flood water after *looting* a grocery store in New Orleans on Tuesday, Aug. 30, 2005. ...

Chris Graythen/Agence France-Presse/Getty

Two residents wade through chest-deep water after *finding* bread and soda from a local grocery store after Hurricane Katrina came through the area in New Orleans, Louisiana.

While *Yahoo!* printed both pictures as captioned, they were written by two different individuals at two different agencies, and not by *Yahoo!*. Nevertheless, the disparity — reflecting the racial mindsets — is both typical and stunning. To quote Wilhelm Reich: "The Question is not why hungry people steal food, it's why they don't." – MC

to get out during the first few days. Every single one of them was *white*.

Some tourists, on the other hand — most of them white — were trapped in the Monteleone Hotel. They pooled their funds and paid $25,000 for 10 buses to get them out. The buses were sent, but *the military confiscated all ten of them* en route, regardless. The tourists were not allowed to leave the city and were ordered to the Convention Center.

Evacuating the 100,000 people trapped in the city should

not have been that difficult. There was, for example, no shortage of available buses — why didn't the government use them before the hurricane hit, and throughout the week? But it didn't. Similarly, AMTRAK says it offered free rides out of town but City officials never got back to them to finalize arrangements. Even without AMTRAK or private cars, it would have taken at most 3,000 buses to get everyone out, fewer than come into Washington D.C. for some of the giant anti-war demonstrations. Even at $2,500 a pop — highway robbery — that would only cost a total of $7.5 million for transporting out of harm's way *all* of those who did not have the means to leave.

The government made no reasonable provisions for the poorest residents who were trapped in the city (primarily Blacks but many poor Whites as well), nor for those thousands who were refusing to evacuate without their pets. Those who refused or were blocked from leaving the City were locked in the SuperDome and *not allowed to leave* — five days of hell. Those who survived the first dome were then — finally! — bussed out of the area to another stadium, the AstroDome in Houston. Call them "People of the Dome."

So Who DID Help?
The Grassroots Organizes Itself

The story above is but half the tale. The other half is how entire communities of people from all walks of life took direct action to help their fellow human beings abandoned by government and corporate America. And, as usual, it's a story that for the most part continues to go unnoted by the national media.

Gulf Coast resident Latosha Brown reports that the first group to send emergency supplies was TOPS, The Ordinary Peoples Society, a prison ministry in Dothan, Alabama, founded and staffed by ex-offenders. They organized food, pooled their money for additional goods and brought the supplies to a second organization of former prisoners in Mobile who distributed them, while the first group went back to Dothan for more supplies. "That's why we tell everybody now that it was felons who were the first to feed, the first to respond to need, the first to get up and do something. They didn't wait for permission or for a contract. That's real leadership."[108]

Volunteer medics established free clinics with the Common Ground Collective (www.commongroundrelief.org) in defiance of governmental edicts and machine guns. Common Ground also mobilized thousands of young people from all over the country to go to New Orleans and help with the rebuilding, while using non-toxic alternative methods of mold removal and prevention that they developed.

Others, working in solidarity with tribal leaders, created a dedicated relief effort for Native American communities

---

[108] Bruce Dixon, "Rescue Came from the Grassroots: The People, Not FEMA, Saved Themselves," *The Black Commentator*.

(www.intuitivepath.org/relief.html). *Food Not Bombs* volunteers fed people all over the region, with no help from the government *or* the Red Cross (www.foodnotbombs.net/dollar_for_peace.html).

On the other hand, from Day One huge war profiteering corporations such as Halliburton, Bechtel and other private contractors began descending on the region, their pockets stuffed with billions of dollars in government handouts. Thousands of poor homeowners and rental tenants — including those unable to return to New Orleans, having been evacuated to the far away domed stadiums — were evicted and their homes confiscated and torn down, says Mike Howell, who continues to organize tenants to resist eviction.

The phony "reconstruction" of New Orleans began with the land grab, and with the Mayor proposing gambling casinos, which he says would "rescue" the city, while destroying the remaining wetlands. Wetlands are nature's way of protecting large areas from floods. Paving them over prior to Katrina contributed to the devastation experienced by New Orleans and the Mississippi Delta. The city, meanwhile, sprayed massive amounts of cancer-causing pesticides over the entire flooded areas.

Many people are resisting the blatant confiscation of their lands and homes. As the resistance grows, New Orleans may soon become known as the first battle of the new American revolution. *(September, 2005)*

Occupy Heads into the Spring

Mad, Passionate Love — and Violence

by Rebecca Solnit

When you fall in love, it's all about what you have in common, and you can hardly imagine that there are differences, let alone that you will quarrel over them, or weep about them, or be torn apart by them — or if all goes well, struggle, learn, and bond more strongly because of, rather than despite, them. The Occupy movement had its glorious honeymoon when old and young, liberal and radical, comfortable and desperate, homeless and tenured all found that what they had in common was so compelling the differences hardly seemed to matter.

Until they did.

Revolutions are always like this: at first all men are brothers and anything is possible, and then, if you're lucky, the romance of that heady moment ripens into a relationship, instead of a breakup, an abusive marriage, or a murder-suicide. Occupy had its golden age, when those who never before imagined living side-by-side with homeless people found themselves in adjoining tents in public squares.

All sorts of other equalizing forces were present, not least the police brutality that battered the privileged the way that inner-city kids are used to being battered all the time. Part of what we had in common was what we were against: the current economy and the principle of insatiable greed that made it run, as well as the emotional and economic privatization that accompanied it.

This is a system that damages people, and its devastation was on display as never before in the early months of Occupy and related phenomena like the "We are the 99%" website. When it was people facing foreclosure, or who'd lost their jobs, or were thrashing around under avalanches of college or medical debt, they weren't hard to accept as *us*, and not *them*.

And then came the people who'd been damaged far more, the psychologically fragile, the marginal, and the homeless — some of them endlessly needy and with a huge capacity for disruption. People who had come to fight the power found themselves staying on to figure out available mental-health resources, while others who had wanted to experience a democratic society on a grand scale found themselves trying to solve sanitation problems.

And then there was the violence.

The Faces of Violence

The most important direct violence Occupy faced was,

of course, from the state, in the form of the police using maximum sub-lethal force on sleepers in tents, mothers with children, unarmed pedestrians, young women already penned up, unresisting seated students, poets, professors, pregnant women, wheelchair-bound Occupyers, and octogenarians. It has been a sustained campaign of police brutality from Wall Street to Washington State the likes of which we haven't seen in 40 years.

On the part of activists, there were also a few notable incidents of violence in the hundreds of camps, especially violence against women. The mainstream media seemed to think this damned the Occupy movement, though it made the camps, at worst, a whole lot like the rest of the planet, which, in case you hadn't noticed, seethes with violence against women. But these were isolated incidents.

That old line of songster Woody Guthrie is always handy in situations like this: "Some will rob you with a six-gun, some with a fountain pen." The police have been going after Occupyers with projectile weapons, clubs, and tear gas, sending some of them to the hospital and leaving more than a few others traumatized and fearful. That's the six-gun here.

But it all began with the fountain pens, slashing through peoples' lives, through national and international economies, through the global markets. These were wielded by the banksters, the "vampire squid," the deregulators in D.C., the men — and with the rarest of exceptions they were men — who stole the world.

That's what Occupy came together to oppose, the grandest violence by scale, the least obvious by impact. No one on Wall Street ever had to get his suit besmirched by carrying out a foreclosure eviction himself. Cities provided that service for free to the banks (thereby further impoverishing themselves as they created new paupers out of old taxpayers). And the police clubbed their opponents for them, over and over, everywhere across the United States.

The grand thieves invented ever more ingenious methods, including those sliced and diced derivatives, to crush the hopes and livelihoods of the many. This is the terrible violence that Occupy was formed to oppose. Don't ever lose sight of that.

Oakland's Beautiful Nonviolence

Now that we're done remembering the major violence, let's talk about Occupy Oakland. A great deal of fuss has been made about two incidents in which mostly young people affiliated with Occupy Oakland damaged some property and raised some hell.

The mainstream media and some faraway pundits weighed in on those Bay Area incidents as though they determined the meaning and future of the transnational Occupy phenomenon. Perhaps some of them even hoped, consciously or otherwise, that harped on enough these might divide or destroy the movement. So it's important to recall that the initial impact of Occupy Oakland was the very opposite of violent, stunningly so, in ways that were intentionally suppressed.

Occupy Oakland began in early October as a vibrant, multiracial gathering. A camp was built at Oscar Grant/Frank Ogawa Plaza, and thousands received much-needed meals and health care for free from well-organized volunteers. Sometimes called the Oakland Commune, it was consciously descended from some of the finer aspects of an earlier movement born in Oakland, the Black Panthers, whose free breakfast programs should perhaps be as well-remembered and more admired than their macho posturing.

A compelling and generous-spirited General Assembly took place nightly and then biweekly in which the most important things on Earth were discussed by wildly different participants. Once, for instance, I was in a breakout discussion group that included Native American, white, Latino, and able-bodied and disabled Occupyers, and in which I was likely the eldest participant; another time, a bunch of peacenik grandmothers dominated my group.

This country is segregated in so many terrible ways — and then it wasn't for those glorious weeks when civil society awoke and fell in love with itself. Everyone showed up;

everyone talked to everyone else; and in little tastes, in fleeting moments, the old divides no longer divided us and we felt like we could imagine ourselves as one society. This was the dream of the promised land — this land, that is, without its bitter divides. Honey never tasted sweeter, and power never felt better.

Now here's something astonishing. While the camp was in existence, crime went down 19% in Oakland, a statistic the city was careful to conceal. "It may be counter to our statement that the Occupy movement is negatively impacting crime in Oakland," the police chief wrote to the mayor in an email that local news station KTVU later obtained and released to little fanfare. Pay attention: Occupy was so powerful a force for nonviolence that it was already solving Oakland's chronic crime and violence problems just by giving people hope and meals and solidarity and conversation.

The police attacking the camp knew what the rest of us

didn't: Occupy was abating crime, including violent crime, in this gritty, crime-ridden city. "You gotta give them hope," said an elected official across the bay once upon a time — a city supervisor named Harvey Milk. Occupy was hope we gave ourselves, the dream come true. The city did its best to take the hope away violently at 5 a.m. on October 25th. The sleepers were assaulted; their belongings confiscated and trashed. Then, Occupy Oakland rose again. Many thousands of nonviolent marchers shut down the Port of Oakland in a stunning display of popular power on November 2nd.

That night, some kids did the smashy-smashy stuff that everyone gets really excited about. (They even spray-painted "smashy" on a Rite Aid drugstore in giant letters.) When we talk about people who spray-paint and break windows and start

> Let's keep one thing in mind: they didn't send anyone to the hospital, drive any seniors from their homes, spread despair and debt among the young, snatch food and medicine from the desperate, or destroy the global economy.

bonfires in the street and shove people and scream and run around, making a demonstration into something way too much like the punk rock shows of my youth, let's keep one thing in mind: they didn't send anyone to the hospital, drive any seniors from their homes, spread despair and debt among the young, snatch food and medicine from the desperate, or destroy the global economy.

That said, they are still a problem. They are the bait the police take and the media go to town with. They create a situation a whole lot of us don't like and that drives away many who might otherwise participate or sympathize. They are, that is, incredibly bad for a movement, and represent a form of segregation by intimidation.

But don't confuse the pro-vandalism Occupyers with the vampire squid or the up-armored robocops who have gone after us almost everywhere. Though their means are deeply flawed, their ends are not so different than yours. There's no question that they should improve their tactics or maybe just act tactically, let alone strategically, and there's no question that a lot of other people should stop being so apocalyptic about it.

Those who advocate for nonviolence at Occupy should remember that nonviolence is at best a great spirit of love and generosity, not a prissy enforcement squad. After all, the Reverend Martin Luther King, Jr., who gets invoked all the time when such issues come up, didn't go around saying grumpy things about Malcolm X and the Black Panthers.

Violence Against the Truth

Of course, a lot of people responding to these incidents in Oakland are actually responding to fictional versions of them. In such cases, you could even say that some journalists were doing violence against the truth of what happened in Oakland on November 2nd and January 28th.

The *San Francisco Chronicle,* for example, reported on the day's events this way:

"Among the most violent incidents that occurred Saturday night was in front of the YMCA at 23rd Street and Broadway. Police corralled protesters in front of the building and several dozen protesters stormed into the Y, apparently to escape from the police, city officials and protesters said. Protesters damaged a door and a few fixtures, and frightened those inside the gym working out, said Robert Wilkins, president of the YMCA of the East Bay."[108]

Wilkins was apparently not in the building, and first-person testimony recounts that a YMCA staff member welcomed the surrounded and battered protesters, and once inside, some were so terrified [of the police violence] they pretended to work out on exercise machines to blend in.

I wrote this to the journalists who described the incident

---

[108] "Jean Quan plans to call national Occupy leaders," *San Francisco Chronicle*, Jan. 30, 2012.

so peculiarly: "What was violent about [activists] fleeing police engaging in wholesale arrests and aggressive behavior? Even the YMCA official who complains about it adds, 'The damage appears pretty minimal.' And you call it violence? That's sloppy."

The reporter who responded apologized for what she called her "poor word choice" and said the phrase was meant to convey police violence as well.

When the police are violent against activists, journalists tend to frame it as though there was violence in some vaguely unascribable sense that implicates the clobbered as well as the clobberers. In, for example, the build-up to the 2004 Republican National Convention in New York City, the mainstream media kept portraying the right of the people peaceably to assemble as tantamount to terrorism and describing all the terrible things that the government or the media themselves speculated we might want to do (but never did).

Some of this was based on the fiction of tremendous activist violence in Seattle in 1999 that the *New York Times* in particular devoted itself to promulgating. That the police smashed up nonviolent demonstrators and constitutional rights pretty badly in both Seattle and New York didn't excite them nearly as much. Don't forget that before the obsession with violence arose, the smearing of Occupy was focused on the idea that people weren't washing very much, and before that the framework for marginalization was that Occupy had "no demands." There's always something.

Keep in mind as well that Oakland's police department is on the brink of federal receivership for not having made real amends for old and well-documented problems of violence, corruption, and mismanagement, and that it was the police department, not the Occupy Oakland demonstrators, which used tear gas, clubs, smoke grenades, and rubber bullets on January 28th. It's true that a small group vandalized City Hall after the considerable police violence, but that's hardly what the plans were at the outset of the day.

The action on January 28th that resulted in 400 arrests and a media conflagration was called Move-In Day. There was a handmade patchwork banner that proclaimed "Another Oakland Is Possible" and a children's contingent with pennants, balloons, and strollers. Occupy Oakland was seeking to take over an abandoned building so that it could reestablish the community, the food programs, and the medical clinic it had set up last fall. It may not have been well planned or well executed, but it was idealistic.

Despite this, many people who had no firsthand contact with Occupy Oakland inveighed against it or even against the whole Occupy movement. If only that intensity of fury were to be directed at the root cause of it all, the colossal economic violence that surrounds us.

All of which is to say, for anyone who hadn't noticed, that the honeymoon is over.

Now for the Real Work

The honeymoon is, of course, the period when you're so in love you don't notice differences that will eventually have to be worked out one way or another. Most relationships begin as though you were coasting downhill. Then come the flatlands, followed by the hills where you're going to have to pedal hard, if you don't just abandon the bike.

Occupy might just be the name we've put on a great groundswell of popular outrage and a rebirth of civil society too deep, too broad, to be a movement. A movement is an ocean wave: this is the whole tide turning from Cairo to Moscow to Athens to Santiago to Chicago. Nevertheless, the American swell in this tide involves a delicate alliance between liberals and radicals, people who want to reform the

> **If the radicals should frighten the liberals as little as possible, surely the liberals have an equal obligation to get fiercer and more willing to confront — and to remember that nonviolence, even in its purest form, is not the same as being nice.**

government and campaign for particular gains, and people who wish the government didn't exist and mostly want to work outside the system.

Surely the only possible answer to the tired question of where Occupy should go from here (as though a few public figures get to decide) is: *everywhere*. I keep being asked what Occupy should do next, but it's already doing it. It *is* everywhere.

In many cities, outside the limelight, people are still occupying public space in tents and holding General Assemblies. February 20th, for instance, was a national day of Occupy solidarity with prisoners. Occupyers are organizing on many fronts and planning for May Day, and a great many foreclosure defenses from Nashville to San Francisco have kept people in their homes and made banks renegotiate. Campus activism is reinvigorated, and creative and fierce discussions about college costs and student debt are underway, as is a deeper conversation about economics and ethics that rejects conventional wisdom about what is fair and possible.

Occupy is one catalyst or facet of the populist will you can see in a host of recent victories. The campaign against corporate personhood seems to be gaining momentum. A popular environmental campaign made President Obama reject the Keystone XL tar sands pipeline from Canada, despite immense Republican and corporate pressure.[109] In response to widespread outrage, the Susan B. Komen Foundation reversed its decision to defund cancer detection at Planned Parenthood. Online campaigns have forced Apple to address its hideous labor issues, and the ever-heroic Coalition of Immokalee Workers at last brought Trader Joe's into line with its fair wages for farmworkers campaign.

These genuine gains come thanks to relatively modest exercises of popular power. They should act as reminders that we do have power and that its exercise can be popular. Some of last fall's exhilarating conversations have faltered, but the great conversation that is civil society awake and arisen hasn't stopped.

What happens now depends on vigorous participation, including yours, in thinking aloud together about who we are, what we want, and how we get there, and then acting upon it. Go occupy the possibilities and don't stop pedaling. And remember, it started with mad, passionate love.

Published in *Le Monde Diplomatique,* February 22, 2012.

---

[109] Not quite. As many activists predicted, this "victory" was temporary, and President Obama is negotiating with the corporations involved for a slight change in the route, but hardly a cancellation of the pipeline.

Report from San Francisco

Overthrowing the Ruling Class by Farce

by Jeff Goldthorpe

In the late '70s and early '80s, many movements for social justice partook in the doing of — and theorizing about — direct action. This essay, published in "Deadly Connections" in 1985 and drawing on those separate movements, was an important contribution towards "pulling it all together." It was widely discussed in autonomous circles in the Left in the U.S. It is reprinted here without revision, so that new generations of radical activists can understand their roots and perhaps help to answer some of the questions left unresolved.

The Reagan Revolution sought to teach the Left the **three R's:** retreat, retrenchment and retrogression. Predictably, most of the Left in 1984 opted for electoral activism in the realm of the Democratic Party and was given the ultimate punishment: having to half-heartedly suggest that people vote for *what's-his-name*, anybody but Reagan. This made for a boring, lethargic brand of activism, which was particularly apparent in the larger "progressive events" around the Democratic Convention in San Francisco in July 1984. An AFL-CIO rally the Sunday before the convention saw some 150,000 union members march up Market Street in a "curiously quiet demonstration. ... Generally the mood was in keeping with the amorphous theme of the affair, 'We can do it!' ('Do what?' some marchers were heard to ask.)"[110]

As the Convention opened the next day, there was a "Vote Peace" rally, intended mainly to influence convention delegates to adopt a pro-Freeze, anti-intervention platform. The *San Francisco Chronicle* commented that

> in contrast to the anti-war demonstrators outside the 1968 Democratic Convention in Chicago, the mood was friendly and peaceful toward the Democrats.[111]

The *Guardian* noted,

> The dominant political message of the rally was non-intervention in Central America. All the speakers contrived to avoid mentioning Mondale's name, urging the audience to "vote for peace" or "give peace a chance."[112]

In contrast, on the last day of the Convention, the downtown rush was stilled for a moment by a funeral procession of 750 people for the victims of Salvadoran death squads, organized by *Casa El Salvador–Farabundo Marti*. The mourners, dressed in black, carrying coffins, flowers and posters of

---

[110] *The Guardian*, 25 July 1984, p7.

[111] *San Francisco Chronicle*, 17 Jul 1984.

[112] *The Guardian*, op. cit.

Salvadoran victims, chanted dirge-like. The emotional intensity generated seemed to overwhelm even the participants, as well as many of the bystanders, said one account.[113]

Later that same day over a thousand people spontaneously marched to the City Jail, to protest the mass arrests earlier in the week of demonstrators associated with the Democratic War Chest Tours. They marched behind a ten-foot Trojan donkey, which had been the centerpiece of a skit on the Democratic Party (the donkey was fed money and votes and excreted bombs and soldiers, accompanied by a leaflet entitled "Beware of Geeks Bearing Gifts.") The War Chest Tours group had formed to point out the links between banks and corporations involved in military production and the "party of peace" of 1984. Their chief activity had been to lead groups of "tourists" through the business district, exposing corporate crimes and doing occasional screaming "die-ins" on sidewalks, in the streets and at times in corporate lobbies. Their youthful composition and the preponderance of "peace punks" in their ranks had made them conspicuous targets for police arrest throughout the week.

Merging Creative Art With Public Protest

This contrast in appearance between the events at the beginning and end of the Convention is not accidental. The

---

[113] *It's About Times,* Aug-Sept. 1984, p5.

"Vote Peace" mode of protest is the dominant one in the current anti-war movement. The funeral procession and the War Chest Tours represent an alternative style of political protest that has arisen in the past five years. This latter approach is distinctive in its rejection of divisions basic to late capitalist culture, in several ways: (1) its synthesis of creative art with public protest; (2) its rejection of the artist/non-artist distinction; (3) its assertion of grief, rage and sarcasm in the field of "rational" political protest; and, (4) its violation of the norms of capitalist daily life, often pushing a certain subcultural vision of life into the public eye. Although it exists unevenly across the country, it is definitely a national phenomenon. (My focus on the Bay Area is simply due to limited time and resources.) What is aimed at here is only a cursory review of these creative modes of protest and the role of subcultures within these protests.[114] I will also include some tentative conclusions on the importance of this activity and the response to it by the Marxist left.

Note well: the focus here is not on "cultural work in the Left." It is not about singers on rally podiums. Nor is it about artist activism as such. The focus is on moments when creative

---

[114] There are few "primary sources" of cultural theory listed here. Generally, I follow the stress of *Radical America* and *Cultural Correspondence* on popular culture as contested terrain, where buried emancipatory impulses can arise. See also Dick Hebdidge, *Subculture: The Meaning of Style* (New York: Methuen, 1979) and Lucy Lippard, *Get the Message? A Decade of Art for Social Change* (New York: E.P Dutton, 1984).

expression *merges* with political protest, when "art" leaps out of its gilded cage into the mundane reality of daily life. While creative artists have often participated in such actions, they are not necessarily responsible for the nature of the actions. The whole point here is that *anyone is* capable of creating them.

I can sense already some furrowed brows among my readers, some skeptical eyes. They detect the faint odor of Yippie-ism, LSD in the water supply and perhaps their own youthful follies. They are thinking of working hard, organizing a rally and overhearing some impetuous purist muttering, "Well, another boring demonstration!" (The guy must think he deserves a Las Vegas floor show.) Does this, writer believe that clever theatrics equals good politics? Well, yes and no.

Boring From Within, or Just Boring?

A mainstay of traditional left practice is the big national rally, sponsored by a broad coalition. Such coalitions are typically top-down affairs. A steering committee picks speakers to maintain a political balance, set a tone and garner media attention. Building up pressure for a particular reform goal takes precedence over the content of the organizing process. The march, the only time when most participants can directly shape the event, is usually quite orchestrated. Creative performers are added to the rally speakers to spice up the bill.

After 20 years of mobilizations for civil rights, gay rights,

ERA; after marches against union busting, nuclear war, the Vietnam war and intervention in Central America, we know what to expect. National marches are now a part of the institutionalized functioning of bourgeois politics. Authorities have formal methods and set strategies for handling them. Movement leaders are pressured to exert crowd discipline in conjunction with official crowd control plans. The resources of liberal institutions, such as unions, churches and professional associations (for Social Responsibility), and, of course, politicians are brought to bear on the national mobilization staffs to guarantee a suitably moderate orientation.

As a result of this kind of organizing process, these events are rarely able to satisfy the participants' desires for new experience and communion with others. Although mass demonstrations have been used to symbolize a collective power (or threat),[115] they quite often leave participants with a vague, impotent feeling, lost in a sea of people.

One perceptive observer of the anti-nuclear movement has written,

> The movement has been powered by fear and indignation. As emotional fuel, these feelings burn hot, but fast. The initial horror wears off, to be replaced by creeping numbness, an exhaustion under

---

[115] On demonstration as theatrical threat, see John Berger, "The Nature of Mass Demonstrations," in *The Look of Things* (New York: Viking Press, 1974), pp245-250. For an interesting journalistic account of the politics of the 1967 March on the Pentagon, see Norman Mailer's *Armies of the Night*.

> the barrage of atrocities howling from the headlines. For the seasoned activist ... bitterness is tamped down, along with guilt and defiance, finally becoming force of habit. Protest turns into a way of life. A culture develops around it, a cluster of attitudes and behaviors that isolate the activist from 'ordinary people.'[116]

When "protest becomes a way of life," activists often lose touch with the deepest motivations that originally provoked them to act. Then — faction battles, movement monitors and idiotic adventurism aside — rallies begin to resemble our daily lives, which are not only lonely, oppressive and grueling, but where each day looks like the next, where a premium is put on predictability and time is finely measured. Perhaps that is too strong, but the tendency of these events toward routinization is very real.

In addition to the national reform organizations — single-issue peace groups and progressive politicians who exercise control over the mobilizations — a much wider spectrum of local activists is involved in organizing these events. Given current realities, these grassroots activists are preoccupied with defensive reform struggles on the job, at school, in their communities, or in some other political arena.

Correspondingly, most Marxist groupings have adopted a "boring from within" strategy, concentrating their efforts on exerting leadership within these institutional arenas and in traditional reform organizations. A natural corollary for Marx-

---

[116] "Beyond Playing Dead-Playing to Win" (leaflet). Shock Troupe, October 1983.

ists in this position is to mute controversial elements of their social lives, which might offend their intended constituency. Even with the strongest individuals, under the best circumstances, this pressure takes its toll. In times of quiescence, the tendency is to succumb to the mores of the hegemonic culture.

Reading the Bible Backwards

Sure I'm a Marxist —
A Groucho Marxist

An intent common to many creative forms of protest is to undermine some norm of everyday life by setting askew an advertisement, a wall, a product, a certain social expectation, with the goal of jolting the observer into new perception. This is reminiscent of the fabled methods of black magic cultists: summoning up the devil by reading "God's Word" backwards, or using religious articles or rituals in blasphemous combinations. While this method was given its most coherent formulation by the Situationist concept of "detournement," its widespread use in the '60s was rooted, not so much in a theory, but in a popular, rebellious mood. Indeed one could argue that this bent is derived more from childhood experience of popular cultural traditions of "offending the bourgeois," exemplified by the Three Stooges and the Marx Brothers, than from any theory.[117]

---

[117] See Franklin Rosemont, *Surrealism and Its Popular Accomplices* (San Francisco: City Lights, 1980). On situationism, see *Situationst Anthology,*

One morning in 1982, 30 people simultaneously boarded Bay Area Rapid Transit trains and posted instructions "In Case of Nuclear Attack." The posters were designed to fit over normal evacuation instructions. Its design used those lovable generic cookie cut-out people who are always seen on instructions and logos. But the instructions had the proper dosage of the morbid and the absurd to unsettle even the most naive viewer: for example, "Have Food and Water for Several Weeks of Isolation." The design was later picked up by *Workers Democracy* in St. Louis for a notice on PCB contamination.[118]

Graffiti, having become a popular art form on New York subway trains and the barrio walls of the Southwest, can be used to inflame a long-smouldering neighborhood issue. During the summer of 1983, a wall was painted beside a vacant lot, on a busy corner in San Francisco's Mission district. Out of red and orange leaping flames emerged the large, black letters: GARTLAND HOTEL FIRE 1975 12 DEAD LANDLORD ARSON. The deed was acclaimed in bilingual posted flyers titled: "This Is Not Vandalism — This is a Public Service."

Politically it refueled controversy over landlord and city complicity in the disaster and the property's future use. Then "the pit" became a graveyard with cardboard tombstones, and was lauded by the *Chronicle's* art critic. Finally the graffiti were

---

edited and translated by, Ken Knabb, Bureau of Pubic Secrets, Berkeley.

[118] BART poster reprinted in *Processed World,* summer 1983, p38. Dioxin poster in *Labor's Joke Book,* edited by Paul Buhle (WD Press, 1985), p58.

painted over, but activity at "the pit" continued: a candlelight vigil, and movie and slide showings on its walls. Later, even the black paint over the original graffiti was painted over in large red letters: ARSON FOR PROFIT. In a capitalist world of the eternal now, the graffiti engendered a sense of community memory.[119]

Street theater, a popular form of action in the '60s, and born again in the late '70s, has given rise to many new groupings. One of these was the Union of Concerned Commies (UCC), which specialized in using irony "to create an interference in the 'normal' rigid patterns of understanding."[120] During the Iranian hostage crisis, the UCC did a skit parodying ABC's "America Held Hostage" reports. A skit participant recounted: "A narrator describes a series of episodes depicting the captivity of 'James Workman, Hostage.' The action is simultaneously mimicked by performers and the effect is quite humorous. By the end of the skit it is obvious that what is being described is the daily life of the typical American working man." While not claiming that the audience was transformed by the skit, the performers suggest that "the next time they hear the same words or are faced with the images on TV, echoes of what they saw in the skit will come back to them. ... A space for critical

---

[119] *Community Murals,* Fall 1983, p27.
[120] Unpublished paper on UCC activity, July 1980, p9.

thought will have been created."[121]

A distinctive feature of the UCC's practice was its distribution of popularly written but substantial anti-capitalist statements based on the skits. Although formally disbanded in 1980, the group still occasionally mounts actions. Some of the UCC went on to publish *Processed World,* the "magazine with the bad attitude," which focuses on the high-tech office world and is filled with clever satire and commentaries. The Radical Humor Festival, held in New York in the spring of 1982, also contributed to this sensibility in the Left.[122]

Given this development, and the recent revival of the "new patriotism," it would seem inevitable that we would witness the emergence of the farcical demonstration. Thus, shortly after the invasion of Grenada in October 1983, an impromptu coalition launched a flotilla of boats into the San Francisco Bay in order to root out suspected Cuban terrorists on nearby Angel Island. While the terrorists eluded the invaders' grasp, the invaders did run into the news media, receiving some coverage. More recently, at the height of Reagan's re-election popularity, *Casa El Salvador-Farabundo Marti* initiated a Rally to Re-elect Reagan. Marchers snaked through the streets of downtown San Francisco in demonic Reagan masks, or dressed as their favorite war criminals.

---

[121] *Ibid.,* p10.

[122] *Processed World.* On the Radical Humor Festival, see *Cultural Correspondence* Number 2 (new series).

Chants followed the beat of a patriotic marching band: "*1-2-3-4 We* can't wait to go to war, *4-3-2-1* Nicaragua looks like fun!" Red, white and blue flyers were handed out offering a serious explanation for the mock event.

A similar sort of gallows humor led to the organization of the "End of the World's Fair" (held on the same day as the opening of the World's Fair in New Orleans in 1984). It drew 3000 participants for the day-long parade and festival, which turned out more like a punkish, multi-cultural Mardi Gras than the nihilist funeral that some of the Left expected. Floats included a "Prisoners of Daily Life" truck pulled forward by two "wage slaves" harnessed like horses, a Rube Goldberg-type "Amerikan Lobotomy Machine," as well as floats supporting the people of El Salvador and the Native Americans at Big Mountain, Arizona. Costumes ranged from someone outfitted in a giant computer disk labeled "very important senseless data," to a post-holocaust cockroach couple handing out play money. "'What are you symbolizing?'" a man asked as he passed the pair. "Nothing," said Gonsales (one of the roaches), adjusting her fur collar. 'We're into survival.'"[123] Rather than having a strict political focus, the Fair sought to further popularize an irreverent, anti-authoritarian cultural style with a direct action orientation.

As with a typical picket line or rally, the impact of such

---

[123] *San Francisco Examiner Chronicle,* 13 May 1984, p3.

events is hard to gauge. What is clear is that the *participants* in cultural actions find them enjoyable, energizing and even cathartic. This is of no small importance in a demoralized left where many profess feelings of boredom and futility when they attend actions. While some people may be put off by cultural actions, others are attracted to them who would never attend a standard event. This was certainly the case with the Fair.

This was also the experience of the Campaign for Nuclear Disarmament skit at San Francisco State University. In the spring of 1985 CND organized a multimedia art performance show and other theatrical activities instead of its previous focus on standard educationals and rallies. As a result, a new wave of people reinvigorated the group.

Another sign of a successful action is the ripple effect when others spontaneously perform a similar action. For example, the previously-mentioned funeral procession for Salvadoran death squad victims has been repeated in other cities. Women have attended events dressed as "mothers of the disappeared," carrying photos of actual *"desparecidos"* from El Salvador.

Obviously, some of these actions are more intelligent, better planned or more successful than others. They are all prey to the same political problems, misjudgments and mistakes made by organizers of more routine events. Since these actions are rarely done in conjunction with ongoing organizing, it is difficult to make a strictly empirical assessment of their effect. But again, can activists who specialize in petitioning, leafleting, picket lines, rallies and electioneering claim a better record in reaching new people and involving them?[124]

Community Roots

Popular festivals, rooted in the culture of a given area, can have a great effect on the appeal of the ritual processions described above. One major precedent for San Francisco has been Gay Freedom Day, commemorating the 1969 Stonewall riot, with its myriad forms of self-expression anathema to the homophobic world. It has partly been organized like a traditional political event with a set march and rally including established speakers and entertainment; but few will contest that the main event is the parade itself and not on the podium. The gay community in San Francisco has also adopted Halloween as its own, a night where fantasy becomes flesh and people shake off their normal social roles.

A similar modem tradition is the Latin-Caribbean "Carnaval," first celebrated in San Francisco in the mid-'70s, which has a liberatory, anti-racist cast that attracts tens of thousands every year not just to watch but to join in. It is no accident that the Mission Cultural Center, a progressive

---

[124] Those who see cultural actions as simply middle-class phenomena should refer to Steve Golin's essay on the pageant performed by the 1911 Paterson, N.J. textile works strikers, led by the IWW. (Steve Golin, "The Paterson Pageant: Success or Failure?," *Socialist Review,* Number 69, pp45-78.)

community arts center in the predominantly Latin Mission district, has been a major locus of activity for past Carnaval preparation. The MCC, along with *La Pena* in Berkeley (a cultural center organized by Chilean exiles and solidarity activists after Pinochet's coup in 1973) has been an important channel through which the political culture of Latino exiles has been diffused in the community through music, poetry, chants, dance, graphic arts and the community mural movement.

Colorful, dancing contingents in demonstrations led by a Caribbean drumbeat are one kind of synthesis of this influence. The funeral procession, modeled on funerals in El Salvador (for a brief period the only possible means of protest in that country) is another. Salvadoran refugees have also organized long group walks around Northern California, reminiscent of traditional Catholic pilgrimages, to dramatize their condition. Finally there is the homegrown urban youth sub-culture of second and third generation Latinos, of the *cholos* and low riders, which combines with '60s-derived Chicano nationalism at annual commemorations of the martyrs of the 1970 Chicano Moratorium. In sum, this development is different than the Vietnam period; the growth of a culture of resistance to U.S. imperialism is spreading into the US directly from the war zone.

Revolting Sub-Cultures and Direct Action

The shared values, rituals and language of a sub-culture

can often provide the foundation for a successful direct action (defined as a disruption or seizure of an institution, negating its authority). Such actions, commonly organized on the basis of affinity groups, are often able to express a "holistic" concept of opposition, linking the focal issue with a critique of capitalism, not just in rhetoric, *but in the very form of action*. Frequently, though, these same rituals, values and language can be a source of alienation to those participants who do not fit neatly into the sub-culture. This contradiction of empowerment versus alienation (or direct action versus education) is quite unavoidable. The trick is to grasp, in each phase of a mass movement, whether a given sub-culture stultifies or opens possibilities for mass direct action.

The genesis of the War Chest Tours, mentioned at the beginning of this article, is interesting in this respect. The Hall of Shame Tours, first sponsored by the Abalone Alliance on March 22, 1982, sought to publicize the role of corporate capital in the arms race and in nuclear power. "Tour guides" led crowds of "tourists" around downtown San Francisco, stopping at bank and corporate headquarters, where small groups performed skits or held forth, soapbox style, on the role of the particular institution in the nuclear industry. Flyers were handed out to bystanders and sometimes the "tourists" went into the buildings to confront corporate officers. A rally of a few thousand was held outside the headquarters of Bechtel and Pacific Gas and Electric, where there were more skits and a type of collective group dancing. The latter ritual manifested the influence of "new age" culture in the Abalone network. The ritual that was alienating for some was an act of political self-affirmation for others.

Much of the same "new age" culture, and a strong dose of Christian pacifism, was carried into the Livermore Action Group (LAG). By 1983, LAG had come to the forefront of the Bay Area direct action anti-nuclear movement. Thousands joined in LAG's blockades of the Livermore Labs, which required that participants pledge to obey a quite narrowly defined "nonviolence code," which had been adopted from the Abalone Alliance. The rigidly stationary, arrest-oriented mode of civil disobedience, which had been popularized as the only kind of direct action, became subject to criticism in the Bay Area movement for promoting the same kind of passive acceptance of authority as traditional reformism. This criticism inevitably included criticism of the "tofu politics" of new age sub-culture, particularly its middle-class bias.[125] But this critique, much of it raised by "sixties new leftists" uncomfortable with pacifism, was insufficient to create alternative tactics.

The turn towards a rowdier, more confrontational style

---

[125] For earlier critiques of 'tofu politics,' see *It's About Times,* January 1982 and June-July 1983.

of direct action can be traced to a second Hall of Shame Tour on October 24, 1983, when "peace punk" affinity groups did roving "die-ins" in intersections and corporate lobbies, catching the police off guard. Another tour was launched in the spring of 1984 on Tax Day, again with a "peace punk" flavor, with a hundred people listening to denunciations of corporate crimes and doing screaming die-ins in front of perplexed executives and office workers. Later that day they spread their innovative approach at a large demonstration protesting the visit of Henry Kissinger.[126] Following the Tour actions during the 1984 Democratic and Republican conventions, the tactic spread across the country, attracting a new constituency of white youth, typically relying on a freewheeling anarchism akin to that practiced in the larger movements in Italy, England and West Germany. These tactics were the original impetus for the "No Business As Usual" day of April 29, 1985 (although some might believe it was sparked by a flash of divine inspiration by Revolutionary Communist Party leader Bob Avakian).

The cohesion of the punk milieu allowed bolder, more active and participatory tactics to emerge (e.g. mobile blockades and avoidance of arrest), reinforcing the Left critique of traditional civil disobedience. Yet, as the tactics spread, their

---

[126] On the Hall of Shame Tour, see *It's About Times,* April 1982 p9. On later actions, (Oct. 24, 1983); Tax Day 1984; and the Conventions, see *Direct Action* (Livermore Action Group), September 1984.

sub-cultural origin limited their effectiveness. The confinement of outreach literature (if it was prepared at all) to the simple negativity of punk protest, the frequent lack of concern for dialogue with "straight" types and the impoverished organizing strategies among anarchists revealed the limits of a simplistic "direct action as *the* strategy" approach. By early 1985 it was clear that, despite its advance over new age pacifism, punk protest was not growing. Cracked skulls, jail time and endless legal procedures sapped the energy of these new activists, courageous though they were. Unfortunately, the older generation of revolutionary socialists was rarely able to establish a fruitful dialogue with the young rebels, which might have led to a transcendence of the punks' sub-cultural limits.

Mostly Vegetarian, Except When Devouring Men

The most significant wave of culturally-infused direct action may be, in the long run, feminist peace activism along the lines of the women's peace camp in Greenham Common in England. Writer and muralist Eva Cockroft has described the feminist approach as "creating a new feminist culture" amidst an action, where "a ritualistic structure at least momentarily unites a disparate group" by means of "emotional unity; discipline through rigid control of the types of behavior permitted; and the transformation of the

MissileDickChicks in NY. The troupe grew to 30 womyn in glam-fem wigs & bras (and those missiles!), gender-bending anti-capitalist songs and choreographed dances at anti-war protests and truck stops, en route to Crawford, TX.

every mundane into art."[127] The style here is the flip side of the punk, ironic forms of protest described above. The predominant political influence, at least in the US, would seem to be radical feminism, with its recollection of pre-modernist rituals which some find purifying but others find unconvincing in its unifying power.

---

[127] "Artist Activism in the '80s," *Cultural Correspondence* Number 3 (new series). This issue gives an interesting overview as a "Directory of Arts Activism". The latest issue is a how-to booklet on the art of demonstration.

The Women's Pentagon Action of November 1981 illustrates this well. The day before the action was devoted to communal preparations in a large hall. Women talked, sang, constructed props and tied together fabrics they had all brought with which to ring the Pentagon. The next day 3,500 women assembled and grouped around four large *papier mâché* puppets. The puppets symbolized the ritualized emotions enacted during the march: mourning, rage, empowerment and defiance. Some have spoken of the power of this ritual to "simultaneously reflect, reinforce and create a new personal and political consciousness."[128] Many women carried cardboard tombstones representing victims of male violence and planted them in front of the Pentagon. Some examples: "My mother. Died of an illegal abortion in 1964," and "Three unknown Vietnamese women. Killed by my son."[129] There were also more general ones, dedicated to the women of Chile and Northern Ireland. While the ritual unity did not hold once the civil disobedience began, there was an ending ceremony where bread was shared and seeds were planted.

Across the US, women have made tenacious efforts to set up ongoing peace camps at military and corporate facilities. They have attempted to balance the work of maintain-

---

[128] Rhoda Linton and Michele Whitham, "With Mourning, Rage, Empowerment and Defiance: The 1981 Women's Pentagon Action," *Socialist Review* Number 63-64, p13.

[129] *Ibid.* pp18-19.

ing a feminist community and upholding a high level of visibility and outreach. This basic model was followed at the Seneca Falls women's peace camp in the summer of 1983, with strict nonviolence, consensus decision-making and a feminist approach to internationalism and militarism. In rural Seneca Falls, this led to virulent lesbian-baiting and near-violent confrontations from the nearby small town residents. Eventually though, a significant minority of townspeople broke through the intimidation and established a positive dialogue with the campers.[130]

Yet the problem of sub-cultural politics, the codes of language, dress and behavior that repel the feminist from the punk from the new-ager (not to mention the "mainstream"), continues to divide the anti-war struggle. Hostility to the "mainstream" seems to breed a tendency in each subculture to rigidify its insights and habits into a narrow code or ideology. The women of Greenham Common seem to have gone beyond this dilemma. Without giving up their all-female camps, with all the profound questions of gender they provoke, they have coalesced into an open social movement, which acts like a magnet attracting almost all sectors of society who question the militarist order. Within such an atmosphere women and men of very different backgrounds

---

[130] Lois Hayes, "Separatism and Disobedience: The Seneca Women's Peace Encampment," *Radical America*, July-Aug 1983, pp55-64.

can meet face to face, beyond their respective ghettoes and the media's stereotypes. Thus the Greenham women sing to parody their media image as namby-pamby pacifists who are also fire-breathing feminists. "We're mostly vegetarian / except when devouring men."[131]

Demonstration as the Medium

It would be mistaken to see these creative forms of protest as mutually exclusive of the more traditional modes. They exist together, albeit in tension with one another. A march on Washington called by CISPES for November 12, 1983 is a good example of this. When a New York network called Ad/Hoc Artists pulled together to work on this action, they argued that "we were to be political organizers in the ongoing effort, not decorators. From the first meeting we began a discussion (with the other organizers) of the *form* of the demonstration."[132]

By organizing different "feeder demonstrations" at various federal buildings, they hoped to emphasize the interlocking issues of immigration, racial discrimination and intervention. By facilitating a participatory dance to a Latin drumbeat at one of the feeder sites, distributing a song sheet and setting up a "People's Monument" decorated by the

---

[131] Ann Snitow. "Holding the Line at Greenham," *Mother Jones*, Feb-Mar, 1985, p43.

[132] Charles Fredrick, "November 12th Anti-Intervention Demonstration: A Description of the Making of a Work of Art," *Cultural Correspondence,* Number 3, pp110-112.

demonstrators themselves, they sought to overcome the mass passivity of large protest marches.

One participant spoke of a "theoretical threshold in art making," which they had tried to surmount. In practice, of course, they fell short of their original goals. Aside from the typical foul-ups in organizing a mass event, the Ad/Hoc Artists were still working within a protest ritual that always ends up focusing on a central stage and major speakers. Most of the thousands of people who came to the event came expecting a "rally," not a participatory event. The habits of at least 20 years are not broken easily.

It appears that that "threshold" was breached even further by artist activists in the April 20th, 1985 rally in Washington, D.C. Four stages were set up (symbolizing the four demands of the multi-issue rally), on which poets, musicians, break dancers and theater groups played a major role. According to the *Guardian*, this "lent the event a participatory, festive air different from the more passive speech-listening of many demonstrations."[133]

Metaphor and Reality

Typically, the cultural actions described above seek to jolt the observer out of passivity by cracking the shell of "eternal" capitalist norms. The goal is to provoke people to

---

[133] *The Guardian*, 15 May 1985, p10.

see the normal as abnormal, the everyday as barbarian, and the unknown change as self-affirming and imminent in each human being. Yet there are definite limits to this approach, as one student of the subject has noted: "It is precisely the metaphorical nature of cultural images that makes them both powerful and confusing at the same time. Part of the power of art is that the observer participates in the process, creating something other than what the artist produced. But it is also in this arena that the specific intent of the artist can be lost. Metaphors are powerful, but they are exactly that: allusions to something else."[134]

The metaphorical images of a cultural action can only acquire meaning when they are associated with the observer's feelings and experiences. Surely most observers of these actions are too atomized, too caught up in the maze of appearances of capitalist daily life, or too distant in language and discourse from the cultural interventionists to make the connections outside their "mundane shell." On the other hand, cultural interventionists have often been quick to interpret an audience's indifference as proof of hopeless brainwashing. The logical endpoint of this view (of people as, mere dupes of ideology) is an elitist concept of social change. If we embrace instead the idea that working people possess, in a fragmentary and unarticulated form, human

---

[134] Lance Hill, unpublished correspondence.

potentials which prefigure the new society, then our cultural actions must aim to distinguish and clarify those precious emancipatory potentials, not just to lambaste the illusion and hypocrisy of capitalist ideology.

Whatever the approach, the problem remains that most observers' experience of these potentials is too meager and submerged for them to make the connections. This is the limitation of cultural action. Most people will only begin to think about a new society after circumstances force them to take collective direct action beyond the normal limits of bourgeois legality and rationality. As it is, neither cultural interventionists nor organizers adequately grasp the centrality of the experience of collective empowerment and individual subjectivity when it arises.

We Must Dream: Problems of the Marxist Left

The confusion of metaphor and reality is easily blurred in a time of weakened class struggle, and political strategy in this period can appear as irrelevant to many activists. This problem can be illustrated in a recent action at Greenham Common. One major activity of the Greenham women has been to violate the base's security as often as possible, to defy and harass the nuclear guardians. You may have seen a delightful photo taken at Greenham when a large group of women "invaded" the base and did a circle dance on a missile silo. Trespassing onto a nuclear equipped military base is, on one level, a real, not symbolic action. But on another level, it can be a very illusory victory, because we are still so far from having any power to stop that base and those missiles if the authorities want to use them. The governments must be disarmed in order to dispose of those weapons. The workers and soldiers who operate the military apparatus must be won over at some point, which in turn requires a mass movement that uproots the mass passivity of millions with a struggle for self-emancipation. What is the fastest way to get there? A strategy must be developed, and I believe Marxists have something to contribute here. As one stodgy, balding Bolshevik once said: we must dream.

But many Marxists have forgotten how to dream. Why? Well, revolutions are the high points of history, showing us the enormous potential of human creativity and endurance. That old Bolshevik was right again when he said that revolutions are festivals of the oppressed. But we don't seem to be at a high point of history in the US right now. For over a decade we seem to have been in the trough of history. This trough is more like a schoolroom of the oppressed, with a sadistic master of the Historical Present giving us whippings for exhibiting any reckless, visionary tendencies. Some of us of the ultra-left bent have engaged in frenzied activity with messianic fervor, before being jailed or burning out. Most of us partially adapt. Our activity becomes relatively stale. Not immune to the capitalist division of labor, we specialize, we are patient, we "relate to people where they are at."

Nurturing a culture of resistance is a necessary antidote to the "boring from within" dilemma we find ourselves in. But we also have long experience teaching us that there is no oasis of liberation within the universal marketplace. Creative action is life-giving because there is no solution to the routinization and falsification of radical politics without a permanent revolution of criticism and learning. And we cannot conduct this latter task without utilizing irony, humor, sorrow, rage, utopian flights of fantasy, linguistic open endedness and inventiveness of discourse, so as to avoid the tunnel vision and reabsorption of our work by the capitalist consciousness industry.[135]

Jeff Goldthorpe is a teacher and activist in Oakland, He was an organizer of San Francisco's End of the World Fair in 1984.

---

[135] Paraphrased from Louis Michaelson's unpublished paper "Notes From a Mutant," May 1983.

A Response to Chris Hedges

Violence, Tactics, and Revolutionary Strategy

by Mitchel Cohen

I was not going to comment further on Chris Hedges' widely published essay, "The Cancer in Occupy,"[136] concerning tactics for Occupy Oakland (and by extension Occupy Wall Street). In that article, Hedges condemned tactics he attributed to the Black Bloc at the January 28, 2012 "Move-In Day" march where, according to one of many similar reports,[137] Occupy Oakland unsuccessfully attempted to take over the long disused Henry J. Kaiser Convention Center with the intent of converting it into a community center. The peaceful protest of 2,000 was disrupted by police firing tear gas, smoke and pepper bombs into the crowd. It ended with police "kettling" marchers in a public park and in front of a YMCA. But Hedges appeared on May Day on Democracy Now! and renewed his condemnations without reflecting at all on what folks in Occupy had been saying to him, so I decided to publish this review.

---

[136] Chris Hedges, "The Cancer in Occupy," *TruthDig*, Feb. 6, 2012.

[137] "Occupy, Black Bloc & Liberal Pacifism: The Politics of Confrontation," *1917: Journal of the International Bolshevik Tendency*, May 2012.

Chris Hedges has and continues to make valuable and often blistering critiques of what he calls "corporate capitalism," and the role of both the Democratic and Republican parties in crushing civil liberties, enacting imperialist wars and ravaging the planet in the service of the 1 percent. He is an inspiring ally (and, strangely, "not a member," in his own words) of the Occupy Wall Street movement. But he has zero experience as part of a radical organization or even an affinity group, and it shows, especially when it comes to how to address differences of opinion and other concerns within a movement.

In fact, Hedges exhibits tremendous disdain for left movements that don't conform to his increasingly moralistic mold. His book, *Death of the Liberal Class,* "is one of the worst misreadings of history by an acclaimed writer on the Left that I've ever seen," says Brian Tokar, a veteran participant in numerous direct action campaigns and also a professor at the Institute for Social Ecology and of environmental studies at the University of Vermont. "Hedges honestly believes that the New Left accomplished almost nothing, except for some key figures he likes, such as Howard Zinn and the Berrigans."

In *Death of the Liberal Class,* Hedges (incredibly, to me) condemns the New Left for having "no political vision. Herman Hesse's *Siddhartha,* with its narrator's search for enlightenment, became emblematic of the moral hollowness of the New Left." And he continues:

> Protest in the 1960s found its ideological roots in the disengagement championed earlier by Beats such [as] by Jack Kerouac, Allen Ginsberg, and William Borroughs. It was a movement that, while it incorporated a healthy dose of disrespect for authority, focused again on self-indulgent schemes for inner peace and fulfillment. ... These movements, and the counterculture celebrities that led them such as the Yippie leader Abbie Hoffman, sought and catered to the stage set for them by the television cameras. Protest and court trials became street theater. Dissent became another media spectacle. Anti-war protesters in Berkeley switched from singing "Solidarity Forever" to "Yellow Submarine." [138]

Even if the New Left *had* focused on achieving inner peace and fulfillment, what would be wrong with that? But at any rate Hedges is just wrong; he misses completely the numerous contributions by participants in anti-war, Women's, Black & Gay liberation, cultural, social justice and ecological movements of the last 50 years; he somehow also misses the free breakfast programs, clinics, community institutions and other forms of what we called "dual power strategies for revolutionary societal transformation" built by key sectors of the supposedly "self-indulgent" New Left (many of those projects crushed or co-opted by the State).

What Hedges chastizes as "self-indulgent" the New Left

---

[138] Chris Hedges, *Death of the Liberal Class*, Nation Books: 2010. pp110-111.

characterized as *alienation* from all aspects of capitalist society. That alienation that so marked the New Left is invisible in Hedges' critique. Hedges turns the '60s generation's struggle against one's own oppression into, in his view, a contemptible and immoral rejection of self-sacrifice on behalf of "others":

> The civil-rights movement, which was rooted in the moral and religious imperatives of justice and self-sacrifice, what Dwight Macdonald called nonhistorical values, was largely eclipsed by the self-centeredness of the New Left, especially after the assassinations of Malcolm X in 1967 [*sic* — Malcolm was killed on February 21, 1965, not '67 – MC] and Martin Luther King Jr. a year later. And once the Vietnam War ended, once middle-class men no longer had to go to war, the movement disintegrated. The political and moral void within the counterculture meant it was an easy transition from college radical to a member of the liberal class.[139]

Many did sacrifice for others and for principles of social justice. But that portrait of martyrdom is all Hedges desires in viewing his snapshots of the New Left movements of the 1960s and '70s. He echoes the false duality of "altruism" vs. "self-interest" as the two antagonistic threads of social behavior, which is the mainstay of liberal social-psychology, a false duality that critical theorists on the Left and in the Women's Liberation Movement scathingly rejected. ("The personal is political" was just one of the key synopses of

---

[139] *Ibid.*

those movements.)

Hedges is at best confused. He reduces the complexities of human actions and motivations to simplistic "either/or" categories. You either give up yourself in the fight for "others" (altruism) or you're a selfish, immoral narcissist (or worse!). Thus, the civil rights, trade union and antiwar movements are powerfully attractive to Hedges largely because they were rooted, he imagines, in Christ-like self-sacrifice. But that kind of historical summary borders on the pathological. It's as though Black people trying to register to vote; farmworkers trying to organize into a union; Vietnamese fighting against their country being bombed and their countryside poisoned had no self-interest in those movements, and for Hedges there'd be something wrong with them if they did. Hedges sits atop his judgmental throne unable to deal with the fact that huge numbers of people were seeking *not* to sacrifice their lives but to *improve* them, by participating in movements that would also improve the lot of everyone else. In fact, he offers such a cartoonish one-dimensional portrayal of the New Left and of what motivated its participants, that those who chose to fight for their own liberation as well as for others become, in his flawed framework, betrayers of the dream. Hedges' martyr-filled conception of history distorts his understanding; his becomes the umbrage of the "sectarian betrayed."

Hedges' misreading of the history of social movements in the U.S. frames his conception of Occupy Wall Street — at least in his writings under review here — from which grow his proposals for effecting societal transformation. Here, for instance, is how he sees what he calls the "failure" of the Black Panthers and other groups:

> The Black Panthers, the Nation of Islam, and the Weather Underground Organization, severed from the daily concerns of the working class, became as infected with the lust for violence, quest for ideological purity, crippling paranoia, self-exaltation, and internal repression as the state apparatus they defied.[140]

"Lust for violence?" Here, as elsewhere, Hedges — the fine reporter in the context of the *New York Times* — morphs into a terrible historian of social movements. He equates the State's repression — two million human beings murdered outright in Vietnam, 20-30 Panthers assassinated here at home, the earth held hostage — with windows broken by some protesters! The sheer magnitude of the daily horror was something that militant pacifist Dave Dellinger, who was (unlike Hedges) a strong supporter of the Black Panther Party, always distinguished from frustrated people's sometimes trivial or pointless venting. Had he bothered to put his reportorial skills to work and actually interview activists who were part of organizations engaged in what

---

[140] *Ibid.* p110.

Hedges would call mindless "violence", he might have learned that far from a "lust for violence", most leftists involved in property damage were very circumspect about their actions and took pains to ensure that no people were injured thereby. (In transforming himself from a *NY Times* reporter to a commentator of radical movements, the lack of first-hand interviewing is a recurring problem in Hedges' work.) While no one involved in those organizations would claim that they had overcome their serious problems and internal contradictions — contradictions within Left strategy and non-violent theory and practice that Dellinger, for one, never stopped exploring and was always trying to resolve — Hedges issues such blanket (and smug) dismissals, denouncing groups that do not tow his line, substituting his own goals for what the groups themselves say they are trying to accomplish, and basing it all on sweeping (and wrong) generalizations concerning U.S. history, that one has no choice but to question his *honesty* as he rewrites history to draw from it the "lessons" he has apparently already decided to promulgate.[141]

> Radical violent groups cling like parasites to popular protests. The Black Panthers, the American Indi-

---

[141] There are dozens of excellent and readily available writings that examine the contributions as well as the contradictions of those organizations in detail, and for Hedges — an experienced journalist — to have missed all of that in his research on the New Left makes the entirety of his historical analysis untrustworthy. For starters, see Mitchel Cohen, *Those Not Busy Born are Busy Dying*, a Red Balloon Collective pamphlet in the *Zen-Marxism* series.

> an Movement, the Weather Underground, the Red Brigades and the Symbionese Liberation Army arose in the ferment of the 1960s. Violent radicals are used by the state to justify harsh repression. They scare the mainstream from the movement. They thwart the goal of all revolutions, which is to turn the majority against an isolated and discredited ruling class.[142]

Here Hedges skews the history of the groups he mentions, especially the Black Panther Party. He blames the trivial violence of some radical groups for the harsh repressive measures of the State, as though the extremely violent measures the capitalist state employs are in response to the minimal property damage caused by radical organizations and not the system's need to police its everyday thievery of labor and resources globally. Hedges himself has taken courageous stands against the new and I dare say "fascist" legislation of the Bush and Obama administrations. Why then is he unable to see state violence for what it is: the norm perpetrated by the State in the course of its daily functioning? What "violence" by social activists in the U.S. "provoked" Obama to deploy drones to target individuals for assassination at the President's personal edict? What leftist violence prompted legislation granting the State authority to arrest and indefinitely detain U.S. citizens, as authorized in the National Defense Authorization Act strongly pushed by President Obama?

---

[142] "Why the Occupy Movement Frightens the Corporate Elite," *op cit.*

In fact, NDAA's co-sponsor, Senator Carl Levin (a Democrat), reported that it was the Obama administration, not the Republicans, that demanded removal from the bill language that would have at least protected American citizens from being subject to indefinite detention — not that anyone should be subjected to such Nazi-like roundups without trial.

"The language which precluded the application of Section 1031 to American citizens was in the bill that we originally approved ... and the administration asked us to remove the language which says that U.S. citizens and lawful residents would not be subject to this section," Levin said.

Levin, who Chairs the Armed Services Committee, continued: "It was the administration that asked us to remove the very language which we had in the bill which passed the committee ... we removed it at the request of the administration," said Levin, emphasizing, "It was the administration which asked us to remove the very language the absence of which is now objected to."

No "violent leftist groups" were needed for the State to take such measures, as I'm sure Chris Hedges knows. So why is his analysis of Occupy Wall Street and the Left such a muddle?

Hedges' invention of an intervening liberal class

Hedges pulls no punches in excoriating the behavior of liberals today (and I agree with him there), but because he never gets to the root of liberalism as the ideology of U.S. capitalism in its decades of global expansion (now at an end) he ends up unable to explain the roots of its collapse and its ramifications. And so, he invents a non-existent liberal "class" (the same sector he rips into elsewhere) and expects its members to take up the revolution's cause.

> The real danger to the elite comes from déclassé intellectuals, those educated middle-class men and women who are barred by a calcified system from advancement. Artists without studios or theaters, teachers without classrooms, lawyers without clients, doctors without patients and journalists without newspapers descend economically. They become, as they mingle with the underclass, a bridge between the worlds of the elite and the oppressed. And they are the dynamite that triggers revolt.[143]

Hedges offers here a pale shadow of V.I. Lenin's early argument (later modified) in *What Is To Be Done?*, where Lenin posits the need for a "third party" made up of professional revolutionaries drawn primarily from the intelligentsia, to bring socialist consciousness into the working class movement that could not on its own develop a socialist consciousness.[144] For Marx and Engels, on the other hand, consciousness is not some state of individual enlightenment to be at-

---

[143] Chris Hedges, "Why the Occupy Movement Frightens the Corporate Elite," *TruthDig*, May 14, 2012.

[144] Mitchel Cohen, *The Shortcomings of Traditional Leftist Strategy*, Zen-Marxism #7, Red Balloon pamphlet series.

tained from outside workers' struggles as a class but is *part of an objective process inherent in, bound up with and emerging from those struggles.* For Hedges, as with the early (and mistaken) V.I. Lenin, consciousness come from elsewhere.[145]

Hedges posits a "liberal class" as that "somewhere else." But he does so glibly, using terminology that doesn't take into account the centuries of thought and political/philosophical stances that came before, which make up the history of the argument that Hedges now joins. In his book, *Death of the Liberal Class*, he offers the proposition that progressive changes have historically occurred when a sector of the U.S. intelligentsia — which he incorrectly assigns to be a "class" separate from both the working class and the rulers — took up certain programs and forced society to adopt them. He blames the liberal class' demise on its failure to become more radical. His goal, thus, is to radicalize it in order to save it. To achieve a radicalization of the "Liberal Class" and not alienate its members, Hedges proposes that

---

[145] "What is class class consciousness and where does it come from?" was (and remains) a fundamental question for the New Left. Hedges *assumes* a certain "of course-ness" to how he answers it, reflecting his lack of familiarity with the perhaps unexpected historical as well as philosophical intricacies of that question. For some discussion of this, see Mitchel Cohen, *Zen-Marxism 9: Out in Front of a Dozen Dead Oceans — Some theoretical and philosophical advances of the new left,* and *Zen-Marxism 7: The Shortcomings of Traditional Leftist Strategy,* both published as booklets by the Red Balloon Collective. Also, see Georg Lucás, *History and Class Consciousness,* and, Wilhelm Reich, *What is Class Consciousness?,* in *Sex-Pol.*

Occupy adopt a strategy of nonviolent civil disobedience. But he errs in assuming (or hoping) that radicalizing or even reaching out to the "Liberal Class" is Occupy's goal. It's not.

Therein lies the first disconnect. Hedges ends up hoping to achieve one set of goals for a movement he specifies he's not part of (thank you very much!), while much of the Occupy movement does not accept that such a "liberal class" exists, let alone that Occupy is or should formulate tactics in order to influence it. Occupy is working towards different goals that require different and even antithetical strategies and tactics.

That disconnect underlies Hedges' royal denunciation of the black bloc sector within the Occupy movement. He fears that by engaging in window-breaking and other forms of property destruction, the Black Bloc undermines the moral suasion of symbolic civil disobedience on the "liberal class," which, says Hedges, is the motor for social change.

Was there ever a "liberal 'class' "?

Is it true that, as Hedges argues, up until World War I there was a liberal "class" in the U.S. that served as an effective and powerful advocate for social movements, and that after World War I that model abruptly unraveled? Hedges fails to offer substantive analysis of the interaction between liberal advocates and the rise and fall of the working class (and other radical movements) in those periods.[146] While there were certainly influential public intellectuals who denounced capitalist conditions and supported radical movements, at no time was liberalism a positive "intervention" by a *class* of individuals (as defined by their categorical relationship to the relations of production and reproduction) on behalf of social movements. Nevertheless, Hedges views it as essential to win over liberals who do not participate, but who are potentially sympathetic and influential, and who — as the primary agents of social change — would then presumably take on the demands of the 99 percent, just as (according to Hedges) they had done in the past, had they not been driven away by the militancy of protesters:

> The danger the corporate state faces does not come from the poor. The poor, those Karl Marx dismissed as the Lumpenproletariat, do not mount revolutions, although they join them and often become cannon fodder. ... In every revolutionary movement I covered in Latin America, Africa and the Middle East, the leadership emerged from déclassé intellectuals. The leaders were usually young or middle-aged, educated and always unable to meet their professional and personal aspirations. They were never part of the power elite, although often their parents had been. They were conversant in the language of power as well as the language of oppression. It is the

---

[146] See, for example, Meredith Tax, *The Rising of the Women,* which details the interaction between mostly desperate immigrant garment workers organizing into unions at the turn of the 20th century and the upper class women in the suffragette movement.

> presence of large numbers of déclassé intellectuals that makes the uprisings in Spain, Egypt, Greece and finally the United States threatening to the overlords at Goldman Sachs, ExxonMobil and JPMorgan Chase. They must face down opponents who understand, in a way the uneducated often do not, the lies disseminated on behalf of corporations by the public relations industry. These déclassé intellectuals, because they are conversant in economics and political theory, grasp that those who hold power, real power, are not the elected mandarins in Washington but the criminal class on Wall Street.[147]

But while liberal leadership may emerge from among déclassé intellectuals who constitute, for Hedges, "the real danger to the elite" (and that raises the question of how can they act as a "class" if they are "déclassé") — and please forgive me the repetition here — liberalism was *never* the province of a separate class, let alone one that interceded in the U.S. (positive or otherwise); rather, *it was the ideology of the dominant arm of the U.S. ruling class itself during capitalism's long period of expansion.* Whether a liberal sector of civil society interceded with the state on behalf of the working class (as Hedges argues) or whether liberal rearrangement of the workplace and related social policies were promulgated by the ruling class itself as a matter of its own economic class interest, is *not* a distinction without a difference. The institutions resulting from what Hedges sees as proof of historical

---

[147] "Why the Occupy Movement Frightens the Corporate Elite," *op cit.*

"progress" in actuality were put into place to *curtail* radical influence and *manage* working class rebellions, not assist them.[148] Issues like an end to racial slavery, the legalization of trade unions, and recognition of women's and Black people's right to vote were won by militant mass movements during which workers took *direct action*, even where they led to alienating intellectuals and capitalists.[149] The 1917 Russian revolution — which no doubt alienated *many* — was also hugely inspiring to working class struggles everywhere. By the mid-1930s, workers occupied Ford and General Motors factories in Flint, Michigan, and were threatening to overturn the whole capitalist applecart.

The Roosevelt administration saved capitalism, by (in part) granting workers the right to legally unionize. That was a tremendous victory for workers everywhere. But over time it turned out to be a mixed blessing. The 1935 National Labor Relations Act and other federal laws allowed workers, for the first time, legal recognition to negotiate with their employers over a narrow range of areas, but only in exchange

---

[148] See Silvia Federici, *Caliban and the Witch,* for an examination of the function of capitalism in thwarting radical social movements via "managing" them, going all the way back to the transition from feudalism to capitalism.

[149] Joy James, in *Transcending the Talented Tenth: Black Leaders and American Intellectuals,* examines the history of the anti-lynching movement and its prominent leader, Ida B. Wells, when faced with the possibility of alienating other Black leaders. Similar contradictions erupted in the anti-slavery movement when women demanded their rights as well, leading up to Sojourner Truth's historic speech, "Ain't I a Woman"?

for accepting the legitimacy of the factory form of production, against which, historically, there had been massive struggles. The organized working class was required to recognize and accept the boundaries circumscribed in the new social compact, particularly the alleged "right" of capitalists to fully own the product of the day's labor and to dispense it in any way they wished — a "right" taken for granted today but over which huge battles had been and would continue to be fought, before capitalism finally gained widespread acceptance in the 1950s of its full privatization of the labor product.

The liberal industrial and banking sector of the bourgeoisie, represented politically by Franklin Roosevelt in the 1930s and early 1940s, desperately needed the support of the working class to defeat the policies of other capitalist sectors and consolidate its hegemony over them. This battle between competing capitalist sectors had been going on for many years — each had their own way of organizing production, requiring different and often contradictory mechanisms of control and social policies. Roosevelt, on behalf of industrial and banking capital, took control of the mechanisms of the state, with the help of organized labor and avowedly Communist organizations singing the praises of the new liberal ideology.

The New Deal succeeded in salvaging capitalism by completing a process that had begun in the early 1900s with the Rockefeller-assisted ascension of the American Federation of Labor, which — with the consequent defeat of the radical Knights of Labor, Western Federation of Miners, and Industrial Workers of the World — codified certain union forms and stamped them with official state approval at the expense of other far more radical working class organizations, which allowed industrial capital, oil and high finance to gain hegemony over competing capitalist sectors.

To the extent that the liberal ideology began seeping into the ideological pores of the system, it helped forge a national consensus behind the socio-economic approach of the most advanced wing of capital. A new "labor-management partnership" (discussed below, in the paragraphs pertaining to the Hawthorne studies) provided Roosevelt with the "scientific" rationale he needed to legalize unions (under narrow conditions) and generate an alliance with them, enabling industrial and banking capital to wrest control of the federal state apparatus away from other competing sectors while systematizing production, investment and the flow of profits. In a sense, legalizing the right of workers to organize within well-defined boundaries co-opted working class struggles and upheld only those forms that were more amenable to the long-term interests of capital. Today, we call such legitimated working class formations "corporate unions." Most Marxists and other socialists have expended immense energy defending workers' struggles over the length of their chains, and no longer over the existence of the chain itself.

American History Belies Hedges' Claim

In actuality, what today we consider to be liberal "victories" came about in the period of expansionary U.S. capitalism, a result of the most advanced sector of U.S. capital fighting in its own self-interest against more backward sectors, and not as a result of the interventions of a separate liberal class standing outside of the interests of corporate capitalism.

Even the Civil War (and this is half-a-century earlier than the periods Hedges refers to) was fought essentially to provide cheap labor for expanding industrial capitalism vs. the expense to rural agriculture of maintaining a slave labor system. Already in his famous treatise, *Wealth of Nations* (1776), Adam Smith had shown that slavery had become more expensive for the owner than wage labor. Whatever the indisputable moral imperative in the fight to abolish chattel slavery, eventually the freeing of the slaves served the interests of industrial capital. Freed slaves bolstered the Union's depleted forces and then joined the burgeoning industrial workforce, where they were used to drive down wages. My point is that even in cases where such a stark moral imperative for social justice captured the imaginations and consciousness of much of humanity, capital's economic imperatives were dominant, and not the other way around.

Such was the case, too, when a few decades later the Workers' Compensation board was established. This new arrangement grew out of the fight between different sectors of capital with competing interests, not working class demands. The owners of giant factories, refineries, railroads and mines needed to systematize the increasing payouts to workers for their many injuries as a result of the new machinery;[150] in fact, no working class organizer except the bought-off Samuel Gompers had been demanding such a "reform". It is a serious error for us today to claim such a policy as "a victory" for the working class (it wasn't). The ideological battles fought out within the ruling class had little to do with the needs of workers or other radicals, but were propagandized in time-honored fashion to win large sectors of the working class do the bidding of one or another faction of capital. Famed robber baron and multi-millionaire power-broker Jay Gould (not to be confused with the wonderful science essayist Stephen Jay Gould a century later) bragged in the late 1800s: "I can hire one-half of the working class to kill the other half."

In the early 1900s Frederick Taylor introduced his Time-and-Motion studies into industry and examined the fragmentary repetitive motions of the industrial labor process with the aim of increasing output and efficiency by subdivid-

---

[150] James Weinstein, *The Corporate Ideal & the Liberal State: 1900-1918*, Beacon:1968.

ing each task and reducing each worker's movements as much as possible to mimic the mechanical motions of a machine.[151] One of the corporations adopting such methods was Western Electric, which had just built a huge factory in Hawthorne, Illinois. Workers there and elsewhere organized against the terrible conditions, culminating in new forms of rebellion at Hawthorne and by the mid-1930s brazen sit-down occupations of auto plants in Michigan and Ohio.

Western Electric commissioned a series of experiments that became known as the Hawthorne studies, to see if it was possible to offset workplace tensions and thereby lessen rebellions affecting capital's bottom line by instituting more sophisticated industrial managerial techniques — which they called "progress" and "liberalization" of the workplace. At no point did "progress" at Hawthorne entail altering the basic class relations of ownership and control of capital.

The Hawthorne studies propagated the myth that workers and bosses shared in the good fortunes of the company.[152] The emergent new "science" of the industrial labor

---

[151] Even V.I. Lenin enthused over this new "scientific approach" to the production process.

[152] This was a bit difficult to do, as no one at the time could forget the 1915 disaster — one of the worst accidents in Chicago history — when the *Eastland*, a vessel filled with Western Electric/ Hawthorne employees and their family members attending the company's annual outing, capsized at its dock in the Chicago River, killing more than 800 people. See also Robert Tressell's novel, *The Ragged Trousered Philanthropists*, which dispels the myth of "we're all in this together."

process propagated this liberal ideology. It averred that the capitalist relations of production, exploitation, and the factory form were good for worker and capitalist alike.[153]

Class harmony over allegedly common interests (within capitalism), said Mayo and Roethlisberger — the chief Hawthorne researchers — must replace class struggle over exploitation. Liberal management techniques were designed to foster that illusion; they soon congealed into a new dominant paradigm — that of the "partnership" between labor and capital — which offered a "democratic" framework for intensifying exploitation and profit. All of this was, once again, not the positive result of working class organizing nor intervention by a liberal class (as Hedges would have it), but of the most advanced sector of capital pursuing its own self-interest.

It was essential, from the point of view of an expanding U.S.-based industrial capital, that all resistance to exploitation be framed as an *individual* problem. This enabled capital to isolate and co-opt workers' sense of meaninglessness and anger which rose from their increasingly Chaplinesque robot-like work, before it could erupt into systematic and organized hatred of the ruling class. The Hawthorne studies' misinterpretation and false portrayal of data filled that important *ideological* function. It helped to rationalize a

---

[153] See Mitchel Cohen, *Big Science, the Fragmenting of Work & the Left's Curious Notion of Progress, Zen-Marxism #10,* Red Balloon Books: 1997.

vile exploitative system, laying the ideological basis for the corporate liberalism — which included the cooptation of industrial unions — in the years to follow.[154]

But today, as the production base in the U.S. declines and neoliberalism's "structural adjustment plans" and massive working class debt have become the norm, there is hardly room to win reforms within the disintegrating framework of the liberal expansive capitalism that used-to-be. The bright side, if we can call it that, is that as unions come under attack with such officials as Republican Vice Presidential candidate Paul Ryan and Wisconsin Governor Scott Walker threatening their legal right to exist, more and more unions are recognizing that they are less and less bound by the restrictions of that 1935 social compact, and new possibilities open up. In fact, a number of unions have mobilized their members in solidarity with Occupy Wall Street and other social movements, and are even probing, however gingerly, the possibility of raising environmental, anti-war and other social policy issues for the first time.[155]

Getting from Here to There?

Earlier, I quoted Chris Hedges as follows: "[Groups engaging in violence] thwart the goal of all revolutions, which

---

[154] *Ibid.*

[155] I discuss much of the new openings for unions in my book, *What Is Direct Action?*

is to turn the majority against an isolated and discredited ruling class," and argued that Hedges was wrong historically in portraying the Black Panthers or the occasional (and insignificant) property damage done by the Black Bloc as "violent" and discrediting to those movements — especially in contrast to the overwhelming (and often hidden) violence that defines the everyday norm under capitalism and imperialism. But there is something else about Hedges' statement I'd now like to discuss.

Is it true that "turn[ing] the majority against an isolated and discredited ruling class" is the primary "goal of all revolutions" at all stages in their development? If so — and let me for the sake of argument allow Hedges his assertion without challenge for the moment — what mechanism does he propose to enable the economic and social unease of the majority to congeal into actual revolution? How is that mechanism created, and by whom? How does Hedges understand that process? He writes:

> Acts of resistance are moral acts. They take place because people of conscience understand the moral, rather than the practical, imperative of rebellion. They should be carried out not because they are effective, but because they are right. ... [They are] the supreme act of faith, the highest form of spirituality ... [that] cannot be measured by its utilitarian effect.[156]

---

[156] *Death of the Liberal Class,* p205.

Well, *perhaps*, but that just begs the question: "What must the so-called 'liberal class' actually *do* to replace the system?"

Hedges is infuriatingly vague about this. How does one get to be in a position to even address questions about revolutionary process — by proving one's moral commitment to self-sacrifice? That's certainly not evident in the history of revolutionary movements in this or any century. Are civil disobedient actions able to flip the conscience of those in power against their own class interests, or at least their agents of repression *en masse*, as Hedges believes? As someone who has participated and been arrested in many civil disobedience actions, I view CD as a symbolic tactic that is obviously useful in many circumstances and at certain stages — especially for calling public attention to particular inequities — but of and by itself it is not and has never been a vehicle through which systemic change in the United States takes place.

There is thus a 2nd disconnect, this time not only between Hedges' goals and those of the Occupy movement, but between the tactics Hedges promotes and the goals he wants them to achieve. And what to learn from those who actually succeeded in building revolutions? Undaunted, Hedges here continues his sweeping moralistic claims. He writes:

> These violent fringe groups are seductive to those who yearn for personal empowerment through hyper-masculinity and violence, but they do little to ad-

vance the cause. The primary role of radical extremists, such as Maximilien Robespierre and Vladimir Lenin, is to hijack successful revolutions. They unleash a reign of terror, primarily against fellow revolutionaries, which often outdoes the repression of the old regime. They often do not play much of a role in building a revolution.[157]

Neither Robespierre nor Lenin "hijack[ed] successful revolutions ... [and did] not play much of a role in building a revolution." Whatever you think of the outcome, they were both instrumental in *making* those revolutions. But Hedges' falsified history and simply appalling judgment lead him to proffer ineffective and disempowering strategies and tactics for Occupy today. In fact, the closest he comes to providing a potentially helpful overview of the revolutionary process is in his essay *Why the Occupy Movement Frightens the Corporate Elite*:

> The end of these regimes comes when old beliefs die and the organs of security, especially the police and military, abandon the elites and join the revolutionaries. This is true in every successful revolution. It does not matter how sophisticated the repressive apparatus. Once those who handle the tools of repression become demoralized, the security and surveillance state is impotent. Regimes, when they die, are like a great ocean liner sinking in minutes on the horizon. And no one, including the purported leaders of the opposition, can predict the moment of death. Revolutions have an innate, mysterious life force that defies comprehension. They are living entities.

---

[157] "Why the Occupy Movement Frightens the Corporate Elite," *op cit.*

Yes, revolutions are indeed living entities. And yes, large sectors of the military and repressive apparatus must come over to the revolution if it is to succeed, or at least refuse to follow orders. But instead of learning from such masterful works as Karl Marx's *The 18th Brumaire of Louis Bonaparte* and *The Civil War In France,* Hedges throws up his hands and declares that the revolutionary process "defies comprehension", abandoning any hope for understanding what one needs to do to help nurture revolutionary movements, and leading him to make destructive errors.

A Question of "Violence"

In "The Cancer in Occupy," Hedges equates the codewords "property damage" and "violence," and then blames the black bloc for all random acts of property damage. This is simply wrong, as:

a) like it or not, damaging corporate property is not the same as violence against people and other living beings, and should not invoke the same vituperative response;

b) members of the black bloc *do not* generally engage in random acts of property damage; and,

c) much of the property damage is done by cops wearing masks and posing as protesters, especially to Occupy-friendly local businesses (which *is* a legitimate concern that Hedges raises).

To me, this latter is the most serious and legitimate concern, and the black bloc *does* need to take responsibility for examining ways of preventing police agents in sheep's clothing from wrecking the movement.[158] But why assume that it is not doing so? (I've talked with many black bloc members who are concerned about that. There are many ways to root out, expose or contain police agents in our midst.) Hedges' public denunciation of all of those involved in some form of militant tactic is not constructive criticism.

In fact, Hedges calls on the Occupy movement to *purge* the relatively few individuals engaging in minimal property damage (such as breaking a few windows), going so far as to label them the "cancer of the occupy movement." (We all know what the western prescription for "cancer" is, I reckon. It's not homeopathy.) And for what grievous act are we to spend endless months debating how to set up committees of public safety to police our own movement? A kid who throws a soda can against a window? An occasional individual who spraypaints graffiti on a friendly business? Even if one disagrees with or deplores such actions, does that make it okay to wreck a kid's life by turning her over to the police (as a few folks did at the anti-World Trade Organization protests in Seattle, 1999) or purging her from the Occupy movement? Where's the morality (let alone the "non-violence") in

---

[158] See Brian Glick, *War at Home*, South End Press.

that? Think of the time and energy it would take to argue over and set up mechanisms for purges. Couldn't it be spent more productively and compassionately? Hasn't the Left been down that road before?

Our movements need to clarify the distinction between property destruction and physical violence against people — a distinction Hedges strangely fails to make; we should not use the same word "violence" for both. Had Hedges written about the futility of breaking a window here or there during a march as a tactical issue (as opposed to making it a question of morality) and brought it up for discussion within Occupy, surely I and most others would have agreed with him that the vandalism was counterproductive (depending on the target, timing and circumstances), although I wouldn't have thought it to be that big a deal. But Hedges turned his annoyance into a crusade and fed the mainstream media's frenzy to tar Occupy, especially those in the black bloc who generally do good work and don't engage in the random vandalism — let alone "violence" — that Hedges is attributing to them.

Strangely, Hedges deplores the property damage in Oakland but applauds the far greater property damage engaged in by rioting and often-masked comrades in Greece (his May 2010 article in *TruthDig* praising rioters in Greece is accompanied by a photograph of fires raging):

> Here's to the Greeks. They know what to do when

corporations pillage and loot their country. They know what to do when Goldman Sachs and international bankers collude with their power elite to falsify economic data and then make billions betting that the Greek economy will collapse. They know what to do when they are told their pensions, benefits and jobs have to be cut to pay corporate banks, which screwed them in the first place. Call a general strike. Riot. Shut down the city centers. Toss the bastards out. Do not be afraid of the language of class warfare — the rich versus the poor, the oligarchs versus the citizens, the capitalists versus the proletariat. The Greeks, unlike most of us, get it. ... Barack Obama is simply the latest face that masks the corporate state. His administration serves corporate interests, not ours.[159]

Wow. Exactly right in terms of understanding that Obama "is simply the latest face that masks the corporate state." But not so fast, Chris Hedges, with the rest of it! Class consciousness entails identifying Goldman Sachs and the international bankers as *part of* the enemy, which is the *system* of capitalism based, as it is, on the exploitation of the labor of the 99 percent, production of commodities for private profit, the pillaging of Nature and private accumulation of resources — and control of the state apparatus to ensure the system's ongoing authority. It is only when participants identify the source of the problems we face that we can take measures to prevent capitalism from reproducing itself through our own actions, social relations and commentaries.

---

[159] Chris Hedges, "The Greeks Get It," *TruthDig,* May 24, 2010.

The Dangers in *not* Naming the System

In Greece, there is an increasingly organized and growing fascist movement participating in the anti-austerity strikes, riots, occupations and shut-downs alongside their arch-enemy: the socialist, anarchist and communist Left.[160] Hedges makes the mistake of praising the rebellions in Greece and Egypt while scolding activists in the U.S. who damage corporate property, calling them a "cancer" that must be extirpated. Hedges, who lived for several years in Egypt and reported on events there for the *New York Times,* has praised the armed bodyguards that accompanied him there and in some of the world's other hot spots. It was only their training in violence, and their machine guns, that protected him and allowed him to write his articles. He does make a point that he is not a pacifist, and in fairness he does makes the important distinction between the use of violence for individual self defense and "violence" as the prevailing theme for a social movement. But he fails to consider that, compared with Greece, there has been virtually no violence *against people* perpetrated by the Occupy movement.

Writing from Cyprus, Petros Evdokas explores the on-the-ground manifestations such confusion leads to, in a more des-

---

[160] George Caffentzis, *Greek Diary,* August 2012; Alex Steiner, *Athens: A View of the General Strike,* http://forum.permanent-revolution.org, September 26, 2012; *Greece in Flames: Prelude to European Revolution? A Debate Within the Left,* posted to http://www.mitchelcohen.com.

perate stage of the resistance than exists currently in the U.S.

Popular leaders like Glezos and Theodorakis are the visible part of a humongous majority of activist-oriented millions of people in the country who have been organizing (and recently calling openly) for an uprising. The majority of people are behind this sentiment and support it, BUT, also the majority of people have the political maturity to desire an uprising that is as peaceful and mindful as possible.

The arson attacks against more than forty buildings on Sunday that burned down a large number of shops and buildings that have *nothing* to do with the regime of Corporate and State oppressors, took place against the wishes of the people-in-rebellion. They are actions of conscious and unconscious agents of the regime — the truth is all in the photos.[161] Are these masked protesters "revolutionaries"?

There is nothing "revolutionary" about burning down classical architecture buildings that people love and identify with, cafés and movie theaters that constitute some of the last remaining humane parts of the City's downtown.[162]

At this time, the debate among true and honest revolutionary networks has not yet concluded on what is the best way to revolution in *this* juncture. Strikes are more and more organized and well-attended, but takeover strikes (occupations) are only now in this last year beginning to appear, and only on a very small scale. Armed response teams capable

---

[161] If you think this claim is too extreme, please see the top photo of the new Cyprus IndyMedia article titled *This is who burned down Athens*, http://cyprus.indymedia.org/node/88 .

[162] I am reminded of the fires set during the 1992 LA Rebellion, in which buildings were "coincidentally" set ablaze all along the route of a proposed subway, making it much easier and less costly for the developers to lay claim to that land.

of delivering meaningful blows to the regime (meaningful in the political sense), or capable of defending strikes, occupations, and protests from the regime, or capable of enforcing direct actions such as liberation and distribution of food in the cities or the countryside have not yet been formed because the people still do not support such a move. It might come to that, but popular awareness, desire and willingness to engage in the revolution is the one and most important factor that we need to be in tune with. The only ones engaged in armed actions in the last few years are the same fake anarchists and regime provocateurs who repeatedly pull off highly destructive (and sometimes lethal) actions that erode the peoples' morale.

Nobody wants to be part of a revolution that kills workers, attacks leftist demonstrators and firebombs small shops, and the people have repeatedly in the last few years immediately responded to these actions by pulling away from mass mobilizations. That is *exactly* the reason why the regime seeks to instigate such actions, with the help of a few hundred brainless idiots who think that such behaviour is "revolutionary."[163]

While Petros Evdokas' critique might appear to lend support to Chris Hedges' view, the concerns that go into it are very different. Petros starts from the point of how to successfully organize ourselves into a revolutionary force and whether the tactics attributed to the black bloc in Greece (in which three people were killed in a firebomb attack on a bank while people were inside) contribute to doing that. Hedges, on the other hand, is primarily concerned with cre-

---

[163] Petros Evdokas, private letter to author.

ating a moralistic and almost religious approach so as not to alienate the liberal class.

Drawing Baseless Conclusions

Chris Hedges' tactical assessment of the black bloc is based on fiction, on (mis)information garnered from the same incendiary news broadcasts he elsewhere lambastes. Surprisingly, Hedges doesn't bother to check their sources, but "confirms" his already-drawn conclusions by quoting one (and only one) obscure teenager (*nom de guerre* "Venomous Butterfly") writing in an equally obscure anarchist journal, *Green Anarchy*, 11 years ago — an article that at the time had *every* anarchist I know protesting its statements.[164] *He did not talk to actual participants at Occupy Oakland,* an ongoing problem in Hedges' widely promulgated assumptions. Had he done so I suspect he would have been able to see the black bloc as a specific *political* formation around a strategy of dual power[165] and not of symbolic tactics (although

---

[164] John Zerzan, an editor of *Green Anarchy,* writes: "Hedges finds it scandalous that *Green Anarchy* magazine published a brief article years ago (GA #5, Spring 2001) criticizing the Zapatista EZLN from an anarchist perspective. As an editor of GA at the time, I recall that we weren't thrilled by the piece, but we ran it in the interest of provoking discussion. Hedges is evidently not in favor of open discussion, and neither was the EZLN, which sent us a rather angry response (GA #8, Spring 2002). If it is scandalous to think critically about what is going on in Chiapas, it is worse to fail to learn from the evidence, from the record." *Fifth Estate*, "Vagaries of the Left: John Zerzan answers liberal columnist Chris Hedges who charges the Black Bloc has 'hi-jacked' the Occupy Movement," Spring 2012.

[165] See Mitchel Cohen, *What Is Direct Action? Op cit.*; *Zen-Marxism #8: A*

some might conclude — with good reason — that the black bloc's "militancy" itself remains in the realm of the symbolic, too!); he would have been hard-pressed not to qualify or even withdraw the pronouncements he made about them.

Posing False Alternatives

Hedges sets up a flawed framework in which the poles of debate are either black bloc "violence" or non-violent civil disobedience. There is no such thing as "violence" in the abstract or "non-violence" in the abstract. Many proponents of symbolic nonviolent civil disobedience seize on the misleadingly portrayed "nonviolent" revolution in Egypt as an argument for what we need to do here, while not recognizing that almost 900 people were killed and 6,400 injured by government forces in the first two weeks of the "peaceful" occupation of Tahrir Square.[166] Nor were the Occupyers united in nonviolence, especially when faced with needing to defend themselves. A letter of solidarity from Tahrir Square to Occupy Wall Street focuses on setting that record straight:

> Those who said that the Egyptian revolution was peaceful did not see the horrors that police visited upon us, nor did they see the resistance and even force that revolutionaries used against the police to

---

Headful of Ideas that are Driving Me Insane; and *Zen-Marxism #13: Fear & the Art of Neurosis Maintenance* for discussions about Dual Consciousness and Dual Power.

[166] Jessica Rettig, "Death Toll of Arab Spring," *U.S. News & World Report*.

defend their tentative occupations and spaces. By the government's own admission 99 police stations were put to the torch, thousands of police cars were destroyed, and all of the ruling party's offices around Egypt were burned down. Barricades were erected, officers were beaten back and pelted with rocks even as they fired tear gas and live ammunition on us. But at the end of the day on the 28th of January they retreated, and we had won our cities.

It is not our desire to participate in violence, but it is even less our desire to lose. If we do not resist, actively, when they come to take what we have won back, then we will surely lose. Do not confuse the tactics that we used when we shouted "peaceful" with fetishizing nonviolence; if the state had given up immediately we would have been overjoyed, but as they sought to abuse us, beat us, kill us, we knew that there was no other option than to fight back. Had we laid down and allowed ourselves to be arrested, tortured, and martyred to "make a point," we would be no less bloodied, beaten and dead. Be prepared to defend these things you have occupied, that you are building, because, after everything else has been taken from us, these reclaimed spaces are so very precious.[167]

How to Welcome Different Views

The absolutist poles Hedges sets up with regard to Occupy Oakland are devoid of context. They present us with a false, moralistic and decontextualized narrative. Amin Husein, an organizer with Occupy Wall Street and editor of its

---

[167] http://infrontandcenter.wordpress.com/2011/10/25/letter-of-solidarity-to-ows-from-tahrir/

theoretical journal, *Tidal,* spoke directly to Chris Hedges about all of this in a discussion broadcast on *Democracy Now*:

> It's an oversimplification to just say that the movement needs to make a decision [on the black bloc] without really kind of rethinking how we work. ... In this context of [Hedges'] article, though very good points [were made] and many people in the movement felt it was good because it sparked a conversation, it came at a time when it almost derailed us. And we worked with each other, you know, on the issue of Trinity and Duarte Square. ... We would have appreciated a phone call, because we would have facilitated these conversations, which needed to happen.[168]

Occupy activist and attorney Marina Sitrin hammers home the difference between discussing a tactic *within* Occupy and publicly blasting its proponents. The movement, she said, democratically decided to accept the diversity of tactics that Hedges opposed:

> It's actually not useful at all, from the outside, to tell the movements what to do, especially by people who have access to publish in certain places. And there's quite a few. [Some are] well-meaning people [like Hedges and] Zizek, telling us we must be serious revolutionaries and anti-capitalists and do this, that and the other. And, you know, with all respect, either engage in the discussion, because it is open — all of it is open, and we need to have these conversations, and we'd love to have more intellectuals who relate to the movements relating to us directly and having the discussions, not telling us what to do.[169]

---

[168] Democracy Now! May 1, 2012.

[169] *ibid*.

The question of tactics is an ongoing discussion within the Occupy movement, as Husein and Sitrin explained. Unlike journalists (however supportive of a movement they may be), participants in movements engage each other in such discussions all the time. As a participant, Hedges' views would have been welcome, just like everyone else's. But Hedges makes clear he is "not part" of it, and so his thunderbolts are issued from afar, rather than put up for internal discussion. The fact that Hedges used his access to the media as the venue for this "fight" while others do not have such access, and called for the purging of those whose alleged actions he did not agree with, was extremely disruptive to the movement he supports.

Tactics "should not be about abstract principles of using violence or not," writes Les Evenchick, a community organizer in New Orleans. "Initiating violence serves the interest of the ruling classes *unless you are in a position to win.* And it should not be about trashing property but about *seizing* property. And the property that needs to be seized are the banks, the seats of government, the means of communication, and the centers of police and military organization."

Would Hedges consider defense of seized property — say, a health clinic or library — to be violent? With violence pervading the entire society, the water we drink, the air we breathe, would removing the oppressor's boot from one's throat not be the nonviolent alternative, even if it takes some "force" to remove it? As beat poet Diane DiPrima succinctly put it: "Get your cut throat off my knife!"

Petros Evdokas adds:

> Something that is almost always forgotten, is that *organized* revolutionary violence [as opposed to chaotic individual violence] is *always* the most peaceful solution. By comparison to a Corporate State regime's otherwise unchecked, perennial, chaotic and barbaric violence, organized revolutionary violence is the non-violent alternative. But in order to fulfill those criteria, in addition to what Les correctly points out above, [Petros continues], revolutionary violence:
> 1. Must be organized.
> 2. Must be under tight and disciplined control by a morally uncompromisable and politically aware leadership.
> 3. Must have clear, transparent goals, plus a strategy and tactics worked out beforehand.
> 4. Must have the support — or tolerance — of the majority of the population.

In other words, militancy in achieving a strategic objective is not the same as indiscriminate property destruction, even though some outside observers may fail to distinguish the difference.

Occupying Property

What triggered Hedges' ire was Occupy Oakland's attempt to seize an abandoned city-owned property and use it to provide much needed social services for the community, devastated by cutbacks in jobs and social services that were part of the neoliberal structural adjustment program enacted by the Democratic Party politicians running that city. The cutbacks and layoffs were enacted only through violence, although it is a violence that is so much the norm it remains invisible and accepted in our everyday lives. Occupy Oakland's shutdown of the ports and its attempts to occupy and open up abandoned city-owned property uncloaked that violent reality. Occupy was no longer simply engaging in symbolic civil disobedience but acting to establish and defend actual spaces for people to use to meet their needs through direct action.

Some politicians disagree. Attorney Mal Burnstein — a wheeler-dealer for the "Save KPFA" faction on KPFA radio's local board, member of the Wellstone Renewal Democratic Party club and co-chair of the California Progressive Democrats Caucus — introduced a resolution *not* to the Occupy Oakland group but *to his Democratic Party club* pressuring *Occupy* to support Oakland Mayor Jean Quan, who unleashed the police against Occupy and whom Burnstein supports, and to

> honor previous decisions that have been democratically arrived at, such as the election of local officials, while never abdicating the right to challenge them on issues,[170]

basically calling on Occupy to surrender its *raison d'être* and

---

[170] Resolution introduced to the Wellstone Democratic Party Club by Mal Burnstein and Pamela Drake, as reported on IndyBay.org on March 13, 2012.

everything it has fought for. Contra Burnstein, the community has not only the right but the responsibility to establish its own processes through which it will work — whether outsiders agree with them or not — and to physically defend those seized buildings and the embryonic network of new people's institutions attempting to be born.

Physical Force vs. "Violence"

Occupations and organized physical defense of reclaimed community property require all sorts of tactics, different ones at different times. We have to stop falling into the trap of arguing about the use of force and property damage in the abstract, as forms of violence.

The reality is, the "violence" Hedges deplores does not exist in the Occupy movement in the U.S. Almost all of the actual violence has been perpetrated by the police, in defense of the property relations of the 1 percent. Long time radical activist Chris Kinder reported from Oakland last October 25, 2011, as the Oakland Police Department, under orders from Mayor Jean Quan, cleared the encampments and attacked the ensuing march:

> We marched and marched, seeing no cops, and getting enthusiastic welcome from the drivers whose cars were stuck at intersections that the march was passing through. In the streets the whole way, this march had grown as people heard news reports on KPFA and came down to join it. Very hard to say,

but I think its peak could have been 3,000.

After a stop at Snow Park, on the shore of Lake Merritt (the site of a second encampment, which was also removed early Tuesday morning), marchers headed back up to 14th and Broadway. That's when the serious battle erupted. This time, after the usual warning, marchers held their ground, and the cops unleashed a huge barrage of tear gas, which sent most of us off in different directions. At least one demonstrator was struck in the head by a tear gas canister.

The police were later quoted on local TV news as saying that they acted in self-defense, since they were being bombarded with rocks, bottles, and even knives. This is crap. I was watching the whole time from the outer edge of the crowd, and saw exactly one piece of something flying toward the cops. It was now about 8 pm, and my companion and I escaped the tear gas and called it a night. But many marchers, fewer in number each time, kept returning to the scene at 14th and Broadway. According to news reports, three more barrages of tear gas were fired at ever smaller groups of protesters, the last one around 11 pm. And the maddening drone of helicopters never seems to stop, just one price of living in a war zone.[171]

Tactics utilized in self-defense of a hospital or a community center that has been occupied and "opened up" for the community have a different purpose than tactics employed for the purposes of symbolically calling attention to an issue. In engaging in symbolic civil disobedience as a form of lobbying for changes in policy, one is in effect accepting — even if

---

[171] Chris Kinder, Oakland Occupy Dispersed, but then ... Oakland Erupts!, Oct. 26, 2011, posted to http://www.MitchelCohen.com.

just for that moment — the authority of those in power, even while despising it. Without transformative strategy (such as the occupation of buildings and the creation of institutions of dual power), one ends up relying on tactics that futilely try to shame the ruling class into "doing the right thing," even though the bankers and their enablers could not care less about self-sacrifice and civil disobedience as a moral force.

Outside Agitators?

Who's to blame for inspiring the black bloc's actions? Again, Hedges fails to do his proper research. He writes that "primitive anarchist" author John Zerzan is the outside-agitator leader of the Oakland black bloc. Even stranger, Hedges alleges that the black bloc anarchists disparage the Zapatistas, which is so much the opposite of the truth as to be laughable. Both declarations would be news to the 99 percent (so to speak) of its participants — something Hedges would have known had he bothered to interview actual participants, or even to read the decades-old arguments *within anarchism* between Zerzan and the *Fifth Estate* or *Love & Rage* newspaper collectives, let alone those between Murray Bookchin's school of social ecology anarcho-ecologists and *Earth-First!* He might then have been surprised to learn that the anarchists he condemns were actually not only among the most active supporters of the Zapatistas, but published many of the early communiqués and essential writings of Commandante Marcos following the January 1994 uprising in Chiapas.[172] In fact, the Zapatistas' very elongated decision-making process was one of the great influences on Occupy's (and the black bloc's) consensus-based procedures. For someone of Hedges' stature to fail to confirm sources or read the historical debates is not only poor journalism but a serious breach of the whole idea of Occupy Wall Street's horizontal communication. As such, his assertions read simply as smears.

Meanwhile, the Oakland Police Department and city officials, like so many before them, claim that Occupy Oakland is made up of outsiders who are not from Oakland. It's true that many of the participants come from around the Bay Area and not Oakland proper. The Occupation there acts as a magnet for people trying to create new, non-commodified ways of relating to each other, and the attraction of meaningful ways of relating and living knows no municipal boundaries. But here's what the press reports fail to mention: *93 percent of the Oakland Police Department lives outside Oakland.* The cops come into the city each day as part of a different sort of "occupation" — that of an occupying army, which is the way the Maoist organization that Oakland Mayor Jean Quan had once belonged to, put it.

---

[172] See, for example, *Zapatistas: Documents of the New American Revolution*, Autonomedia: 1994.

Remember, 43 years ago the media was similarly replete with accusations that the Occupyers *then* were "outside agitators." In May, 1969, people from all over the region converged on People's Park in Berkeley to defend it from the University's so-called "development" bulldozers — they wanted to "pave paradise and put up a parking lot" . . . literally! One observer, James Rector, was shot and killed by police while sitting and watching from a nearby roof; the tear-gassing went on for weeks. Years later, 17-year-old Rosebud was shot and killed by a lone trigger-happy cop after she'd snuck into the Chancellor's house — which turned out to be empty! — hoping to discuss the University's eviction of her friends from People's Park. The struggle over People's Park and the role of U.C. Berkeley as a corporate and "developmental" powerhouse has been going on for decades.

The violence committed by the State, as Bay Area writer and activist Rebecca Solnit points out,[173] has been over-the-top, immoral, and costly; it reveals the lengths to which the State is willing to go to protect the sanctity of corporate property when it is threatened — even if only ideologically — by peaceful activists seeking to have a say over how that property is used. The conclusion some are drawing — that Occupy should stop its seizing of abandoned municipal pro-

---

[173] "Occupy Heads into the Spring: Mad, Passionate Love — and Violence," *Le Monde Diplomatique,* February 22, 2012.

perty for the public good because they "cause" the police to react violently in defending the private profits of corporations and the authority of the State — is exactly the opposite of what needs to happen. **Occupations need to expand.** They need to seize back the municipal and private corporate properties that the 1 percent and its government have stolen, and put them to use in the service of the 99 percent.

In addition to occupying parks and public spaces across the country, Occupy Wall Street has begun to reclaim a few of the ten million homes and farms that the banks foreclosed on in the last few years, returning them to those who'd been evicted from them. What if we begin occupying and directly opening up those schools, libraries, hospitals, firehouses, subway stations and post offices that the government has shut down?

Imagine occupying and re-opening the essential St. Vincent's Hospital in NYC's Greenwich Village — shuttered by Republican Mayor Michael Bloomberg, with the support of the Democrats[174] — and inviting health care providers from around the world to come and treat people, as occurred last year in Greece and Chicago! Or, to start with something smaller, occupy a library whose hours have been cut, keep it open 24/7, and move the People's Library into it, as Occupy

---

[174] Christine Quinn, a Democrat mayoral candidate and current chair of the City Council, received large campaign contributions from real estate magnate Scott Rudin, who fêted her at banquets. It was Quinn's approval, along with the Mayor's, that was indispensable in closing the hospital and giving Rudin the go-ahead to turn it into private luxury condos.

Oakland is doing in the Fruitvale section of that city.

"Occupy, Reclaim and Open-Up" is a direct response to the cutbacks, shutdowns and foreclosures forced on us through the everyday violence of the system, by those owning and administering wealth in this country. It's the kind of direct action that we "99 percenters," and maybe even some of the 1 percent, could get behind and participate in, involving wider sectors of society.

I urge Chris Hedges — and all of us! — to keep focus on who is the real enemy, and who is committing the real violence. ◆

Oakland police, before firing the tear gas shell that hit Iraqi veteran and antiwar activist Scott Olson in the head at close range.

The Violent Peace-Police

An Open Letter to Chris Hedges

by David Graeber

I am writing this on the premise that you are a well-meaning person who wishes Occupy Wall Street to succeed. I am also writing as someone who was deeply involved in the early stages of planning Occupy in New York.

I am also an anarchist who has participated in many black blocs. While I have never personally engaged in acts of property destruction, I have on more than one occasion taken part in Blocs where property damage has occurred. (I have taken part in even more Blocs that did not engage in such tactics. It is a common fallacy that this is what black blocs are all about. It isn't.)

I was hardly the only black bloc veteran who took part in planning the initial strategy for Occupy Wall Street. In fact, anarchists like myself were the real core of the group that came up with the idea of occupying Zuccotti Park, the "99%" slogan, the General Assembly process, and, in fact, who collectively decided that we would adopt a strategy of Gandhian non-violence and eschew acts of property damage. Many of us had taken part in black blocs. We just didn't feel that was an appropriate tactic for the situation we were in.

This is why I feel compelled to respond to your statement "The Cancer in Occupy." This statement is not only factually inaccurate, it is quite literally dangerous. This is the sort of misinformation that really can get people killed. In fact, it is far more likely to do so, in my estimation, than anything done by any black-clad teenager throwing rocks.

Let me just lay out a few initial facts:

1. black bloc is a tactic, not a group. It is a tactic where activists don masks and black clothing (originally leather jackets in Germany, later, hoodies in America), as a gesture of anonymity, solidarity, and to indicate to others that they are prepared, if the situation calls for it, for militant action. The very nature of the tactic belies the accusation that they are trying to hijack a movement and endanger others. One of the ideas of having a black bloc is that everyone who comes to a protest should know where the people likely to engage in militant action are, and thus easily be able to avoid it if that's what they wish to do.

2. black blocs do not represent any specific ideological, or for that matter anti-ideological position. Black blocs have tended in the past to be made up primarily of anarchists but most contain participants whose politics vary from Maoism to Social Democracy. They are not united by ideology, or lack of ideology, but merely a common feeling that creating a bloc of people with explicitly revolutionary politics and ready to confront the forces of the order through more militant tactics if required, is, on the particular occasion when they assemble, a useful thing to do. It follows one can no more speak of "black bloc Anarchists," as a group with an identifiable ideology, than one can speak of "Sign-Carrying Anarchists" or "Mic-Checking Anarchists."

3. Even if you must select a tiny, ultra-radical minority within the black bloc and pretend their views are representative of anyone who ever put on a hoodie, you could at least be up-to-date about it. It was back in 1999 that people used to pretend "the black bloc" was made up of nihilistic primitivist followers of John Zerzan opposed to all forms of organization. Nowadays, the preferred approach is to pretend "the black bloc" is made up of nihilistic insurrectionary followers of The Invisible Committee, opposed to all forms of organization. Both are absurd slurs. Yours is also 12 years out of date.

4. Your comment about black bloc'ers hating the Zapatistas is one of the weirdest I've ever seen. Sure, if you dig around, you can find *someone* saying almost anything. But I'm guessing that, despite the ideological diversity, if you took a poll of participants in the average black bloc and asked what political movement in the world inspired them the most, the EZLN would get about 80% of the vote. In fact I'd be willing to wager that at least a third of participants in the average black bloc are wearing or carrying at least one item of Zapatista paraphernalia. (Have you ever actually *talked* to someone who has taken part in a black bloc? Or just to people who dislike them?)

5. "Diversity of tactics" is not a "black bloc" idea. The original GA in Tompkins Square Park that planned the original occupation, if I remember, adopted the principle of diversity of tactics (at least it was discussed in a very approving fashion), at the same time as we all also concurred that a Gandhian approach would be the best way to go. This is not a contradiction: "diversity of tactics" means leaving such matters up to individual conscience, rather than imposing a code on anyone. Partly, this is because imposing such a code invariably backfires. In practice, it means some groups break off in indignation and do even more militant things than they would have otherwise, without coordinating with anyone else — as happened, for instance, in Seattle. The results are usually disastrous. After the fiasco of Seattle, of watching some activists actively turning others over to the police — we quickly decided we needed to ensure this never happened again. What we found that if we declared "we shall all be in solidarity with one another. We will not turn in fellow protesters to the police. We will treat you as brothers and sisters. But we expect you to do the same to us" — then, those who might be disposed to more militant tactics will act in solidarity as well, either by not engaging in militant actions at all for fear they will endanger others (as in many later Global Justice Actions, where black blocs merely helped protect the lockdowns, or in Zuccotti Park, where mostly people didn't bloc up at all) or doing so in ways that run the least risk of endangering fellow activists.

All this is secondary. Mainly I am writing as an appeal to conscience. Your conscience, since clearly you are a sincere and well-meaning person who wishes this movement to succeed. I beg you: Please consider what I am saying. Please bear in mind as I say this that I am not a crazy nihilist, but a reasonable person who is one (if just one) of the original authors of the Gandhian strategy OWS adopted — as well as a student of social movements, who has spent many years both participating in such movements, and trying to understand their history and dynamics.

I am appealing to you because I really do believe the kind of statement you made is profoundly dangerous.

The reason I say this is because, whatever your intentions, it is very hard to read your statement as anything but an appeal to violence. After all, what are you basically saying about what you call "black bloc anarchists"?

1) they are not part of us

2) they are consciously malevolent in their intentions
3) they are violent
4) they cannot be reasoned with
5) they are all the same
6) they wish to destroy us
7) they are a cancer that must be excised

Surely you must recognize, when it's laid out in this fashion, that this is precisely the sort of language and argument that, historically, has been invoked by those encouraging one group of people to physically attack, ethnically cleanse, or exterminate another — in fact, the sort of language and argument that is almost never invoked in any other circumstance. After all, if a group is made up exclusively of violent fanatics who cannot be reasoned with, intent on our destruction, what else can we really do? This is the language of violence in its purest form. Far more than "fuck the police." To see this kind of language employed by someone who claims to be speaking in the name of non-violence is genuinely extraordinary. I recognize that you've managed to find certain peculiar fringe elements in anarchism saying some pretty extreme things, it's not hard to do, especially since such people are much easier to find on the internet than in real life, but it would be difficult to come up with any "black bloc anarchist" making a statement as extreme as this.

Even if you did not intend this statement as a call to violence, which I suspect you did not, how can you honestly believe that many will not read it as such?

In my experience, when I point this sort of thing out, the first reaction I normally get from pacifists is along the lines of "what are you talking about? Of course I'm not in favor of attacking anyone! I am non-violent! I am merely calling for non-violently confronting such elements and excluding them from the group!" The problem is that in practice this is almost never what actually happens. Time after time, what it has actually meant in practice is either a) turning fellow activists over to the police, i.e., turning them over to people with weapons who will physically assault, shackle, and imprison them, or b) actual physical activist-on-activist assault. Such things *have* happened. There have been physical assaults by activists on other activists, and, to my knowledge, they have never been perpetrated by anyone in the black bloc, but invariably by purported pacifists against those who dare to pull a hood over their heads or a bandanna over their faces, or, simply, against anarchists who adopt tactics someone else thinks are going too far. (Not — I should note — even *potentially* violent tactics. During one 15-minute period in Occupy Austin, I was threatened first with arrest, then with assault, by fellow campers because I was expressing verbal solidarity with, and then standing in passive resistance beside, a small group of anarchists who were raising what was considered to be an unauthorized tent.)

This situation often produces extraordinary ironies. In Seattle, the only incidents of actual physical assault by protesters on other individuals were not attacks on the police, since these did not occur at all, but attacks by "pacifists" on black bloc'ers engaged in acts of property damage. Since the black bloc'ers had collectively agreed on a strict policy of non-violence (which they defined as never doing anything to harm another living being), they uniformly refused to strike back. In many recent occupations, self-appointed "Peace Police" have manhandled activists who showed up to marches in black clothing and hoodies, ripped their masks off, shoved and kicked them — always, without the victims themselves having engaged in any act of violence, always, with the victims refusing, on moral grounds, to shove or kick back.

The kind of rhetoric you are engaging in, if it disseminates widely, will ensure this kind of violence becomes much, much more severe.

Perhaps you do not believe me, or do not believe these events to be particularly significant. If so, let me put the matter in a larger historical context.

If I understand your argument, it seems to come down to this:

1. OWS has been successful because it has followed a

Gandhian strategy of showing how, even in the face of strictly non-violent opposition, the state will respond with illegal violence.

2. Black bloc elements who do not act according to principles of Gandhian non-violence are destroying the movement because they provide retroactive justification for state repression, especially in the eyes of the media.

3. Therefore, the black bloc elements must be somehow rooted out.

As one of the authors of the original Gandhian strategy, I can recall how well-aware we were, when we framed this strategy, that we were taking an enormous risk. Gandhian strategies have not historically worked in the U.S.; in fact, they haven't really worked on a mass scale since the civil rights movement. This is because the U.S. media is simply constitutionally incapable of reporting acts of police repression as "violence." (One reason the civil rights movement was an exception is so many Americans at the time didn't view the Deep South as part of the same country.) Many of the young men and women who formed the famous black bloc in Seattle were in fact eco-activists who had been involved in tree-sits and forest defense lock-downs that operated on purely Gandhian principles — only to find that in the U.S. of the 1990s, non-violent protesters could be brutalized, tortured (have pepper spray directly rubbed in their eyes), or even killed, without serious objection from the national media. So they turned to other tactics. We knew all this. We decided it was worth the risk.

However, we are also aware that when the repression begins, some will break ranks and respond with greater militancy. Even if this doesn't happen in a systematic and organized fashion, some violent acts will take place. You write that black bloc'ers smashed up a "locally owned coffee shop"; I doubted this when I read it, since most black blocs agree on a strict policy of not damaging owner-operated enterprises, and I now find in Susie Cagle's response to your article that, in fact, it was a chain coffee shop, and the property destruction was carried out by someone not in black. But still, you're right: A few such incidents will inevitably occur. The question is how one responds.

If the police decide to attack a group of protesters, they will claim to have been provoked, and the media will repeat whatever the police say, no matter how implausible, as the basic initial facts of what happened. This will happen whether or not anyone at the protest does anything that can be remotely described as violence. Many police claims will be obviously ridiculous — as at the recent Oakland march where police accused participants of throwing "improvised explosive devices" — but no matter how many times the police lie about such matters, the national media will still report their claims as true, and it will be up to protesters to provide evidence to the contrary. Sometimes, with the help of social media, we can demonstrate that particular police attacks were absolutely unjustified, as with the famous Tony Bologna pepper-spray incident. But we cannot by definition prove all police attacks were unjustified, even all attacks at one particular march; it's simply physically impossible to film everything that happens from every possible angle all the time. Therefore we can expect that whatever we do, the media will dutifully report "protesters engaged in clashes with police" rather than "police attacked non-violent protesters." What's more, when someone does throw back a tear-gas canister, or toss a bottle, or even spray-paint something, we can assume that act will be employed as retroactive justification for whatever police violence occurred before the act took place.

All this will be true whether or not a black bloc is present.

If the moral question is "is it defensible to threaten physical harm against those who do no direct harm to others," one might say the pragmatic, tactical question is, "even if it were somehow possible to create a Peace Police capable of preventing any act that could even be interpreted as 'violent' by the corporate media, by anyone at or near a protest, no matter what the provocation, would it have any meaningful effect?" That is, would it create a situation where the police would feel they couldn't use arbitrary force against non-violent protesters? The example of Zuccotti Park, where we achieved pretty consistent non-violence, suggests this is profoundly unlikely. And perhaps most importantly of all, even if it *were* somehow possible to create some kind of Peace Police that would prevent anyone under gas attack from so much as tossing a bottle, so that we could justly claim that no one had done anything to warrant the sort of attack that police have routinely brought, would the marginally better media coverage we would thus obtain really be worth the cost in freedom and democracy that would inevitably follow from creating such an internal police force to begin with?

These are not hypothetical questions. Every major movement of mass non-violent civil disobedience has had to grapple with them in one form or another. How inclusive should you be with those who have different ideas about what tactics are appropriate? What do you do about those who go beyond what most people consider acceptable limits? What do you do when the government and its media allies hold up their actions as justification — even retroactive justification — for violent and repressive acts?

Successful movements have understood that it's absolutely essential not to fall into the trap set out by the authorities and spend one's time condemning and attempting to police other activists. One makes one's own principles clear. One expresses what solidarity one can with others who share the same struggle, and if one cannot, tries one's best to ignore or avoid them, but above all, one keeps the focus on the *actual source of violence*, without doing or saying anything that might seem to justify that violence because of tactical disagreements you have with fellow activists.

I remember my surprise and amusement, the first time I met activists from the April 6 Youth Movement from Egypt, when the issue of non-violence came up. "Of course we were non-violent," said one of the original organizers, a young man of liberal politics who actually worked at a bank. "No one ever used firearms, or anything like that. We never did anything more militant than throwing rocks!"

Here was a man who understood what it takes to win a non-violent revolution! He knew that if the police start aiming tear-gas canisters directly at people's heads, beating them with truncheons, arresting and torturing people, and you have thousands of protesters, then some of them will fight back. There's no way to absolutely prevent this. The appropriate response is to keep reminding everyone of the violence of the state authorities, and never, ever, start writing long denunciations of fellow activists, claiming they are part of an insane fanatic malevolent cabal. (Even though I am quite sure that if a hypothetical Egyptian activist had wanted to make a case that, say, violent Salafis, or even Trotskyists, were trying to subvert the revolution, and adopted standards of evidence as broad as yours, looking around for inflammatory statements wherever they could find them and pretending they were typical of everyone who threw a rock, they could easily have made a case.) This is why most of us are aware that Mubarak's regime attacked non-violent protesters, and are not aware that many responded by throwing rocks.

Egyptian activists, in other words, understood what playing into the hands of the police *really* means.

Actually, why limit ourselves to Egypt? Since we are talking about Gandhian tactics here, why not consider the case of Gandhi himself? He had to deal with what to say about people who went much further than rock-throwing (even though Egyptians throwing rocks at police were already going much further than any U.S. black bloc has). Gandhi was part of a very broad anti-colonial movement that included elements that actually were using firearms, in fact, elements engaged in outright terrorism. He first began to frame his own strategy of mass non-violent civil resistance in response to a debate over the act of an Indian nationalist who walked into the office of a British official and shot him five times in the face, killing him instantly. Gandhi made it clear that while he was opposed to murder under any circumstances, he also refused to denounce the murderer. This was a man who was trying to do the right thing, to act against an historical injustice, but did it in the wrong way because he was "drunk with a mad idea."

Over the course of the next 40 years, Gandhi and his movement were regularly denounced in the media, just as non-violent anarchists are also always denounced in the media (and I might remark here that while not an anarchist himself, Gandhi was strongly influenced by anarchists like Kropotkin and Tolstoy), as a mere front for more violent, terroristic elements, with whom he was said to be secretly collaborating. He was regularly challenged to prove his non-violent credentials by assisting the authorities in suppressing such elements. Here Gandhi remained resolute. It is always morally superior, he insisted, to oppose injustice through non-violent means than through violent means. However, to oppose injustice through violent means is still morally superior to not doing anything to oppose injustice at all.

And Gandhi was talking about people who were blowing up trains, or assassinating government officials. Not damaging windows or spray-painting rude things about the police.

The Black Freedom Movement

Chris Hedges' Misuse of History

by Jay Moore

"We want freedom now, but we're not going to get it saying 'We Shall Overcome.' We've got to fight until we overcome." — Malcolm X

"A social movement that only moves people is merely a revolt. A movement that changes both people and institutions is a revolution."
— Dr. Martin Luther King, Jr.

On the night of January 18, 1958, the Ku Klux Klan, which the previous week had held cross-burnings on the lawns of a mixed-race couple and of a Lumbee Indian family who had moved into a white neighborhood, tried to hold a rally against race "mongrelization" in Robeson County, North Carolina. But when the fifty Klan members showed up, they were confronted with ten times that many Lumbee Indians led by World War II veterans and armed with stick and guns. Shots were fired, and the Klansmen scattered in fright through the woods and swamps never to return.

The same year of 1958, a couple of counties away in Monroe, North Carolina, another World War II vet, the local NAACP head Robert F. Williams, was also organizing armed defense against the Klan. Williams would later write a memoir about his experiences entitled *Negroes with Guns*. A few years later, in the Deep South, some other ex-soldiers formed the Deacons for Defense and Justice to furnish armed protection from racists for that part of the movement who were engaged in sit-ins and other forms of non-violent resistance. (A movie has been made about the Deacons for Defense.)

Certainly most school kids in this country know a little bit about Martin Luther King and Rosa Parks and perhaps Thurgood Marshall. They should! But do they know anything about any of the above? That's because the history of the Black Freedom Movement (*aka* Civil Rights Movement) is presented as a sweet little feel-good fairy tale somewhat along these lines: There were once bad white people down South (we don't hear much if at all in this fairy tale about the white racists in the North) who were all too willing to unleash violence in the form of shootings, beatings, fire hoses, dogs, and jailings — the horrors of lynching are rarely mentioned — against anybody of the wrong color who was thought to be the least bit "uppity," not to mention those who might have wanted to rock the segregationist boat. It was a tough uphill struggle. But the story has a happy and uplifting ending: Due to the actions of people like King and Parks, we are able to live today in a country with freedom and justice for all — because the power of non-violence and of loving your fellow man was all that was really needed, along with a good dollop of courage. Goodness (and being well-mannered and well-groomed, and always remembering to turn the other cheek) was able to triumph over Evil.

We'll leave aside the question of why this movement history is generally retold in such a selective and disarming kind of way, let alone the question of whether this country has truly gained full and genuine racial equality. Not only does the school kids' fairy tale leave out the exceptional circumstances of the Cold War during the 1950s and '60s — when the U.S. and the Soviet Union were vying to appeal to the colored peoples of the newly-independent colonial countries — that arguably gave peaceful protest in this country more leverage than it has ever had before or since; but also, in reality, the Black Freedom Movement had always proceeded on two tracks — two tracks that were both necessary for its success.

One freedom path was always angry and militant and it did not eschew the use of force, if necessary. We can go all the way back to the anti-slavery movement before the Civil War. In 1829 David Walker, a free black man in Boston issued an "Appeal to the Coloured Citizens of the World." In this incendiary pamphlet, Walker went beyond the usual moral criticisms of slavery; he denounced America for its hypocrisy, especially singling out Thomas Jefferson, and suggested that slaves might rebel against their masters if the country did not start living up to its professions of all men being created equal.

This was too much for the white liberal humanitarians of the day. William Lloyd Garrison, the great abolitionist newspaper editor who had condemned slavery as the greatest sin of the age and demanded immediate emancipation and national repentance, decried what Walker had said. Garrison lectured the men and women in bondage that, rather than rising up in revolt, they should suffer evil "unresistingly," as had Jesus and his apostles, in the expectation that divine justice would come. Walker was a devoutly religious man himself who likewise believed in the inevitability of divine justice, but he also believed that "you must go to work and prepare the way of the Lord."

Walker's "Appeal," followed in 1831 by the slave revolt in Virginia led by Nat Turner, reverberated throughout the South for slaves and slave-owners alike. Southern whites totally freaked, trying to suppress the "Appeal" from reaching slaves. Walker used black sailors to smuggle it into the South. New laws were enacted forbidding slaves from being taught to read and write. The next no-holds-barred black radical after Walker (who died in 1830) was Henry Highland Garnet, who addressed the National Negro Convention in Buffalo in 1843 and issued an outright call for slaves to rebel. "Arise, arise! Strike for your lives and liberties. Now is the day and hour." Again, this was too much for the "moral suasion" (pacifist) abolitionists, including Frederick Douglass. But, with the passage of the Fugitive Slave Act in 1850, Douglass changed his mind and argued that it might be justifiable to kill a slave catcher to save an escaped slave from being taken back into slavery. And Douglass, along with a number of prominent white abolitionists, became secret supporters of John Brown's bold plan to take the fight to the South by attacking the federal arsenal at Harpers Ferry, Virginia — an act which catalyzed the Civil War and ended slavery as many African-Americans, free and slave, took up arms. For southern slave-owners, this was the feared apocalyptic slave rebellion.

In the first half of the 20th Century, of course, we had the radical black nationalist Marcus Garvey and his numerous followers and the Communist Party which launched the international campaigns to save Angelo Herndon and the Scottsboro Boys. As Glenda Gilmore has detailed in her excellent recent book on the deeper radical roots of the Civil Rights Movement,[175] the sometimes underground organizing

---

[175] Glenda Gilmore, *Defying Dixie: The Radical Roots of Civil Rights, 1919-*

work of the Communist Party and other hard-core left-wing radicals in the South was a key ingredient to what was able to happen subsequently in Montgomery and elsewhere. Yet, as I discover repeatedly as a college teacher with my students who express surprise at learning about these things (and then turning in some cases to anger about never being told before), practically none of this history is included in the fairy tale fed to American school children and the general public.

The current controversy over strategy and tactics in the Occupy Wall Street Movement, spurred by Chris Hedges' ill-informed, poorly-researched essay in *TruthDig* setting up the "black bloc" as a supposedly mindlessly-violent, window-breaking anarchist strawman to promote his moralizing pacifist agenda, is an echo of earlier movement differences and debates. Although Hedges has expressed support for rioting in Greece, he seems to think that any kind of militant actions *here* are *ipso facto* "violent" and thus illegitimate. Hedges (as well as others like him) likes to wrap his politics in the mantle of Martin Luther King and Gandhi. But King, while following his own heartfelt path and despite his own strong philosophical differences with Malcolm X and others in the Black Freedom Movement, never publicly criticized those who espoused a more militant in-your-face approach. Martin was able to understand where people like Malcolm

---

1950, W. W. Norton & Company, January 2008.

were coming from, given the severe history of racist repression in the black community. Many of our youth of all colors today, in this hollow materialistic capitalist world which is busy destroying the planet, also feel the same fury and uncompromising determination to stand up to Evil.

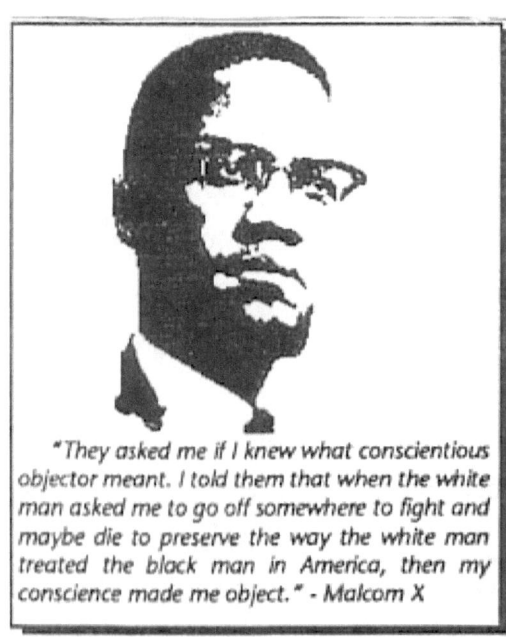

"They asked me if I knew what conscientious objector meant. I told them that when the white man asked me to go off somewhere to fight and maybe die to preserve the way the white man treated the black man in America, then my conscience made me object." - Malcom X

During the Sixties, it was these two paths together that enabled significant change to happen. Yes, sometimes they would be at odds, but at the same time they mutually reinforced each other, the one personified by King and the other personified by Malcolm X (and subsequently by the Black Panther Party for Self-Defense, by H. Rap Brown and

Stokely Carmichael).[176] Malcolm visited Selma, Alabama in 1965 to show support for the movement there and for King who had been jailed. He spoke frankly as to how this was a sort of good-cop/bad-cop approach. If the white racists did not want to deal reasonably with King, then beware; the alternative was having to deal with people like Malcolm X. Some members of the ruling elite got the message — King had told Kennedy on a visit to the White House that the black masses were losing their patience with him — and the Civil Rights Acts went through.

We could find similar parallels in the Women's and Gay Liberation and the environmental movements where those who were in favor of using step-by-step means appealing to those in power to do the right thing and those calling for the System to be dismantled lock, stock, and barrel "by any means necessary" (Malcolm's language) — the equivalent of today's "diversity of tactics" — were able to deliver a one-two punch and make changes happen, if not necessarily to bring about an all-around revolution that the militants (and some of the pacifists like King himself at the end) desired. We radicals can generally appreciate the sometime usefulness of liberals and their reformist approach — Malcolm X supported the black voter registration drives in the South, al-

---

[176] For some of the latter history, see the new Swedish-made Black Power Mixtape documentary.)

though considering them naive on the nature of who really rules America and what ultimately needs to be done.

This is not to advocate "violence" — non-violent direct action seems to be the best tactical choice under most current circumstances except when there is a need to defend ourselves against Oakland-style police brutality — but it is to affirm the angry, impassioned side or path which we also need to win short-term gains against inequality and corruption as well as to build for the revolutionary future.

Jay Moore is a radical historian who lives and teaches (when he can find work) in rural Vermont.

Occupy Theory, Occupy Strategy

Pulling the Emergency Brake

by Marina Sitrin

"Marx said that revolutions are the locomotive of world history. But perhaps things are very different. It may be that revolutions are the act by which the human race traveling in the train applies the emergency brake." Walter Benjamin's words perfectly fit what has been going on around the globe throughout 2011 — and in many places before this, and much further south, from Chiapas and Oaxaca Mexico to Argentina. Our movements are about the shouting of No! The *Ya Basta!* The *Que Se Vayan Todos!* — our collective refusal to remain passive in an untenable situation. And so we pull the emergency brake, and in that space we freeze time and begin to open up and create something new. We are not even sure what exactly it is. We know we want to create open free spaces. What that looks like we are all discovering together, as we create it, which is also how we are creating it together, horizontally and with affect. What we are doing and how we are doing it are inextricably linked, and are all a part of this prefigurative movement.

A Few Dangers in Openness

In moments of crisis people frequently come together, look to one another, and create new supportive relationships. These moments can be some of the most beautiful and solidarious that we ever experience. What happens again and again, however, is that after a period of time, these new relationships get repressed and co-opted by institutional power, or implode from within. Often our previous ways of relating return. How can we prevent this? Under what circumstances is this less likely to occur? How can we bring about moments where history breaks open, our imaginations are freed and we are able to envision and create new landscapes towards new horizons? Below I begin to address just a few of the many potential challenges we can face as a movement. I use the examples of left political parties and the State, but the challenges are many, and the point is to begin a more open conversation about challenges so as to overcome them, or even better, avoid them. I use Argentina as a means for delving into the examples since the autonomous movements there now have ten years of experience.

Political Party Disruption

The relationships we are creating in our movements attempt to open space for all people, who generally agree with a set of emancipatory principles. Occupy does not create structures of membership or behavior modes — most anyone is welcome. This is both our strength and a potential weakness if we do not think carefully about what can happen in these open spaces and organize accordingly.

In Argentina after the 2001 popular rebellion, hundreds of neighborhood assemblies were formed, all using *horizontalidad*, resembling to a large extent what the Occupy movements are attempting to create with general assemblies in neighborhoods, towns and cities — forming new relationships while striving to meet basic needs. While the neighborhood assembly movement faced numerous challenges, one of the most destabilizing according to participants at the time, was left political party disruption. This was done in various ways, from trying to control the assemblies' agenda; loading the speakers list with their members so as to dominate the conversation, thereby exhausting many people who came to the assembly; and when that did not work, organizing disruption campaigns, especially in the *interbarrial* (the assembly of assemblies where many hundreds of assemblies came together to make decisions). In this last case, Party members would mobilize to disrupt an assembly, shouting out of turn, making demands, such as the end to imperialism now, or the need for a 10 point plan for women's liberation, all to be decided that night. And most devious — they often would not identify as members of a group, so they appeared to be just regular passionate participants. This of course then brings out the most wonderful of our democratic impulses, which is to make sure they are fully heard. But if their agenda is not sincere, is it democratic to allow them the space to make demands on the group? (This behavior is not that different from political police — but that is the topic for another day.)

Elections & the State

Another area that created a great deal of disorientation and demobilization in Argentina was the national elections. The 2001 rebellion forced out five consecutive governments with popular power. The legitimacy of the State was in question. People organized assemblies in neighborhoods, unemployed workers movements grew exponentially, and workers, using horizontalidad, recuperated workplaces, without bosses or hierarchy. The State responded with direct repression, cooptation and attempts at reinstitutionalization. The strategy with regard to legitimacy was elections. Movements had planned to boycott the elections and form assemblies of assemblies, creating a potential dual power situation. Then, a far-right candidate was put on the ballot, one responsible for the last decade of privatization, and who ran on a ticket of "law and order." This created fear amongst many in the movements, and the conversations shifted to what to do, vote, not vote, organize against the candidates, etc., sidetracking the movement agenda to that of the State and the State's agenda. In the end, the center candidate won, resulting in a number of positive effects, from human rights to international relations. The point and danger however is not related to the specific politics of the new government but that it became the central point of reference for many in the movements, with people positioning themselves in relationship to the possibilities and real offerings of the State. The movements continued to organize, but lost a lot of momentum, and the conversation in society shifted from the alternative powers being developed by the movements to the institutional power of the State.

Now, years later, many reflect on the question of elections and the State in a different way. The perspective is not a total boycott, but that the most important thing is to maintain the movement's agenda, and from the point of reference of the movement, decide how and if there is a relationship to institutional power. Some have referred to this strategy as "With, Against and Beyond the State." Along these lines, at the time of the latest elections, one movement participant explained that their perspective was to "vote and run". Having no illusions in the State, but also not wanting the right-wing to win. She explained that there were intentionally few conversations about the elections taking place in the assemblies. Similarly, their perspective on material support is to take what they can get only as long as they maintain their own agenda. As soon as the State puts demands or qualifiers on the offer, the movement walks away.

The politics of our movements necessarily means that the State cannot fix the problems of society. Experience has shown that the State, whether capitalist or socialist, cannot be the emancipatory agent of change. And, when we as movements try and work outside the State without a conscious engagement with it, the State will always engage us, through direct repression or countless more covert tactics. The movement's point of reference should continue to be one another — creating the most directly democratic spaces, but we also must find ways to negotiate issues of institutional power — all the while maintaining our agenda.

Reprinted from Tidal #2, March 2012

May Day Highlight

The Loving Embrace of Black Bloc

by Isis Feral

On the eve of May Day a black-clad crowd indiscriminately smashed up a neighborhood in San Francisco's Mission District, and continued unhindered even after they hit the police station. In a sensationalistic frenzy, the bourgeois media denounced anarchists as the ones to blame, but there were reports that no one among local anarchists and black bloc participants knew the vandals. In fact, comrades in black bloc explicitly distanced themselves from the vandalism, and most left the scene as soon as they realized that the action was without direction and not principled. In the days following, Occupy San Francisco, which includes anarchists and black bloc, condemned the action and offered help to repair the damage to homes and small local businesses.

Wearing black and masks, and smashing things, does not a black bloc make.

May Day itself was an amazing day here in the Bay Area. While it was not a traditional general strike, several unions did go on strike, including janitors, nurses and ferry workers, while longshore workers effectively shut down the ports for a contractual stop-work meeting. Immigrant workers marched as they have every year since May Day 2006, a national day without immigrants, the first general strike in the U.S. since Oakland 1946 and the union busting Taft-Hartley Act that followed in 1947. It really felt like International Workers Day, a holiday observed in most of the world except in this country, where it originated when the 1886 general strike in Chicago won the 8-hour work day.

We left Oakland at 2:30 am for the Larkspur ferry terminal in Marin County, to picket there with the striking inland boatmen. The Golden Gate district officially canceled the ferries that morning, but we'd heard that they had lied in a previous strike, so we didn't take any chances, and showed up early to help defend the strike.

The picket line was slow to start, but when a driver threatened to run me over, more workers got pissed off and finally picketed in earnest, until a union bureaucrat showed up and ordered everyone not to block cars. I didn't violate her wishes, but did challenge her, hoping that the rank and file might follow my example in the long run. Too many unions are neutered by the rank and file relying on their bureaucracies to make decisions for them that are not in their own best interest. Rather than take her word for it, I asked how we can be sure that none of the drivers are scabs, and told her that if she asks me to come to a picket, I'll picket, but if she asks me to come to a protest, I'm not showing up at 4 o'clock in the morning.

As the sun came up the rally was bolstered by a teamsters' big rig, blasting Marianne Faithful's version of *Which Side Are You On*. They also brought a giant inflatable fat cat grabbing a worker by the throat. We left the party atmosphere behind by around 9 am, and headed to Berkeley to support the striking nurses.

Though the hospital was surrounded by nurses, they weren't too clear on the concept of picketing either. I asked some of them whether they were really picketing, or were they just protesting and letting people through. They said they stop only union workers. They let non-union scabs go in to fill the jobs they had walked out of. Something obviously got lost in the translation. How sad when THE militant direct action strategy in defense of the working class is so woefully misunderstood, and its effectiveness diminished by catering to laws that were written to enslave.

At noon we left the nurses and went to Oscar Grant Plaza, the center of activity for Occupy Oakland. We arrived just after the first police riot, when they discharged teargas and snatched individuals out of the crowd. I later saw video footage, and at one point cops were surrounded by angry protesters. *If* Occupy really was violent, those cops would have gotten seriously hurt, but all the crowd did was yell, 'we are not afraid'. And *if* Occupy really was violent, it wouldn't have been just bottles and paint that were thrown at cops later that evening, when they lined up to clear the plaza long before curfew, as a peaceful crowd milled about. Not one of the cops in their armored riot gear got hurt. They did not even react to the shattering glass, and seemed more concerned about the paint stains on their uniforms. They went after Occupyers quite some time later, so their actions were most definitely not in 'self-defense'. The violence originated ENTIRELY from the cops, who were armed to their teeth.

We hung out at the plaza for a couple of hours, a very chilled out scene, nothing illegal going on that I could see. It didn't even smell like pot! We were using the plaza for its intended purpose. But then we heard the familiar sound of a police projectile exploding about a block away, and a little later, someone came up saying that the cops had announced (out of earshot, in a side street) that they would arrest everyone at the plaza, so most of us left. A few people stayed behind to test it out, and were not arrested after all. But looking down from the nearby parking garage, we saw a huge crowd in the intersection, which looked like a very large protest. All riot cops! It looked like there were hundreds of them. This was around 3 pm.

We came back a couple of hours later, after lunch, and

people were back at the plaza, waiting for the permitted immigrants rights march to arrive. The cops took down the banners while we waited, and I saw one of them reach for the pink pig piñata with a police badge on its chest, hanging out of reach. Some Occupyers were all too happy to assist, and smashed the piñata to shreds, with candy and fake money flying everywhere. The only 'violence' from protesters that I saw was against a papier-mâché pig. The cops decided not to interfere.[177]

We left around 8:30pm, right before another police projectile exploded in the intersection. In footage I saw later, the cops pushed the crowd away from the plaza up Broadway, at one point with a line of motorcycles with all sirens blaring. In one video a red SUV turned onto a street in my neighborhood, several blocks away from the plaza, and riot cops spilled out of it, and jumped a guy just standing on the sidewalk. The protest crowd was nowhere to be seen.

There is also footage of two Alameda County Sheriffs (the notorious, and aptly named 'blue meanies') with M4 assault rifles in front of city hall earlier in the afternoon. They drove through downtown with an armored personnel carrier, which appeared to have on its roof an as of yet unused LRAD (long range acoustic device, which can make you deaf), apparently trying to intimidate the crowd. When I was at the plaza in the

---

[177] You can see a short, satisfying video of the piñata meeting its demise, with comrades singing 'no more pigs in the community — no more brothers/sisters in jail' at youtube.com/ watch?v=eB7sw8_e8sl.

evening, I saw a group of about five Oakland cops patrolling the park, and one had his hand firmly placed on his pistol with live ammunition.

With the overwhelming and threatening presence of ever more militarized riot cops, the highlight of my day was when we approached a small cluster of black bloc at the plaza. My comrade was distributing his organization's critical defense of black bloc in response to Chris Hedges' article of condemnation, and we stopped to talk for a while. I told one of them that I've been defending them a lot in recent months, because I know that in the face of police violence it's usually black bloc, whether individuals or in a group, who shield others, preventing a lot of injuries and arrests. I don't have to agree with every smashed window to stand up for those who have my back.

I wish someone had taken a photo, because what happened next should disintegrate all the stereotypes of black bloc being out of control thugs. This completely cloaked ninja-like figure, whose eyes were all I could see, and whom I will likely never recognize again, quietly spread his arms out wide, then wrapped them around me in a loving embrace.

It was a snapshot that encompasses the way I've always experienced black bloc: Loving towards their community, concerned for our safety, and ready to defend us. When the explosion went off in the afternoon, black bloc participants were right in the front of the crowd that swarmed to help our

Peace, Love and Anarchism, Occupy Oakland Black Bloc, May 1, 2012.

comrades under attack.

Some of us have been calling for 'Workers Defense Guards' for decades, but few among organized labor have heeded the call. Until workers organize such defense guards, black bloc is the only group of people who mobilize to do this necessary work, who put their own bodies on the line to defend our comrades from the direct violence of state repression. I love them for it, and from now on I just may start all my participation in actions by first hugging everyone in black bloc.

The morning after May Day my neighbors found one of the black bloc shields, which the City of Oakland has since attempted to ban as a 'Tool of Violence': a plastic garbage can, cut in half, with a big heart painted on it, abandoned on the sidewalk in our neighborhood, battered, like so many more of us would be, if it wasn't for the courage of a few anonymous comrades.

PEOPLE'S PARK, BERKELEY, 1969.
It's not as though the police violence against Occupy is something new, though many participants may not be aware of their own movement's history.

What Did Occupy Achieve?

Occupy Wall Street and The Meanings of Success

by Marina Sitrin

It is late August 2012. Dozens of people are sitting and standing in a circle in Tompkins Square Park, planning the actions to commemorate the one year anniversary of Occupy Wall Street. We are literally in the same place, even under the same tree, where the assemblies to plan the initial September 17 occupation took place a year ago. There are a few of the same faces, and many many new ones. As I stand there reflecting on what it means to be in exactly the same geographic spot, yet in an entirely different world, a young man bounces up to me. He is an artist and has played a consistent role in organizing Occupy since last summer. He almost always bounces rather than walks, and his eyes usually glisten with happiness. After a long hug by way of greeting he asks me, "Do you think we should be depressed?" His eyes are not sparkling as much as usual, and I am taken aback by the question. Depressed? Why? I had just been thinking about how far we had come.

Many people think Occupy has been a failure, he says.

Hundreds of parks and plazas around the country are no longer occupied, and we are no longer in the mainstream news, and people are saying that we do not have a plan.

But, I say, and he also says, and we both agree: these seem like the wrong metrics. At the same time, what would the right metrics be?

The conversation was a familiar one. In June I traveled to Athens, Greece. Almost immediately after saying hello, a friend from a neighborhood assembly said to me, "Marina, you have to understand, the situation here is much worse, it is not like we thought it would be, we are not succeeding." Only *half* the population of Athens was refusing to pay the newly imposed tax on the electric bill, he said. And the coordination among the more than 50 neighborhood assemblies in Athens was not as concrete as it should be, and, even more frustrating, many neighbors were coming to their local assemblies for support, but were no longer participating regularly. Maybe I looked like I was going to laugh, because he proceeded to remind me that in November of 2011, the expectations for the movement were quite high: some spoke of dual power and others even of revolutionary situations. By comparison, half the population engaging in direct action and another significant sector looking to the neighborhood assembly as the local power, but not directly participating regularly, was disappointing. After a long conversation I agreed that, based on his definition of success, the movement had not "succeeded"; but I also argued that it did not mean that they had been unsuccessful.

What does success mean? Who decides? By what standards? What has taken place over the course of this last year?

September 17, 2011, marked the beginning of a new refusal in the US. Joining our sisters and brothers around the globe, who in the years prior were declaring *Enough is Enough!*, as in Mexico and Greece, to *Kefaya!* (Enough) in Egypt, and *They All Must Go!* in Argentina. Together we are not only refusing — we are not just saying no! In each place, in ways that are unique and remarkably similar at the same time, we are affirming ourselves and our power. This is the power of the slogan We are *the 99%* or *Real Democracy Ya!* It is a claim of who we are and a recognition of that power.

Around the world there has been a move from the occupation of large plazas to the creation of neighborhood assemblies, weaving assemblies and actions into the fabric of everyday life. The movements have left the large public plazas to root themselves in workplaces and schools. In Greece, the refusal to pay the new electricity tax is organized through local neighborhood assemblies. Then, when the electricity is cut, it is also the neighborhood assembly that reconnects it. Sometimes the assembly breaks into the records office of the electric company and destroys records of debt.

This is all done through local assemblies coordinating on regional levels. Similar actions are also taking place with regard to increased costs to basic health care. Again the neighborhood assemblies block the cashiers in the hospitals so that people do not have to pay. Additionally people are organizing barter networks, through local assemblies that then have more regional connections.

Here in New York we have seen the appearance of numerous local assemblies, which in some cases work directly to defend neighbors from evictions or to support their struggle for the right to affordable and dignified housing, as in Sunset Park, Brooklyn. Occupy assemblies have appeared in each of the college and university campuses of the public city university system in New York, coordinating together to resist cuts and proposed tuition increases, as well as to create a space for a "free university" where new forms of education and pedagogy are experimented with, led, and coordinated by students.

Throughout the United States, in large cities and small towns, people inspired by the politics and tactics of Occupy have been organizing to defend people from evictions, from the neighborhood of Bernal Heights in San Francisco to suburbs in Midwestern Minnesota and Iowa. The form is the same. Neighbors come together, sometimes going door to door, sometimes meeting in a person's home, and discuss who is at risk of foreclosure and what to do about it, often physically defending homes from eviction as well as petitioning for new terms for living in the home with the bank. Anyone who has been to one of these home defenses, or even looked at the photos, will quickly get a sense of what this means: teenagers in sports jackets, mothers holding children, grandparents and neighbors and activists, all together gather to prevent an eviction or foreclosure from taking place. In most cases they win, forcing the banks to allow people to keep their homes instead of being cast out on the street.

For example, in the Bernal Heights neighborhood of San Francisco, a few neighbors came together first to help defend a longtime resident who was facing foreclosure. After a long battle, they were able to force the bank to renegotiate his mortgage to one that he could afford. From there, a number of women began a door knocking campaign where they went house to house asking if people were facing foreclosure and if they wanted to fight. As Molly, one of the first participants in Occupy Bernal explained,

> Well, we've stopped a lot of auctions — that's kind of a last-ditch effort, once the home is getting auctioned off. We're trying to stop the foreclosures before that. And now we're starting think about we need to talk to people before they even get in to foreclosure, because the more time we have the better it is, if we're really trying to save people's homes.... A lot of people were skeptical at first, but there are peo-

ple who've gotten their loans modified through work that we've done — their home would have been auctioned off; they would have been evicted. We feel like we're doing something for our neighbors at least. And one thing that I found out, once we started at who was in foreclosure — we found out who they were: they were almost all people of color. This is a very diverse neighborhood, but I would say most of the people who live here were white people; so that people of color were the ones who the bank targeted for these bad loans. So it feels to me like — this is the main reason that I'm active in this — that the face of my neighborhood is getting changed every day by the banks, these big banks that made fraudulent loans to my neighbors. I'm just outraged. I'm outraged all the time anyway, but this is really outrageous.

Similar stories are being told throughout the US, and many housing defenses are taking place that I am sure are not known about, that are not in the media or even the alternative press. As Molly and others from Occupy Bernal explain, they began to organize to defend their neighbors. It was and is the most basic thing to do — to speak with the person living next to you and organize together. This sort of direct action, facilitated by neighborhood assemblies, is part of what Occupy has inspired. This is where Occupy has come in less than a year.

Within workplaces the movement is still beginning, but the relationship of the Occupy movement to those involved in labor struggles is deepening and profound. Labor laws that threaten workers for taking action on the job have created such fear that there is often little fighting back within a workplace during business hours. However, there has been an increasing relationship with workers in struggle and movement participants. For example, in my neighborhood in Kensington Brooklyn, a local community group, together with the new Occupy in the neighborhood, have begun to support worker's efforts to organize a union. The workers themselves fear losing their jobs, so they do not join the picket and flyering outside, but the movement has been successfully keeping neighbors from shopping in the grocery store (Golden Farms) and is increasing the pressure on the owners to recognize workers rights. Just last week, workers have won at Hot and Crusty, a cafe on the Upper East Side of Manhattan, where they have been organizing a union for almost a year. This victory would not have taken place without the support of community groups, labor and Occupy. Workers from the cafe began coming to Occupy meetings last fall, and with the support of the community and movements have maintained pressure inside the workplace. Then, once they were locked out, workers received movement participants' support in maintaining an ongoing action outside the café, handing out food and coffee on a donation basis, as well as educating the neighborhood as to what was taking place. Finally, due to the pressure, the owners now have agreed to recognize the union and will reopen the cafe as a union shop. These are huge victories that demonstrate the powerful relationship between workers in struggle and Occupy. Similarly in Spain, when there is a struggle and workers ask for support, movement participants will sometimes physically block all people from entering a workplace so that it is effectively shut down, even if the workers cannot "legally" strike. In this way direct action by the movement directly supports the struggle of the workers, yet without placing the workers in any danger. The effect of strike has still occurred with solidarity action.

Not Just *What*, But *How*

There is no question as to the amount of Occupy-inspired actions across the country. What I have mentioned above is only the tip of the iceberg. But more important than making a list of *what* is happening under the umbrella of Occupy is *how* it is all taking place. People are coming together in horizontal assemblies and deciding what to do. No one is waiting on a political party or a boss or leader to come and tell them what to do and how, but we are looking to one another and figuring it out together. It is not about asking but about doing. It is from a point of affirming our power together and not from a position of weakness.

In Argentina, ten years after the popular rebellion, an interesting phenomenon arose with regard to the question of success of the movements. Young people, and even those in their 30s, who were generally teens or in their 20s during the rebellion, have begun to refer to themselves as *Hijos* (children) of the 19th and 20th. What they mean by this is not that they became political during the rebellion of December 19th and 20th, 2001, though many of them did. What they mean is that the way that they organize today, with assemblies, using *horizontalidad*, was created by the rebellion. What it means to be a child of the 19th and 20th lies in the forms of social relationships and the seeing of means as a part of the ends. Nicolas and Gisela, two movement participants explained this as follows in 2010: "[We say] we are the children of 2001 because we were formed by everything we lived within — the assemblies, the factories, and everything that happened in the streets. It is there that we learned these cooperative principles of *horizontalidad*."

Can One Measure a Dream?

Social movements are made up of people. People with ideas and dreams, dreams for themselves, dreams for the collective, and dreams for the movements and the world. Sometimes these movement dreams and goals measure up with those of social scientists who study movements, claiming to know what a successful movement is. Which I guess is like saying they know the dreams of the movement participants. Some theorists argue, for example, that the Occupy movement must ultimately take state and institutional power to be successful. Some Occupy movement participants however often say that dignity and freedom in their relationships is what they desire and dream. Who is right? Are the people who tell me that I need to own a home and have a well-paying job to be happy truly arguing I am not happy because I do not? Can one really argue that a movement is not successful because it did not meet the goals a person has imposed on the movement?

Who decides success? Success has to be decided by those people in struggle, those who are fighting or organizing for something.

Success of a movement, movement goals and people's desires come from those people, those social actors, not those studying them or politically desiring to lead them. In fact, it is against this way of thinking and organizing that the Occupy movement was born. It was a rupture with people telling us what to do and how to do it. This includes not only governments and politicians, but also left political parties, journalists, and scholars.

One year after Occupy we have a success already. When people begin to organize all over the country they are doing so with assemblies, struggling against hierarchy, thinking about the question of leadership and power, and trying to create ways where all can be leaders. When people are organizing today it might not always be with the word Occupy, but the spirit of assemblies, direct action, and creating power together is there for sure. The mark of Occupy is there for sure.

The Future of Occupy

The Wonderful, Unpredictable Life of the Occupy Movement

by Arun Gupta

I met Nomi on a bus in Baltimore. She was from Wisconsin and had been involved with Occupy Wall Street. She was part of Occupy Judaism and fondly recalled the *Yom Kippur* services she attended at the Wall Street occupation with hundreds of other people.[178] Nomi said that, for the first time, she and her friends felt like they could combine the religious and radical dimensions of Judaism. The conversation fell silent as the bus rolled along. Suddenly she turned to me and excitedly announced that she met her girlfriend at Liberty Plaza. I smiled and responded, "That's why Occupy Wall Street matters."

---

[178] There were so many people who showed up that the service had to move across Broadway to the giant cube plaza, in front of Brown Brothers Harriman. Around 800 to 1,000 people took part, mic-checking every phrase so that everyone could hear. The irony: Brown Brothers Harriman worked with Prescott Bush (George H.W. Bush's father) to launder money for Hitler and the Nazis. One rabbi said, "we're not praying to that building." Most people, unaware of that history, just took the Rabbi's statement as a joke they didn't quite understand. [note by Mitchel Cohen]

Photo: Sunset Parkerpix

Occupy Wall Street demonstration, New York City, March 15, 2012.

By enabling people to find fulfillment in all parts of their lives, whether romantic, spiritual, political or cultural, the Occupy movement is more than a movement. It is life-changing. People experience themselves as complete social beings, not just as angry, alienated protesters. Nomi said she was no longer involved in the movement, which I thought was more evidence of why the actual occupations were so important — they provided socio-cultural spaces in which participants were able to forge bonds while also allowing them to feel part of the broader OWS movement.

The emergence of every mass movement makes sense in hindsight, but no one could have predicted hundreds of occupations and thousands of groups would pop up across the United States just weeks after a ragged encampment secured a tenuous foothold on Wall Street last September. Sure, anger was boiling over prior to the takeover of Zuccotti Park in downtown Manhattan, but the occupation crystallized who is to blame for the economic crisis and who are the legitimate people. Anyone could walk into the public space, share their stories, find people with similar grievances and help build micro-societies. Occupy wasn't just a rejection of Washington and Wall Street. It revealed the failings of liberals, unions and the Left. New activists didn't first have to master volumes of social and cultural theory, attend grueling anti-oppression workshops and learn how to pepper their comments with academic jargon before joining. Nor did the movement require consultants, focus groups or polling to occupy the center of American politics with a radical left message. And the form was not the same old rallies with canned chants, pre-printed protest signs and preaching to the choir.

It's worth considering why Occupy Wall Street was such a smashing success last fall, as well as where it is headed. While the media lens has shifted away, Occupy has spawned a menagerie of energized movements and ambitious plans. Veteran organizer David Solnit, who is involved with Bay Area Occupy movements, sums up the current state: "The numbers showing up at GAs have dropped. Any movement has its mass mobilization and its in-between times. The organizing a lot of people are doing around housing and education is less visible but goes much deeper. We need a better measuring tape than numbers and public space and whether it's amplified through media owned by the 1 percent."

Like plants that lay dormant for the winter conserving energy, many occupations are blossoming anew with ambitious plans now that it's spring. Solnit says in San Francisco the movement is defending a dozen families in foreclosure, and is working toward a citywide moratorium on bank foreclosures and evictions. In Los Angeles, organizers say plans include large-scale marches by immigrants and unions, rolling street blockades and even an attempt to disrupt the main airport. In New York and around the country, a campaign has been launched called "*F the Banks*" to force the government to dismantle Bank of America, which is still receiving taxpayer subsidies. In Chicago, after the G8 summit set for May was moved to Camp David because of fear of large-scale protests, activists organized tens of thousands to protest the North Atlantic Treaty Organization (NATO) meeting that same month.

Challenging the status quo comes with costs. As the Occupy movement struggles to effect radical social change, it faces persistent police attacks and cooptation by Democratic Party forces from the outside and divisions over identity politics, militancy, localism and diffusion from the inside.

Rethinking Democracy

Occupy Wall Street is foremost a democratic uprising from the Left because it advocates for the downward and outward distribution of wealth and political power. Tying political democracy to economic democracy has made class relevant again for millions of people. As for the form, occupying public space is an old tactic. Since the early 20th century, examples include the Wobbly free-speech campaign, the automobile factory sit-down strikes, lunch-counter sit-ins, the Columbia University student takeover and Cindy Sheehan's vigil outside of Bush's Texas ranch. The need for democratic forums is greater than ever as public space is ever-more surveilled, regulated and commodified.

Occupy also challenges the notion that workers are the sole agent of revolution. Clearly, labor's power is unmatched in potentially bringing capitalism to a halt, but in actuality, collective action on the shop or office floor has been crippled by a lack of working-class consciousness, timid and self-serving union bureaucracies, and the legal and repressive tools of the corporate-state hybrid. Occupations of public space by activists, intellectuals and marginal workers — as shown by Egypt's Tahrir Square, Oakland's November 2, 2011 general strike and the December 12, 2011 West Coast port blockades — can attack capital from unexpected directions, creating space for organized labor to take more militant action.

In terms of development, the Occupy movement has gone through a series of stages, though they are not so much distinct phases as overlapping and intermingling trends where one stage may take prominence over the others at different times. First, the occupation created an awareness of a group that could be called "the people," which is often invoked with the now-ubiquitous chant, "We are the 99 percent." The flipside of "the people" is those who are not a legitimate part of the community: "the 1 percent," in this case. Both categories are social and psychological concepts that mobilize rather than analytical terms that accurately describe social forces. Segments of the 99 percent, such as white-collar managers, small-business owners and the police, generally act as the social and physical enforcers for the elite, while the real owning class is perhaps the top .01 percent. But "We are the 99.99 percent" is hardly a catchy slogan. In this respect, Occupy Wall Street is similar to the Tea Party, which invokes its legitimate community with slogans like, "We the people," "Take back America" and "Founding Fathers." For Tea Partyers, however, nearly everyone else is illegitimate — unions, immigrants, Muslims, liberals, welfare recipients (code for blacks and Latinos), feminists, environmentalists, socialists, and gays and lesbians.

Combine a public organizing space with "the people," and the second stage follows: assault the citadels of illegitimate power. As one organizer told me about Zuccotti Park,

"At any moment, you could call for an impromptu march on Goldman Sachs and a hundred people would join you." The night of October 5, 2011, was an exhilarating example of this. After a union-led rally in downtown Manhattan, thousands of people surged through the financial district in breakaway marches for hours. With so many people in the streets feeling the wind of public support at their backs, the police were taxed to hold the line. Wall Street was no longer an impenetrable bastion and the New York Police Department (NYPD) was no longer omnipotent. They felt fragile and under siege.

The occupation was a focal point for the media as well, and, surprisingly, many corporate media outlets gave the movement favorable press at times. Some observers have suggested that one lesson is not to see the corporate media as *the* enemy. Rather, it should be treated as a battleground, albeit one that is tilted toward the interests of the wealthy and the imperial state. The physical occupation also served a valuable role in making "politicians realize there are people watching what they are doing," says Anne Gemmell, political director of the labor-backed community group Fight for Philly.

The Carnival of the Imagination

The third stage is carnival. After years of clichéd protests bearing witness to power, street politics had become futile and predictable. Leaders of the anti-Iraq War movement excelled at polite marches on weekends with no risk and little impact, and adjusted its politics to the election cycle, leading to its demise by 2007. Occupy Wall Street hit the big time because it is innovative political theater, a quality shared by the civil rights movement, the AIDS Coalition to Unleash Power (ACT UP), the global justice movement and the Arab Spring before it. I would stand on the steps of Zuccotti Park and watch as hundreds of people below exchanged food, art, knowledge, books, politics, health care, bedding, anger, ideas, skills and love. Not one exchange was mediated by money (of course, the goods were paid for at some point). It felt like being able to breathe for the first time, because relations were being forged according to human needs and concerns, not according to the logic of the market. Revolutionary consciousness was being born through collective, democratic political action, which is essential to igniting a new era of activism and organization.

The occupation made a different world real, one without corporations, authoritarian politics and the police state. As Michael Premo of Occupy Wall Street's housing group, puts it: "You don't know how to dream unless you see it sometimes. The occupation unlocked the creative, radical imagination." Seeing new and different ways of organizing work, family and community drew throngs of first-time as well as wayward activists to the movement. If it was the Left organizing the Left, Occupy Wall Street would have failed because experienced activists, no matter how well intentioned, come bearing heavy allegiances, ideologies and interpersonal baggage that inevitably sink left re-foundation projects. A movement must coalesce around the previously nonpolitical to forge meaningful social change.

Whose Community?

The fourth stage is creating genuine community. The cultural life of occupations and the experience of working and living together bonded Occupyers together. What community involves is thorny, however. For example, at the occupation in Portland Oregon, organizers say the encampment diverged from the general assembly because those sleeping in the park, many of whom were homeless, were not present at the general assembly meetings, also known as GAs. As a result, the GA was approving decisions about the occupation with few actual Occupyers present. A related case occurred in Austin, Texas, where one organizer told me that, by December, the GA was trying to end the encampment on the steps of Austin City Hall, while the Occupyers, again mainly homeless, blocked the action because they said they had no other safe place to live. (Eventually, the city of Austin shut it down by force in early February.) Other cities encountered a similar phenomenon, and frequently enough that "home-based Occupyers" is now a common term used to refer to those who are active in the movement but do not sleep in the camp.

The idea of community is also a proxy for long-simmering debates over whether the goal is to take over the system or to build a new world in the shell of the old. As occupations and enthusiasm spread, many activists yearned to construct sustainable economies to meet the needs of daily life. Occupations ran on their communal stomach, so community gardens, recycling and grey-water systems were often first on the agenda. It didn't take long for the dreams to outrun reality, however. Last fall, I was approached by Occupyers looking to form a printing cooperative. They planned to start with photocopies and progress to newspapers such as *The Indypendent* and *The Occupied Wall Street Journal*, both of which I co-founded. I was stunned. Photocopying flyers is one thing, but printing 50,000 copies of a four-color newspaper is another. I explained it would require a warehouse-sized space, millions of dollars in capital, sophisticated press equipment and digital technology, experienced workers to run the facility and business savvy to survive in a printing industry with razor-thin margins. I never heard from them again.[179] Currently, many occupations are pursuing small-scale projects such as urban farming and communal living, but this runs the risk of utopian separatism. The dream of gathering the righteous and

---

[179] The Occupy Publishing Collective survived and, with the donation it received of multilith printing equipment resides on Atlantic Avenue in Brooklyn directly below an acupuncture and meditation center. In the best spirit of Occupy, they have to work out time-sharing arrangements so as not to disturb the acupuncture clients, which they've successfully achieved.

starting anew in uncharted territory or creating a new social space is the story of America, after all. Withdrawing from society is tempting, but a sign of defeat.

Now that nearly every occupation that popped up last fall has been evicted from their common space, it's tempting to say that "Occupy 2.0" is underway. There are energized movements around housing, finance, labor, food, art, gender and ecology. Nonetheless, the loss of public space is an undeniable setback: it glued the movement together.

Nathan Schneider, who has chronicled Occupy Wall Street from the pre-planning stages, says that, since the occupation was routed from Zuccotti Park, decision-making power has devolved from the general assembly to the spokescouncil to working groups to campaigns. In March, I queried about 15 Occupy Wall Street organizers, and not one had been to a GA meeting in the prior month. Some rolled their eyes at mention of the GA and told of constant disruptions and occasional fistfights. A few claimed paid provocateurs were stirring up the pot. No one could offer any proof of government agents, which is admittedly difficult to come by, but the infighting is all too real. When hundreds were living on Wall Street's doorstep, the target was obvious: banks like Goldman Sachs and their lapdogs in the media and politics. Without an occupation as an anchor, vessels like the general assembly and spokescouncil can drift aimlessly, making it tempting to turn on your fellow crewmates.

With the occupations over, most newcomers have wandered away. Ruth Fowler, a writer who works with Occupy Los Angeles, says: "Occupy is very odd right now. The people who have stayed are the cream of the crap, and the brilliant. The rank-and-file in between are at home ... It's an interesting dynamic. Not entirely comfortable. Lots of loonies floating around."

The lack of community means struggling with who is the subject and what is the purpose of the decision-making bodies. Michael Premo of Occupy Wall Street says organizers understand there is a need for physical space, "to build on the things that worked and think about what didn't work." He adds that Occupy Wall Street is, "planning on creating a clearinghouse for people to come together, build community and organize actions."

The Roads Ahead

New York is a showcase for the possibilities and pitfalls of Occupy Wall Street, which still bubbles with creativity. On March 28, 2012, Occupy Wall Street (claiming support of transit workers) took credit for chaining open 20 subway stations, allowing thousands of straphangers to ride for free so as to call attention to Wall Street's profiteering off of the city's perpetual mass transit follies. On March 15, a few hundred people outfitted with songs, banners and facades of foreclosed homes and costumed as bankers and police joined "*F the Banks.*" At turns festive and angry, the procession snaked through downtown Manhattan, halting at bailed-out banks to deliver a dose of displeasure. The highlight was an attempt to occupy a Bank of America branch with furniture. It being New York, police pounced as sofas, tables and bookcases were arranged outside the bank. Within minutes, scores of cops had quarantined the area and were carting away a handful of smiling protesters in cuffs.

The police strategy is to suffocate any outbreak of democracy, and it shows signs of working as long as the rank and file has vanished. Elites want images of heavy-handed policing because the narrative shifts from inequality to streetfighting, scaring off potential supporters. On March 17, the six-month anniversary of Occupy Wall Street, a completely peaceful attempt to re-occupy Zuccotti was aggressively evicted. The occupation shifted to Union Square, but after a few days, hundreds of police swept in to enforce rarely employed restrictions on overnight activity. Other than a protest against the killing of Trayvon Martin, most recent Occupy Wall Street events have attracted less than 500 people. (In the case of the Martin protest, criticism was rife that some Occupyers tried to turn it into an Occupy event to retake space, rather than focusing on police violence against and profiling of communities of color.) The protest-a-day mode can backfire because police swarm smaller protests, however peaceful and theatrical they may be. The antidote is greater numbers, but because any working group or campaign can call a protest, the movement risks spiraling downward into diffusion, unsustainable activity, burnout and shrinking crowds.

Occupy Comes Home

Despite these problems, Occupy has an enviable brand, significant public support, a plethora of movements and an unqualified success in reorienting the national debate from austerity to inequality. The secret of Occupy Wall Street's strength is disrupting power in ways both simple, such as the "mic check," and grand, such as by occupying public space. Even if that space is now a rarity, Occupy Wall Street retains a disruptive capacity that defies prediction. It can be seen from Occupy the SEC (Securities and Exchange Commission), which released a stunning 325-page critique of the Volcker Rule[180] (which seeks to curb banks from gambling with government-insured money), to Occupy Our Homes, which has successfully engaged in dozens of successful foreclosure and eviction defenses nationwide since November.

These are symbolic victories that put financial regulators on notice that they are being watched, and they are real victories

---

[180] http://www.occupythesec.org/letter/OSEC-OCC-2011-14-CommentLetter.pdf.

that keep families in their homes. Victories are essential because they sustain the movement. Occupy Our Homes has pioneered singing demonstrations to disrupt public auctions of foreclosed homes, having closed down two in Brooklyn in recent months, and the tactic is spreading throughout the city and country.

Beth Stephens and Annie Sprinkle, artists and social justice activists who describe themselves as "eco-sexual domestic partners," have made their Bay Area neighborhood of Bernal a model of the anti-foreclosure movement. Their movement began out of "neighborly love" for a 72-year-old African-American homeowner and veteran who is facing eviction. They say David Solnit was the catalyst, introducing them to two dynamic organizers — Buck Bagot and Stardust (in Human Form) — who helped them found Occupy Bernal to defend homeowners. Stephens said: "The heart of the group is door-knocking. We have a list of foreclosures, and once a week, members go out to these homes and tell them we will help." Stephens says 85 households, mostly of people of color, are facing foreclosure in their area, and Occupy Bernal explains they can assist them with free legal help.

"We are trying to mitigate the shame in this," Stephens says. "If they don't feel shame, they can understand where the blame is. They've been taken of advantage of by the banks." She adds that Occupy Bernal is actively defending 13 homeowners against eviction, has disrupted auctions and protests regularly — including in a group called "wild old women" who are in front of the banks every week — but the threat of eviction remains. So Occupy Bernal is pushing the San Francisco City Board of Supervisors "to pass a resolution calling for a moratorium on all foreclosures until the big banks are investigated" for fraud in lending and foreclosure activity. Sprinkle emphasizes that while the work is "deadly serious, we are also having fun doing it."

Nonetheless, the anti-foreclosure movement has a long way to go compared to the scale of the problem today, with 4 million families having lost their homes to foreclosures since 2007,[181] and compared to the scope of resistance in the past, with some historians claiming that, during the first eight months of 1932 in New York City, 77,000 evicted families were moved back into their homes by activists.

Laboring for Victories

To notch far-reaching victories, the Occupy movement needs allies with millions of members and access to resources — in short, the beleaguered labor movement, which has found a lifeline in Occupy. Organized labor seems to understand that laws and court rulings have blunted its most potent weapon: the strike. Labor organizers across the country are unbridled in their support for the movement, saying Occupyers

---

[181] http://topics.nytimes.com/top/reference/timestopics/subjects/f/foreclosures/index.html. Others have put the figure at 10 million.

can take risks unions are unable or unwilling to. Gemmell of Fight for Philly says, "There are no leashes holding the energy of the Occupy movement back." She says it has had a "positive spillover effect," and cited two instances where workers settled contracts on better-than-expected terms while Occupy Philadelphia was entrenched outside City Hall. Occupy Wall Street was a factor in the repeal last fall of Ohio's law that would have decimated public-sector unions, though the tens of millions of dollars labor poured into the effort did not hurt.

By moving beyond the workplace as the locus of struggle between labor and capital, Occupy has introduced creative tensions that benefit unions even if they feel their toes are being stepped on. The December 12, 2011 West Coast port shutdowns organized by the Occupy movement generated friction with leaders of the International Longshore and Warehouse Union (ILWU), who opposed the blockade attempts from Long Beach, California, to Vancouver, Canada. Occupyers then began organizing flying pickets to help the ILWU block a union-busting ship scheduled to come into Longview under military escort. Paul Glavin, an Occupy organizer in Oregon, says various occupations were "going to send hundreds of people, if not more."

"It was going to be very big," said Glavin. Before the confrontation occurred, grain export terminal operator EGT blinked and signed a contract with the ILWU.

The next test for labor and Occupy is May Day, with Occupy Los Angeles calling for a general strike. Michael Novick, a retired school teacher and anti-racist organizer, says, "There is a bunch of labor actions for May Day in LA," including one by recycling workers in San Fernando Valley and possibly at attempt by workers to disrupt traffic to LAX, the most active airport on the West Coast. Students are discussing shutting down a freeway, and Novick says there will, "be two different immigrant rights marches in downtown, which reflects a lot of historical divisions in the movement."

"Occupy is doing a car and bike caravan moving slowly across L.A. from four different directions," said Novick.

One troubling development is the formation of a "99 percent table" by Los Angeles labor organizers who are allegedly siphoning unions and faith-based groups away from the Occupy movement while also excluding some members of Occupy Los Angeles who have criticized what they see as attempts to poach the movement. Novick says Occupy's strategy is to work with everyone, and the day will end with an occupation of some sort in downtown Los Angeles.

Many other cities are gearing up for a range of marches and protests on May Day, though anything approaching a general strike seems highly unlikely. "Occupy Portland is planning for a spring offensive with May Day as the focus," said Glavin. "The Portland Liberation Organization Council is organizing to take over a building May 1. May Day will be part of a longer struggle. The strategy is to get organized in working-class neighborhoods to work toward a general strike."

Austin, Texas, is a different story. Dave Cortez, a community organizer whose focus is on energy and jobs, is part of Occupy Austin's working group on banks. Since Occupy Austin was cleared off the City Hall steps in early February, activities include organizing local, small businesses and nonprofits to move their money from Wall Street banks to community institutions.

"We are working toward getting the city, the county government, the transportation and school board to shift their money from the big banks to credit unions, and local banks," said Cortez. "Since October, we've tracked $1.6 million moved from largely personal accounts into credit accounts." But as for May Day, "We are one of the few Occupy movements not calling for a general strike on May Day. We've built a large coalition of immigrant rights, socialists, students, communities, faith, anarchists and environmental groups." Cortez says union members support Occupy Austin, but it does not have any official union support. "It was clear from the get-go we would not be able to get buy-in for a general strike. It's difficult for workers to participate because Texas is a right-to-work state. If they called in sick and participated, they could very easily be fired."

Occupy and organized labor may also find themselves on opposing sides as unions throw money and troops into President Obama's re-election battle while Occupy Wall Street mobilizes to occupy the Democratic National Convention, and the Republican counterpart, as well as making its presence known on the fall campaign trail.

Occupy the Election

When Occupy became a national sensation, Obama and the Democratic Party tried to co-opt it, and failed. At this point, the liberal strategy is more sophisticated. Democratic Party front groups like MoveOn and Rebuild the Dream have glommed onto the "99 percent," trying to steal Occupy's thunder while distancing themselves from the movement. Obama, meanwhile, is running even farther away by employing squishy language about "economic fairness," while Democrats are delighted that Mitt Romney is all but assured of the Republican nomination. Organized labor and liberals are already branding Romney as "Mr. 1 Percent," as if Obama isn't a gold-plated member of the 1 percent or been their greatest benefactor during the last three years.

Having interviewed hundreds of Occupyers across the country, it's fairly safe to say they fall into three camps regarding the 2012 election. There are those who didn't support Obama in 2008 and certainly won't this time; those who voted for him last time, but say they will not this time; and the plurality, those who say they will hold their nose and vote for

Obama. Few Occupyers, if any, will join Obama's campaign, because all agree that the electoral system is broken, which is exactly why they flocked to the movement as an alternative method of building and leveraging power. But at the same time, the Occupy movement needs to create a compelling counternarrative to the electoral process. It could be sidelined if it adopts a knee-jerk "pox on everyone's house" response and tries to occupy the Republican and Democratic National Conventions in the face of certain police thuggery.

There are some in the movement who do want to enlist in policy battles and electoral campaigns, but visiting an active occupation affirms that the heart of the movement is about creating societies that embrace the limitless possibilities of everyday life instead of allowing our passions to be manipulated into support for a venal system and our desires to be ground into grist for cheap trinkets.

In February my partner, Michelle Fawcett, and I heard that Occupy Fullerton in Orange County was holding an "Occupalooza." It was a warm, sunny day, like it almost always is in the O.C., so we cruised Fullerton's banal architecture until we happened upon an incongruous tent village. It was a familiar scene: about 40 tents, most shielded by blue tarps, and small knots of people playing music, smoking and lounging in the afternoon sun. The party was on top of the hill overlooking the Occupy Fullerton Camp, we were told.

Before hiking up the hill we met Wolf, a 25-year-old transgender native of Fullerton. Wolf was new to the movement, yet already immersed in it. He explained how Occupy Fullerton is lobbying the City Council to pass resolutions on issues ranging from Citizens United to predatory debt. His coolheaded explanation of how credit card companies trap unsuspecting college students in a cycle of debt gave way to a passionate embrace of the Occupy movement as a welcoming space for him and his intersex partner.

As we interviewed Wolf, John Park hung on the edge. When we turned to talk to Park, a Korean-American with two children in college, he launched into a blistering critique of the ideology of free trade, expertly citing the academic literature on the subject. That a middle-aged, immigrant computer programmer who is organizing around the outsourcing of jobs has found common cause with a transgender youth activist speaks to the raw ideological and emotional power of the twin slogans, *We are the 99 percent* and *Occupy Wall Street.*

When we clambered up the hill, we found a bowl-shaped grass amphitheater fringed by palm trees, a house band jamming with a few dozen people grooving to the music. True to the California setting, there were frisbees, sun bathers and stoners. Since it was winter, kids were sledding, even though that meant bouncing along a dirt gully gouged from the hillside. Lupe Barrios, eyeing our camera and notepad, sauntered over to talk. He said he was from Tucson, his right calf proclaimed "Hecho en San Diego" and he was here for "fun, not politics." But within a minute, he was talking about how, "immigrant rights are workers' rights," and told us, "My mother lives in a cage wherever she goes because of social and class oppressions."

The party was festive and giddy and unpredictable. The left is abundant in anger; the Occupy movement has turned that into joy. This country is floundering in despair; Occupy has given countless people hope. Within the Occupy movement, questions of inclusiveness, cooperation, compassion and democracy are foremost on people's minds. People want work, but they want it to be meaningful. They want the good life however they define it: liberatory, intellectual, libidinous or spiritual.

These emotional and philosophical truths make all the difference. If the movement becomes predictable, the faces all look familiar and the organizing feels like drudgery, then it will have lost. For now, no one knows what will happen next. And that's a wonderful thing.

Arun Gupta is covering the Occupy movement nationwide for Salon. *A version of this article was published in the May 2012 issue of* Z Magazine. *This article is from* Truthout.

Part Six.
OCCUPY SANDY

Todd Maisel, *New York Daily News*

Gravesend Bay, Brooklyn, looking northwest towards the Verrazano Bridge and Staten Island. October 29, 2012.

There is no "Planet B". Copenhagen, Denmark, 2009.

Southern Brooklyn "Sandy" Diary

by Mitchel Cohen

I live on the 7th floor of a 160-household apartment building on the southern edge of Bensonhurst, right next to (but not included in) the mandatory Evacuation Zone. There is a large park between my building and Gravesend Bay. SuperStorm Sandy's winds whipped the Bay into a frenzy; the waters smashed repeatedly into the pilings, esplanade, boat pier just across the Belt Parkway from my apartment.

The parkway had eerily emptied of traffic hours earlier. Suddenly, along with Coney Island, Brighton and Manhattan Beaches, it's under water and mostly dark. Emmons Ave. in Sheepshead Bay was reported to have been flooded by a wave 10-feet high, carrying away a number of cars as well as pouring into houses and local restaurants.

The waters came within 5 feet of my building, flooded the parking lot when the sewers on Cropsey Avenue backed up with scathingly polluted water ... and then stopped!

Dreier-Offerman park across the highway *would have* absorbed much of the water from the bay had New York City, in its infinite wisdom, not flattened the hills and replaced the natural soil and trees with artificial turf a year ago. The water rolled over the synthetic turf like marbles of mercury on Teflon without being absorbed and came cascading across the Belt Parkway, even though there was hardly any rain with this storm.

As I walked the next day in Brighton Beach, there were long lines at the public pay telephones — if you could find one! My favorite scene: Into the mountain of sand that the storm deposited on the Coney Island Boardwalk, someone carved a heart with the name "Sandy" in the center. "I ♥ Sandy!" Made me smile. Brooklynites maintain their sarcasm at all costs.

Four Days Later

Ida Sanoff had been trapped in her apartment in Brighton Beach. Like so many others, she and her husband Jeff have difficulty trudging the 8 flights of pitch black hallways and stairs a few times a day. "We have no water and our apartment is freezing. Both of our cars have been totaled, so getting around is next to impossible. Many people in our building have no flashlights & are feeling their way up & down the stairs in the dark. 311 is the biggest joke of all — either the line is busy & you can't get through, or you finally do get through & you wait & wait & wait & no one ever picks up.

"On Brighton Beach Ave., the mud line is half way up the facade of the stores. The building around the corner from me started pumping water out of their basement today.

"On top of everything else, we had to put our almost 22 year old cat down today. Our truck driver took us in his car. We could not get out to her regular vet, the cat specialist in Queens so we went to the emergency vet on Flatbush Ave. & Ave. R. They had no power either and were functioning on an emergency generator. We met people from Gerritsen Beach who had only the clothes on their back, their home had been flooded & they lost everything."

The Red Cross? FEMA? Nowhere to be found. I was about to walk the 2½ miles to Brighton with a bag of groceries for Ida when I finally hear from her. She writes:

> omg omg omg
>
> Finally got to go up on the Boardwalk today & walk around my block. Looks like half of Breezy is on my beach. Chairs, tables, wooden steps, huge sections of piers, a blue rowboat stenciled RPYC or BPYC. can't tell. All sorts of metal, a refrigerator. Toys. A rocking chair facing the shoreline.
>
> Warbasse houses will not have power for weeks. Coney Island Creek which is loaded with hideous sediments, including coal tars, flooded it. Loads of seniors 20+ floors up in the cold & dark & with no water.
>
> Two buildings of the Oceana/Millennium luxury condos at Coney Island Ave. have had major damage to their mechanicals and have been evacuated.

Behind my building, there was a lovely older co-op building. Lobby was a lovingly preserved time capsule of high-end design, circa 1960. Several steps up to the lobby so I thought they'd be OK. Went in with my friend who lives there. Everything had already been ripped out because it was soaked, walls, floors, everything. The high water mark was over my head. My friend said that on the first floor, people barely escaped the rising water in their apartments. In the condo building next door which is adjacent to the Boardwalk, the cars on the first floor garage level are buried several feet in sand. The windows on the first floor blew out & the whole place flooded. Sand piles 6 feet high on Ocean Parkway, a BobCat trying to at least clear the sidewalk. Mountains of sand on sidewalks that should be put back onto the beach & no way or no one to do it. Anyone have some dump trucks?

Several trees down in Seaside Park. Both synagogues on Sea Breeze Ave have several feet of sand in their lobbies.

Several stores open on Brighton Beach Ave. but no one is clear on whether or not the food they are selling is fresh, has defrosted or was soaked by flood waters. My friend bought some anyway. Rocco's pizza being made by the light of a generator. I was so hungry, but again, not sure if the food had been compromised. Rocco's deli said that they will get fresh cold cuts & cheese tomorrow. Hope they don't sell out by the time I get there.

People waiting on lines for food.

The handball players shoveled the courts at West 5th and are having a grand time!

No one, but no one, here has a car. Rumor is that insurance companies are not even sending adjusters, they are just assuming that the cars are totaled. Need to see a doctor for the stitches in my finger & no way to get to one. Some folks I know nearby have cars, but don't have gas. My truck driver got on a gas line in East NY at 4:30 AM & was told that gas was on the way. He gave up around 5 PM & found a station nearby that has gas and he is on the line & praying they don't run out.

No subway service until Kings Hwy. Buses are packed & don't stop. No way to get to Waldbaum's on Ocean Ave & Voorhies which reportedly has reopened.

My block is "No Standing Fire Zone" & everyone is parked here with no one to give tickets. If there is a fire we will fry. Tried calling 311 — WHAT A JOKE!!!!!

But a few blocks north of here, everything is perfectly normal. People can't understand why we are so upset.

Election Day & after

A few days ago I attended a very moving and huge memorial service in Park Slope for Jessie Streich-Kest, the young animal rights and ACORN activist who was killed along with her friend Jacob Vogelman by a falling tree, as they walked outside with her dog Max.

I'm heading down to Coney Island after I vote to see what more I can do to help. So many people whose homes, boats, and lives are in ruins. This is a very great tragedy, just as it has been for decades for poorer people, homeless or near-homeless. Many large houses in the gated community of Sea Gate, on Coney's tip, are gone. Can they continue to work together, these wealthy and these poor, in this great spirit of cooperation that sweeps over New York and everywhere else in responding to tragedy?

I talk to a man re-charging his cellphone on a generator set up on the edge of the Coney Island projects. He is wondering about all the birds — where do they go? Did they survive the vicious winds? He's brought some nuts and crumbs for the birds, but — I hadn't noticed this until he mentioned it — like the Red Cross and FEMA, there are few birds to be seen. He's extremely concerned. They've disappeared!

I ask an electrician working on replacing equipment in the projects why is it that the private apartment building right next door had power restored a week ago? He just looks at me quizically, maybe bemused, more likely "is this guy (me) really so clueless?," and says: "If you have to ask, you already know the answer."

Howard Brandstein — one of those who certainly knows

that answer and is trying to do something about it — reports from the Sixth Street Community Center on the Lower East Side (built, over the decades, in the shell of a century-old abandoned synagogue that still retains some of the beautiful marble tablets inside), that they had hundreds of volunteers over the weekend making sandwiches and distributing them door-to-door in nearby public housing projects. The basement had been flooded, but Citlalic Jeffers, the young Coordinator of the Community Supported Agriculture project that runs out of the Center, is organizing emergency daily food distributions for the neighborhood in conjunction with Good Old Lower East Side (GOLES).

Everywhere, people are trying to help each other. Occupy Wall Street is doing a tremendous amount. They've morphed into "Occupy Sandy"; the OWS network of committed organizers kicked into high gear immediately, which says a great deal not only about who really gives a shit but about the benefits of lateral organizing. One friend from Occupy lived in Rockaway and her house was burned to the ground. I often see her collecting supplies to distribute. Beauty is everywhere amidst tragedy. Despite the Breezy Point section of Rockaway's long history of exclusionary and racist housing and access policies, volunteers are nevertheless rallying to its assistance, demonstrating the ability of the human spirit to sweep aside prejudices in times of social crisis, at least temporarily. Perhaps not surprisingly, none of the media have discussed the nature and history of Breezy Point, as Mark Rausher points out:

> As a child, I grew up on the Southern shore of Brooklyn, within sight of the Rockaway Peninsula which juts into the Atlantic Ocean from Jamaica Bay. I frequently took a ferry from Sheepshead Bay to Rockaway, driving my mother crazy with my desire to ride on the water and breathe the sea air. Growing up, I heard about Breezy Point, an early gated community on Rockaway which for decades had discriminated against Jews, Blacks, Italians, Hispanics, Asians and other groups. Unlike the über-rich gated communities we hear so much about, this was an Irish enclave of small beachfront cottages, private and self-contained with a volunteer fire department and a large private security force, paying limited property taxes and not subject to anti-discrimination laws.
>
> The devastating fires which consumed over 100 of these homes during Hurricane Sandy's brief visit, in conjunction with a tornado that touched down there earlier this year, seem to me to be classic examples of karmic retribution; it also highlights the hypocrisy which surrounds our new economic reality — despite the fact that Breezy Point residents paid practically no taxes and flouted local laws (and morality), when the fires started, city, state and Federal funds were used to bring first responders to Breezy Point, to fight the fires and try to assist residents who had failed to honor the mandatory evacuation order. These residents, mostly middle-class, took advantage of America's fierce support for individual/property rights when it suited them, but were more than glad to grab those services (and the public financial support which

makes them available) when *they* needed them.¹⁸²

Occupy Sandy, as the upcoming stories in this book relate, is spending a great deal of time and effort in the Rockaways, not only at Breezy Point but most especially in the Federal housing projects to the East which are neglected by public services, just as they are elsewhere. Volunteers are going up and down the stairs door-to-door to each and every one of the tens of thousands of apartments there and in Coney Island, just to check on people, provide some relief, water, food, blankets and batteries. In fact, several people have already been discovered dead, apparently for days or even weeks, in their apartments.

Occupy — with so many dedicated participants — has proven in practice that non-hierarchal networking is capable of organizing a very quick volunteer response. But one question especially lingers: Will Occupy be able to mobilize the same desperate people it is now assisting, when it comes to direct action protests, especially as it appears that the City is intentionally denying assistance to poor people in order to drive them out of the projects and confiscate that prime ocean-front real estate for luxury homes, hotels and playgrounds for the rich and famous? That is exactly what occurred in New Orleans, with tens of thousands of people never being able to return to their homes. Can Occupy Sandy switch

---

¹⁸² Mark Rausher, private letter.

gears from being a "salvation army" type of activity, crucial though it has been, into a radical or even revolutionary movement *with* the thousands of people they are helping?

* * *

Since I've never "upgraded" my internet connection from my land line "dial-up", I am one of the few in my building whose internet access and phone service remains intact, even though our electricity never went out. So I can get and send email, and watch the News on TV thanks to my ancient indoor rabbit ears antenna, news that I relay to my neighbors when I see them in the elevator, to their astonished exclamations of "You're kidding me!" I tell them about independent mobilizations providing mutual aid that are occurring all over the place.[183]

In Coney Island, FEMA finally opened a center — a full four days after the storm. They ran out of supplies a few days ago. Today there's a line of around 65 people outside, and soldiers and police, who are all over the FEMA warehouse, are not letting people in. I ask "why not?" A soldier points to his wrist, and says "It's not time, yet."

On the *Democracy Now!* radio show, Mike Burke asks Rockaway organizer Catherine Yeager how her efforts with Occupy are different than FEMA's. Her testy response is em-

---

[183] Check out http://interoccupy.net/occupysandy/ for info about how to organize assistance in your area.

blematic of the best of direct action organizing:

> **MIKE BURKE:** Now, how are the relief efforts that are taking place here different from what we're seeing with FEMA and the National Guard down the street?
>
> **CATHERINE YEAGER:** FEMA down the street, from what I understand, is handing out pieces of paper that tell you to call a phone number to get help. Here, you come, and you get help immediately.[184]

There are many people, mostly from the nearby NYC Housing Authority projects, who still have no electricity more than two weeks after the storm, no running water, no bathroom facilities, no food — and NYCHA (the housing authority) is still charging them full rent, and was about to proceed with evictions for nonpayment until Occupy and many others raised a stink. I'm sick of the stagnant, militarized FEMA facility. I decide to walk west on Neptune Avenue to West 29th Street, across from a deserted Kaiser Field, where neighborhood resident Pam Harris has turned her front yard into a relief center with Occupy Sandy. She tells me she didn't know who they were, she just found the Occupy Relief website by doing a google search when she was able to access the internet. Now she's filled with nothing but praise for all the young committed folks who've poured into Coney Island from all over the City to lend a hand. In

---

[184] http://www.democracynow.org/2012/11/5/after_sandy_occupy_movement_re_emerges

front of her house, a steady stream of people drop off supplies, while others pick up blankets, winter clothing, batteries, flashlights and diapers. Occupy has set up a generator for people to charge their cellphones and computer batteries. And now, every day another team of chefs come from restaurants around the City to serve hot meals for free to whoever wants one, no standing on ceremony, just come and take what you need, eat your fill of great food, and drop off supplies for others. There are no forms to fill out, no one is keeping track ... and yet, Pam knows exactly where everything is and how much of this or that is available. "We'll be running out of blankets tomorrow," she tells me. "If you can get the word out, that would be great." We'd just met; already, like a born organizer, she's giving me an assignment, and I am all too grateful for the chance to help out. Across the street, the church is serving as a depot for clothing and an even bigger daily feeding operation is underway.

Radio station WBAI, which airs an "Occupy Wall Street" show every weeknight at 6:30 pm and which is part of the listener-sponsored non–commercial Pacifica network, is pretty much alone among media in pointing out the racial and class discrepancies in government and Red Cross assistance. But it is on and off the air sporadically during the storm. As Chair of the Local Board for the last four years, I'm involved up to my ears in trying to get the station to remain on the air, not the least reason so that we can use the station to help give voice to the needs of our neighbors and mobilize assistance. WBAI's General Manager Berthold Reimers reports that after the NYC transit system was shut down the evening before the storm, a crew of seven WBAI producers and volunteers chose to disregard the mandatory evacuation orders and camped out at the station at its headquarters at 120 Wall Street so that they could provide round-the-clock live coverage of Hurricane Sandy, as Wall Street flooded 10 stories below them.

By Monday evening October 29th — ominously the date of the 1929 stock market crash(!) — the East River decided to race into the building and up the stairs on the ground floor, and then six feet or so higher, filling the lobby of the 34-story building. Generators exploded, and Con Ed — which had been taking shortcuts in protecting its equipment over the last few years and laying off hundreds of workers — had to shut off the power, and along with it WBAI's ability to broadcast from that location. Announcer Michael G. Haskins was able to continue broadcasting for several hours from a remote location, using Comrex equipment that allows for remote broadcasting.

The WBAI crew, meanwhile, was trapped. While the view from the 10th floor is spectacular, it was not exactly for that reason that they stuck it out until Tuesday morning when the waters receded. Meanwhile, WBAI's broadcast was interrupted late Monday night and again on Tuesday morning when Verizon lost its connection to the antenna atop the Empire State Building, and WBAI went silent.

WBAI was not able to come back on the air until late Tuesday night, and only with archival recordings. By Wednesday afternoon, the station was again broadcasting live, but sporadically, from the studios of Gary Null's internet Progressive Radio Network on Manhattan's Upper West Side.

All day Sunday and Monday, WBAI ran interviews with New Yorkers, and focused on questions that, at the time, were going unasked by the corporate media, Reimers said, proudly. Are the nuclear power plants at Indian Point in jeopardy, and should they be shut down immediately? Why did New York City shut off electricity, water and elevators more than 24 hours before the storm hit to the tens of thousands of poor and working class people living in public housing? Was the City trying to drive people out for good? What effect did global climate change have on this storm, and on future ones?

Nowhere else in the media could you hear that kind of questioning, which continues in a long train of searching out the truth in complicated stories. WBAI airs a biweekly show covering the global ecological crisis and climate change in the tradition of the station's coverage of the protests against the Vietnam War in the '60s, the Gulf War in the '90s, and the endless 'War on Terror' in 2001 and since. WBAI covered the events of 9/11 live, and stayed at the mic round-the-clock reporting from downtown Manhattan.

Democracy Now!, hosted by Amy Goodman and Juan Gonzalez, which broadcasts over WBAI in New York City, carried stirring interviews on Monday November 5th, with Occupy Sandy activists; that same night, Mimi Rosenberg and Ken Nash provided the first comprehensive coverage of the situation in Coney Island, which was pretty much being ignored in the mainstream media. And Esther Armah, Ken Gale and Tony Ryan were unrelenting in their coverage of global climate change and especially the threat from the combination of the storm and New York's nuclear power plants, which no one else was talking about.

In fact in the days leading up to the storm, a number of us were apoplectic over the possibility of radiation releases at NYC's nuclear power plants. The government shut the subways. They shut the schools. They shut the parks, tunnels, bridges and even the electricity as generators exploded right near WBAI. But the nuclear power generators at Indian Point, just 26 miles north of New York City? *Those* they kept running.

Are they insane? Should the waters of the Hudson flood into the plant, that would be an unprecedented disaster, on the scale of Fukushima or worse. Should any of the spent fuel rods foolishly stored in pools at Indian Point be washed into the Hudson, we can kiss New York City goodbye. (How's that for an early morning TV show — "Goodbye New York"?)

There were 16 nuclear power plants in the path of hurricane Sandy, as it whipped its way back from the Atlantic and up the coast. The Nuclear Regulatory Commission put additional observers at the sites and claimed they could shut down the nukes on just a few hours notice if they had to, so "don't worry."

Ken Gale, producer of the show "EcoLogic," presented the frightening scenario on WBAI. Hundreds of listeners called the governor and the NRC, begging them to shut down the Indian Point nuclear power plant at least for the storm's duration. WBAI provided phone numbers to call. And all of that concern had an effect. A spokesperson for the NRC was able to get through to me at home — a first! — and we had a long conversation. She agreed to discuss it live on the radio the next morning, but then WBAI was again knocked off the air.

The Obama-Nukes Connection

The nuclear nightmare is entirely man–made and profit–driven. There is nothing "natural" about it. It is the result not just of technology gone "inexplicably" haywire but, predictably, of a *certain kind* of technology — a centralized, metered and capitalist technology,[185] very expensive and made

---

[185] Just because nuclear power was used by the former Soviet Union and is widespread in China, etc., does not make it less of a "capitalist technolo-

economically profitable only by a boatload of government subsidies to the nuclear industry.[186]

And yet, even amidst the current catastrophe, and even as the government of Venezuela halts its own nuclear program in response to public requests to reconsider the direction for society in light of Fukushima,[187] **the U.S. government is dead-set on shoring up the industry and constructing new nuclear power plants**. Along with Wall Street brokerage house Goldman Sachs, nuclear reactor operator Exelon Inc. — one of the largest employers in Illinois where Obama was Senator (a state that gets approximately half of its electricity from nuclear power, more than

---

gy." It is true that some leftists argue that nuclear power (like genetic engineering) is only a problem under capitalism and if only workers had control over it in a truly socialist society, it would be safe. Some discussion of that concept can be found in Mitchel Cohen, *The Capitalist Infesto: Is Marx's Critique of Science and Technology Radical Enough?*, Red Balloon Pamphlets, 2010; also, by the same author, *Big Science, and the Left's Curious Notion of Progress* (2005).

[186] $13 billion in cradle-to-grave subsidies and tax breaks, as well as unlimited taxpayer-backed loan guarantees, limited liability in the case of an accident, and other incentives have been approved this year to go to the nuclear industry to build new nuclear reactors. *Public Citizen*. Also, note that the designer of the Fukushima nuclear reactors as well as many here in the U.S., the General Electric Company, paid no taxes at all in 2010 even though it made billions in profits.

[187] Venezuela is suspending development of a nuclear power program following the catastrophe at the nuclear complex in Japan, President Hugo Chavez announced. *Reuters,* March 16, 2011. Venezuela "had hoped that a planned Russian-built nuclear power plant would provide 4,000 megawatts (MW) and be ready in about a decade. But Chavez said events in Japan showed the risks associated with nuclear power were too great. 'For now, I have ordered the freezing of the plans we have been developing … for a peaceful nuclear program,' he said during a televised meeting with Chinese investors."

any other state) — was a top contributor to Barack Obama's campaigns, officially donating over $269,000.

The company currently operates 10 reactors at six sites. The Quad-cities Nuclear Power Plant, located on the banks of the Mississippi River, is a GE Mark-1 plant, with the identical design and nearly the same age as the Fukushima reactors. Exelon barely averted disaster at its Braidwood nuke in Joliet, IL last year, caused by several problems that the company had refused to correct — including a poor design that led to repeated floods in buildings housing safety equipment. The company allowed vented steam to rip metal siding off containment walls and used undersized electrical fuses for vital safety equipment, according to the NRC.[188]

As candidate for president, Obama knew about the deadly dangers of nuclear power. "I start off with the premise that nuclear energy is not optimal and so I am not a nuclear energy proponent," Obama said at a campaign stop in Newton, Iowa on December 30, 2007. "My general view is that until we can make certain that nuclear power plants are safe. ... I don't think that's the best option. I am much more interested in solar and wind and bio-diesel and strategies [for] alternative fuels."[189]

---

[188] Union of Concerned Scientists, "The NRC and Nuclear Power Plant Safety in 2010," March 2011.

[189] Karl Grossman, "Behind the Hydrogen Explosion at the Fukushima Nuclear Plant," http://www.KarlGrossman.blogspot.com.

As he told the editorial board of the *Keene Sentinel* in New Hampshire on November 25, 2007: "I don't think there's anything that we inevitably dislike about nuclear power. We just dislike the fact that it might blow up ... and irradiate us ... and kill us. That's the problem." But as president, Obama hired a nuclear power proponent out of the national nuclear laboratory system, **Steven Chu**, as his energy secretary. Chu, who had been director of the Lawrence Berkeley National Laboratory, minimizes the impacts of radioactivity, as do many of the atomic physicists in the national laboratory system. Obama's two top White House aides, meanwhile, had been deeply involved with Exelon — the utility operating more nuclear power plants than any other in the U.S. **Rahm Emanuel**, his former chief of staff and now Mayor of Chicago, was an investment banker central to the $8.2 billion corporate merger in 1999 that produced Exelon. **David Axelrod**, senior advisor and Obama's chief political strategist, was an Exelon PR consultant. **Frank M. Clark**, who runs ComEd, helped advise Obama before he ran for President and is one of Obama's largest fundraisers. Candidate Obama received sizable contributions from Exelon president and CEO **John Rowe**, who in 2007 also became chairman of the Nuclear Energy Institute, the nuclear industry's main trade group. As *Forbes* magazine wrote, "Ties are tight between Exelon and the Obama administration," noting Exelon's political contributions and Emanuel's and Axelrod's Exelon links.[190] Upon becoming President, Obama appointed Rowe to his Blue Ribbon Commission on America's Energy Future.

The revolving door between government and industry rotates just as fast in Japan as it does in the U.S. In fact, the former director general of METI left the agency and joined TEPCO as a senior adviser. Another METI board member became executive vice president at TEPCO.[191]

Not surprisingly, given who funded his campaigns, as president Obama betrayed his campaign statements and began promoting "safe, clean nuclear power." He pushed for multi-billion dollar taxpayer subsidies for the construction of new nuclear plants, and made them a central part of his energy policy. **He now proposes allocating $36 billion in federal loan guarantees** to jump-start the construction of new nuclear reactors. Unfortunately, he has maneuvered some who have argued fervently for the need to cut greenhouse gas emissions and to reduce or reverse global warming, such as NASA scientist James Hansen, into supporting his pro-nuclear policies by falsely posing coal mining and se-

---

[190] Jonathan Fahey, "The President's Utility," *Forbes*, January 18, 2010. Rahm Emanuel "was hired by Rowe to help broker the $8.2 billion deal between Unicom and Peco when Emanuel was at the investment bank Wasserstein Perella (now Dresdner Kleinwort). In his two-year career there Emanuel earned $16.2 million, according to congressional disclosures. His biggest deal was the Exelon merger."

[191] John Bussey, "Japan Will Rebuild From Quake But Faces Other Daunting Tests," *The Wall Street Journal*, March 25, 2011.

questration, mountaintop removal, deep sea oil drilling, and hydro-fracking for natural gas as the options to nuclear power — *all* of which the Obama administration is aggressively promoting. Opponents of nuclear power, in contrast, vigorously oppose *every* one of those Obama proposals and argue instead for funding for development of decentralized sustainable energy alternatives like solar and wind power. Contrary to the claims of nuclear supporters, anti-nuke activists also strongly oppose expansion of oil and coal-burning power plants and support phasing them out, as they are rightly seen as prime contributors to air pollution, asthma and greenhouse gases involved in global climate change. Nuclear power is not the answer.

John Rowe's Nuclear Energy Institute praises legislation that would facilitate the development of smaller, scalable nuclear reactors. The legislation, sponsored by Democrats as well as Republicans,

> was introduced March 8 2011 in the U.S. Senate. The Nuclear Power 2021 Act (S. 512) was introduced by Senate Energy and Natural Resources Committee Chairman Jeff Bingaman (D-N.M.) and Sens. Lisa Murkowski (R-Alaska) and Mark Udall (D-Colo.), along with Sens. Mike Crapo (R-Idaho), Mary Landrieu (D-La.) and Mark Pryor (D-Ark.). The legislation directs the Secretary of Energy to implement programs to develop and demonstrate two reactor designs, one fewer than 300 megawatts of electric generating capacity and the other fewer than 50

megawatts. This public-private, cost-shared program would facilitate the design certification by the Nuclear Regulatory Commission of two small reactor designs by the end of 2017 and the licensing of the reactors by the end of 2020.[192]

Even as the nuclear nightmare plays out in Japan and the odds in favor of the nightmare scenario happening in New York and at other nukes as global climate change generates stronger and much larger storms that threaten the plants, the President, the nuclear industry and its proponents in Congress bull ahead, disregarding the potential for causing global catastrophic events. Just as one of former President Bush's first acts in office was to increase allowable arsenic in drinking water when that water was found to already have higher arsenic levels than expected (waters used, now, in the growing of rice which is now said to be replete with high levels of arsenic), the U.S. Environmental Protection Agency under Obama **is preparing to dramatically increase permissible radioactive releases in water, food and soil,** in preparation for what they are calling 'radiological incidents.'[193]

This is taking place entirely behind closed doors, warns the Public Employees for Environmental Responsibility

---

[192] "NEI Welcomes Senators' Legislation to Advance Development of Small Reactors," *Nuclear Energy Institute*, March 09, 2011. http://www.nei.org

[193] Public Employees for Environmental Responsibility (PEER), "Radiation Exposure Debate Rages Inside EPA," April 5, 2011, http://www.peer.org/news/news_id.php?row_id=1325

(PEER). Because this plan is considered 'guidance' it does not require public notice as a normal regulation would. The radiation guides (called Protective Action Guides or PAGs) "are protocols for responding to radiological events ranging from nuclear power-plant accidents to 'dirty' bombs." Under the new guides, nuclear energy plants would be allowed to vent much higher levels of radioactive isotopes into the water supply and expose many more people to higher doses of radiation, including

- A nearly 1000-fold increase in strontium-90;
- A 3000 to 100,000-fold hike for iodine-131; and
- An almost 25,000 rise for nickel-63.

The new radiation guidelines would also allow long-term cleanup standards thousands of times more lax than anything EPA has ever before accepted, **permitting doses to the public that EPA itself estimates would cause cancer in as many as every fourth person exposed.**[194] These relaxations of radiation protection requirements are favored by the nuclear industry and allies in the Nuclear Regulatory Commission and Energy Department.

Fortunately, there are some in the regulatory agencies resisting the proposed increase in allowable radiation guides. The idea that there could be *any* "acceptable level"

---

[194] *ibid.* Also, Brian Moench, MD, "Radiation: Nothing to See Here?" *Truthout,* March 25, 2011 — a popular compilation of the dangers of radiation.

of radiation — let alone these drastically "enhanced" levels — is being vigorously opposed by public health professionals inside EPA where a critical debate is now taking place, according to documents PEER obtained by suing the EPA under the Freedom of Information Act. Even Exelon CEO John Rowe said lawmakers shouldn't *expand* U.S. guarantees for loans for new reactors, and that he is reassessing a $3.65-billion plan to boost output by upgrading Exelon's existing reactors[195] — not for any newfound moral, environmental or health-related concern but as a smokescreen for reducing corporate expenditures.

Meanwhile, as the chaos and destruction generated by Hurricane Sandy make all too clear, we dodged a bullet this time with regard to the Indian Point nuclear power plant. We might not be so "lucky" next year, or the year after that, when the storms of increasing magnitude are likely to strike again.

---

[195] John McCormick, "Nuclear Illinois Helped Shape Obama View on Energy in Dealings With Exelon," *Bloomberg News,* March 23, 2011.

Changing the Political Climate

by John Tarleton

The Consolidated Edison substation that lit up the Manhattan sky so spectacularly on the night Hurricane Sandy arrived is a part of a massive, hulking power plant complex that has been sealed to all car and foot traffic since the 9/11 attacks.

In 2001 the nearby exit from FDR Drive was closed, and the east end of 14th Street was abruptly terminated with a chain-link fence at Avenue C, roughly a quarter-mile from the freeway.

When I lived in the East Village, I rode by the power plant many times on my bike, often stopping to stare up at the four giant smokestacks that loom high over the surrounding neighborhood. Under the prevailing norms of post-9/11 life, such precautions to thwart a possible terrorist attack seemed sensible.

Now, of course, we know that it was the ocean, supercharged by global warming, that was coming for Con Edison's power plant — not Al Qaeda.

The same goes for our wounded subway system, which saw many miles of track submerged by the storm and will likely require many months and billions of dollars to fully repair.

Protecting the subways from terrorists has been central to counterterrorism efforts in New York City, amid fears stoked in part by the 2004 arrest of the "Herald Square bomber." The suspect, Shahawar Matin Siraj, was goaded and guided at every step by a New York Police Department informant until the government was ready to scoop him up. He was sent to prison for 30 years.

World Trade Center 1 (the "Freedom Tower") has been rebuilt with special blast-proof materials and will be the most heavily guarded building in the country when it finally opens. None of this spared the World Trade Center reconstruction site itself from the surging seas that poured down West Street and filled the lower level of the site with millions of gallons of salt water. Port Authority officials are still assessing the situation. According to Crain's New York Business, the flooding "could potentially cause costly damage to equipment and electrical systems at the multibillion-dollar construction project."

What happens when more powerful storms occur in the future?

For the past 11 years, we've been told that no effort or expense should be spared in the War on Terror lest "they" strike the "homeland" again. Combined spending on the military and domestic security agencies now approaches a trillion dollars per year.

Climate scientists first informed politicians in the late 1980s about the threats posed by growing levels of heat-trapping gases in the atmosphere. Levels of carbon dioxide, the main greenhouse gas, have continued to climb each year. Scientists warn that, as temperatures rise, we are approaching a tipping point after which runaway global warming will destabilize life as we know it.

According to Munich Re, one of the world's leading reinsurance firms, the number of "weather-related loss events" in North America has increased by 500 percent over the past three decades.

In the past year, we have seen the hottest annual temperature in U.S. history, record melting of the Arctic ice cap, a summer drought that affected 80 percent of farmland in the Midwest and the Great Plains and now Sandy. This follows 332 consecutive months, dating back to March 1985, in which average global monthly temperatures have been higher than the overall 20th-century average.

Yet nothing changes, as the oil and gas industries go on reaping many billions of dollars in profits.

Faced with projections of more climate chaos in the decades ahead, both major-party presidential candidates ignored climate change throughout the campaign. Instead, they advocated an all-out assault on untapped fossil fuel resources from upstate New York to the Arctic Sea.

It has been convenient for politicians and the corporate media to fix the public's attention on small bands of scary Islamic extremists on the other side of the world. But the real danger lies much closer to home.

In one sense, the threat is in the changing physics and chemistry of the planet — warmer ocean waters, higher levels of moisture in the atmosphere, melting icecaps — but those are merely symptoms. The real threat lies in the fossil fuel industries that will, if unfettered, lock us permanently into a dirty-energy future that will fry the planet — and a capitalist system that rewards the short-term profiteering of the few at the expense of the many as well as of the natural world.

If "green capitalism" is possible, let's see it soon. However, to have a viable future, it increasingly looks like we will have to make a more dramatic shift to an environmentally centered democratic socialism — yes, the S-word — that places key sectors of the economy under public control, enacts a green deal, places a new emphasis on local and regional economies, gives people dignified jobs, promotes participatory democracy and makes a decisive break with the capitalist ideology of economic growth at all costs. Otherwise, we can expect planetary ecosystems to unravel further as we descend into a world in which desperate battles are fought over dwindling resources amid widespread social disintegration.

System change or climate change? That will be our fundamental choice in the decades ahead. Conventional political wisdom says the former is impossible. But the rapidly changing environment we live in suggests it's essential — and that we fail to make it happen at our peril.

from The Indypendent, Nov. 22 – Dec. 19, 2012

Occupy Springs Into Action

by Sarah Jaffe

For those of us who've spent the last few years covering the struggles of everyday people against the financial and corporate giants who've consolidated wealth to unheard-of levels, the aftermath of Hurricane Sandy has been an exercise in "Where the hell have you been?"

The comparisons to Katrina have been everywhere, of course, but for me they hit home when, safe and warm in my Crown Heights apartment, I saw friends and acquaintances who'd been involved with Occupy Wall Street tweeting their relief activities under the hashtag #OccupySandy. As they set up their hub in Red Hook I couldn't help but think of New Orleans' mutual aid after the storm, and how leftists and radicals (such as Malik Rahim, who learned about community care from the Black Panthers' free food and tutoring programs) step quietly into the spaces left vacant by cuts to social programs and city budgets.

Julieta Salgado, a Brooklyn College student and organizer, told me that it started with a text message from a handful of folks working with the Free University. That group wound up at the Red Hook Initiative and from there fanned out into the streets of wealthy, dry Carroll Gardens to seek donations.

"We just walked from door to door and every single person responded, no one turned us down," Salgado said. "People were thanking us for coming. I think we gave an entryway to some folks who didn't know how to help."

The aftermath of disaster, particularly in a neoliberal state whose safety net has been shredded, is a void waiting to be filled by mutual aid. When the state simply isn't there, people step up to take care of each other — not just looking out for themselves as our libertarian friends would have it, but working together as communities in solidarity. The idea of mutual aid was as much at the foundation of the Occupy movement as its hotly debated horizontalism and opposition to the banks.

The Friday after Sandy, not long after cultural historian Thomas Frank declared Occupy dead, I walked into St. Jacobi Church in Sunset Park and saw familiar faces from Zuccotti Park. They weren't sitting around debating how to talk about the revolution, as Frank would have it; they were doing hard, necessary, practical work to feed, clothe and support swathes of the city reeling from the superstorm. The obituaries of Occupy had never seemed so wrong.

The church basement was filled with volunteers standing around tables, some preparing food, some sorting donations and putting together boxes, like the Kitchen and Comfort stations many of us remember from Occupy Wall Street. All would be fed. All would be clothed. Instead of waiting for those in need to arrive, as they had at Zuccotti, volunteers were now loading cars filled with precious gasoline to drive to Coney Island, to the Rockaways, to anywhere people weren't being cared for.

"It's amazing how organized we are. It's amazing how much so many people involved with the social movement have learned about themselves, about each other, about how to put these values into practice," said Michael Premo, one of the Occupy organizers in Sunset Park.

I'd seen lines around the block for food, diapers, blankets, flashlights and water, as the Red Hook Initiative/Occupy Sandy effort expanded to more buildings. The public housing all around us was still cold and without power, but there were so many volunteers that they didn't know what to do with us all. Salgado showed up again the next day and saw two people whose doors she'd knocked on the night before. They were there to help.

Political Organizing

Community groups that jumped into action for Sandy — organizers who make their (meager) livings providing services to people facing foreclosure, to immigrant workers fighting wage theft, to neighborhoods trying to keep out the corporate-backed charter schools — have played a vital role in the relief effort. Political organizing and mutual aid go hand in hand, or they should. The early labor movement wasn't just about organizing on the job, but organizing in neighborhoods. The folks still trying to build an anticapitalist movement in this country know that shell-shocked people can't organize until their basic needs have been met.

Rebecca Solnit has written eloquently of the communities that arise in disaster. Occupy Wall Street was a response to a disaster, too: the slow-moving financial hurricane that destroyed homes as surely as the storm. So it shouldn't be surprising that after Sandy moved through, the first people to jump into action were the same ones who made things run in the park. Observers all agree that the movement suffered from a lack of focus after the encampments were cleared out, but Sandy provided an immediate and critical focus. Within hours, Occupy was already using pre-existing social networks to kick off the relief effort.

"We scaled up in 24 hours. It's really a testament to how this specific set of values was able to really get us organized with one clear, focused vision," Premo said.

Sense of Urgency

As I finished up a 10-hour day volunteering in Sunset Park, cars were departing, volunteers were leaving and more coming to replace them, familiar faces running in with news of possible staging locations in other parts of the city. The rhythm was different than Zuccotti Park, the sense of urgency more acute, with reports pouring in of neighborhoods desperately in need of support. But the work was the same, even if the motivation was different. Meet people's needs, help them solve their problems.

Blackouts provided just a temporary respite from the daily hustle of late-capitalist New York City, but in that space there was room for something else.

As Salgado put it: "The cops are still doing what we expected them to do, Bloomberg is still doing what we expected him to do, and we're still doing what we expected us to do — but no one else did."

from The Indypendent, *Nov. 22-Dec. 19, 2012*
Originally published in Jacobin Magazine

On the Waterfront

by Tom Angotti

Sandy has triggered a public debate about how to protect the city in the future given the growing consensus that powerful storms and sea level rise are inevitable. But who will be protected? And who will pay?

Gov. Andrew Cuomo thinks New York City needs floodgates. Mayor Michael Bloomberg thinks other drastic measures have to be taken. Both of them have joined the chorus linking Sandy's devastation with global climate change. But neither of them has suggested he would stray from government's long tradition of protecting big real estate interests and abandoning those living at the margins, such as the tenants in the public housing projects of the Rockaways, Coney Island and Red Hook.

There needs to be a more equitable strategy going forward that forces the powerful real estate giants in Manhattan to pay the steep price of fortifying their luxury enclaves and puts public funds into protecting the most vulnerable working people.

The Cuomo and Bloomberg proposals are examples of short-term thinking dressed up in green rhetoric. They fail to look deeply at the long-term sustainability of the city. They obscure the basic questions of who benefits and who pays. If the chief beneficiaries of expensive dikes and other greening measures are downtown and waterfront property owners, why shouldn't they foot their fair share of the bill? If the captains of the growth machine took the risk with their capital, why should government have to bail them out?

On the other hand, if the city and state administrations seriously want to address climate change, they might begin to limit development in flood-prone areas instead of promoting it. They could also put more money into preserving and retrofitting the city's housing stock, especially public housing and homes in vulnerable areas, instead of wasting money to protect lavish new developments.

Protecting Investors

The corporate press has been quick to hail the declarations of the mayor and governor as evidence of necessary change in a world where climate change deniers, heavily funded by the fossil fuel lobby, have managed to prevent serious action. But on closer look, the Cuomo-Bloomberg discussion is mostly about protecting existing and future investments in New York City's most valuable real estate, including Mayor Bloomberg's signature development projects located along the most vulnerable upscale waterfronts. For them, the underlying issue isn't really climate change but how to get government to put up the massive expenditures needed to protect "the real estate capital of the world." By wrapping themselves in a green mantle of climate change adaptation, they can convince others that they're saving the world.

Up till now Bloomberg has been skeptical of proposals to build hugely expensive barriers in the harbor. Many high-end real estate interests, after all, are on high ground, and the newer projects are likely to be built to withstand the worst. Bloomberg has also been a forceful advocate for building more, not less, on the city's waterfront, leaving it to engineers and architects to deal with protections against storm surges. Ambitious measures to protect the less fortunate living in low-lying Zone A, however, were never contemplated. City Hall's policy has been to make these areas more attractive for private developers on the assumption they will do the job themselves. Budget cuts in Washington are bleeding public housing to death all over the country, so the long-term trend is for the privatization or demolition of the giant public housing projects in these areas. (an attempt was already made in the Rockaways under the federal government's HOPE VI program but failed in part due to tenant resistance.)

As an alternative to building barriers, the city administration has favored more modest long-term measures such as rebuilding wetlands or creating new ones, and improving the ability to divert and absorb storm water overflows. After Sandy, however, this option appears to be quite limited.

Legacy Projects

Bloomberg's "legacy" development projects are mostly on the waterfront, and they have received millions of dollars in subsidies from the city's Economic Development Corporation. The mayor has publicly touted the planned multi-billion-dollar Hudson Yards redevelopment on Manhattan's west side as his trophy project. He is using his last year in office to try to set in stone the more controversial developments, such as Willets Point and Hunters Point in Queens. Other projects, including cruise terminals in Manhattan and Brooklyn and commercial recreation areas such as Brooklyn Bridge Park, are in place or under development.

The Bloomberg strategy goes beyond direct city subsidies for waterfront projects. In the last decade the administration passed more than 110 rezoning proposals around the city, including many in formerly industrial waterfront areas, that created windfall profits for private landowners and ushered in massive new construction.

Bloomberg's rezoning of Coney Island included new opportunities for condos near the waterfront. He has been outspoken in his support for new condos in Gowanus and Newtown Creek, areas located in the flood plains of Brooklyn and saturated with toxic waste. Ignoring calls from community activists to clean up the area before promoting new residential development, the administration opposed a federally funded Superfund cleanup and refuses to question an ambitious new condo project in Gowanus. The mayor argues that the best hope for cleaning up the toxic land and water lies in private real estate development, which would improve each site as it develops. However, this would only shift the problem from one property to another and would still expose new residents and workers to toxic waste.

In perhaps the most dramatic rezoning, the city overcame substantial opposition by neighborhood groups and in 2005 rezoned the waterfront in Brooklyn's Williamsburg. This unleashed a frenzy of luxury condo development on the waterfront, resulted in the displacement of thousands of industrial jobs and virtually wiped out one of the last remaining city neighborhoods to combine industry and housing. A similar process evolved in Long Island City, Queens, over the last two decades. In the thrall of big real estate money and waterfront views, City Hall never questioned the wisdom of lining the waterfront with more towers.

Growth Machine

Let's not blame it all on Bloomberg. The frenzy to build in the flood zones began in earnest in the 1980s. The aging port facilities had closed and moved to New Jersey by the early 1970s but the city's fiscal crisis froze any efforts to redevelop the waterfront. By the 1980s the real estate market began to boom again. In 1993, the city completed a comprehensive waterfront plan and new waterfront zoning regulations. Now the big investment trusts, equity funds and banks that put up the money for the new waterfront properties in Brooklyn and Queens, along with towers in lower Manhattan that got submerged by Sandy, are facing threats to their lower floors and bottom lines. They will certainly not pay for the repairs to the city's streets, sewers and subway systems. But if the flooding continues they will have to pay to fix their buildings.

Could the selfish interests of the real estate growth machine actually benefit all the rest of us, following traditional trickle-down economics? After all, some argue, it was real estate interests that made possible construction of the nation's largest subway system, and even though it was an unintended consequence, the subway has drastically reduced the need for burning carbon. Perhaps so, but imagine if the subway had been a truly public transit system from the start, as it is in many other big cities of the world. Then there may not have been a need for a public buyout of the first two private companies in the 1930s after they were milked dry by their investors. Imagine if instead of having three separate systems that all converge in Manhattan's overblown real estate market, and several separate suburban rail systems, there had been a region-wide system that served the vast majority of the population in the tri-state area, which live, after all, in the suburbs and not in New York City.

It's this kind of holistic, long-term thinking that is urgently needed as New Yorkers look to a future of rising sea waters and more storms like Sandy.

Tom Angotti is Director of the Hunter College Center for Community Planning & Development and author of New York for Sale: Community Planning Confronts Global Real Estate *(MIT Press, 2008).*

from The Indypendent, *Nov. 22-Dec. 19, 2012*

Healing a Stricken City & Greening the Planet

by Chris Williams

The Maldives are a country in peril. The collection of 1200 islands and atolls, the highest point of which is a mere five feet above sea-level, were put on the map of world consciousness by the first democratically-elected president, Mohammed Nasheed. Until overthrown in a military coup by a regime unwilling to countenance democracy, Nasheed became famous when he held a Cabinet meeting under water to highlight the plight of his country. He was the subject of the documentary *The Island President* for his efforts to raise awareness of climate change and the resulting sea-level rise that will likely make his nation the first to disappear beneath the waves.

The Maldives, better known for its exclusive resorts than the fact that 320,000 people currently call the islands home, is in danger of being overwhelmed by the Indian Ocean this century. But what if, instead of the remote island paradise, it's a major city that goes first?

Of course we could and should have been engaged with this question after Katrina flooded 80% of New Orleans in 2005. Two weeks after Frankenstorm Sandy, with dozens dead, many thousands of New Yorkers still struggling without power, running water or heat and 40,000 people made homeless, now is another good time to be looking for answers.

How should New York, brought to its knees by Sandy, rebuild to make it a beacon to other coastal cities around the world, the inhabitants of which are watching the suffering of our city with horror and, after a quick glance at climate change data for their region, a deepening sense of foreboding?

There has been much debate about the extent to which Hurricane Sandy may have been made larger and stronger and, in an unusual deviation for this time of year, pushed onto land to devastate the Northeast coast rather than moving back out to sea. As associate editor of *Scientific American* David Biello argued:

> Global warming didn't spawn Sandy but it certainly contributed to the impact, with a couple of features definitely worsening it. ... Higher sea surface temperatures have made the storm surge stronger. ... Normally hurricanes come up to the coast and turn right back into the ocean, but as a consequence of the major meltdown of Arctic sea ice this summer,

there was a weather pattern preventing Sandy from taking that course, and [it] steered it back into land.

In August, the director of the NASA Goddard Institute for Space Studies, James Hansen, who testified to Congress in 1988 about the reality of human-induced climate change, wrote in the *Washington Post*:

"Our analysis shows that it is no longer enough to say that global warming will increase the likelihood of extreme weather and to repeat the caveat that no individual weather event can be directly linked to climate change. To the contrary, our analysis shows that, for the extreme hot weather of the recent past, there is virtually no explanation other than climate change."

Reviewing some of the extreme weather events around the world over the last few years, Hansen went on to say:

> These weather events are not simply an example of what climate change could bring. They are caused by climate change. The odds that natural variability created these extremes are minuscule, vanishingly small. To count on those odds would be like quitting your job and playing the lottery every morning to pay the bills.

Ultimately however, we are asking the wrong question. The issue of whether this or that extreme weather event such as Sandy or the massive US drought this year, was exacerbated by climate change is overshadowed by the knowledge that we only have a single planet.

We know for a fact that carbon dioxide, a compound linked through many scientific studies to global warming, is being pumped in vast quantities into the atmosphere. In confirmation of this, witness the tragic irony of people in the Northeast waiting for hours to fill up their gas tanks with the stuff that is largely responsible for increasing the concentrations of that compound and thereby altering the heat balance of the planet. It makes no sense to think that humans can extract and burn 80 million barrels of oil every day and it will have no impact on the composition of the air we breathe, or that increasing the concentration of a climate-regulating gas such as carbon dioxide will not have global implications for the climate.

We also know for a fact that New York has seen a 12-inch increase in sea-level over the last century, alongside an average increase of 2.5 degrees Fahrenheit. We also know that a 600-mile stretch of the East Coast of the United States is a regional "hot spot" for sea-level rise, which is getting higher 3 to 4 times faster than the global average. Thus, with two hurricanes in the northeast in two years, what we are looking at is more of the same. No doubt that is why 95% of cities in Latin America are making contingency plans for climate change and its impact on their locations.

Therefore, just on the basis of the Precautionary Principle and knowing that there is no Planet B, we need to systematically and rapidly move to reduce our dependence, not on foreign oil, but on all oil, gas, coal and uranium. Furthermore, instead of continuing on our current path toward greater oil consumption, which will cause global warming to spin out of control, we urgently need to investigate ways of living more in-tune with our natural surroundings, before we lose control of our destiny. On current projections, oil consumption is predicted to rise to 110 million barrels by 2020 while carbon dioxide emissions rose by 2.5 percent last year.

What would our city look like if it were built to withstand and accommodate the kind of monster storms that are becoming more prevalent due to climate change? What would our city look like if it were made for people, not cars?

There are two quite different sets of answers to those questions. On the one hand, like some medieval fortress, we could spend approximately $10-17 billion building sea fortifications. On the other hand, rather than adopting a siege mentality, shielding ourselves from the blows raining down from an enraged Mother Nature by encasing New York in ring of iron and steel revetments, we could build a city that is a genuine testament to forward-thinking, long-term-planning worthy of the 21st century.

Building sea-walls and oceanic sea gates that would open and close as needed isn't unprecedented; several cities have built large and small versions, including Holland, which is a country that is largely below sea level to begin with. But there are some unique and complex challenges to building such gates on the scale required to protect a city of eight million located on a series of low-lying islands off the coast of the North Atlantic.

First, such a scheme, from planning to implementation, would take decades to be operational; clearly, New York City does not have decades. Second, if one is going to build sea-walls, the water still has to go somewhere. Hence, planning to save some areas of New York may end up simply shifting the water elsewhere and inundating, for example, New Jersey. There is also the fact that all of the pollution run-off and raw sewage from overwhelmed sanitation systems would then be trapped on the city-side of the gates. Third, while the Netherlands recently completed a storm surge barrier that takes into account such an unlikely possibility as a once-in-ten-thousand-years weather event, the United States, with its short-term planning predicated on cutting state and federal budgets on infrastructure and elevating short-term corporate profits is unlikely to come up with the resources to pull off a project like this. It is highly likely therefore, that whatever is planned and built today will skimp on costs and be inadequate for storm surges of the future. As things currently stand, a not unrealistic foot-and-a-half sea-level rise by 2050 combined with a storm surge would require New York to evacuate three million people. Lastly, there's the enormous economic cost for such a technological fix, which may not effectively address the long-term issues we face and come with unexpected and undesirable outcomes.

Given the self-evident inadequacy of New York and New Jersey's storm preparedness in light of Sandy, despite years of scientific reports documenting the possibility of a major storm causing havoc in the area, it seems clear that only one force has enough power to thwart the self-serving and derisory solutions promulgated by politicians in thrall to corporate interests: the power of the people to organize in our own interests. Only by demanding and fighting for substantive change will we be able to live in safety and security in our own city, breathing clean air and drinking pure water.

Our public high school students have some excellent ideas about where to start:

> New York City could build high walls all around to keep out the water, turning us into prisoners in our own city and preventing use of our greatest natural resource. Instead of confining New Yorkers we can find suitable solutions through creating a soft shoreline with native organisms that were heavily populated in this area.
> As aquaculturists at the New York harbor school we grow oysters for environmental restoration. Oysters are a keystone species which means they have a

disproportionate positive effect on their ecosystem. Oyster reefs provide habitat for small marine life and filter water of nitrogen and phosphorous by consuming algae that contain these nutrients.

Oyster reefs act as wave attenuators and benthic stabilizers.

In other words, we can use natural flood defenses, such as the restoration of salt marches and coastal wetlands, along with a well-funded and general campaign to return oysters to New York's estuary, to build natural resilience into New York's ability to cope with large storms and help filter and clean the water. Half of the coastal wetlands of the United States have been lost over the last 50 years.

There are of course smaller things that need doing, such as moving vulnerable electrical equipment above storm surge levels and retrofitting subway stations and tunnels to be more resilient and protected from flooding. Con Edison could have spent the $250 million in investment the company deemed necessary to install submersible switches and move high-voltage transformers above ground level but instead preferred to use the $1 billion in profit it made last year for other purposes.

While the *New York Times* recently reported on some more natural possibilities for increasing the climate resilience of the city, melding ecology with infrastructure was in fact the thesis of an exhibit at MoMA in 2010. Five architectural teams gave their vision to create "soft edges" to New York in order to absorb, rather than repel, storm water. Not only would this create a visually stunning, highly resilient city, but create environments conducive to a more variegated and enriched diversity of animal, plant and human life.

In contrast to the reductive and limited thinking that is illustrated by simply saying let's build more walls, the approach taken by the architects and landscape designers represents a much more holistic philosophy that is far more likely to be successful in terms of allowing New York to weather the next storm, not to mention making the city a much more aesthetically pleasing place to live.

Apart from re-greening coastal areas, the city and region need much more planning with regard to coastal development to prevent the kind of helter-skelter unregulated development of areas that are known flood plains. As an investigative report published in the Huffington Post documented about a local manifestation of the wild-west nature of contemporary capitalism:

> Authorities in New York and New Jersey simply allowed heavy development of at-risk coastal areas to continue largely unabated in recent decades, even as the potential for a massive storm surge in the region became increasingly clear.
>
> In the end, a pell-mell, decades-long rush to throw up housing and businesses along fragile and vulnerable coastlines trumped commonsense concerns about the wisdom of placing hundreds of thousands of closely huddled people in the path of potential cataclysms.

The report places blame for this type of development, which took place in some of the worst hit areas, such as the Jersey Shore and the Rockaways, to the power of capital to sway politicians who knew of the risks, even as they approved of the building frenzy:

> Developers built up parts of the Jersey Shore and the Rockaways, a low-lying peninsula in Queens, N.Y., in similar fashion in recent years, with little effort by local or state officials to mitigate the risk posed by hurricanes, experts said. Real estate developers represent a powerful force in state politics, particularly in New Jersey and New York, where executives and political action committees have been major donors to governors and local officeholders.
>
> This coastal growth took place even as public and private sector leaders in both New York and New Jersey began expressing growing concern over the potential for climate change to intensify storms and accelerate already rising sea levels. New York City officials in particular were well aware of the ways in which climate change would make the potentially destructive effects of a major hurricane worse, scientists said.

Therefore, a radical reevaluation is needed of where buildings are placed. Simply rebuilding what existed before, perhaps jacking up the foundations a bit or requiring extra flood insurance, cannot be the answer. Much stricter regulations on building location and building requirements themselves, such as the location of boilers, flood-proofing basements, etc. are needed.

Buildings themselves are a major source of carbon emissions from heating and cooling. Rather than constructing buildings to require air-conditioning, how could we instead create buildings out of materials (and layouts) that maximize *natural* heating and cooling, including the expanded use of geothermal heat pumps?

We need to vastly increase car-free zones and bring trams back to New York. Many streets in Manhattan should be made into pedestrian-only areas and planted with trees. Whenever sidewalks are replaced, they need to be made from a water-permeable material, as cities such as Chicago have already begun to do.

With many fewer cars in city centers, the concomitant huge expansion of public transit and the creation of a pedestrian- and bike-friendly city, the vast oceans of impermeable concrete that contribute to storm run-off, otherwise known as parking lots, can similarly be transformed into tree-lined water parks.

On average, any given car is only in use around 5 percent of the time, often with a single occupant. On top of that, an internal combustion engine is only about 25 percent efficient. We couldn't have designed a more inefficient use of resources and a better pollution emitter if we had started with that as our actual objective. There are enough non-residential parking spaces in the United States for 800 million cars; in some cities one-third of the total surface area is taken up by parking lots.

As temperatures rise due to global warming, life — and death — in cities that experience a greater number of 90-plus degree days is a critical issue to address. Air conditioning, car engines and concrete all contribute to the urban heat island effect and rising temperatures worsen air quality.

Therefore, taking these measures with regard to buildings, transportation and other aspects of urban infrastructure — all of which will cost less than building sea-walls while simultaneously positively contributing to city dwellers' quality of life and the long-term resilience of cities — are a no-brainer. In even more good news, doing this on a fast timetable will get tens of thousands of people back to meaningful and fulfilling employment that is socially useful and eminently necessary.

However, these things will only occur if we fight against the entrenched economic and political interests and form organizations capable of effectively putting them forward and demanding their implementation.

Chris Williams is author of Ecology and Socialism: Solutions to Capitalist Ecological Crisis.

from The Indypendent, *Nov. 22-Dec. 19, 2012*

Message to the *New* New Left: Occupy the Big Connections

by Mickey Z.

I may be a devout fan of direct action, but I can still recognize how often the means and ends get confused. What we now call the 1% has created such a profound planetary crisis that activists can easily be consumed with putting out urgent fires and thus lose sight of the bigger connections.

This is precisely why I open many of my talks like this:

This is the point in the evening when the speaker typically implores everyone to turn off the cell phones. But, as far as I'm concerned, you can leave yours on. This way, every time someone's phone goes off, we can be reminded of the fact that half the humans on the planet have never made a single phone call.

Or maybe, when a phone rings, we can focus on these

six simple words: "The Democratic Republic of the Congo." We'd do that because one of the primary components of cell phone circuitry is a metallic ore called Columbite-Tantalite —or "coltan." Eighty percent of the world's known coltan can be found in African nation of The Democratic Republic of the Congo (or DRC), which just so happens to be embroiled in a brutal (even by current standards) civil war since the pre-cell phone days of 1994. Over time, all sides in the unrelenting struggles adroitly began using the mining and sale of coltan not only to nourish the West's seemingly insatiable cell phone addiction, but also to fund their inexorable mayhem. Civilian deaths in the DRC during this time— mostly from war-related disease and malnutrition—are estimated not in the hundreds, thousands, or even tens of thousands, but rather in the millions ... making it the world's deadliest military conflict since the Second World War.

And it gets worse. Just ask an Eastern Lowland Gorilla, the world's largest primate, found almost exclusively in the DRC. According to *National Geographic*: "Following a decade of civil war in the Democratic Republic of the Congo, new estimates suggest that the number of eastern lowland gorillas may have plummeted by 70 percent. Conflict, illegal mining for a mineral used for electronic-device components, and the growing bush-meat trade have all taken their toll." The UN Environment Program has reported that the number of eastern lowland gorillas in eight DRC national parks has subsequently declined by 90 percent. We can only hope that some enterprising soul has already recorded the eastern lowland gorilla's call so it can be used as a ring tone long after they're gone.

So yeah, go ahead and leave your phones on…

Post-Sandy Connections

More recently, I've found myself relentlessly reminding activists in the post-Sandy world about other big connections. In a late 2012 article, my colleague Robert Jensen described an "obvious" problem:

"We face multiple, cascading ecological crises that should spur us to rethink our economy, politics, and society, but the existing rules rule out such thinking. If we can't transcend these intellectual limits, it is not clear that an ongoing large-scale human presence on the earth will be possible."

As they say in South Florida: BINGO.

For example, the "intellectual limits" and "existing rules" within the post-Sandy discussions left us choosing between two candidates who dared not utter the words "climate change" during televised debates for fear of angering their corporate owners.

Such limits and rules, even as gasoline lines stretched for blocks, also excluded a meaningful conversation about our lethal love affair with the internal combustion engine — and the petroleum that fuels it.

Then, of course, we have the unyielding intellectual limits on display when acknowledging the number one cause of human-created greenhouse gases loses out to serving factory farmed animals to those impacted by a symptom of climate change.

In my efforts to take advantage of this powerful teaching moment, I'm told (among other things) to not "force" veganism on other people.

I'm told that it's "more important to get people fed with what's available than to make things about diet, health, global warming, or whatever."

I'm told there shouldn't be "any concern about diet politics in the day-to-day efforts" and that it's important we not "adopt dietary codes in social movements."

Please allow me to yet again address this army of straw men...

Deceptively labeling my points as "diet politics" or "dietary codes" doesn't change the fact that what I'm obviously doing is suggesting that those who identify as open-minded activists recognize some documented connections and act accordingly.

The number one cause of events like Hurricane Sandy may be sitting on the plates given to those most impacted; but rather than embracing change, activists waste energy portraying my words as "forcing" some "code" on unsuspecting people who just need to be fed and can't be concerned with "diet politics."

Not only are they underestimating the intelligence and curiosity of those they're helping while ignoring the primary cause of the crisis, activists are also pretending that "codes" don't exist within social movements.

Is a radical kitchen "imposing a code" when insisting on actions like recycling, composting, etc. or is the value of these efforts clear and thus, no further discussion truly needed?

Is it disrespectful when new forms of communication (hands signals, anyone?) usurp more familiar methods? Is this an elite "transmission code" being "forced" upon unprepared people?

Is it a "code" when activists expect their comrades to eschew racist-sexist-homophobic language?

Do I even need to continue on this point?

My articles and posts about the factory farming/Sandy connections are not about codes, politics, or force. As stated above, we have an opening here — a chance to begin a crucial transition to a lifestyle that will help cultivate a much-needed global shift.

Going vegan is a lot more than altering your diet. It's even a lot more than the climate change connection. This choice is also about (among many other things): workplace justice, torture, health care, deforestation, overfishing, poverty, habitat loss, GMOs, ocean dead zones, corporate welfare, Wall Street profits, and so-called free trade agreements.

In addition, when properly practiced, the plant-based life *is* the healthier choice — and without a single utterance of the word "prevention" in Obama's health care giveaway to big business, it's crucial for all of us to take some responsibility for our own health.

P.S. Veganism is the ethical choice, too. I could fill this article with heinous details about fur farms, vivisection labs, circuses, zoos, veal crates, and so much more — but that's what search engines are for, right?

To any activist who incorrectly characterizes the vegan lifestyle as elitist, I'd urge you to examine how your food choices negatively impact the working class you wish to help. Inside the slaughterhouses, the animals are not the only ones suffering.

The meat industry, along with its low wages, long hours, and dehumanizing work, has the highest job-related injury rate and by far the highest rate of serious injury — and at least half the workers are women.

GoVeg.com adds: "According to the U.S. Department of Labor, nearly one in three slaughterhouse workers suffers from illness or injury, compared to one in 10 workers in other manufacturing jobs. Slaughterhouse workers are also 35 times more likely to suffer from repetitive stress injuries than their counterparts in other manufacturing jobs."

Of course, with many undocumented immigrants and poor Americans working such jobs, it remains unknown how many injuries go unreported.

I could go on (and on) to easily counter every rejoinder I've faced but, instead, I'll clarify my stance: I'm not implying that major cultural changes are simple or can happen overnight or must be about purity or litmus tests but, as anyone willing to accept reality knows, we're past the point of no return.

This isn't easy to hear—let alone hear over and over again— so let me close with something aimed at the one retort I haven't yet addressed, the one that typically goes a little something like: "This sanctimonious zeal by some vegans has been one of the main reasons why I've never become a vegan."

Such an emotional and irrational reaction could be easily dismissed, of course. I could simply point how, by the same logic (sic), after dealing with an overzealous anti-war activist, we should all rush out and enlist.

However, there is a very useful and important point to be made here: Just because some passionate vegan activists are perceived as annoying doesn't mean all vegans are and more significantly, *it doesn't mean we're wrong.*

The only "code" being imposed here is that of Hurricane Sandy: *Adapt or perish.*

Is that *direct* enough for ya?

Mickey Z. is the author of 11 books, most recently the novel Darker Shade of Green. Until the laws are changed or the power runs out, he can be found on an obscure website called Facebook.

Mitchel Cohen, as part of the "Clown" affinity group at the action to free Mumia Abu Jamal and Leonard Peltier, at the Liberty Bell in Philadelphia, July 3, 1999. Along with many others, Mitchel was arrested on charges of trespass, disorderly conduct, resisting arrest, and refusing to follow the orders of a policeman (none of the other tourists shown here were arrested, funny how that works) but refused to plead guilty. After a trial that lasted several days, during which the arresting officer was "unavailable" and another police officer testified that Mitchel was dressed "normal" — no mention of the giant glasses, SWAT cap, and wood tie — Judge Rappaport found Mitchel and a co-defendant "guilty", confiscated their passports, sentenced him to 1 year federal supervised probation, monthly urine tests, a $250 fine, and whatever else the judge saw fit to add in. They appealed, and lost.

DEDICATION

I wrote an earlier draft of *What Is Direct Action?* a few days after I learned of the death of Crysta Casey — a wonderful poet and member of the Red Balloon Poetry Conspiracy in the 1970s, and my friend all of these many years. She lived in Seattle, where she succumbed to lung cancer and died on June 24, 2008. It was in her apartment that I stayed during the 1999 "Battle of Seattle" against the World Trade Organization. I hadn't seen her in at least 10 years; yet when I showed up at her door, it was as though no time had passed. We immediately launched into critiquing each other's poetry, pencils in hand. After a few days, she ordered me to find another place to stay as she was deathly worried that some evil would befall me during the protests and she'd end up worrying herself awake all day (Crysta rarely slept at night) as I darted from rally, to march, to conference, to jail support.

Crysta's story is unusual, even for those of us who lived what today seem like "unusual" lives. She spent 30 years in and out of the psychiatric facilities at the Veterans Hospital in Seattle. She'd go off her meds so that she could capture the edges of emotion that she needed to write and paint. And then, of course, she wouldn't want to go back on them, and the havoc they'd caused her all those years would break her open.

Every couple of months for decades she'd call me at 4 in the morning. As soon as the phone rang I knew it was Crysta, even before hearing her raspy, twinkling voice. She'd want to read me her latest poem. She'd sit all night rocking back and forth in her supposedly stationary hard-backed chair, staring, thinking, rhythming, night after night after night. Her phone calls would arrive in the course of these rocking sessions, and I'd ask her what she was doing. "Rocking," was always her answer. That's when she was happiest. Smoking cigarettes and rocking.

Her first poem was about her first time in a gay bar. The images burned smoke rings into the page. She said she wrote it as "an experiment" for a poetry workshop we were both taking at Stony Brook with Kofi Awoonar. Crysta was wearing overalls like a train engineer. "I can't write poetry," she protested when I offered to publish her poem.

For many years, she sent me dozens of revisions of one of her poems about her friend who'd served with her in the Marine Corps, Private Sanchez, who was murdered in a scene eerily similar to that in "A Few Good Men" (the Tom Cruise-Jack Nicholson-Demi Moore film). Then, there was the poem she wrote about a co-worker, Tony — or rather, not so much about him but about his finger, which snapped off in a barricade's rusty hinge, its light blinking like one yellow eye, the finger twitching by Tony's boot. At the psych ward in the V.A. Hospital where she was periodically re-drugged until the shrinks felt it was safe to let her out again, she painted word-portraits of the damaged souls she found there. In poem after poem, rewrite after rewrite, Crysta relived the intense pain and also the joys of those friendships, carefully paring this or that image until she got it exactly "right". She'd call me when she found the right word, after a month's search.

Crysta liked writing about hum-drum subjects, the small encounters in everyday life, and finding meaning in them. Every poem she wrote, even the throw-aways, contained at least one image or one peculiar and insightful phrase that would blow my mind, stopping me in my tracks. I learned early on that it was worth wading through page after page of roughly worded or not-quite-ready-for-prime-time verse in order to get to that one reality-changing image that would open my eyes and clear out the cobwebs in my brain.

It was a trip to hear Crysta read her own work, the struggle, the slightly lithium-slurred speech, the strong caustic and yet love-filled enunciation, sort of like the wonderful experience listening to the Brooklyn-accented poet Enid Dame, a favorite of both of us. Enid died at the end of 2003.

In her last 10 years, Crysta took up water-colors and painted the same way she wrote: tersely, in images from everyday life with always something slightly awry, some quirk that to her was normal but that would jolt realities. I think she painted the same chair — the one she rocked in — over and over and over again. What was it about that chair? What rock did this Sisyphus learn to love as she pushed it eternally up life's incline?

CRYSTA'S LAST LETTER TO ME

Mon, 24 Mar 2008

Hi Mitch,

I've been given the good ole six-month life span... course I've never died before (except once from a suicide attempt) so this is an adventure. I have found a home for all my files. DW will also continue to try and get my completed manuscripts published, so I sleep peacefully at night knowing this. I will add your email to the list of people who should be notified when I die. It would be nice to see you of course, but it doesn't look like either of us is traveling soon, so... Anyway, keep up the struggle for another fallen comrade... love, crysta

KADDISH FOR ANOTHER FALLEN COMRADE

There are those
whose voices
will always ring
with silver clarity

whose tenacity
whose eloquence
still roar
this Atlantic
inside our hearts

There are those
from yesterlives
who somehow
slipped in through
the battened hatch
of memory
and in their confusion
and with their deep
vulnerability
opened us
like rosebuds
their mad lips
hot sticky verse

There are those
who are touchstones
to a past we overthrew
(or so we thought)
to a future
we are shaping still
hounded by police

rising again
like mist
jagging this indigo dungeon
of flesh
of bone

There are those
whose long fingers
squirm through
ancient dust
wringing
the neck of indifference
from beyond the grave
revolutions to make,
worlds yet to change

And there are those
who remain silent
pacing forgotten alley-ways
gray brick walls
grey cement floors
souls lost in the maze
of grimy posters torn
from yesterday's wars
flapping in the wind
the brooding
eyebrows of Winter

ashes to ashes
dust to dust

At the risk
of seeming
ridiculous, Autumn's
carnival of tears
explodes into
magnificent foliage —
look all around you! —
and we
WILL remember
for what we fight
for why we breathe
Freedom! —
those
great feelings
of love

And so
we meet again
regather
our tribes
mourning another
among us
who has fallen
Now, it is Crysta Casey's time

to set aside the colors
that only she could see
metaphors
that she'd cajole,
beg, plead, entreat
and sometimes hold a gun
to their heads until
they leapt across the synapses
between us until
they disrobed and conveyed
their meaning to me, too,
to you, too,
and we, like unsuspecting fishermen,
huddle in our boats
casting nets
into the darkness,
straining on the oars,
rowing
rowing
the bones
ashore

This book is written in memory of Crysta Casey, Saralee Hamilton and John "Tito" Gerassi. Also, Alex Cockburn, Shulamith Firestone, Daniel Simidor (André Elizée), Garda Ghista, Len Weinglass, Dennis Brutus, Manning Marable,

Maria Kuriloff, Fred Friedman, Howard Zinn, Bernie McFall, Dr. Philip Metling, Steffie Brooks, Brad Will, Bob Fitch, Carl Lesnor, Michael Shanker, Kathryn Shay, Tom Angress, Carl Lesnor, Ward Morehouse, Dave Wycoff, Enid Dame, Peggy Dye, Susan Blake, Lenny Cohen, Ralph Klaber, Mike Pahios, Will Miller, Valerie Sheppard, Bryna Eill, Connie Holland, Grandpa Al Lewis, Frieda Zames, Chris Delvecchio, Patty Staib, Kate Berrigan, Shari Nezami, Pat Dalto, Bob Rosado, Gloria Pasin, Iris Burlock, Stephen Becker, David Cline, Judi Bari, William Kunstler, Rachel Corrie, Dorothy Klein, Bernice Linton, Virginia Lerner, Peter Camejo, Gus Reichbach, Al Kutzik, Allen Ginsberg, Tuli Kupferberg, Adrienne Rich, Dave Dellinger, Sol Yurick, Kofi Awoonar, and to my next door neighbor Mollie Goldstein — fallen comrades in the circles in, around and supportive of the Red Balloon Collective at one time or another, oaks in the forest, and most of them my friends who stood up for humanity in an era of robots. And to all of those who confronted the Pentagon in October, 1967. Who would have known back then that *that* demonstration, described so eloquently by Norman Mailer in *Armies of the Night*, would mark the start of the anti-imperialist *resistance* in the United States, as opposed to simply the "anti-war" movement, and baptize a new generation — with great leaps of insight, risk, and imagination — that would shake the entire world?

ABOUT THE AUTHOR

Photo by Cathryn Swan

Mitchel Cohen, distributing his pamphlet *Why I Hate Thanksgiving*, & artist Seth Tobocman at Occupy Wall Street, Thanksgiving 2011. Note the police tower on the Left, recording everything in Zuccotti Park.

Mitchel Cohen lives in Brooklyn, New York, and co-founded the Red Balloon Collective (1969) at SUNY Stony Brook. He chaired the WBAI (99.5 FM) Local Board (2008-2012), organizes with the Brooklyn Greens/Green Party, No Spray Coalition against toxic pesticides, NY State Against Genetic Engineering, Occupy Wall Street, Radical Philosophy Association, Direct Action Network to free Mumia Abu-Jamal and Leonard Peltier, and others. Mitchel hosts a weekly internet radio show, "Steal This Radio," and has written numerous political pamphlets gathered under the aegis of *Zen-Marxism* and *I Was A Teenage Communist*. Check out his two books of poetry, available from his website: http://www.MitchelCohen.com.

Email: mitchelcohen@mindspring.com